Library of
Davidson College

# COMMITTEE ON ABILITY TESTING

WENDELL R. GARNER (*Chair*), Department of Psychology, Yale University
MARCUS ALEXIS, Department of Economics, Northwestern University
WILLIAM BEVAN, Department of Psychology, Duke University
LEE J. CRONBACH, School of Education, Stanford University (psychometrics)
ZVI GRILICHES, Department of Economics, Harvard University
OSCAR HANDLIN, Director of Libraries, Harvard University (history)
DELMOS JONES, Department of Anthropology, City University of New York
LYLE V. JONES, L.L. Thurstone Psychometric Laboratory, University of North Carolina (psychometrics, statistics)
PHILIP B. KURLAND, Law School, University of Chicago
BURKE MARSHALL, Law School, Yale University
MELVIN R. NOVICK, Lindquist Center for Measurement, University of Iowa (statistics, psychometrics)
LAUREN B. RESNICK, Learning Research and Development Center, University of Pittsburgh (psychology, educational psychology)
ALICE ROSSI, Department of Sociology, University of Massachusetts
WILLIAM H. SEWELL, Department of Sociology, University of Wisconsin
JANET T. SPENCE, Department of Psychology, University of Texas
ALAN A. STONE, Law School, Harvard University (psychiatry, law)*
MARY L. TENOPYR, Human Resources Laboratory, American Telephone and Telegraph Company, Morristown, N.J. (industrial psychology)
JOHN W. TUKEY, Bell Telephone Laboratories, Inc., Murray Hill, N.J. (statistics)
E. BELVIN WILLIAMS, Educational Testing Service, Princeton, N.J. (psychology)

ALEXANDRA K. WIGDOR, *Study Director*
SUSAN W. SHERMAN, *Senior Research Associate*
GLADYS R. BOSTICK, *Administrative Secretary*

*Member until 1980.

# Contents

Preface                                                                 vii

## EMPLOYMENT TESTING

History of Employment Testing
   *Matthew Hale*                                         3
Psychological Testing and the Law of Employment Discrimination
   *Alexandra Wigdor*                                     39
Ability Testing: Federal Guidelines and Professional Standards
   *Melvin Novick*                                        70
Current Use of Tests for Employment
   *Toby Friedman* and *E. Belvin Williams*                99

## EDUCATIONAL TESTING

History of Educational Testing
   *Daniel Resnick*                                      173
Legal Context of Educational Testing
   *Patricia Hollander*                                  195
Test Use Today in Elementary and Secondary Schools
   *Beverly Anderson*                                    232
On the Use and Importance of Tests of Ability in Admission to
   Postsecondary Education
   *Rodney Skager*                                       286

Some Aspects of the Use and Misuse of Standardized Aptitude
and Achievement Tests
  *Eric Gardner*                                               315

## PSYCHOMETRIC ISSUES

Ability Testing: Individual Differences, Prediction and
Differential Prediction
  *Robert Linn*                                                335
The Implications of Coaching for Ability Testing
  *Nancy Cole*                                                 389

# Preface

The Committee on Ability Testing was established under the auspices of the National Research Council to conduct a broad examination of the role of testing in American life. The project was conceived at a time of widespread public debate about the use of standardized tests in the schools, for college admissions, and in the workplace. That debate has not been stilled by time.

Advocates of testing consider it the best available means of impartial selection based on ability; many are, in addition, enthusiastic about the value of tests in revealing undiscovered talent and extol their contribution to increased efficiency and accountability in a variety of educational and employment settings. Critics of testing have found the negative effects of testing more compelling. They claim that tests measure too little too narrowly. And some spokesmen for minority interests have attacked standardized tests as artificial barriers to social equality and economic opportunity.

Both high expectations and serious complaints have focused public attention on the underlying questions of what tests actually measure and the meaning to be attached to test scores. The increasing interest of courts, legislatures, and governmental agencies in the way tests are used in selection systems has added a significant new dimension to these questions.

The complexity of the issues and the high emotion generated by testing controversies convinced the sponsors of this project of the need for a dispassionate investigation of testing by a multidisciplinary group of people whose breadth of experience and training would provide the requisite technical mastery, balance, and social understanding. The charge to the Committee was, first, to describe as fully as possible the nature, incidence, and impact of testing practices; second, to identify the fundamental policy questions presented by widespread use of standardized tests; and third, to provide guidance on appropriate use and interpretation of test results. This had led us to pay close attention not only to the status of testing technology, but to the legal, political, and social contexts within which testing takes place.

Our report is not primarily an action document, though there are a number of recommendations; nor is it a highly technical study of mental measurement, written by and for psychometricians. It is, rather, a white paper—a document intended to describe accurately the theory and practice of testing; to illuminate competing interests in a balanced fashion; and, ultimately, to help those who make decisions with tests or about testing to reach better-informed judgments than is now the case. It is to those decision makers—judges, lawmakers and their staffs, educators, employers, personnel administrators and the testing industry—that our efforts have been aimed and to whom this report is addressed. Of course, we also hope that the research community will find it useful.

The Committee was chosen with great care. A majority of the members were drawn from areas unconnected with testing: law, history, anthropology, sociology, economics, experimental psychology, mathematics, and education. The variety of their learning and experiences brought to our discussions of testing issues a constant interplay of different points of view, different ways of asking questions. Among the psychometricians and psychologists who completed the group are scholars who have made important contributions to test theory, as well as practitioners with long experience in test development and personnel selection. All of the members gave freely of their time and their knowledge. Each has helped to form the report, and although individual members may not agree with every point in it, this report represents their consensus.

The content and format of this two-part study of ability testing reflect our decisions about scope, purpose, and audience. Part I, the report of the Committee, presents a wide-ranging discussion of testing issues. Because it is addressed to policy makers and test users, the text has been kept largely free of the critical apparatus of scholarly literature. Chapters 1 through 3 provide an overview of the controversies surrounding testing, an introduction to the concepts, methods, and terminology of ability testing, a brief history of testing in the United States, and a discussion of the proliferation of legal requirements that have come to surround the use of tests. Chapters 4 through 6 describe test use for employment

*Preface* ix

selection and educational purposes, point out common types of misuse, and make recommendations about how tests might be better used to preserve the integrity of the technology while at the same time responding to legitimate social, institutional, and individual goals. Chapter 7 takes a close look at the limitations of standardized tests and then attempts to establish a sense of proportion by placing the controversy over testing within the context of the larger social currents that influence the course of national life. The text and recommendations in Part I are the responsibility of the Committee.

Part II is a set of 11 signed papers. Although the Committee has used the papers liberally and major portions of the report reflect the considerable labors of their authors, the Committee does not necessarily subscribe to the views expressed or interpretations offered in them. But it is here that the interested reader will find a rich introduction to the case law, the research literature, and data sources.

**ACKNOWLEDGMENTS**

This project has been supported with patience and generosity by the Carnegie Corporation of New York, the National Institute of Education, the Office of Personnel Management, the National Institute of Mental Health, and the Ittleson Foundation. In addition to financial support, the Committee is indebted to the Carnegie Corporation, the National Institute of Education, and the Office of Personnel Management for making numerous research reports, data summaries, and other resources available to us.

Our study has been a collaborative venture. In carrying out its work, the Committee met regularly as a whole or in writing groups over a period of 3 years. Individual Committee and staff members produced working papers and position pieces for consideration, two of which appear in Part II. Subcommittees took responsibility for drafting various sections of Part I. The Committee also consulted widely with those who use tests, those who take tests, those who develop tests, and those who regulate testing. In November of 1979, we conducted public hearings in order to give representatives of each group the opportunity to express their point of view and describe their experiences with testing (see Appendix A for a list of participants).

We owe a great deal to the various staff members who have worked with the Committee during its life. Our thanks go first to David A. Goslin, Executive Director of the Assembly of Behavioral and Social Sciences, who has been a source of encouragement and support. Barbara Lerner provided staff leadership in the initial phases of the study and was ably followed by Edwin Hollander. Rita Atkinson, Deborah Coates, and Kathleen Kappy assisted with data collection and produced background pieces for discussion. Martha Feldman and Judy Kron served as research assistants. Susan Sherman helped to develop the project and served as senior research associate throughout our work.

Among those who served as consultants to the Committee, we owe a particular debt to Robert Linn, who gave form to our discussions of technical testing matters, and to Matthew Hale, whose digging into the past provided us with a crucial sense of perspective. Our thanks go as well to the other authors of the signed papers in Part II: Melvin Novick, Toby Friedman and E. Belvin Williams, Daniel Resnick, Patricia Hollander, Beverly Anderson, Rodney Skager, Eric Gardner, and Nancy Cole. A number of others contributed working papers that aided discussion: Michael Rothschild, Carol Gargantiel, C. J. Bartlett, Linda Ingram, Henry Acland, David Martin, Rose Giaconia, and James Richards.

Our acknowledgments would not be complete without special thanks to Eugenia Grohman, whose editing skills were surpassed only by her understanding of the workings of the National Research Council; to Chris McShane, who got us to the press on time; to Jean Savage and Elaine McGarraugh, who worked diligently with the authors of the signed papers to locate lost footnotes and dangling participles; and to Gladys Bostick, administrative secretary, who got everyone to meetings, kept track of innumerable drafts of chapters, and accomplished all with efficiency and tact.

WENDELL R. GARNER, *Chair*
ALEXANDRA K. WIGDOR, *Study Director*
Committee on Ability Testing

# Employment Testing

MATTHEW HALE
# History of Employment Testing

## INTRODUCTION

Employment testing, broadly defined, is probably as old as employment itself. Yet employment tests as we know them today—standardized, objective, and validated examinations based on job analyses—are relatively recent. Not until the late nineteenth century did the U.S. government adopt standardized tests as a way to select civil servants, and only in the second and third decades of this century did private industry use employment tests on anything more than an experimental basis. Employment testing, however, has grown from tentative beginnings early in the century to become a commonplace feature of business and government. By the 1960s, most private businesses, according to several surveys, gave one form of test or another to at least some job candidates; the federal government filled more than 80 percent of all positions by competitive examination; and every state and major city in the United States conducted civil service examinations. Only recently has the use of employment tests begun to decline.

The development of employment testing in the United States, from the first civil service examinations of the nineteenth century to the assessment centers of the 1970s, is closely linked to the emergence of modern industrial society. Two elements of this development deserve special mention: first, employment testing arose as an answer to problems of rapid growth in industrial society and as a way to rationalize a chaotic labor market; and second, employment tests, because they were assumed to reward merit and eliminate special privilege, reflected a general movement in the twentieth century toward "democratizing" American society.

Twentieth-century society, characterized by an increasingly heterogeneous and transient population, large-scale industry, and rapidly expanding bureaucracy, presented problems that neither traditional nor commonsense methods of organization could solve. In response to these problems, Americans embarked at the turn of the century on what Robert Wiebe has called a "search for order": an attempt, through rational and scientific planning, to impose organization and efficiency on a society growing too fast for traditional bonds to hold it together (Wiebe 1967). One manifestation of this search was the use of newly developed ability tests for employee selection. The employer might be able to select job candidates better than the psychologist could, as one critic of testing claimed early in the century, but only if the employer was particularly skilled in judging people and only if the employer's establishment were small. Large enterprises, on the other hand, required a systematic, scientific approach to hiring. Reformers, entrepreneurs, and personnel managers promoted testing as just such an approach; testing, they argued, could overcome the problems of scale, rationalize employee selection, and ensure progress and efficiency.

Not only were businesses larger by the twentieth century, they also required employees with new, specialized skills. Many Americans believed that, in a simpler age, most people could do most jobs (this was the explicit rationale of the spoils system in government), but that, in the modern era, many jobs required special skills or training. Critics pointed to inefficiency in the workplace and high rates of labor turnover as evidence that traditional hiring practices failed to produce a competent work force. Employment tests were seen as a solution. Indeed, dissatisfaction with the "human material" in the labor pool repeatedly spurred the development and application of tests, whether the concerns were over accident-prone trolley drivers or inefficient telephone operators in the 1910s, indecisive or marginally competent managers in the 1940s, or teachers weak in grammar and arithmetic in the 1970s and 1980s. Employment tests, their promoters argued, could identify people with skills or talent and screen out those who lacked the attributes necessary for particular positions.

Many Americans regarded tests not only as a way to identify the most efficient and competent workers, but also as a way to promote democracy by rewarding merit rather than privilege. The acceptance of tests in the Progressive years (and later) reflected the widespread conviction that men—and sometimes women—were to be judged on their individual skills and ability (or, in this case, on test scores assumed to measure skills

## History of Employment Testing

and ability) rather than on appearance, class, heritage, or personal connections. Particularly in the case of civil service examinations, tests were seen as a means of guaranteeing equal opportunity as well as social efficiency.

Very recently, of course, the impact of employment tests on minority groups and the role of tests in perpetuating discrimination, have become major issues. It is impossible to assess this impact historically because the major barriers to equal employment opportunity in the past have been legal and extralegal constraints rather than tests. The civil service examinations, for example, were open to all, but in the early years the hiring official could specify the sex of candidates for specific positions. Many blacks may have scored low on certain employment tests because of their cultural background or because of poor education (if they had taken the tests at all), but in most cases they would not have been eligible for the job even if they had done well. Tests, however, did offer an alternative to the racial and ethnic stereotyping typical of hiring practices throughout the century. Whatever the actual effect of tests, most advocates of testing regarded employment tests as opening jobs to the talented rather than closing them to the underprivileged. Ironically, a tool that was originally seen by its supporters as ensuring selection on the basis of merit rather than privilege has come to be perceived by many as a barrier to social justice.

### CIVIL SERVICE TESTING, 1883–1915

In the United States, the federal government was the first to experiment in a systematic way with employment tests. In 1814, the Army instituted examinations for surgeons, and shortly thereafter the Naval Academy and West Point began to administer tests to prospective students. Certain positions in the federal bureaucracy had testing requirements before the Civil War. The Treasury Department, for example, sporadically conducted examinations for entry into some accounting positions. Candidates were required to write an ordinary business letter, to show themselves acquainted with "the four rules of arithmetic," and "to evince some knowledge of the generally received principles of accounting." And in 1853 Congress required pass-examinations for a large proportion of clerical positions in the District of Columbia. On the whole, however, the spoils system operated without restraint. Government positions, from Cabinet posts to the lowest postal clerkships, were considered prizes for the politically deserving (Van Riper 1958:52-53).

The scandals that shook federal, state, and city governments in the years that followed the Civil War precipitated a movement for reform in government. One of the primary objectives of this movement was to replace the spoils system in civil service with a merit system based on the British method of appointment by competitive examination. In 1871 President Grant set up a civil service commission that conducted examinations for positions in the New York City Customs House and Post Office and in several federal offices in Washington. The experiment proved short-lived, falling before pressure from spoilsmen in 1875, but it served as a model for the Civil Service Commission, established in 1883 in the wake of the assassination of President Garfield by a disappointed office seeker. The heart of the new system was the principle of open competitive examinations, which, presumably, would ensure appointment by merit. The model was largely British, but Congress hoped to escape the academic bias of the English system by requiring that the tests be "practical in character." The tests were designed to allow candidates with eighth-grade educations to compete successfully with college graduates on the basis of merit and experience, not school learning. From the beginning, Congress had hoped to legislate against the creation of a mandarinate in the federal service, and the stipulation that the civil service tests be practical frequently set them apart from psychological testing in private industry (Van Riper 1958, ch. 5).[1]

Initially, only slightly over 10 percent of all federal positions were filled by examination; most of these were clerical positions in Washington and in the nation's largest customs houses. The system, however, grew at a rapid rate until by the end of Theodore Roosevelt's presidency the figure had reached 60 percent. One innovation that allowed the rapid expansion of the system was its extension to certain scientific and technical positions through the nonassembled examination, which substituted ratings based on training and experience for written examinations. By the early twentieth century, the Civil Service Commission administered hundreds of tests to assess proficiency in specific trades and professions; the most common examinations were measures of "general intelligence," which were used in the selection of clerks and messengers and which tested such areas or skills as grammar, arithmetic, general information, and care and accuracy. In the year ending June 1911, according to the Commission's annual report, 105,000 candidates were examined. Of these, 77,000 candidates passed, and 23,000 received positions (U.S. CSC 1912:29; see also, U.S. Congress 1976).

At the same time, civil service reformers extended the merit system to

---

[1] See also U.S. Civil Service Commission (1911, 1912, 1924) for information on the development of the examination system.

state and local governments. New York (1883) and Massachusetts (1884) adopted the merit system with competitive civil service examinations on the federal model shortly after the passage of the Civil Service Act. Before the end of the century, the cities of New York, Albany, Syracuse, Chicago, and Seattle, among others, also adopted the merit system (Shafritz 1975:43). The pace of civil service reform picked up early in the twentieth century, when Progressive reformers adopted efficient government and the recognition of individual merit as major goals. Between 1905 and 1911, Wisconsin, Illinois, Colorado, and New Jersey introduced merit systems; by 1911 6 states, 217 cities, 20 counties, and 7 villages had in part or whole adopted competitive systems of appointment to public service (Lee 1979:22, U.S. CSC 1911:161).

## INDUSTRIAL TESTING BEFORE WORLD WAR I

Leaders of industry in the meantime increasingly turned their attention to the efficient management of personnel. Attempting to rationalize the workplace, employers introduced time cards, job clocks, and other innovations. By the early twentieth century many looked with interest on the work of such efficiency experts as Frederick W. Taylor, who used time-and-motion studies to determine the one best way of performing a task and who advocated piece rates to spur production. In a few cases, mental and physiological tests were adopted as aids in the selection of personnel. Taylor recommended that certain workers be tested before they were hired—the use of reaction-time tests for selecting women in one factory, he suggested, had almost quadrupled productivity and he argued that similar efforts in other factories might produce the same results. At about the same time, several leading corporations, including General Electric and Westinghouse, developed testing and evaluation programs along academic lines in their engineering schools (Nelson 1975, Eilbirt 1959, Haber 1960, Noble 1977). On the whole, however, it was not until the second decade of the century that industrial managers looked seriously at systematic methods of employee selection.

By the 1910s, a turndown in the economy impelled many employers to rethink their hiring policies. Traditionally, hiring had simply been a question of recruiting enough able bodies through newspaper advertisements, fliers, and similar promotional literature. In most businesses, employee recruitment and selection were the prerogative of the individual supervisors. But high rates of labor turnover and industrial accidents—constant themes in the trade and progressive literature of the period—suggested to many that the modern industrial world required a skilled and efficient work force that time-honored hiring practices could no longer guarantee. A manager at Bell Telephone Company, for example, claimed that 1 of 3 of the company's 16,000 operators quit or was dismissed within the first half year of work; another manager blamed human error for 80 percent of the railroad accidents in the United States, in which more than 10,000 people were killed in 1911 (Hale 1980, ch. 10).[2]

To many employers, especially those hiring workers whose jobs required a high degree of care or responsibility, waste and inefficiency in the workplace pointed directly to poor selection procedures. A systematic science of selection, they argued, would go far toward eliminating the disorders of scale—manifested in high rates of labor turnover, strikes, absenteeism, and industrial accidents—that beset modern industry. Indeed, it soon became a central tenet of the new profession of personnel management that all labor problems would be eliminated "when a scheme has been devised which will make it possible to select *the right man for the right place*" (Link 1919:293).

During the 1910s, numerous pseudoscientific systems of employee selection claimed to offer just such schemes. For many managers, racial and ethnic background served as a guide for hiring. For example, a text for a correspondence course (American School of Correspondence 1919, Vol. 2:215) suggested:

It is well known that certain foreign peoples are naturally adapted to certain kinds of work. For instance, Finns, Croatians, and Austrians make good miners; Italians and Swedes are good railroad builders; Russians, Lithuanians, and Poles are good foundry and steel mill workers; Jews, French, and Irish do not take well to monotonous or repetitive work but are particularly adapted to any work requiring action, artistry, and enthusiasm. For all-round rough work, Norwegians, Greeks, Russians, and German Poles are generally recommended.

A particularly popular system was the Blackford Plan of character analysis, devised by Katherine Blackford and popularized in the 1910s in a series of books, including *The Job, the Man, the Boss*, published in 1919. Most psychologists of the day scorned the plan, but many practical businessmen took seriously Blackford's remarks on the character traits of blonds versus brunettes and her advice on reading physiognomy and handwriting. At the same time, a few businessmen turned to systems of mental testing already worked out by psychologists and vocational counselors.

From the 1890s, a growing number of psychologists, led by Francis Galton in England, James McKeen Cattell in the United States, Alfred

---

[2] On labor turnover, see Bureau of Labor Statistics (1917), Eilbirt (1959), Gaudet (1960).

## History of Employment Testing

Binet in France, and Emil Kraepelin in Germany, concentrated on the measurement of individual differences. In doing so, they turned their attention away from the general facts of perception and cognition, which were the central concerns of nineteenth-century experimental psychology. Their predecessors had regarded differences in human aptitude as interesting only insofar as they threw light on the general rules of mind. More practical-minded men like Cattell argued that the measurement of differences, whether in reaction times or in ability to remember nonsense syllables, made possible an applied psychology that could contribute to the progress of civilization as effectively as had engineering. Tests of individual traits conducted in the laboratory or with pencil and paper, Cattell suggested, could serve education, psychotherapy, and vocational guidance (Boring 1942, ch. 18, 19, Young 1923:1-47).

The concern of Cattell and other testers for vocation was typical of the period; vocation had become a central theme of the Progressive years. During this period, according to many social critics, the demands of industrial society had stripped work of its meaning. In the modern world, so the argument went, young boys and girls no longer fell naturally into their proper places in society, but were condemned to live out their lives as misfits. The toll that this situation imposed on society was enormous, for it expressed itself in industrial unrest and personal breakdown. A number of reformers—above all Frank Parsons of Boston—championed scientific vocational guidance as the answer to these social ills. As Parsons and fellow vocational reformers saw it, society was an organism in which each individual had a proper place, determined by his or her special aptitudes and interests. "Men work best," Parsons wrote in 1894, "when they are doing what Nature has especially fitted them for." The function of scientific vocational guidance was to fulfill society's responsibility to put men "as well as timber, stone, and iron in the places for which their natures fit them" (Parsons 1894:69, xvi).[3]

Operating out of the Boston Vocation Bureau early in the twentieth century, Parsons analyzed the aptitudes and interests of young men and women by an eclectic approach that combined interviews, questionnaires, and self-analysis (Parsons 1908:3, Brewer 1942, ch. 5). By 1909, he had enlisted the aid of the German-born and -trained psychologist Hugo Münsterberg of Harvard, a pioneer in applied psychology, to administer psychological tests to his clients and to assist him in his diagnoses (Münsterberg 1910:32-34). Münsterberg widely publicized his work with Parsons. Before long other leading psychologists, including H. L.

---

[3] On Parsons, see Mann (1954:126-144), Davis (1969).

Hollingworth of Barnard and W. D. Scott of Northwestern, had thrown themselves enthusiastically into the design of vocational tests.

Members of the vocational guidance movement, who had strong roots in education and traditional counseling, soon lost interest in mental testing, but at least a few employers and personnel managers recognized that the work of the vocational psychologists had relevance to their own needs. As Hollingworth wrote (1916:79):

> The first definite contribution of vocational psychology is . . . not so much toward the guidance of the individual worker as for the guidance of the employer who may be required to select from a number of applicants those whose general intellectual equipment is most adequate.

By the early 1910s, psychologists were at work developing tests for industry. In 1911, Münsterberg devised a test to eliminate incompetent ship captains at the request of the director of the Hamburg-American shipping line. In the following year the progressive American Association for Labor Legislation, which was financed in part by John D. Rockefeller, asked Münsterberg to develop tests for identifying accident-prone trolley drivers. Münsterberg's tests were unwieldy—although they or modifications of them were used in a number of American and European cities for a decade—and they proved highly controversial (Hale 1980, ch. 10, Münsterberg 1913, ch. 8, 9). Many contemporary psychologists challenged their validity, but as Scott (1913:283) wrote:

> The significant point of it all is that simple tests have been devised and applied in certain typical economic situations and that there is a positive correlation between the standing in the tests and the standing in the practical work.

Almost immediately, other psychologists offered their services to industry. Scott pioneered tests for salesmen for American Tobacco, National Lead Company, Western Electric, and other firms, and he developed the first tests for factory workers for the Joseph and Feiss Company of Cleveland. Edward Thorndike of Columbia University developed tests of salesmanship ability for Metropolitan Life, and Hollingworth and others devised tests for clerks and typists (Baritz 1960:38-39, Viteles 1932, ch. 5, Link 1923:34, Feiss 1915:5-16, Scott 1915). By 1915, according to Hollingworth, tests for twenty types of work had been developed and to one extent or another tried out (1915:919).

Work at the Carnegie Institute of Technology in Pittsburgh also indicated the growing interest of industrial managers and psychologists in employment testing. Administrators at Carnegie, where 50 percent of the students were training for careers in industry and management, recognized a need for "increasing the reliability of selection among applicants

## History of Employment Testing

for employment." To meet this need, they brought in Walter V. D. Bingham from Dartmouth in 1915 as head of a new Division of Applied Psychology (Bingham 1923a:180-181, 1923b:141-159, 1952). The most pressing demand for assistance, according to Bingham, came from sales managers and executives of large manufacturing concerns whose primary responsibility was marketing. How, managers wanted to know, could they select salesmen whose traits of mind and personality most suited them to the job? To conduct research on this question, Bingham set up a Bureau of Salesmanship Research, financed initially by 27 nationally based firms, and he hired Scott to direct it. This cooperative venture, which survived for a decade, not only proved of direct service to industry in developing tests, but it also served as a model for later enterprises.

By 1915, the battle lines on testing were drawn. Enthusiasts like Münsterberg and Scott championed their science. Thorndike wrote with enthusiasm that in two hours of testing a psychologist could diagnose an educated adult's intellectual ability better than could "two teachers or friends who have observed him in the ordinary course of life each for a thousand hours" (Thorndike 1913:139). Early testers claimed that their methods were faster than traditional methods; they also asserted that they were more accurate. Most industrial managers, however, remained skeptical. In response to Münsterberg's description of his trolley driver tests, for instance, a Philadelphia railway man asserted in a trade journal that "the traffic manager will be able to judge of his men a good deal better than Münsterberg or any other of those people who give new names to familiar facts" (see Hale 1980:156). Those who took the tests, apparently, were often no more impressed. Mary Gilson, employment manager at Joseph and Feiss, later recalled that "the girls thought it was a lot of nonsense to have run a needle up a metal alley or do some other 'high jinks'" (see Baritz 1960:39). In this case the women may have had a point. According to the industrial psychologist Henry C. Link, the correlation between productivity and test scores at Joseph and Feiss after 5 years proved to be 0.002. The tests had no value, Link suggested, beyond a rough ability to distinguish left-handedness (1923:34).

## TESTING DURING WORLD WAR I

During World War I, the U.S. Army launched an unprecedented experiment in group testing.[4] For years the military had used academic-style

---

[4] The most complete account of the military testing program in World War I is Yerkes (1921). See also Camfield (1969), Kevles (1968), Samelson (1977), Napoli (1975).

tests to aid in selecting officer candidates, and, in the early years of World War I, European nations, in particular Germany, used psychological tests to select motor transport drivers, pilots, and other specialists (Dorsch 1963:149-150). None of these efforts in military testing, however, approached the scope of the program that the United States launched after the American entry into the war.

War had hardly been declared when in April 1917, Robert M. Yerkes of Harvard, then President of the American Psychological Association, offered the services of his science to the war effort. At Yerkes's urging, the newly founded National Research Council (NRC) of the National Academy of Sciences set up a Committee for Psychology made up of leading psychologists, which immediately set to work on the problem of applying behavioral science to the wartime emergency. Yerkes and others recognized that the selection and classification of recruits was the major personnel problem facing a nation without a large standing army and with no traditions of conscription. To this end, they organized a Committee on the Psychological Examination of Recruits, which included such famous testers as Yerkes, Bingham, and Lewis Terman of Stanford, who had recently adapted Binet's intelligence test for American use.

Working under the Army Surgeon General (because the Army believed that psychological testing was a medical question rather than one of personnel management), the committee undertook the task of classifying "recruits on the basis of intellectual ability, with special reference to the elimination of the unfit and the identification of exceptionally superior ability" (Yerkes 1921:299). Committee members quickly put together the famous Army Alpha test, which was modeled after a number of prewar intelligence tests and which included multiple-choice and true-false questions testing grammar, vocabulary, arithmetic, "common sense," general knowledge, and similar skills or areas. When the testers found in early trials that a large number of recruits could not read or write English, they developed the Army Beta, a test for illiterates that used pictures and diagrams. By early 1918, the tests were being given in recruiting stations around the nation. Within slightly more than a year, according to the official statistics, 1,726,966 men had been tested (Yerkes 1921:99).

Scores on the Alpha or Beta tests became part of each recruit's personnel records. They were available to commanding officers for use in assigning individuals to specific duties, in selecting noncommissioned officers and other special personnel, and in balancing the "intelligence" of military units. The extent to which the results were actually used for these purposes cannot be accurately determined. Many commanders believed that traditional methods of promotion and selection were more reliable than the tests; considerable testimony, however, suggested that test scores did in fact play an important role in many decisions and that many officers came out of the war impressed with the potential of mental testing. One result of the testing program, however, can be identified: Almost 8,000 recruits were recommended for immediate discharge as mentally incompetent, and approximately the same number were assigned to special labor duty (Yoakum and Yerkes 1920:12-13).[5]

Shortly after the organization of the Committee on the Psychological Examination of Recruits, members of the NRC Committee for Psychology organized a Committee on Classification of Personnel (Baritz 1960:46-47, U.S. Adjutant General's Office 1919), which worked out of the office of the Army Adjutant General. The goal of this committee, which included Scott, Bingham, and John B. Watson, the founder of behaviorism, was to assign military personnel to specialized tasks and to rate officers for appointment and promotion. The ordinary methods of industry, they believed, were too slow and unwieldy for the wartime emergency; they hoped instead to develop "a measuring device which can be used *without trade knowledge on the part of the examiner*, for rating in objective, quantitative terms the degree of trade ability possessed by the person under examination" (Chapman 1923:49, 1921). For this purpose they put together batteries of tests based on oral questions about individual trades, questions based on photographs, and sample tasks. These tests were eventually used to rate almost half the personnel in the Army on their abilities, education, and experience. The work of the Committee on Classification, according to a recent historian, represented the first attempt by a large organization, public or private, "to determine the capabilities of all its individual members and to assign them accordingly" (Van Riper 1958:252). Yerkes and Clarence Yoakum wrote that the committee's work "ultimately touched and more or less profoundly modified almost every important aspect of military personnel" (Yoakum and Yerkes 1920:ix).

The Yerkes and Scott committees, always on the verge of open rivalry, represented two different approaches to employment testing, and they foreshadowed a split that emerged in the 1920s and the following decades. Scott and Bingham argued for tests of proficiency in or aptitude for a specific trade; Yerkes contended that "general intelligence," which another psychologist defined as "*the capacity to learn those things of most general use to civilized man*" (Dunlap 1923:74), was the "best available single indication of a person's occupational usefulness" (in

---

[5] For a discussion of the actual use of the testing program in World War I, see Samelson (1977:278-280).

Baritz 1960:65). In the massive analysis of the Army testing program written for the National Academy of Sciences (NAS), Yerkes and his colleagues found what they considered striking differences among the levels of intelligence of men in different occupations. The implication was that occupations could be ordered hierarchically by the degree of intelligence demanded and that the most appropriate selection tests for a given occupation were tests of "general intelligence." That the significant correlation might have been between a high level of education (and therefore a high social status) and a high occupational status was not seriously considered.

Another important result of the Army testing program was its apparent confirmation of racial stereotypes, and therefore, ironically, its validation of employment practices that most psychologists considered prescientific. In a sample of 162,526 soldiers tested, the NAS report found a wide variation in the scores of men born in different countries, the highest scores belonging to recruits from northern and western Europe, the lowest from eastern and southern Europe. Especially striking were the low scores of blacks, most of whom, like a large number of the foreign-born, took the Beta examinations. "The intellectual status of the Negro," according to the report, was "greatly inferior to that of the white" (Samelson 1977:280, Yerkes 1921:564, 693-699, 705-742).[6] These data proved a boon to postwar eugenicists and nativists, who took them as proof of their racial views. They led to a major public debate between psychologists and social commentators like Walter Lippmann over the validity of intelligence testing and the roles of heredity and environment in the development of general intelligence, and they provided ammunition to anti-immigrationists, who successfully pushed through a restrictionist immigration policy in the 1920s.

Psychologists may have disagreed over the relative values of tests of "general intelligence" and of specific aptitudes, and over the relation between intelligence and ethnicity, but almost all emerged from the war convinced that wartime testing techniques would prove invaluable to industry and education. "Great will be our good fortune," Yerkes wrote in 1919, "if the lesson in human engineering which the war has taught us is carried over directly and effectively into our civil institutions and activities" (Yoakum and Yerkes 1920:viii). He need not have worried, for, as Cattell observed, the war put psychology "on the map of the United States" and precipitated a boom in testing that continued for half a decade (in Samelson 1977:275).

---

[6] For a criticism of Yerkes' conclusions by a contemporary psychologist, see Viteles (1928).

## TESTING IN THE 1920s AND 1930s

After the war, the National Research Council and the Army Surgeon General were flooded with requests for information on testing (Baritz 1960:48). The success of the military program alone does not explain the newfound interest of private industry and employment managers in the possibilities of testing. In the final year of the war and in the immediate postwar years, American industry faced an unprecedented level of disruption in the labor market created by a sluggish economy, frequent and often violent strikes, many of which had radical overtones, and the inevitable difficulties that went along with demobilization. Above all, at least in the minds of personnel managers, high rates of absenteeism and turnover disrupted the economy and undermined industrial efficiency. Turnover, which one federal group called "a national menace," was in fact occurring at a startlingly high rate (Federal Board for Vocational Education 1919:9). The U.S. Bureau of Labor Statistics reported that in Detroit the annual turnover rate, defined as the ratio of the total number of separations to the average number of employees, was 300 percent in two of every five firms and 200 percent in four of five. Rates of turnover in other cities were almost as high (Federal Board for Vocational Education 1919:42-49). Some firms, like the Ford Motor Company, successfully cut turnover by raising wages and installing welfare programs for employees, but almost all managers agreed that the careful selection of workers was a prerequisite to reducing turnover to an acceptable level. As in the Progressive years earlier in the century, managers looked to a wide variety of schemes to aid in hiring; the wartime success of the military program made psychological testing a more popular alternative than ever before.

Many professional psychologists, recognizing opportunity when they saw it (and fearing that the market would be taken over by character analysts, graphologists, and other charlatans), enthusiastically offered their services to industry. In 1919, the NRC replaced its Committee for Psychology with a Division for Anthropology and Psychology. The new division promoted personnel psychology and employment testing through the organization of the Personnel Research Foundation and the *Journal of Personnel Research*, soon renamed the *Personnel Journal*.

In the same year, Walter Dill Scott set up the first independent psychological consulting service for industry, the Scott Corporation, which grew directly out of the work of the Committee on Classification of Personnel. Scott's enterprise was short-lived, but in 1921 James McKeen Cattell, with the financial backing of most of the leaders of the science, organized the Psychological Corporation, which for more than 50 years has provided expert consulting in employment testing and other aspects of applied psychology. Other organizations also took up the cause. The Carnegie Institute's Bureau of Salesmanship Research, renamed the Bureau of Personnel Research after the war, continued its work on testing; the Life Insurance Sales Research Bureau, founded as a cooperative enterprise by the Carnegie Institute in 1922, assisted members of the life insurance industry in hiring and rating salesmen (Baritz 1960:51-53, Bingham 1923b:182, Yerkes 1923:172-178, Cattell 1923:165-171, Flinn 1922:7-13).

The psychological profession as a whole reflected this increased concern with the problems of industrial efficiency. By 1920, according to Lewis Terman, more than half of the members of the American Psychological Association worked primarily in applied psychology, and 25 of the 400 members were carrying out studies in industrial psychology (Terman 1919:1-4). Henry Link complained in 1923 that "the use of psychological tests in industry is most conspicuous because it is so rare" (1923:32), but this was not for lack of enthusiasm on the part of psychologists.

Link was speaking of carefully constructed, validated testing programs; in this respect he was correct. In 1921, approximately 32 companies, one survey reported, used employment tests "in a patient and experimental manner." On the other hand, hundreds of companies bought ready-made tests, like the Army Alpha, which was applied with the same indiscriminate enthusiasm as the Blackford Plan and other pseudoscientific schemes (Baritz 1960:67).[7] However much psychologists pleaded for caution, they in fact only encouraged personnel managers to adopt tests as a panacea when, like Cattell, they proclaimed that the direct application of tests already in existence could save certain industries millions of dollars a year (Cattell 1923:169).

Among the more careful attempts at instituting a testing program were Link's at the Winchester Repeating Arms Company, which was called a model of thoroughness and accuracy, E. L. Thorndike's for the Metropolitan Life Insurance Company, Millicent Pond's for the Scovill Manufacturing Company's apprentice school for toolmakers and machinists, Morris Viteles's for the Philadelphia Yellow Cab and Rapid Transit Company, and Bruce V. Moore's for the Westinghouse Educational Department (Borow 1944:71, Moore 1921, Kornhauser and Kingsbury 1924). These and similar programs were significant because the men and women who administered them attempted to analyze the requirements of the jobs for which they were testing and to apply statistical methods to correlate

---

[7] For a criticism of the Blackford plan by contemporary psychologists, see Paterson and Ludgate (1922).

test scores with success on the job—whether defined as high ratings by supervisors, high productivity, or long tenure. These testers often differed over the relative value of tests of "general intelligence," proficiency and trade tests, and tests of aptitude, but they agreed that all programs had to be validated. "The chief problem of employment psychology," Link wrote, "is to determine the value of particular tests when applied to particular tasks. The first step is to *test tests* rather than applicants" (Link 1919:20). Most important, testers agreed that no testing program could by itself be successful. To contribute to rational employment practices, a program had to be part of a general selection process that included such other practices as interviews, application blanks, references, and personal history forms.

The U.S. Civil Service Commission by this time was particularly interested in the new developments in testing. As early as 1917, the Commission's Chief Examiner, George R. Wales, approached Thorndike and Scott for information on their work; after the Armistice, the Commission, with the assistance of Yerkes, administered the Army Alpha test to a sample of its own clerical workers. Although the tests were judged no better than the established civil service tests, they convinced the Commission that the techniques of psychological testing had much to offer. The Commission hired a series of expert psychologists, including Watson and L. L. Thurstone, to assist in streamlining existing tests and developing new ones. By 1922, short-answer, objective tests were introduced for several positions. In 1923 the Commission set up a Research Section in the Office of the Chief Examiner and appointed as its head L. J. O'Rourke of the Air Service Psychological Research Laboratory, an advocate of the latest techniques of mental testing and advanced statistical methods. Under O'Rourke's leadership, the Research Section began immediate work on a broad program of general research, concentrating on measures of "general adaptability" for a wide range of positions and developing shortened examinations for clerks, policemen, firemen, postal workers, and others. In the years that followed, civil service researchers became major contributors to the development of job-specific tests (Van Riper 1958:309-310, Filer and O'Rourke 1923, Kavruk 1956, U.S. Civil Service Commission 1924:xl-xlvii).

Most employers had neither the patience nor the money to adopt testing programs along the lines that Link and other psychologists outlined, especially because psychologists so often disagreed among themselves over the proper techniques and because careful validation programs, when instituted, often showed a low correlation between test scores and job success. In the early 1920s, the Atlantic Refining Company, for example, instituted a program of testing supervisors. After a year, the company found that the correlation between the results of their test and salaries was 0.37, which it considered unacceptably low. As a result, the program was abandoned (Baritz 1960:71-72).[8] Numerous other firms, according to observers at the time, also discovered that the results of their testing programs were not useful. One psychologist estimated that about 90 percent of the companies that began to use tests after World War I found that they did not work (Baritz 1960:71-72). By 1925, according to Morris Viteles, only 4.5 percent of a sample of companies used psychological tests in hiring (Scott et al. 1961). The postwar boom in testing had peaked by 1925.

The decline in employment testing was attributable to more than the failure of many testing programs. The marked upturn in the economy in the early 1920s and the sudden drop in both rates of turnover and concern over turnover also contributed to the decline. Equally important, perhaps, was the growing disenchantment of many industrial psychologists with employment tests (Borow 1944:70-71, Baritz 1960:72-73). Employment psychologists in the 1910s assumed that specific aptitudes or skills were the primary factors in job success, productivity, and—according to some—job satisfaction. By the 1920s, however, psychologists and personnel managers fell increasingly under the sway of functionalists and small-group theorists, who were redefining American sociology. The social context, these sociologists argued, was more important in determining behavior than were the individual traits of the people who made up the society. This theory received startling confirmation toward the end of the decade in the work of industrial sociologists at the Hawthorne Works of the Western Electric Company.

The Hawthorne experiments, which have been called "the first major social science experiment," radically shifted the direction of personnel work and, as the historian Loren Baritz has written, "became standard material for students of industrial sociology and human relations" (1960:77). For more than a decade, scientists from the National Research Council, Massachusetts Institute of Technology, Harvard Business School, and Western Electric closely monitored the work practices of employees in the Hawthorne Works. Their conclusions overturned the individual-centered approach of a previous generation of social theorists. There is no need here to describe the experiments in detail, but it should be emphasized that their results—which are still in dispute—convinced many industrial psychologists and personnel managers that social relations within

---

[8] On the decline of testing in the mid-1920s, see especially Baritz (1960:58-76), Napoli (1975:90), Borow (1944:70-71).

the workplace were more important than individual aptitudes or indeed skills, in determining performance on the job and productivity. According to F. J. Roethlisberger, who participated in the study, the famous bank-wiring room studies of the Hawthorne project demonstrated "no direct relation between performance . . . and capacity to perform as measured by dexterity or intelligence tests" (Roethlisberger and Dickson 1939:445-446). Elton Mayo of Harvard, one of the early leaders of the work, concluded: "The belief that the behavior of an individual within the factory can be predicted before employment upon the basis of a laborious and minute examination by tests of his technical and other capacities is mainly, if not wholly, mistaken" (1945:111; also see Baritz 1960:94).

The Hawthorne experiments, which became widely publicized in the early 1930s, seemed to confirm the conclusions that economic conditions were forcing on personnel managers and industrial psychologists. The use of individual tests for specific skills, particularly clerical and typing skills, remained in practice, but, according to one estimate, 16 percent of the firms that used intelligence tests for selection abandoned them in the first years of the Depression (Baritz 1960:128-129). When mental aptitude tests were given, they were more and more used to eliminate candidates who appeared to be obviously unfit than to find the right person for the right slot. As difficulties with labor grew in the 1930s and as unions gained strength, managers concentrated on personnel counseling—that is, satisfying employees who were already there—instead of on selection techniques. Where managers did use tests, they increasingly emphasized interest and personality inventories, with which they hoped to identify workers who would fit in well with the industrial "team" and who would find their work satisfying.

With millions looking for work, tests of vocational interest and aptitude took on a new importance. In the early 1930s, the Minnesota Employment Stabilization Research Institute set up an occupational analysis clinic that diagnosed thousands of unemployed with an elaborate battery of vocational tests; soon organizations in other areas followed the Minnesota example. In 1933 the National Occupational Conference set up a clearinghouse for information on guidance, promoted research on the measurement of differences in attitudes relevant to vocational success, and commissioned Walter Bingham's classic study *Aptitudes and Aptitude Testing*, which appeared in 1937 (Borow 1944:71-73, Bingham 1937). In 1934 the newly reorganized U.S. Employment Service established an occupational research program that launched a study of the psychological aptitudes required to perform specific jobs. The worker-analysis section of the program began a major project validating aptitude tests then in use in industry, devising new trade tests, and developing an array of research tools and statistical aids. Its report, edited by William Stead (Stead et al. 1940), was the major source of validation studies in the 1940s. As a result of this work, by World War II the Employment Service was able to assist "in the selection of employees by aptitude tests at the specific request of many war plants" (Borow 1944:73).[9]

The use of tests in industry was low in the first years of the Depression. In 1932, the U.S. Bureau of Labor Statistics, which surveyed 224 establishments with a total of 387,826 employees in a wide range of industries, reported that only 14 establishments (6.3 percent) used any kind of intelligence, aptitude, or proficiency tests. Many of the tests were relatively simple. Some companies tested for ability to read English; two publishing firms tested men in the composing room for knowledge of arithmetic, spelling, and geography; a furniture firm tested mechanical efficiency in cabinetmakers; and another company gave intelligence tests, including the Otis test, which had been the basis of the Army Alpha tests, to candidates for executive and supervisory positions. Some firms required aptitude tests for employees who would be using expensive equipment, and a New England firm required an intelligence test for all applicants seeking office positions and a mechanical ability test for factory workers. All of the firms that used tests were happy with them (U.S. Bureau of Labor Statistics 1932:1008).

Walter Dill Scott reported very different results in a 1930 survey of the nation's largest firms: he found that 46 percent of the 195 responding firms gave stenographic or clerical tests, 27 percent gave trade tests, and 17 percent gave "intelligence" tests (Scott et al. 1961:566). A survey of over 2,000 firms by the National Industrial Conference Board (NICB) (1936:23-24) yielded results closer to those of the U.S. Bureau of Labor Statistics. Only 7.3 percent of the firms responding had any kind of testing program. The most common tests were intelligence and aptitude tests for clerical workers, followed by tests for wage earners and trade tests. The difference between Scott's figures and the NICB figures points to the unreliability of the survey methods, but it also reflects Scott's concentration on best-known firms.

A striking trend of the 1930s and 1940s was the increasing use of personality inventories in employment. This trend reflected an effort among personnel managers for stability in the work force during times of considerable labor unrest; it also reflected the emphasis that post-Hawthorne industrial management placed on such intangibles as the willingness of an individual to work as a member of a team.

---

[9] On the U.S. Employment Service, also see Adams 1969, Stead and Masincup 1942:xxx-xxxviii.

Even before World War I, effective personality and interest tests had been the dream of certain testers, particularly Münsterberg, whose German training had alerted him to the "whole personality" of the worker. During the war, Robert S. Woodworth put together a personality development scale, first given in standardized form to recruits to screen out those who would be particularly susceptible to shell shock and other wartime disorders. The scale proved unsuccessful—the same patients who had obtained a median score of 36 hysterical symptoms before Armistice were found to have a median score of 1 after—but Woodworth's work served as a basis for the Thurstone Personality Scale, the Allport Ascendance-Submission Test, and other scales that were adopted for industrial purposes in the 1930s (see especially National Industrial Conference Board 1941:30-37). Shortly after the war, Bruce V. Moore developed interest tests for the Westinghouse Electric Educational Department. According to Moore, these tests could be used together with ratings by interviewers and supervisors to distinguish students who would be successful in design engineering from those who would be successful in sales (Moore 1921).

By the early 1930s, a number of personnel managers began to administer personality and interest inventories to prospective employees in order to cut down rates of turnover and ensure a more cooperative work force. In a depressed economy, much interest focused on salesmen, whose major job qualification—sales ability—was tied closely to personality. Eugen J. Benge, director of personnel for U.S. Gypsum in Chicago and a veteran of the Carnegie Bureau of Salesmanship Research, for example, developed a scale to rate prospective salesmen on their performance in interviews and on the information they supplied in application forms (he gave high scores to married men between 30 and 34 years old). Benge also devised a test for "dominance," "people interest," "judgment," and sales information. Benge claimed that the use of this scale in selecting employees, which was popular in the 1930s and 1940s, increased sales production and reduced turnover (1939:13-14).

By the end of the 1930s, a small group of firms used personality inventories to identify stable, loyal, and productive workers. The most common inventories were the Bernreuter Personality Inventory, which was claimed to measure neurotic tendencies, self-sufficiency, introversion-extroversion, dominance-submission, sociability, and confidence, and the Humm-Wadsworth Temperament Scale, which rated candidates on "general adjustment" and "constructive control of basic temperamental drives" (NICB 1941:35, Wadsworth 1941:58-60). Guy M. Wadsworth, one of the developers of the Humm-Wadsworth, spelled out the intention of his test in 1941:

The worker is, first of all, a person who must fit into the social community in which he works. . . . As recent industrial relations readily attest, the livability of the supervisor-employee relationship is a problem of primary magnitude. We should know something of the prospective employee *as a person*, before he goes out on the job.

Wadsworth claimed that his test could be used to identify those workers who would "enter into the working relationships cooperatively" and to screen out "chronic hot-heads" (Wadsworth 1941:19, 59).

Employers generally echoed the promotional rhetoric of the test designers when they justified personality inventories. A personnel manager at the Atlantic Refining Company, for example, claimed that skill was much less important than " 'personality' and 'interest' factors" for typists (NICB 1939:15). A manager of the Woodward Governor Company of Rockford, Illinois (1941), reported that he could easily find job candidates who were highly skilled, but he wanted ones who would stick. With the assistance of the Personnel Institute of Chicago, the company developed a test that, it was believed, judged ability, strength of character, the power to resist temptation, and "oomph." Another firm, Cherry-Burrell (1941), an equipment supplier for the milk industry in Chicago, tested for the ability to get along with fellow workers.

## TESTING IN WORLD WAR II AND THE POSTWAR YEARS

World War II, which, like World War I, placed extraordinary demands on the personnel systems of industry and government alike, further stimulated the growing interest in testing.[10] The U.S. Army and Navy had dropped their general testing programs in 1919 and retained only a modified personnel classification system left over from Scott's work. As war neared, however, military policymakers and civilian psychologists recognized the need for renewing the testing and classification program; well before American entry into the war, they began a coordinated program to adapt the advances in psychological testing and personnel management to military purposes. The first step was taken in 1940, when the National Research Council, at the request of the War Department, set up a Committee on Classification of Military Personnel. To head the committee, the NRC selected Walter V. Bingham, who soon assumed the title of Chief Psychologist of the Army. Under Bingham's direction, a personnel research section was established in the Office of the Adjutant

---

[10] Unless otherwise noted, the description of employment testing during World War II comes from the following sources: Hunter (1946), Bingham (1944), Baritz (1960, ch. 8).

## History of Employment Testing

General, and staff and civilian psychologists set out to develop a testing program.

Bingham later reported that his "welcome was in sharp contrast to experiences of World War I" (Bingham in Boring et al. 1952, Vol. 4:23)—an indication that the prestige of psychology and employment testing had grown in the previous decades. Under Bingham, new tests were developed to select officer candidates, to determine mechanical and clerical aptitude, to measure aptitude for specific skills such as radiotelegraphy, and to measure knowledge of specific trades. The staff of the personnel research section also developed the Army General Classification Test, which, according to Bingham, made "no pretense of measuring *native* intelligence," but rather was used as "a rough indication of trainability," dividing recruits into five broad categories: very rapid learners, rapid learners, average learners, slow learners, and very slow learners (Bingham in Boring et al. 1952, Vol. 4:22, Bingham 1941, U.S. Adjutant General's Office 1943). By the end of the war, more than 9,000,000 recruits, or one-seventh of the male population of the United States, had taken the test. Unlike the earlier Army Alpha and Beta tests, whose results were often ignored, the Army General Classification Test formed the backbone of Army selection and classification procedures (Napoli 1975:182-183, Partington and Bryant 1946:111).

Early in the war, the College Entrance Examination Board (CEEB), which by the 1930s had become a large-scale and respected enterprise in educational testing, offered its services to the military. John M. Stalnaker, Associate Secretary of the Board, was appointed chairman of the NRC Committee on Service Personnel—Selection and Training, and he subsequently took a position in the Navy. Assuming that tests used to select college students would be appropriate for selecting officers, Stalnaker and testing experts from the CEEB put together the V-12 and the A-12 tests for officer candidates in the Army and Navy (Fuess 1950:162-178). The CEEB, under contract, administered and scored the tests throughout the war.

One of the most successful testing programs in World War II was the Army Air Forces' selection procedures for pilot and air crew trainees (Flanagan 1948, Thorndike 1949, Napoli 1975:183-187). Before the war, the air forces had relied on medical examinations, psychiatric interviews, and educational records to select candidates for pilot training. Because of a shortage of qualified medical examiners and because of the success of other Army testing programs, however, the air forces began psychological testing in 1941, and John C. Flanagan of the University of Pittsburgh was appointed to head the new Psychological Research Agency in the medical division. Under Flanagan's direction, Air Force psychologists and consultants developed a battery of mental and physiological tests that predicted the success of pilot cadets in the training program. It was later estimated that these tests saved the Air Force $1,000 for every dollar spent on pilot training (Lawshe and Balma 1946:7). Before the war was over, the testing program was expanded to include other members of flight crews.

A major concern of the military was to devise effective ways of assessing the qualities of leadership and reliability. The Office of Strategic Services (OSS) conducted the most striking experiment in testing for these qualities, primarily at Station S in northern Virginia. The plan was modeled on German and British programs in which military psychologists set up retreats where candidates for positions of high responsibility took batteries of tests, but the OSS added to this plan an emphasis on situational tests. Between 1943 and 1945, more than 5,000 candidates for the OSS passed through three-day testing sessions at Station S or one-day sessions at other sites. The candidates assumed false identities and cover stories and were then subjected to specially designed mental and personality tests. Central to this program were the situational tests, including such exercises as the famous "brook" test, in which a group of men were to transport a delicate range-finder, "skillfully camouflaged as a log," and a box of percussion caps, camouflaged as a rock, across an eight-foot brook, using only a few short boards, three lengths of rope, and a barrel without a bottom. During this and other exercises, OSS psychologists observed and rated the recruits. Men were then selected for overseas duty on the basis of the ratings of the assessors (U.S. OSS 1948, ch. 3).

The OSS tests departed from previous tests in the United States. Borrowing from the group interaction theory of Kurt Lewin, who was one of the people responsible for developing the program, OSS psychologists adopted what they called an "organismic" approach, which stressed tests for general "effectiveness," and rejected the "elementalistic" approach of earlier tests, which sought to measure specific traits. By observing how a candidate reacted to a specific situation that simulated the work for which he was training, OSS psychologists hoped to assess the candidate's ability to perceive and interpret a situation properly and "to coordinate his acts and direct them in the proper sequence toward the proper objects." In the situational tests, the psychologist did not measure discrete skills (although these were also tested at Station S), but set up "tasks and situations which cannot be properly solved without organization, since it is the power to organize, as much as any other power, that he wishes to measure." The program, according to the OSS report, *Assessment of Men*, was "the first attempt in America to design and carry out selection procedures in conformity with the so-called *organismic* (Gestalt) principles." The effectiveness of the program has been questioned, but the psychologists involved were convinced that it offered a model for selecting people for positions of responsibility in the civilian as well as the military world (U.S. OSS 1948:3, 38-39).

Wartime conditions also fostered interest in testing in private industry. As in World War I, war disrupted the labor market; it necessitated the hiring of people, including women and blacks, who had not traditionally been in the job market; and it led to high rates of turnover and absenteeism. At Sears Roebuck, for example, 17,000 employees entered military service during the war years, representing nearly one-half the company's total male personnel in 1941 (Worthy 1951:8). In an RCA plant in Camden, New Jersey, 22 percent of a group of 212 workers hired in 1944 had left within a month and more than 50 percent had left by six months. Both companies instituted tests to stabilize their work force (Bolanovich 1948).

In the immediate postwar years, new techniques of machine scoring, developed in the 1930s, made the mass use of tests more economical. Psychological consulting services and the U.S. Employment Service, at the same time, promoted ready-made tests for many different occupations. In 1947, 560 commercial tests were available, and from 1949 to 1954 the sale of test blanks tripled (Baritz 1960:156, Habbe 1948:3, Whyte 1954:118). A large testing industry had also arisen to service companies that found it too expensive or time-consuming to develop their own programs. Such new firms as Klein Institute for Aptitude Testing and Rohrer, Hibler and Replogle, which in the late 1960s employed 91 Ph.D.s in psychology, joined established organizations like the Psychological Corporation in developing tests and evaluating personnel (*Business Week* 1965:74, Whyte 1954:118-119, Klaw 1950:107). Also during the war and afterward, the U.S. Employment Service made standard tests available to companies at no cost if they would report their results to the Service. In 1949 approximately 300 companies made use of these services (Baritz 1960:156).

Surveys by Walter Dill Scott and the National Industrial Conference Board indicated an increase in testing in private industry in the late 1940s and early 1950s. In a survey published in 1940, Scott reported that 26 percent of a sample of "best-known" companies gave intelligence tests for selection and promotion; in a 1947 survey, the figure had increased to 38 percent and in 1953 to 56 percent. From 1947 to 1953, the use of tests of all types grew from 66 percent to 75 percent (Scott et al. 1961:566). (Scott did report that testing in general, and clerical, trade, and performance tests in particular, declined from 1940 to 1947. Perhaps the return to the labor market of veterans trained in clerical, skilled, and semiskilled

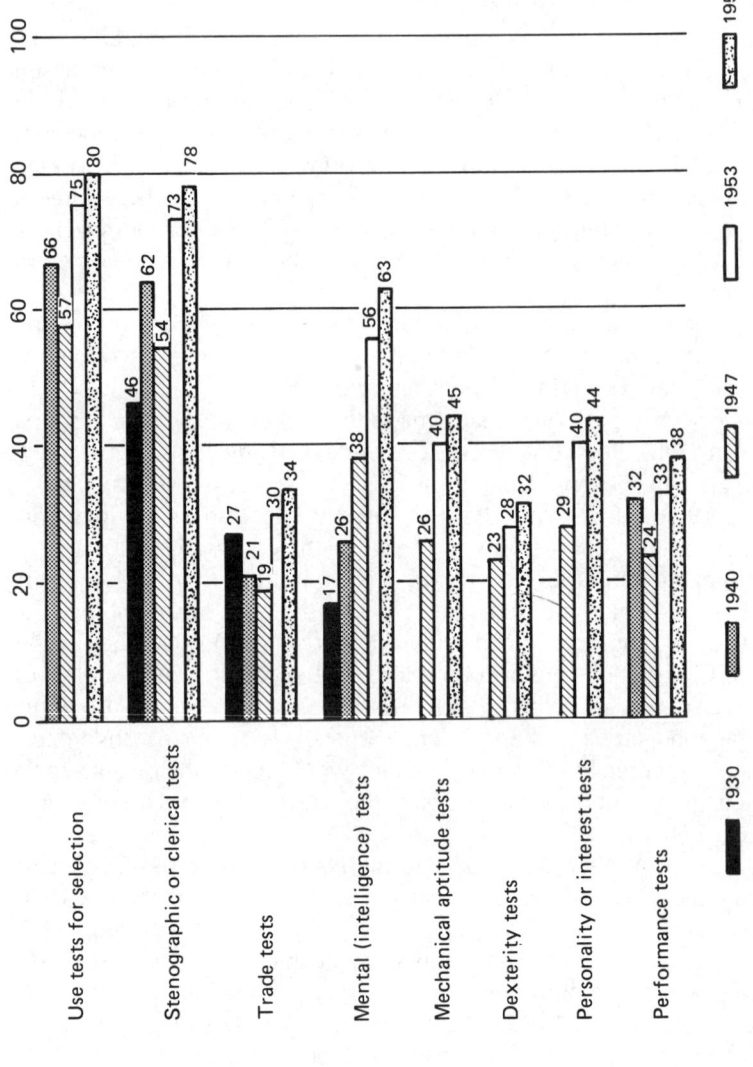

**FIGURE 1** Use of tests for selection and placement by well-known companies. SOURCE: Scott et al. (1961:566).

# History of Employment Testing

work reduced the need for these job-specific tests.) Results of Scott's surveys from 1930 to 1957 are given in Figure 1. In 1946 the NICB, in a broader survey, found testing less prevalent than Scott had: 16.8 percent of 3,498 firms responding in the survey used tests of one form or another. Although the figures were lower than Scott's, they were almost twice those reported by the NICB in the 1930s (NICB 1947:13, 32).

The use of tests in private industry grew steadily through the 1950s and 1960s. In an NICB survey of 1954, 37 percent of respondents claimed to use one form or another of test, generally in selecting or promoting employees. By 1964, the number had increased sharply to 80 percent. In the 1964 survey, insurance companies, banks, and utilities were the most likely to test, and trade firms the least (NICB 1964a,b,c). The most common tests were clerical, followed by intelligence, mechanical ability, personality, and interest. Other surveys, for example by the Bureau of National Affairs (BNA), reported even higher percentages (Bureau of National Affairs 1958, 1963).

In the postwar years, state merit systems also expanded rapidly. In the 1930s, the U.S. Employment Service had promoted examinations in state employment services—in fiscal year 1934, 65,000 persons took written examinations in 38 states (Hohenstein 1956:274)—and several states, including Maine, Michigan, and Connecticut, enacted civil service laws. The most important stimulus to state civil service testing, however, was a 1939 amendment to the Social Security Act. To combat inefficiency and political abuse in the state administration of federal funds, Congress required in this amendment that states establish and maintain merit systems for employees in social security programs. This requirement was soon extended to other federal grant programs. The State Technical Advisory Board of the Social Security Administration (later replaced by the Office of Merit Systems of the Department of Health, Education, and Welfare) assisted states in developing "practical written tests," and its illustrative booklet provided material used in many state examinations (Aronson 1973:134-141, Adkins 1956:260-61). The results of the testing requirement and of federal assistance were striking. By 1949, all but two states had merit systems for public assistance and public health programs. By the 1960s, states with comprehensive merit systems for the first time outnumbered states with systems limited primarily to federally funded programs (Hohenstein 1956:296, Aronson 1973:142).

## ASSESSING MANAGERIAL POTENTIAL

One of the most important trends during the postwar years was the increasing use of psychological tests to select management personnel. At least since Bruce Moore's work for Westinghouse in 1919, leading corporations had experimented with psychological testing as part of programs for selecting managers, either from college recruits or from their own work force. Until the 1940s, however, relatively few companies used tests in any systematic fashion to identify managerial talent. Most relied on personnel records if the potential manager were already a member of the company and references and interviews if he were not.

The situation changed in the 1940s and 1950s, as managers came to play an increasingly prominent role in the corporate structure. By the 1930s, several social commentators, following the argument in Adolf A. Berle's and Gardiner C. Means's *The Modern Corporation and Private Property*, had come to distinguish between ownership and management and to stress the key role of management in the modern, technical world. In 1941 James Burnham suggested in *The Managerial Revolution* that a class of engineers, salesmen, minor executives, and social workers ran the United States. Others argued that a key elite, directing a select group of corporations, was the "dominant force" in society. Whatever the case, the message was the same: American industry and the American economy were held together by a core of talented managers (or not so talented, according to some critics); the American future depended on the recruitment of talent into managerial ranks.

At the same time, as many observers were proclaiming a managerial revolution, the number of managers grew markedly. In the late 1950s, Frederick Harbison of Princeton reported an average increase of 32 percent in the supervisory ranks of two-thirds of a group of companies that he had studied for several years. According to another estimate, the number of nonproduction workers increased 52 percent from 1947 to 1957, while the number of production employees increased only 1 percent; according to still another, the number of professional and technical employees in business increased 200 percent from 1947 to 1957 (Spencer 1959). This rapid increase in managers and professionals precipitated what many called a crisis in talent. From the mid-1940s to the present, the shortage of technical and managerial talent has been a constant theme of industrial analysts. "The unavailability of competent men to make organizational decisions," Felix Lopez wrote in 1967, "represents a crisis in the survival and growth, not just of individual organizations, but of whole societies" (Lopez 1970:4, Hinrichs 1969:425).

During the 1940s, many managers, aware of the military programs for testing officer candidates, hoped to apply tests to the solution of their own problems in selecting management personnel. In 1941, a Lockheed personnel man (Irwin 1942:105) suggested:

## History of Employment Testing

One of the key advantages of testing is its help in the selection of leaders and supervisors, men with the capacity to get along well with those under them, command their respect, and co-operate to get the job done thoroughly and pleasantly.

One of the earliest and most comprehensive testing systems was inaugurated during the war years by Sears Roebuck, which had been particularly affected by loss of personnel to the military. With the help of L. L. Thurstone of the University of Chicago, Sears installed a comprehensive testing program, including tests of intelligence, personality, and vocational interest, to assist in the selection of a reserve group of managers from its own ranks (Worthy 1951:8-17, Emmet and Jeuck 1950:555-558). The standard Sears executive battery, it was claimed, could uncover outstanding mental qualities that might be obscured in certain situations, and it could detect "a basic instability or a deep-seated temperamental maladjustment that might not become evident except in periods of stress" (Worthy 1951:16). By the end of 1950, the tests had been administered to 10,000 people.

In their testing programs, companies like Sears demonstrated an interest in selecting managers with appropriate personal traits as well as skills. Indeed, personality inventories became increasingly popular in the selection of both managers and nonmanagers. In the 1940s, two editions of the National Industrial Conference Board's *Experience with Psychological Tests* devoted considerable space to discussions of the Humm-Wadsworth scale and other personality measures (National Industrial Conference Board 1941, 1948). By the 1950s, the Minnesota Multiphasic Personality Inventory (MMPI), developed to identify certain types of mental illness, and the Bernreuter Personality Inventory, which had sold a million copies by 1953, were in even wider use (Hathaway 1964, Whyte 1954:119). According to Walter Dill Scott, 44 percent of a sample of the best-known firms used personality inventories in 1953, up from 29 percent in 1947; a *Fortune* survey published a year later revealed that 63 percent of a sample of corporations, including General Electric, Sears Roebuck, and Westinghouse, used personality tests in selecting managers (Whyte 1954:117).[11]

Many professional psychologists and personnel managers had long questioned the use of these inventories, and by the mid-1950s they came under open attack. The social critic Walter Whyte launched the attack in his article, "The Fallacies of 'Personality' Testing," published in *Fortune*

---

[11] On the use of projective tests in employment, see especially Kinslinger (1966).

in 1954 and later included in *The Organization Man*. According to Whyte, the tests screened for the traits of tranquility, contentment, and stability, and they eliminated extremes of any sort. They were designed, he argued, to create an organization of yes-men. "If the tests were rigorously applied across the board today," he wrote, "half of the most dynamic men in business would be out walking the streets for a job" (Whyte 1954:118). To the annoyance of many of the testers, he included a section on how to cheat on the most common inventories then in use. Several other attacks followed Whyte's, most notably Martin Gross's *The Brain Watchers* in 1962. By the mid-1960s, personality testers were on the defensive.

The attacks of Whyte, Gross, and others anticipated congressional hearings in 1964 on the use of personality inventories by the government. To be sure, the U.S. Civil Service Commission, committed to job-specific, practical tests, had never adopted personality inventories. In 1965, John W. Macy, Jr., then Civil Service Commissioner, testified to Congress that, "measured against technical standards or against standards of acceptability, present personality tests and inventories do not justify use as selection methods" (Macy 1965a,b). Other federal agencies, however, used personality inventories as screening devices. The Peace Corps, for example, administered the MMPI to all trainees to identify those who possibly had latent mental disorders or "personality deficiencies" (Shriver 1965:876, Carp 1965:917). "From the beginning," one psychologist wrote, "the Peace Corps selection and training have been dominated by psychological findings as has no other Government agency, not even the Air Force" (Amrine 1965:869). The State Department gave the MMPI in the early 1960s to personnel who were to be stationed overseas, and the Defense Department required personality inventories for certain people in sensitive positions. City police forces also experimented with the use of personality inventories (Amrine 1965:867, Lopez 1970:14-16). Interest in personality testing had already peaked, however, in part because validation studies generally showed them to be poor predictors of success, and in part because, according to critics, they violated the rights to privacy of those tested.

By the mid-1950s, personnel managers in several leading corporations sought more effective ways of assessing managerial potential. One obvious model was the multiple assessment technique applied by the OSS in World War II. In 1956, American Telephone and Telegraph initiated a Management Progress Study to test the value of the OSS approach in selecting managers. In this program, new college-educated employees and noncollege first-level managers participated in three-day retreats, during which they took what has become a standard battery of tests, including group and in-basket exercises, paper-and-pencil ability tests,

# History of Employment Testing

personality questionnaires, and projective tests. The theory was to adopt a "holistic" approach to testing on the grounds that "a complex of personal characteristics is more predictive of progress than any single characteristic." In a follow-up study eight years later, Douglas Bray and Donald L. Grant reported that the assessors "were clearly able to identify those more likely to advance in their organizations" (1966:1, 18).[12]

Long before the results of this follow-up study were published, a number of businesses had put assessment centers into practice in the selection of managers. As a result of the Management Progress Study, the technique of assessment centers spread rapidly through the Bell System and soon was adopted by IBM, Standard Oil (Ohio), Sears Roebuck, Kodak, and other leading corporations. By the early 1970s, approximately 1,000 companies in the United States operated some kind of assessment center; these centers had become, according to a recent observer, "one of the more phenomenal success stories of applied psychology and organizational psychology and personnel administration" (Hinrichs 1978:596).

## TESTING AND EQUAL EMPLOYMENT

The success of assessment centers in the 1970s coincided with widespread criticism of employment tests by members of the public, government agencies, and the courts. Many tests, claimed these critics, discriminated against certain groups protected by the Civil Rights Act of 1964, particularly blacks, and stood in the way of equal opportunity for employment. As discussed in other sections of this report, the Civil Rights Act of 1964, and the interpretation of that act by the courts and the Equal Employment Opportunity Commission, made employment testing a public issue in the 1970s. Employers have been asked to prove, often in court, that their tests are valid and job-related—a task that, given the high standards of proof required, has often been difficult. This situation has led to an increased emphasis on techniques of validation and on job-specific tests, and it has induced many companies, especially small businesses, to curtail testing programs or to abandon them entirely. For the first time since the 1920s, the use of employment tests appears to be on the decline (Siegel 1968, McCormick and Tiffin 1975:173, Petersen 1974).

## SUMMARY

From its origins early in the century, modern employment testing has grown into a major business, practiced by a wide variety of employers

---

[12] On assessment centers, also see *Business Week* (1965), Huck (1973).

and promoted by scores of test developers and consulting firms. Employment testing began as a tool for rationalizing hiring practices—in this respect, it reflected a twentieth century drive for order and progress through the application of science to social problems. Tests, enthusiasts claimed, could provide an objective measure of human potential where the commonsense judgments of individual employers were sure to create chaos. Tests, it was also assumed, promoted fair competition for jobs and therefore equal opportunity.

Throughout the century, the practice of employment testing increased in scope and sophistication as well as in size. Before World War I, the Civil Service Commission maintained an extensive program of "practical" testing, for the most part based on written examinations assessing job-specific knowledge and experience. A few businessmen, concerned with high rates of labor turnover, experimented with the work of early psychological testers, including tests designed to measure aptitude and "trainability." It was the U.S. Army in World War I, however, that introduced testing on a modern scale—particularly group testing and short-answer, objective examinations.

In the years immediately after the war, employment testing enjoyed a short-lived boom. Many businessmen hailed tests as ensuring industrial efficiency and enthusiastically applied them to the selection of employees. By the late 1920s, however, the postwar testing boom had collapsed, in part because tests had failed to live up to the expectations of many who had adopted them. More important in the long run was the work of psychologists and personnel management specialists in the 1920s and 1930s, who for the first time seriously attempted to develop techniques for testing tests and for correlating success on tests with success on the job.

During the Depression, testers concentrated more on vocational testing than on employment testing. Late in the 1930s, however, the use of tests for employee selection was once again on the increase, and, stimulated by the military testing program of World War II, employment testing emerged as a central feature of personnel management in the postwar years. From the 1940s on, with the introduction of machine scoring and the availability of ready-made tests, both from private test developers and the federal government, the use of tests grew rapidly. In general, the pattern of testing was similar to what it had been since the 1920s: white-collar workers were the most frequently tested, and clerical and stenographic tests, followed by intelligence tests, were most frequently given. Large companies tested more often and more extensively than small companies. The 1940s and 1950s, however, saw a new development: a sharp increase in the use of interest and personality inventories, which many personnel managers hoped would ensure satisfied and loyal as well as efficient workers. The vogue of personality inventories for the most part died down in the 1960s, but another development of the 1940s—the use of tests to identify management potential—has proved more durable and remains an important element in personnel selection and promotion practices.

The recent concern for equal employment opportunity has dampened the enthusiasm for the testing of the 1950s and 1960s. As in the 1920s, the use of testing in the 1970s was apparently on the decline. In the earlier period, the promotion of tests as a panacea for all industrial ills led to disillusionment and the abandonment of testing by a number of companies. The failure of many tests to yield useful results, however, did not prevent psychologists and personnel specialists from directing their attention to careful test construction and validation. Indeed, it may have fostered these activities. In the same way, some businesses in the 1970s have cut back or abandoned testing programs, particularly programs whose validity was hard to demonstrate. Others, however, in the interest of developing more valid tests, have supported large-scale programs of research, not only in testing but in all aspects of personnel selection and promotion. Whether these programs will succeed in developing more effective, and legally acceptable, procedures of personnel selection waits to be seen.

## REFERENCES

Adams, L. P. (1969) *The Public Employment Service in Transition, 1933-1968: Evolution of a Placement Service into a Manpower Agency.* Cornell Studies in Industrial and Labor Relations No. 16. Ithaca, N.Y.: New York State School of Industrial and Labor Relations, Cornell University.

Adkins, D. C. (1956) Selecting public employees. *Public Personnel Review* 17:260-261.

American School of Correspondence (1919) *Employment Management and Safety Engineering: A Practical Reading Course,* 7 vols. Chicago: American School of Correspondence.

Amrine, M. (1965) The 1965 congressional inquiry into testing. *American Psychologist* 20:869.

Aronson, A. H. (1973) *Biography of an Ideal: A History of the Federal Civil Service.* Washington, D.C.: U.S. Government Printing Office.

Baritz, L. (1960) *Servants of Power: A History of the Use of Social Science in American Industry.* Middletown, Conn.: Wesleyan University Press.

Benge, E. J. (1939) *The Use of Tests in Employment and Promotion.* Studies in Personnel Policy No. 14. New York: National Industrial Conference Board.

Berle, A. A., and Means, G. C. (1932) *The Modern Corporation and Private Property.* Chicago, Ill.: Commerce Clearinghouse.

Bingham, W. V. (1923a) Psychology applied. *Scientific Monthly* 16.

Bingham, W. V. (1923b) Cooperative business research. *Annals of the American Academy of Political Science* 110.

Bingham, W. V. (1937) *Aptitudes and Aptitude Testing.* New York: Harper and Brothers.

Bingham, W. V. (1941) Report of the committee on classification of military personnel advisory to the Adjutant General's office. *Science* n.s. 93:572-574.

Bingham, W. V. (1944) Personnel classification in the Army. *Science* n.s. 100:275-280.

Bingham, W. V. (1952) In E. G. Boring, H. S. Langfield, H. Warner, and R. M. Yerkes, eds., *A History of Psychology in Autobiography.* New York: Russell and Russell.

Blackford, K. M. H., and Newcomb, A. (1919) *The Job, the Man, the Boss.* New York: Doubleday, Page and Co.

Bolanovich, D. J. (1948) Interest tests reduce factory turnover. *Personnel Psychology* 1:81-92.

Boring, E. G. (1942) *A History of Experimental Psychology*, 2d ed. New York: Appleton-Century-Crofts.

Boring, E. G., Langfeld, H. S., Warner, H., and Yerkes, R. M., eds. (1952) *A History of Psychology in Autobiography.* New York: Russell and Russell.

Borow, H. C. (1944) The growth and present status of occupational testing. *Journal of Consulting Psychology* 8:70-73.

Bray, D. W., and Grant, D. L. (1966) The assessment center in the measurement of potential for business management. *Psychological Monographs* 80, Whole number.

Brewer, J. M. (1942) *History of Vocational Guidance: Origins and Early Development.* New York: Harper and Brothers.

Bureau of National Affairs (1958) *Supervisory Selection Procedures.* Personnel Policies Forum No. 48. Washington, D.C.: Bureau of National Affairs.

Bureau of National Affairs (1963) *Employee Selection Procedures.* Personnel Policies Forum No. 70. Washington, D.C.: Bureau of National Affairs.

Burnham, J. (1941) *The Managerial Revolution: What is Happening in the World.* New York: John Day Co., Inc.

*Business Week.* (1965) Sharper tools for the talent hunt. March 27:70-74.

Camfield, T. M. (1969) Psychologists at War: The History of American Psychology and the First World War. Ph.D. dissertation, University of Texas at Austin.

Carp, A. (1965) Testimony before the Senate Subcommittee on Constitutional Rights of the Committee on the Judiciary, June 7-10. *American Psychologist* 20:917.

Cattell, J. M. (1923) The psychological corporation. *Annals of the American Academy of Political Science* 110:165-171.

Chapman, J. C. (1921) *Trade Tests: The Scientific Measurement of Trade Proficiency.* New York: H. Holt and Co.

Chapman, J. C. (1923) Tests for trade proficiency. *Annals of the American Academy of Political Science* 110.

Cherry-Burrell (1941) Square peg 'problem employees' find square holes with aptitude tests. *Sales Management* 48:19-20.

Davis, H. V. (1969) *Frank Parsons: Prophet, Innovator, Counselor.* Carbondale, Ill.: University of Southern Illinois Press.

Dorsch, F. (1963) *Geschichte und Probleme der angewandten Psychologie.* Stuttgart: Verlag Franz Huber.

Dunlap, K. (1923) Fact and fable in character analysis. *Annals of the American Academy of Political Science* 110:74-80.

Eilbirt, H. (1959) The development of personnel management in the United States. *Business History Review* 33:345-64.

Emmet, B., and Jeuck, J. E. (1950) *Catalogues and Counters: A History of Sears, Roebuck and Company.* Chicago: University of Chicago Press.

Federal Board for Vocational Education (1919) *The Turnover of Labor.* Employment Management Series No. 46. Washington, D.C.: U.S. Government Printing Office.

Feiss, R. A. (1915) Personal relationships as a basis of scientific management. *Bulletin of the Society to Promote the Science of Management* 1.

Filer, H. A., and O'Rourke, L. J. (1923) Progress in civil service tests. *Journal of Personnel Research* 1:484-493.

Flanagan, J. C., ed. (1948) *The Aviation Psychology Program in the Army Air Forces.* Army Air Forces Aviation Psychology Research Reports No. 1. Washington, D.C.: U.S. Government Printing Office.

Flinn, A. D. (1922) Development of the Personnel Research Federation. *Journal of Personnel Psychology* 1:7-13.

Fuess, C. M. (1950) *The College Board: Its First Fifty Years.* New York: Columbia University.

Gaudet, F. J. (1960) *Labor Turnover: Calculation and Cost,* American Management Association Research Study 39. New York: American Management Association.

Gross, M. L. (1962) *The Brain Watchers.* New York: Random House.

Habbe, S. (1948) Introduction in *Experience with Psychological Tests.* Studies in Personnel Policy No. 92. New York: National Industrial Conference Board.

Haber, S. (1960) *Efficiency and Uplift: Scientific Management in the Progressive Era.* Chicago, Ill.: University of Chicago Press.

Hale, M., Jr. (1980) *Human Science and Social Order: Hugo Münsterberg and the Origins of Applied Psychology.* Philadelphia, Pa.: Temple University Press.

Hathaway, S. R. (1964) MMPI: Professional use by professional people. *American Psychologist* 19:204-210.

Hinrichs, J. R. (1969) Comparison of "real life" assessments of management potential with situational exercises, paper-and-pencil ability tests, and personality inventories. *Journal of Applied Psychology* 53:425.

Hinrichs, J. R. (1978) An eight-year follow-up of a management assessment center. *Journal of Applied Psychology* 63:596.

Hohenstein, W. V.. (1956) National Influence and Control over State and Local Personnel Practices in the United States. Ph.D. dissertation, University of Minnesota.

Hollingworth, H. L. (1915) Specialized vocational tests and methods. *School and Society* 1.

Hollingworth, H. L. (1916) *Vocational Psychology: Its Problems and Methods.* New York: D. Appleton and Co.

Huck, J. R. (1973) Assessment centers: A review of the external and internal validities. *Personnel Psychology* 26:191-212.

Hunter, W. S. (1946) Psychology in the war. *American Psychologist* 1:479-492.

Irwin, R. R. (1942) Lockheed's full testing program. *Personnel Journal* 21:103-106.

Kavruk, S. (1956) Thirty-three years of test research: A short history of test development in the U.S. Civil Service Commission. *American Psychologist* 11:329-333.

Kevles, D. M. (1968) Testing the Army's intelligence: Psychologists and the military in World War I. *Journal of American History* 55:565-581.

Kinslinger, H. J. (1966) Application of projective techniques in personnel psychology since 1940. *Psychological Bulletin* 66:134-149.

Klaw, S. (1950) The management psychologists have landed. *Fortune* 81:107.

Kornhauser, A. W., and Kingsbury, F. W. (1924) *Psychological Tests in Business.* Chicago: University of Chicago Press.

Lawshe, C. H., and Balma, M.J. (1946) *Principles of Personnel Testing,* 2d ed. New York: McGraw-Hill Book Co.

Lee, R. D., Jr. (1979) *Public Personnel Systems.* Baltimore, Md.: University Park Press.
Link, H. C. (1919) *Employment Psychology: The Application of Scientific Methods to the Selection, Training and Grading of Employees.* New York: Macmillan Co.
Link, H. C. (1923) Psychological tests in industry. *Annals of the American Academy of Political Science* 110.
Lopez, F. M. (1970) *The Making of a Manager: Guidelines to His Selection and Promotion.* New York: American Management Association.
Macy, J. W. (1965a) Psychological Testing. *American Psychologist* 20:883-884.
Macy, J. W. (1965b) Testimony before the Senate Subcommittee on Constitutional Rights of the Committee on the Judiciary, June 7-10. *American Psychologist* 20:931-932.
Mann, A. (1954) *Yankee Reformers in the Urban Age.* Cambridge, Mass.: Harvard University Press.
Mayo, E. (1945) *The Social Problems of an Industrial Civilization.* Boston: Graduate School of Business Administration, Harvard University.
McCormick, E. J., and Tiffin, J. (1975) *Industrial Psychology.* London: George Allen and Unwin.
Moore, B. V. (1921) Personnel selection of graduate engineers: The differentiation of apprentice engineers for training as salesmen, designers, and executives of production. *Psychological Monographs* 30:1-84.
Münsterberg, H. (1910) *American Problems from the Point of View of a Psychologist.* New York: Moffat, Yard and Co.
Münsterberg, H. (1913) *Psychology and Industrial Efficiency.* New York: Houghton Mifflin Co.
Napoli, D. S. (1975) The Architects of Adjustment: The Practice and Professionalization of American Psychology, chapter 5. Ph.D. dissertation, University of California at Davis.
National Industrial Conference Board (1936) *What Employers Are Doing for Employees: A Survey of Voluntary Activities for Improvement of Working Conditions in American Business Concerns.* New York: National Industrial Conference Board.
National Industrial Conference Board (1939) *The Use of Tests in Employment and Promotion.* Studies in Personnel Policy No. 14. New York: National Industrial Conference Board.
National Industrial Conference Board (1941) *Experience with Employment Tests.* Studies in Personnel Policy No. 32. New York: National Industrial Conference Board.
National Industrial Conference Board (1947) *Personnel Activities in American Business.* Studies in Personnel Policy No. 86. New York: National Industrial Conference Board.
National Industrial Conference Board (1948) *Experience with Employment Tests.* Studies in Personnel Policy No. 92. New York: National Industrial Conference Board.
National Industrial Conference Board (1964a) *Personnel Practices in Factory and Office.* Studies in Personnel Policy No. 145. New York: National Industrial Conference Board.
National Industrial Conference Board (1964b) *Personnel Practices in Factory and Office: Manufacturing.* Studies in Personnel Policy No. 194. New York: National Industrial Conference Board.
National Industrial Conference Board (1964c) *Office Personnel Practices: Nonmanufacturing.* Studies in Personnel Policy No. 197. New York: National Industrial Conference Board.
Nelson, D. M. (1975) *Managers and Workers: Origins of the New Factory System in the United States, 1880-1920.* Madison, Wis.: University of Wisconsin Press.
Noble, D. A. (1977) *America by Design: Science, Technology, and the Rise of Corporate Capitalism.* New York: Alfred A. Knopf.

Parsons, F. (1894) *Our Country's Needs: Or the Development of a Scientific Industrialism.* Boston: Arena Publishing Co.

Parsons, F. (1908) The vocation bureau. *Arena* 40.

Partington, J. E., and Bryant, T. R. (1946) The personnel consultant and psychological testing at armed forces induction stations. *American Psychologist* 1:111.

Paterson, D. G., and Ludgate, K. E. (1922) Blond and brunette traits: A quantitative study. *Personnel Research* 1:122-27.

Petersen, D. J. (1974) The impact of *Duke Power* on testing. *Personnel* 51:30-37.

Roethlisberger, F. J., and Dickson, W. J. (1939) *Management and the Worker: An Account of a Research Program Conducted by the Western Electric Company, Hawthorne Works, Chicago.* Cambridge, Mass.: Harvard University Press.

Samelson, F. (1977) World War I intelligence testing and the development of psychology. *Journal of the History of the Behavioral Sciences* 13:274-282.

Scott, W. D. (1913) Review of Hugo Münsterberg, *Psychology and Industrial Efficiency. Psychological Bulletin* 10.

Scott, W. D. (1915) The scientific selection of salesmen. *Advertising and Selling* 24(October):5-6, 94-96. (November):11, 55. (December):11, 69-70.

Scott, W. D., Clothier, R. C., and Spriegel, W. R. (1961) *Personnel Management: Principles, Practices, and a Point of View*, 6th ed. New York: McGraw-Hill Book Co.

Shafritz, J. M. (1975) *Public Personnel Management: The Heritage of Civil Service Reform.* New York: Praeger.

Shriver, S. (1965) Suggestions to the American Psychological Association. *American Psychologist* 20:876-877.

Siegel, J. B. (1968) The use of psychological testing in industry. *Pittsburgh Business Review* 38:1-3.

Spencer, L. M. (1959) What's the score now with psychological tests. *American Business* 29:7-10.

Stead, W. H., Shartle, C. L., and Otis, J. L. (1940) *Occupational Counseling Techniques.* U.S.E.S. study. New York: American Book Company.

Stead, W. H., and Masincup, W. E. (1942) *The Occupational Research Program of the United States Employment Service.* Chicago, Ill.: Public Administration Service.

Terman, L. (1919) The status of applied psychology in the United States. *Journal of Applied Psychology* 5:1-4.

Thorndike, E. L. (1913) Educational Diagnosis. *Science*, n.s., 37.

Thorndike, R. L. (1949) *Personnel Selection: Test and Measurement Techniques.* New York: John Wiley & Sons.

U.S. Adjutant General's Office (1919) *The Personnel System of the United States Army.* Vol. 1: *History of the Personnel System.* Committee on Classification of Personnel in the Army. Washington, D.C.: U.S. Government Printing Office.

U.S. Adjutant General's Office (1943) Personnel Research in the Army. Personnel Research Section, War Department. *Personnel Journal* 21:352.

U.S. Bureau of Labor Statistics (1917) *Proceedings of the Employment Managers' Conference*, Philadelphia, Pa. Bulletin no. 227. Washington, D.C.: U.S. Department of Labor.

U.S. Bureau of Labor Statistics (1932) Hiring and separation methods in American factories. *Monthly Labor Review* 35:1008.

U.S. Civil Service Commission (1911) *Twenty-Seventh Annual Report of the United States Civil Service Commission for the Fiscal Year Ending June 30, 1910.* Washington, D.C.: U.S. Government Printing Office.

U.S. Civil Service Commission (1912) *Twenty-Eighth Annual Report of the United States*

Civil Service Commission for the Fiscal Year Ending June 30, 1911. Washington, D.C.: U.S. Government Printing Office.

U.S. Civil Service Commission (1924) *Fortieth Annual Report of the United States Civil Service Commission for the Fiscal Year Ending June 30, 1923.* Washington, D.C.: U.S. Government Printing Office.

U.S. Congress (1976) *History of Civil Service Merit Systems of the United States and Selected Foreign Countries.* Subcommittee on Manpower and Civil Service. Committee on Post Office and Civil Service, U.S. House of Representatives. 94th Congress, 2d session. Washington, D.C.: U.S. Government Printing Office.

U.S. Office of Strategic Services (1948) *Assessment of Men: Selection of Personnel for the Office of Strategic Services.* New York: Rinehart and Co.

Van Riper, P. (1958) *History of the United States Civil Service.* Evanston, Ill: Row, Peterson and Co.

Viteles, M. (1928) The mental status of the Negro. *Annals of the American Academy of Political Science* 140:166-177.

Viteles, M. (1932) *Industrial Psychology.* New York: W. W. Norton and Co.

Wadsworth, G. W., Jr. (1941) Humm-Wadsworth Temperament Scale. In Experience with Employment Tests. Studies in Personnel Policy No. 32. New York: National Industrial Conference Board 1941.

Whyte, W. H., Jr. (1954) The fallacies of 'personality' testing. *Fortune* 50:118-119.

Wiebe, R. (1967) *The Search for Order, 1877-1920.* New York: Hill and Wang.

Woodward Governor Company (1941) How and why Woodward Governor Co. uses aptitude tests for employes. *Sales Management* 48:66-67.

Worthy, J. C. (1951) "Planned executive development: The experience of Sears, Roebuck and Co." *Personnel Series* 137. New York: American Management Association.

Yerkes, R. M., ed. (1921) *Psychological Examining in the United States Army.* Memoirs of the National Academy of Sciences 15. Washington, D.C.: U.S. Government Printing Office.

Yerkes, R. M. (1923) Psychological work of the National Research Council. *Annals of the American Academy of Political Science* 110:172-78.

Yoakum, C. S., and Yerkes, R. M., eds. (1920) *Army Mental Tests.* New York: Henry Holt and Co.

Young, K. (1923) The history of mental testing. *Pedagogical Seminary* 31:1-47.

ALEXANDRA WIGDOR
# Psychological Testing and the Law of Employment Discrimination

## INTRODUCTION

Americans are of a legalistic turn of mind. They tend to conceive of fundamental social and economic arrangements as legal relationships and to address social problems in the language of civil rights. It is fitting, therefore, that the first major federal program designed to improve the economic status of blacks and certain other minorities was enacted as a part of the omnibus Civil Rights Act of 1964.[1] In Title VII of the Act, entitled "Equal Employment Opportunity," Congress sought to break the pattern of poverty and disadvantage that characterized the lives of black Americans by prohibiting discrimination in employment practices.[2]

The statute suggested that racial discrimination was the fundamental cause of black economic disadvantage, and it held out the promise that civil rights measures would foster economic betterment just as antidiscrimination reforms had promoted greater black participation in American political life. By interpreting the economic distress of blacks as an element in a more general denial of civil rights, the sponsors of the Act were able to draw upon the growing public support for ending discriminatory legal arrangements and to enlist the great vitality that characterized civil rights doctrine in the postwar era.

---

[1] Public Law 88-352.
[2] The Act was, of course, broader than that; it extended protection against discrimination on the basis of "race, color, religion, sex, or national origin."

At the same time, the approach has had its drawbacks. It has placed severe constraints on our public understanding of the consequences of economic deprivation by focusing the governmental effort on a single, simplistic causal factor: discrimination.

## CONGRESSIONAL INTENT

Although congressional intent is seldom uniform, there was a sedulous effort during the course of debate on Title VII to establish the premise that the law intended to eliminate discrimination, was entirely negative in character, and would effect a more equitable occupational distribution by ensuring the conditions that would permit individuals to sort themselves out by ability. As a result, Title VII is essentially an enumeration of unlawful employment practices, addressed to employers, employment agencies, and labor organizations. It was designed to produce equal treatment by prohibiting considerations of race, color, religion, sex, or national origin from entering into employment decisions or from influencing the conditions of labor.

While there may have been those who questioned the efficacy of equal treatment in a situation produced by conditions of severe, long-term inequality, the sponsors of Title VII did not attempt to move their colleagues beyond that essentially negative position, nor to qualify the employer's role in setting the standards for his work force. A decision rendered by the Illinois Fair Employment Practices Commission in *Myart* v. *Motorola, Inc.*[3] occasioned congressional discussion of these points. The Illinois Commission found that an adequate response to fair employment concerns would involve the adoption of procedures that promote the identification and employment of those formerly deprived because of race or national origin:

> Selection techniques may have to be modified at the outset in the light of experience, education, or attitudes of the group. . . . The employer may have to establish in-plant training programs and employ the heretofore disadvantaged persons as learners, placing them under such supervision that will enable them to achieve job success (see Larson 1977:15-13).

Although this sounds very close to the position the federal government has reached through a long process of administrative and judicial inter-

---

[3] Charge No. 63 C-127. The text of the decision was entered into the Congressional Record and was discussed during Senate debate on Title VII. See 110 *Cong. Rec.* 5662-64, 6415-16 (1964).

## The Law of Employment Discrimination

pretation of the Act, proponents of the bill argued against any such implications. Senators Case and Clark submitted an interpretative memorandum, which read in part:

There is no requirement in Title VII that employers abandon bona fide qualification tests where, because of differences in background and education, members of some groups are able to perform better on these tests than members of other groups. An employer may set his qualifications as high as he likes, he may test to determine which applicants have these qualifications, and he may hire, assign, and promote on the basis of test performance.[4]

Senator Tower, desirous of some formal recognition of the position, successfully offered an amendment to the bill excepting from the list of unlawful practices use of "any professionally developed ability test" provided that it is not used to discriminate.[5]

The Act further reinforced the principle of equal treatment by specifically stating that nothing in the title should be interpreted to "require" any employer to

grant preferential treatment to any individual or to any group . . . on account of an imbalance which may exist with respect to the total number or percentage of persons of any race, color, religion, sex, or national origin employed by any employer.[6]

The hope was that prohibiting consciously exclusionary selection procedures would substantially alter employment patterns in America; that is, that ruling out race, color, religion, sex, or national origin as screening criteria would effect the desired amelioration in the condition of the groups offered protection by the statute.

### THE EQUAL EMPLOYMENT OPPORTUNITY COMMISSION

During the course of administrative and judicial interpretation, the operating premise of Title VII shifted to the position that there is a uniform distribution of skill or ability among the various groups comprising the larger society, which one ought to see reflected in the makeup of occupational categories. The "underrepresentation" of blacks, women, etc.

---

[4] 110 *Cong. Rec.* 7213 (1964).
[5] PL 88-352, §703(h).
[6] *Ibid.*, §703(j). (The word "require" is important. Recent case law makes clear that if Title VII does not require, it also does not prohibit preferential treatment to overcome the effects of past discrimination: *United Steelworkers of America* v. *Weber*, 47 LW 4851 (1979); *Detroit Police Officers' Association* v. *Young* (CA 6), 48 LW 3558 (1979).

in most segments of the work force was ascribed to discrimination, and the weight of the federal government was gradually applied to effecting occupational redistribution.[7]

The primary author of this change in course was the agency created by the Act to oversee its implementation. The Equal Employment Opportunity Commission (EEOC) was established as a five-member body with education and conciliation functions. It was empowered to provide those subject to the Act with technical assistance, to further their compliance activities,[8] and to conduct technical studies that would be of general usefulness in promoting compliance. In addition, the agency was given the authority to conduct compliance reviews, summon witnesses, and conciliate employment discrimination conflicts.

From these modest beginnings, the EEOC rapidly developed into an extremely powerful agency with an aggressive conception of its mandate. Although its powers were initially limited to the "informal methods of conference, conciliation, and persuasion,"[9] the Commission was empowered by the 1972 Amendments to the Civil Rights Act to bring civil suits against private employers in the event that a conciliation agreement satisfactory to the Commission could not be reached.[10] EEOC's position vis-à-vis other federal agencies has also been enhanced over the years so that it is significantly more than one among several agencies with equal employment opportunity jurisdiction. This primacy was formally recognized by Executive Order 12067 (June 30, 1978); it grants the Commission authority to coordinate all federal equal employment opportunity programs, which by one count involves eighteen different agencies enforcing some forty EEO laws.[11]

In 1966, the newly formed Equal Employment Opportunity Commis-

---

[7] See, for example, *Teamsters v. United States* 431 U.S. 324, 340 n. 20 (1977) (". . . absent explanation, it is ordinarily to be expected that nondiscriminatory hiring practices will in time result in a work force more or less representative of the racial and ethnic composition of the population in the community from which employees are hired.")

[8] In regard to testing, this power has been interpreted by the agency to mean assisting employers in finding alternatives to written tests that will serve the business needs but avoid the adverse impact typical of tests. The agency does not help employers develop acceptable testing programs. (*Letter*, Ethel Bent Walsh, Acting Chairman, EEOC, to Director, Federal Personnel Compensation Division, General Accounting Office, August 18, 1976, entitled "Answers to 15 Specific Questions Submitted by GAO," p. 5.)

[9] PL 88-352, §706(a).

[10] PL 92-261, §706(f) (March 24, 1972). The 1972 Act extended Title VII requirements to public employers as well, but placed the power to bring suit against recalcitrant governmental units with the Attorney General. That power is both to initiate civil actions and to bring suit in matters referred by EEOC. See Executive Order 12068 (June 30, 1978).

[11] 47 LW 2023.

## The Law of Employment Discrimination

sion, in what was probably its single most important policy decision, interpreted Title VII discrimination to consist not merely of employment practices where the intent was to discriminate or where people of protected status were treated differently from others, but also of those practices that had an adverse impact on members of the protected classes.[12] (Adverse impact meant simply a rate of selection that worked to the disadvantage of members of the protected groups.)

The first set of EEOC *Guidelines on Employment Testing Procedures* was used as the vehicle for announcing the Commission's definition of discrimination, which indicates how quickly it was realized that tests would be at the center of the fair employment practices debate. The *Guidelines* struck the basic formula for federal oversight of personnel selection: if an employer, union, or employment agency uses a test or other selection device that results in proportionately lower selection rates for minorities or females than for white males, the procedure will be considered discriminatory and declared unlawful unless the employer can "validate" the test to the Commission's satisfaction and show its business necessity. The 1966 *Guidelines*, elaborated in 1970 and again in 1978, provide test users with a complex set of technical validation procedures against which the agency judges the sufficiency of an employer's selection system. (For a full discussion of federal employment selection guidelines see Novick, "Ability Testing: Federal Guidelines and Professional Standards," in this volume.)

By sidestepping the question of volition in its definition of discrimination and focusing instead on the results of hiring and promotion decisions, EEOC policy placed employment testing and other so-called objective selection procedures at the center of controversy. Since tests with a heavy cognitive content almost invariably screen out blacks and Hispanics in much higher proportions than whites, tests became suspect by definition. As a consequence, the question of their use has come to absorb a tremendous amount of time and energy on the part of bureaucrats with compliance authority, judges, psychologists, personnel managers, and, of course, employers.

EEOC's guidelines for validating the use of a test are formidable—stringent is a word often used to describe them. The 1970 version was informed by the professional thinking of psychologists. It expressly cited the testing standards adopted by the American Psychological Association (APA) in 1966 as appropriate minimum standards for validation under Title VII. The APA is the major professional organization of psychologists

---

[12] For a brief account of that decision, see Robertson (1976:1-2).

holding a Ph.D., and the *Standards For Psychological Tests and Manuals* (see APA et al. 1966) represent the interests and concerns of the academic, research, and test development communities. While the *Standards* reflect the best in measurement theory, they are, perhaps, rarified for the everyday world of employment testing. Most test users—teachers and personnel managers—are not psychologists, and it takes a psychologist with an interest in psychometrics to fully understand the *Standards*.

By using the *Standards* as the point of departure in defining its validation requirements, EEOC transformed them from a statement of the best professional judgment, intended to serve as a model for the profession, into ground rules for an employer's compliance with the Civil Rights Act.[13] As a result, questions of technical adequacy find their answer in compliance review proceedings or the courtroom; questions of economic feasibility simply don't enter in.

While the use of professional test validation standards as a minimum requirement of fair employment practices has had some problematical consequences, the incorporation of a politically attractive but untested theory in the *Guidelines*—namely, the notion of differential validity—was unsound. The requirement for differential validity studies was based on the hypothesis that conventionally developed tests would systematically underestimate the performance level of black and other minority job candidates. In order to reveal and counteract alleged systematic errors in the predictive validity of test scores, separate validation studies were prescribed for black and white employees so that scores could be interpreted according to a test taker's group classification.[14]

Although extremely plausible, within a few years it became clear that the theory was not supported by the accumulating evidence; most studies showed that test scores either bore the same relationship to performance for blacks and whites, or in some cases, overpredicted for blacks.[15] But as psychometricians were abandoning the idea, the courts, out of def-

---

[13] Aware of the possibility of overambitious use of the *Standards* given the prominence of testing issues in litigation, the authors of the 1974 revision cautioned in the introduction: "This document is prepared as a technical guide for those within the sponsoring professions; it is *not* written as law. An evaluation of (a test user's) competence does not rest on the literal satisfaction of every relevant provision of this document. The individual standards are statements of ideals or goals, some having priority over others" (APA et al. 1974:8). The *Principles for the Validation and Use of Personnel Selection Procedures*, published by the Division of Industrial-Organizational Psychology of APA in 1975, repeats that caution.
[14] 29 C.F.R. §1607.5(b).
[15] For a discussion of differential validity and differential prediction, see Linn, Ability Testing: Individual Differences, Prediction and Differential Prediction, in this volume.

## The Law of Employment Discrimination

erence to the *Guidelines*, were adjudging it a requirement of the law.[16] A commentator remarked on the situation in 1976 (see Balog 1976:106):

During this period in which the courts have been steadfast in their acceptance of the differential validity theory, many experts are having doubts that such a phenomenon does exist. The theory had wide appeal a decade ago and appeared to gain strength in the courts just as the experts were disproving it. The possible unreliability of differential validity was first acknowledged judicially by the Fifth Circuit in UNITED STATES v. GEORGIA POWER CO., but it chose instead to adopt the EEOC Guidelines.

A final hurdle presented by the *Guidelines* put test users in the position of having to prove a negative. If an employer were able to satisfy all of the positive requirements for proof of job relatedness, there would still be the further necessity of showing that there is no alternative procedure that would predict as well, while having less adverse impact on blacks or members of other protected classes.

In an early response to the 1970 *Guidelines*, the *Harvard Law Review* (1971:1131) surmised that they were

designed to scare employers away from any objective standards which have differential impact on minority groups because, applied strictly, the testing requirements are impossible for many employers to follow.[17]

It is certainly the case that, where the courts have adhered strictly to the *Guidelines*, tests (and other selection procedures) have not usually survived challenge. In those instances where the use of a test has been upheld under Title VII, the court has usually either relied on expert testimony or decided that "deference" does not require adherence to the detail of the *Guidelines*.

---

[16] See *U.S. v. Georgia Power*, 474 F. 2d 906 (1973); *Rogers v. International Paper Co.*, 510 F. 2d 1340 (1975); *EEOC v. Detroit Edison Co.* 515 F. 2d 301 (1975); *U.S. v. City of Chicago*, 549 F. 2d 415 (1977); *Commonwealth v. O'Neill*, 19 FEP Cases 55 (1979).

[17] As late as 1976, David L. Rose, chief of the Employment Section of the Civil Rights Division of the Department of Justice, expressed a similar concern about the EEOC Guidelines. He was quoted in the Bureau of National Affairs *Daily Labor Report* as saying: "Under the present EEOC guidelines, few employers are able to show the validity of any of their selection procedures, and the risk of their being held unlawful is high. Since not only tests, but all other procedures must be validated, the thrust of the present guidelines is to place almost all test users in a posture of noncompliance; to give great discretion to enforcement personnel to determine who should be prosecuted; and to set aside objective procedures in favor of numerical hiring." Rose considered the proposed *Uniform Guidelines*, in contrast, to provide standards that would enable employers to bring themselves into compliance with federal law (Bureau of National Affairs 1976:AA-2 to AA-4).

Although the focus of the *Guidelines* is on the development and use of tests, EEOC has no intrinsic interest in test validation. Its sole mission is the elimination of discriminatory employment practices, and it accepts adverse impact as evidence of discriminatory practices. If an employer voluntarily institutes a selection system that eliminates adverse impact, he does not, from the Commission's point of view, have to become involved in the business of test validation. Conversely, use of even the most carefully validated selection device might constitute discrimination where adverse impact exists.[18]

The policy of the Equal Employment Opportunity Commission has been to make the justification of test use as demanding as possible so long as the tests continue to select in differential proportions. And, because of the legacy of racial discrimination that weighs upon the nation, the agency has received a good deal of backing for this policy from the courts, which are the final arbiters of the meaning of Title VII discrimination. As the following discussion of the judicial interpretation of Title VII of the Civil Rights Act will demonstrate, the major policy determination of the Commission, concerning the nature of discrimination, has been accorded the status of law.

## TESTING FOR HIRING AND PROMOTION: THE GRIGGS FORMULA

Within the larger area of employment discrimination law, a discrete body of testing case law has emerged in the last decade. The judicial standards for applying Title VII to employment tests were blocked out in the Supreme Court opinion handed down in *Griggs v. Duke Power Co.*[19] in March of 1971, which established the basic two-step process of Title VII testing litigation: the plaintiff carries the burden of establishing a prima facie case of discrimination, which, once established, places upon the defendant-employer the burden of demonstrating that the test is a "reasonable measure of job performance."[20]

The centrality of *Griggs* warrants a fairly close examination of the case. The Duke Power Company traditionally limited the employment of blacks at its Dan River Steam Station in Draper, North Carolina, to jobs in its

---
[18] Robertson (1976:30-32); Letter, EEOC Acting Chairman Ethel Bent Walsh to H. L. Krieger, GAO, 18 Aug., 1976, p. 1, 5.
[19] *Griggs v. Duke Power Co.*, 401 U.S. 424 (1971).
[20] *Ibid.*, 436.

## The Law of Employment Discrimination

labor department, which had the lowest level and lowest paid jobs.[21] Indeed, the highest paying jobs in the labor department paid less than the lowest paying jobs in the other four departments.[22]

On July 2, 1965, the day Title VII of the Civil Rights Acts of 1964 went into effect, the Duke Power Company gave up its policy of restricting black employees to the labor department. To its previous requirement that employees in all departments except the labor department possess a high school diploma, the company now added the requirement that applicants for jobs in all other departments pass the Wonderlic Personnel Test, a measure of general intelligence, and the Bennett Mechanical Comprehension Test. Those already employed in the labor department could transfer elsewhere only by fulfilling one of the two requirements.

Thirteen of the fourteen black employees in the labor department brought a class action suit challenging the diploma and testing requirements on the grounds that they were not intended to measure a candidate's ability to learn to perform a particular job or class of jobs; that the practical effect was to freeze blacks in lower level jobs; and that the pre-Act diploma requirement had been applied so as to give whites preferential treatment.

The progress of the *Griggs* case through the courts provides a dramatic summary of how the judicial response to equal employment problems has evolved. In the first years after the passage of the Civil Rights Act, it was generally assumed that the basic problem was racism and other forms of bias—that is, the problem lay with the attitudes of the employer. Consequently, the initial focus of judicial scrutiny was on the motivation of the employer, which, it was soon articulated, could be inferred from evidence of disparate treatment. It was discerned only gradually that, even if evil motive and disparate treatment were eliminated, the impulse for equality of opportunity that informed the Civil Rights Act would be frustrated by the deeper effects of past discrimination. From this realization came the theory of disparate impact.

The District Court in *Griggs* found that, while the Power Company had followed a policy of overt racial discrimination before the passage of the Civil Rights Act, it had renounced that policy. The court found no evidence that the newly instituted requirements stemmed from discriminatory intentions. The court also held that because the Civil Rights Act was

---

[21] The other departments were coal handling, operations, maintenance and laboratory, and test.
[22] *Griggs*, 401 U.S. 424, 427 (1971).

prospective, it authorized no remedy to offset the effects of past discrimination.

The Court of Appeals agreed with the lower court's analysis that the question of the employer's intent is determinative in Title VII litigation and rejected plaintiff's argument that employment tests must be job related.[23] The appellate court also upheld the District Court's conclusion that, in the case before it, there was no persuasive evidence of discriminatory intent since the new diploma and testing requirements affected applicants uniformly.

On the question of mitigating the present effects of past discrimination, however, the Court of Appeals reversed the lower court's holding. The court ruled that blacks employed in the labor department before the institution of the diploma or test requirement for transfer into the other departments, could not now be subject to those requirements, for the reason that whites hired in those departments at the time had not been subject to any such requirements. But relief was denied to black employees hired since the institution of the education requirement in 1955, because the requirement was uniformly applied to all employees, regardless of racial identification.

The Supreme Court recognized the fluid nature of equal employment opportunity law: "The Court of Appeals was confronted with a question of first impression, as are we, concerning the meaning of Title VII."[24] And it came to very different conclusions, reversing the lower courts on the centrality of intent under Title VII and spelling out the ground rules that have provided the analytical framework of subsequent litigation.[25] It replaced the lower courts' focus upon motive and disparate treatment with a new focus upon disparate impact, proof of which triggers the employer's burden of showing the assessment device to be job related.

Taking it as axiomatic that Congress had as an objective in the Civil Rights Act the achievement of equality of employment opportunities, the Court concluded that the Act requires the elimination of any "artificial, arbitrary, and unnecessary barriers to employment"[26] *if* these operate to discriminate on the basis of a racial or other classification enumerated

---

[23] "At no place in the Act or in its legislative history does there appear a requirement that employers use only those tests which measure the ability or skill required by a specific job or group of jobs." 420 F. 2d 1225, 1235.

[24] *Griggs*, 401 U.S. 424, 428.

[25] Some cases, including individual actions, continue to be brought on grounds of disparate treatment, but most pattern or practice suits and class actions use the adverse impact approach.

[26] *Griggs*, 401 U.S. 424, 431.

## The Law of Employment Discrimination

in the Act, and *if* they cannot be shown to be "demonstrably a reasonable measure of job performance."[27] Tests that produce exclusionary effects must be shown, in other words, to "measure the person for the job, not the person in the abstract."[28]

The question of intent is irrelevant to this formulation, as the Court made clear.[29] The Court's operational definition focuses judicial attention on the *consequences* of hiring and promotion practices and avoids, as Elizabeth I once put it, "making a window into men's hearts." It would be difficult to exaggerate the expansion of the concept of discrimination implicit in this move from a volitional to a statistical definition, an expansion not yet fully realized, but clearly evident in the case law. The involvement of the federal judiciary in the specifics of personnel practices since *Griggs* has placed great pressures on public and private employers and on the courts themselves. It has also begun to make some occupations far more accessible to minorities and women than was previously the case. Litigation involving police and fire fighter positions has been particularly prominent in this regard in recent years.

Although the courts are still very much in the process of evolving the evidentiary requirements of the *Griggs* mechanism, there is a growing body of adverse impact law that provides some sense of the statistical proof needed to establish a prima facie case of discrimination; likewise, there seem to be some areas of consensus on probative evidence of job relatedness. Before turning to examine the case law, however, there is another, ambivalent element in the *Griggs* opinion. It involves the promotion of goals that are theoretically compatible but very difficult to synchronize: that is, the reward of merit and the promotion of full participation in the economy of minorities and women.

In interpreting the Civil Rights Act to require that tests and other selection procedures measure job-related qualifications, the Supreme Court did not deny that the employer may set these qualifications as high as he likes. Indeed, the opinion states in a number of places that the whole purpose of Title VII is to promote selection on the basis of job qualifi-

---

[27] *Ibid.*, 436

[28] *Ibid.*, 436

[29] ". . . good intent or absence of discriminatory intent does not redeem employment procedures or testing mechanisms that operate as 'built-in headwinds' for minority groups and are unrelated to measuring job capability." *Ibid.*, 432. Although the Title VII Amendments of 1972 extended the statute to state and local governments, a question remains as to whether the intent doctrine applies to states and municipalities. The Court denied certiorari in the 1979 term in a case intended to clarify the law (No. 79-390 *City of Anniston, Alabama v. Scott*, 48 LW 3698).

cations rather than race, color, sex, or other forbidden considerations: "Congress has not commanded that the less qualified be preferred over the better qualified simply because of minority origins."[30]

This defense of selection on the basis of ability is rendered ambiguous by other statements in the opinion. It is pointed out that, on the record in the case,[31] blacks did not fare nearly so well as whites under the test and diploma requirements. The Supreme Court concluded that this consequence is "directly traceable" to race and went on to declare that "Basic intelligence must have the means of articulation to manifest itself fairly in a testing process."[32] This would seem to place on employers the burden of overcoming or bypassing with their tests or other assessment devices the disadvantage produced in "inferior education in segregated schools." There is allusion to the fabled offer of milk to the stork and the fox, and the lesson drawn is that Title VII demands that "the vessel in which the milk is proffered be one all seekers can use."[33]

Quite aside from the questionable feasibility of this last, it is important to be aware of the ambivalence that runs through the opinion. It is not peculiar to the Supreme Court, but runs through the whole of American society. It is an ambivalence that, in the name of equal rights, rejects the idea of quotas and, in the name of social justice, requires equal outcomes. So long as disadvantage continues to be concentrated in the classes of people offered protection by the Civil Rights Act, striking an acceptable balance will be a subject of litigation. So long as great disparities in income and status typify our society, the values will need balancing.

## TESTING AND ADVERSE IMPACT: ESTABLISHING THE PRIMA FACIE CASE

As a 1971 *Harvard Law Review* essay on developments in Title VII litigation noted, the comparatively low economic and social status of black

---

[30] Ibid., 436. This position is reaffirmed in *Furnco Construction Company v. Waters*, 46 LW 4969, (1978) (Title VII forbids having as a goal "a work force selected by any proscribed discriminatory practice, but it does not impose a duty to adopt a hiring procedure that maximizes hiring of minority employees.").

[31] As a number of commentators have pointed out, the evidence in the case is extremely thin, consisting mainly of 1960 North Carolina census data showing that 34 percent of white males and 12 percent of black males had high school diplomas and (since Duke Power maintained no records of test results) some EEOC figures from another case which showed differential pass/fail rates on a test battery that included the two tests in question in *Griggs* as well as several others.

[32] *Griggs*, 401 U.S. 424, 430.

[33] Ibid., 431.

## The Law of Employment Discrimination

Americans prompted congressional attention to questions of employment selection. It was widely assumed that there was a direct causal connection between discrimination and low economic status and that prohibiting the one would ameliorate the other. This formulation implied that employment statistics could be used to infer the degree of compliance with Title VII (Harvard Law Review 1971:1116).

The focus of the *Griggs* decision on the consequences of a selection procedure signaled the High Court's acceptance of this approach to employment discrimination litigation, and it has come to dominate class action and pattern and practice cases.[34] Rather than showing evidence of discriminatory intent, the current strategy involves showing either substantially different pass/fail rates or population/work force statistics for groups classified by race, sex, or ethnicity. The test or other selection device has become the fulcrum on which the action depends. The plaintiff can meet the burden of proving a prima facie case of discrimination by showing that the employer's hiring or promotion procedures select "disproportionately," with resulting "adverse impact" upon protected classes.[35] Without a persuasive showing of adverse impact, there is no actionable cause.[36] Finally, a claim of adverse impact alleges only the discriminatory effect of apparently neutral employment practices; it need not speak to the question of intent.[37]

In the years since *Griggs*, statistical proofs have become increasingly important in employment discrimination cases, with plaintiffs presenting statistics to establish the prima facie case, defendants producing other

---

[34] Individual complaints are brought under the theory of disparate treatment, which requires a showing of intent and thus have different standards of proof to satisfy. See *Teamsters v. United States*, 431 U.S. 324, 335 n. 15 (1977).

[35] *Albemarle Paper Company v. Moody*, 401 U.S. 424, 426 (1975) (the tests select in a racial pattern significantly different from that of the pool of applicants); *Dothard v. Rawlingson*, 433 U.S. 321, 329 (1977); *Firefighters Institute for Racial Equality v. St. Louis*, 549 F. 2d 506, 510 (1977); *James v. Stockham Valves and Fittings, Inc.*, 559 F. 2d 310, 328-30 (1977): *United States v. City of Chicago*, 549 F. 2d 415, 427-28 (1977); Schlei and Grossman (1979:316 n.42) see no merit in the contention that the *Griggs* "Disparate Impact" method of analysis has been eroded.

[36] *Hester v. Southern Railway Company*, 497 F. 2d 1374 (1974).

[37] *U.S. v. City of Chicago*, 549 F. 2d 415, 428 (1977). *Firefighters Inst. v. St. Louis*, 549 F. 2d 506, 510 (1977). But see *United States v. County of Fairfax, Virginia*, Civil Action No. 78-862-A, 3 (April 20, 1979), in which the district court states: "This Court adopts the traditional definition of a prima facie case, i.e., a state of facts, from which the most reasonable inference to be drawn is that there was purposeful discrimination." See also Justice Stewart's dissenting opinion in *New York City Board of Ed. v. Harris*, 48 LW 4035 (1979).

statistics in rebuttal,[38] and trial courts having to decide whose statistics are more persuasive. Although the Supreme Court has sanctioned the use of statistical evidence to establish disproportionate impact,[39] many questions remain unresolved about the probative value of various kinds of data, the amount of difference that constitutes substantial adverse impact, and, in cases where evidence of gross disparity in selection rates exists, which party then has the burden of producing specific statistical evidence based on closer analysis of the geographical area from which the employer draws, the qualified labor market, and the relevant time frame.[40]

The basic assumption underlying *Griggs* is that in an entirely neutral marketplace, protected groups will be selected for employment in roughly the same proportion as they are represented in the population. In *Teamsters v. United States*, the Supreme Court gave voice to that assumption: ". . . absent explanation, it is ordinarily to be expected that nondiscriminatory hiring practices will in time result in a work force more or less representative of the racial and ethnic composition of the population in the community from which employees are hired."[41]

The crucial question, aside from the adequacy of the assumption, is the definition of the population to be used as a basis for comparison.[42] Two basic approaches have been used by plaintiffs: comparison of hire/reject rates and population/work force statistics. Hire/reject comparisons are normally made when a specific test or procedure is under attack. There have been, for example, many challenges to examinations used to hire and promote police and fire fighters,[43] based upon statistics showing differential performance on the tests.

---

[38] *Dothard v. Rawlinson*, 433 U.S. 321, 331 (1977) ("If the employer discerns fallacies or deficiencies in the data offered by the plaintiff, he is free to adduce countervailing evidence of his own.")

[39] *Teamsters v. United States*, 431 U.S. 324, 339 (1977) (it is unmistakably clear that statistical analyses will continue to play an important role in cases disputing the existence of discrimination).

[40] Schlei and Grossman (1979:317) point out that some court decisions seem to place the burden on the plaintiff (*EEOC v. Datapoint Corp.*, 570 F. 2d 1264, 1270 (1978); *Croker v. Boeing Co.*, 437 F. Supp. 1138, 1183-85 (1977)), while others appear to expect the defendant to supply more specific statistical data once the plaintiff has given general evidence of gross disparity (*Donnell v. General Motors Corp.*, 576 F. 2d 1292, 1297 (1978); *Parson v. Kaiser Aluminum and Chemical Corp.*, 575 F. 2d 1374, 1386 (1978)).

[41] *Teamsters v. United States*, 431 U.S. 324, 339 (1977).

[42] On the subject of methods of proof in employment discrimination cases, see Schlei and Grossman (1979), Shoben (1978), Schlei and Grossman (1979), Hay (1978).

[43] E.g., *Afro American Patrolmen's League v. Duck*, 503 F. 2d. 294 (1974); *Firefighters Inst. v. City of St. Louis*, 549 F. 2d 506 (1977); *United States v. City of Chicago*, 549 F. 2d 415 (1977); *Vulcan Society NYC Fire Dept. v. Civil Service Commission*, 490 F. 2d 387 (1973).

The most obvious, and probably the most probative kind of hire/reject statistics deal with "actual applicant flow," that is, the number of people in the relevant categories who actually take the test.[44] But there are a number of possible deficiencies with this method of proof, the first of them being that the very existence of the evidence depends on the employer's record-keeping habits. In the early days of Title VII litigation, such records were seldom available, but are now common practice among employers large enough to support a personnel management staff, for reasons of self-protection (to rebut claims of discrimination, as well as to avoid using procedures that exclude disproportionate numbers of candidates in the protected categories).[45] Applicant flow data can have other drawbacks. It does not take into account the qualifications of applicants; it can be manipulated by employer or employees; it can be distorted by an employer's recruitment efforts, penalizing, for example, an employer who has an agressive affirmative action program that draws in large numbers of minority and female applicants, many of whom may not be qualified.[46]

When actual applicant flow data are not available, plaintiffs, beginning with the *Griggs* case, have frequently used "potential applicant flow" data, based not on the performance of actual applicants on a specific criterion, but on the performance of those who might reasonably be considered potential applicants. In *Griggs*, for example, statistics concerning the percentage of white males and black males who were high school graduates in North Carolina were used to establish the disproportionate impact of the diploma requirement. More recently, an Alabama height/weight requirement for prison guards was struck down on the plaintiff's showing that, based on national statistics, 41 percent of adult females, as compared with 3 percent of adult males, would be excluded from the position.[47]

---

[44] The Fifth Circuit called it the "most direct route to proof of racial discrimination in hiring . . ." in *Hester v. Southern Railway Company*, 497 F. 2d 1374, 1379 (1974).

[45] The Equal Employment Opportunity Commission and other federal agencies charged with implementing Title VII have required employers to keep records documenting the impact of their selection procedures and warn that failure to do so, if the employer "underutilizes" a group in a job category in comparison with the representation of the group in the relevant labor market, may cause the enforcement agencies to "draw an inference of adverse impact of the selection process." Uniform Guidelines on Employee Selection Procedures, 43 Fed. Reg. 38290, 38298 (Aug. 25, 1978).

[46] See, e.g., *United States v. County of Fairfax, Virginia*, slip opinion, Civil Action No. 78-862-A (April 20, 1979).

[47] *Dothard v. Rawlinson*, 433 U.S. 321 (1977). But see *Townsend v. Nassau County Medical Center*, 558 F. 2d 117 (1977), in which the Second Circuit rejected potential applicant flow data based on general population statistics where there was no supporting evidence showing actual exclusionary impact on women and minorities.

Whether using actual or potential applicant flow data, the burden on the plaintiff is to show "substantial disparity," a concept propounded in *Griggs*. There is as yet no clear consensus on the ratio that constitutes substantial disparity. The federal agencies have for years used an 80 percent rule, and that formula is incorporated into the 1978 *Uniform Guidelines on Employee Selection Procedures*. A number of courts have also used the 80 percent rule, but it has not been generally accepted (Schlei and Grossman 1979:328). As a result, courts have typically relied on what one commentator has called "intuitive assessments" of the significance of the disparities in particular cases (Shoben 1978:794).[48]

The comparison of population and work force statistics as a method of proving employment discrimination has undergone considerable refinement in recent years. In the 1960s and early 1970s, general population figures (that is, the number of inhabitants in a given area identified by race, gender, or ethnicity) were frequently accepted by the courts as persuasive evidence of adverse impact, although statistical evidence was still considered something of a novelty in the courtroom.[49] The acceptability of general population data was confirmed by the Supreme Court in the *Teamsters* case in 1977, on condition that the job skills in question be widely possessed or readily acquired and the disparity between population and work force figures be gross.[50] And indeed such statistics are commonly used by plaintiffs to show evidence of adverse impact of tests and other selection procedures for entry-level jobs.[51] But that case and several others decided by the Supreme Court in 1977 and 1978[52] introduced substantially more sophisticated standards of proof to population/work force comparisons.

The refinements to the population/work force approach have involved the definition of both "population" and "work force." First, the question of geographical scope is potentially important in determining the appropriate population to use as a basis for comparison. In *U.S. v. County of*

---

[48] For a survey of ratios presented in particular cases, see Schlei and Grossman (1976:73-74 n. 45, 1979:35 n. 27).

[49] In *United States v. Hayes International Corp.*, 456 F. 2d 112, 120 (1972), the court said: "While we abjure any desire to become involved in a numbers game, statistics such as these do have some relevance in a Title VII pattern and practice suit," and went on to find that the "lopsided ratios" were sufficient to establish a prima facie case.

[50] *Teamsters v. United States*, 431 U.S. at 340, n. 20 (1977).

[51] *County of Los Angeles v. Van Davis*, 566 F. 2d 1264 (1978), vacated on other grounds, 47 LW 4317 (March 27, 1979); *Dothard v. Rawlinson*, 433 U.S. 321 (1977).

[52] *Evans v. United Airlines*, 431 U.S. 553 (1977); *Hazelwood School District v. United States*, 433 U.S. 299 (1977); *Dothard v. Rawlinson*, 433 U.S. 321 (1977); *Furnco Construction Corp. v. Waters*, 17 FEP 1062 (1978).

*Fairfax,* for example, the trial court rejected the Standard Metropolitan Statistical Area (SMSA) as the appropriate labor pool because "it is just not an area from which the defendants can be expected to draw any significant number of their employees."[53] (This case presents the ironic situation of defendant's statistics presented in rebuttal convincing the court of the existence of adverse impact, where plaintiff's evidence had failed.)

A second alteration of the population side of the equation has been the determination of the qualified labor pool in cases involving jobs that require special training. The Supreme Court gave recognition to this argument in *Hazelwood,*[54] a case concerning school teachers, by noting that the definition of the relevant labor market is a preliminary step to a comparison of the racial composition of the community and the defendant's work force.

Other refinements of approach to the definition of the relevant population include qualified *and* interested labor market, qualified actual applicant flow data, and relevant time frame; the latter takes into account the appropriate labor pool available when each opening occurred.

Defendants, who, for obvious reasons, have been prime movers in seeking refinements of the statistical analysis brought to bear in employment discrimination cases, have successfully argued for an inspection of the employer's work force over time rather than the earlier static count, in order that their efforts to increase minority representation in the work force be visible. Measurement of the rate of progress in eliminating "underrepresentation" of specified groups has been recognized judicially and is taken by the Equal Employment Opportunity Commission as a sign of good faith in a compliance review.[55]

## THE ELUSIVE QUALITY OF JOB RELATEDNESS*

Title VII litigation has tended to be dominated by the sort of statistical argument concerning the inference of discrimination in employment practices described above. The evidentiary requirements for establishing the presumption of discrimination are fairly well developed. It is more difficult

---

[53] No. 78-862-A, 8 (April 20, 1979); reversed 629, F. 2d 932 (1980).
[54] 433 U.S. at 308, n. 12 (1977): "when special qualifications are required to fill particular jobs, comparisons to the general population . . . may have little probative value."
[55] *Ibid.*; *Evans* v. *United Airlines,* 431 U.S. 553 (1977).

---

* This section has benefited from an unpublished paper by Ms. Deborah Macdonald entitled, "Job Relatedness and Employment Tests."

to discern an authoritative judicial posture concerning the requirements for proving a sufficient relationship between test and job.

Title VII specifically excluded from its litany of unlawful employment practices the use of "any professionally developed ability test," provided that it was not "designed, intended or used to discriminate because of race, color, religion, sex or national origin."[56] In its initial set of guidelines for implementing the Act, the Equal Employment Opportunity Commission (EEOC 1966:2137) interpreted "professionally developed ability test" to mean

. . . a test which fairly measures the knowledge or skills required by the particular job or class of jobs which the applicant seeks, or which fairly affords the employer a chance to measure the applicant's ability to perform a particular job or class of jobs. The fact that a test was prepared by an individual or organization claiming expertise in test preparation does not, without more, justify its use within the meaning of Title VII.

In other words, "professionally developed" was interpreted to mean "job related," the definition of which has been elaborated in subsequent iterations of the *Guidelines*.

The lower courts were divided in their reading of the statute (see *Harvard Law Review* 1971:1132-1139). Some of them followed the EEOC policy, while others, including the Circuit Court that heard the *Griggs* case,[57] rejected that interpretation. In 1971 the Supreme Court accepted an opportunity to settle the issue; it ruled in *Griggs* that Title VII proscribes an employment practice "which operates to exclude Negroes (and) cannot be shown to be related to job performance. . . ."[58] The Court also specifically endorsed the EEOC, saying that the administrative interpretation of the Act by the enforcing agency is entitled to "great deference."[59] The oft-repeated phrase lent tremendous authority to the agency's *Guidelines*, although the Court has subsequently gone out of its way to make clear that guidelines are not legally binding regulations.[60]

In an essay on the law of employment discrimination published while the Supreme Court was considering the Griggs case, the *Harvard Law Review* (1971:1132 n. 107) cautioned that job relatedness was not the same as validation:

Although some courts have held job relatedness a necessary justification for a

---

[56] PL 88-352, §703 (h).
[57] 420 F. 2d 1225.
[58] 401 U.S. 424, 431 (1971).
[59] *Ibid.*, 434.
[60] See *General Electric Co. v. Gilbert*, 429 U.S. 125 (1976).

## The Law of Employment Discrimination

testing program, few have yet required that job relatedness be demonstrated by the technical validation proposed by the Guidelines.

The impact of *Griggs* was to forge that equation. The opinion itself, while clearly placing the burden of proving a manifest relationship between a test and job performance with the employer, did not give specific guidance as to what would satisfy that obligation.[61] But on the basis of the "great deference" language, the lower courts turned to the EEOC *Guidelines* (1970) to provide the standards for judging the adequacy of employment tests. The Fifth Circuit accorded them controlling force.[62]

A second Supreme Court decision, in the case of *Albemarle* v. *Moody*,[63] lent further authority to the *Guidelines*. Certiorari was granted in that case because of Circuit conflict as to the showing required to establish the job relatedness of employment tests.[64] The *Guidelines* were quoted repeatedly and in detail as the source of the methods to be used to prove the relationship.[65]

The tests in question, the Revised Beta Examination (a measure of nonverbal intelligence) and the Wonderlic Personnel Test (a test of verbal skills), were struck down for lack of sufficient evidence of their relationship to important job skills. The company's last-minute validation study was found defective because it did not measure up to the standards set by the *Guidelines*. Among the shortcomings enumerated were failure to conduct a differential validation study, use of subjective supervisory rankings as the criterion measure, and failure to validate each test battery for all of the skilled lines of progression for which it was used.[66]

*Albemarle* is frequently seen as the high point of the Court's endorsement of the *Guidelines*; in two later decisions the Court has drawn limitations on their influence. It is not yet clear whether its revised posture

---

[61] Since the Company had not made any attempt to show that its entry requirements were related to job performance, standards of proof were not at issue in the case. The Court did, however, mention the newly published EEOC *Guidelines on Employee Selection Procedures* (1970) in a footnote.
[62] *U.S.* v. *Georgia Power Co.*, 474 F. 2d 906, 913 (1973).
[63] 422 U.S. 405 (1975).
[64] *Ibid.*, 413.
[65] But see Chief Justice Burger's dissent in which he warns against "slavish adherence" to the methods of test validation proposed by the *Guidelines* on the grounds that these methods "interpret no section of Title VII and are nowhere referred to in its legislative history." *Ibid.*, 451-52.
[66] *Ibid.*, 431-435. The Court did not, however, adhere to the *Guideline*'s requirement that an employer show that there is no alternative test, substantially as valid, but with less adverse impact; rather, this possibility was extended to the complainant.

will effect readjustments in the equation of job relatedness with psychometric validation techniques as well.

In the case of *Washington v. Davis*,[67] which involved a challenge on constitutional grounds to the entry-level police examination in Washington, D.C. (the Civil Rights Act had not yet been extended to public employees at the time the litigation began, but was shortly afterward), the Supreme Court rejected the Circuit Court's application of Title VII standards to constitutional cases, most importantly in the matter of racially discriminatory intent.[68] The Court did, however, endorse the trial judge's reasoning from Title VII standards in ruling the challenged test to be job related. More specifically, it endorsed the District Court's conclusion that a test shown to be directly related to performance in a training program satisfies the job-relatedness requirement, quite aside from its possible relationship to actual performance as a police officer.[69] The district judge's approach to the *Guidelines* was far more flexible than, for example, the Supreme Court's *Albemarle* decision. Indeed, Judge Gesell's ruling was a "commonsense" conclusion based on the plausibility of a substantial relationship between the test and the course.

Lest too much be read into the apparent shift between *Albemarle* and *Washington v. Davis*, it should be emphasized that both the grounds of action and the fact situations were entirely different in the two cases. The latter case was tried under the Fifth Amendment (despite the confusion wrought by the lower courts' application of Title VII requirements), and for that reason the Court approved the trial judge's less rigorous application of the *Guidelines*.[70] In addition, the Albemarle Paper Company had had a history of overt discrimination in the years before the Civil Rights Act, and its accommodations to the Act had had the effect of freezing long-time black employees in low level jobs, since movement into the skilled jobs would mean loss of seniority. The Washington Police Department, on the other hand, had instituted a systematic and affirmative program to attract black police officers in 1969. The dramatically changed racial composition of the police force precluded any intimation of discriminatory intent.

A second case, not a testing case at all, but one involving EEOC guide-

---

[67] 426 U.S. 229 (1976).
[68] *Ibid.*, 239, 246-248.
[69] *Ibid.*, 249-251.
[70] Under the statutory standards, the Court explained, it is insufficient to demonstrate some rational basis for the challenged practices. Title VII requires "a more probing judicial review of, and less deference to, the seemingly reasonable acts of administrators and executives than is appropriate under the Constitution . . ." *Ibid.*, 247.

## The Law of Employment Discrimination

lines, has also been viewed as indicating a retreat from *Albemarle*.[71] In *General Electric v. Gilbert*[72] (1976), the Court decided a question of pregnancy benefits in direct contradiction of the EEOC guideline on the subject, as well as numerous administrative and lower court decisions.

Justice Rehnquist, writing for the Court, discussed the nature of guidelines:

> We are told that this analysis of the congressional purpose underlying Title VII is consistent with the guidelines of the EEOC, which, it is asserted, are entitled to great deference. . . .[73]

He proceeded to explain that, while guidelines may have the power to persuade, they do not have the power to control, quoting from the Court's 1944 opinion in *Skidmore v. Swift & Co.*:[74]

> We consider that the rulings, interpretations and opinions of the Administrator under this Act, while not controlling upon the courts by reason of their authority, do constitute a body of experience and informed judgment to which courts and litigants may properly resort for guidance. The weight of such a judgment in a particular case will depend upon the thoroughness evident in its consideration, the validity of its reasoning, its consistency with earlier and later pronouncements, and all those factors which give it power to persuade, if lacking power to control.[75]

The question that *Washington v. Davis* and *General Electric v. Gilbert* raises is whether (or to what extent) employers can successfully withstand Title VII challenges to tests and other selection devices by offering evidence of job relatedness that, while reasonable or professionally acceptable, is not in full compliance with the *Guidelines*. Since it is unclear that any test currently available could survive a rigorous application of the EEOC standards,[76] the question is important both to the future of employment testing and to the principle of objective selection.

The answer will never be simple, for even validated tests, as the Court noted in *Albemarle*, can be used to mask discriminatory purpose.[77] But the Court does seem to have it in mind to apply the law in a way that will avoid discouraging all test use, as a literal-minded application of the

---

[71] For a discussion of the case and its implications, see Larson (1977: 15-31-15-33).
[72] 429 U.S. 125 (1976).
[73] *Ibid.*, 140.
[74] 323 U.S. 134, 140 (1944).
[75] 429 U.S. 125, 141-142.
[76] The Iowa Supreme Court remarked in 1973 that its extensive research of federal decisions had "failed to disclose a single example of a written test passing muster under the guidelines for validation" (Larson 1977:15-31). Commentators continue to emphasize the difficulty.
[77] 422 U.S. at 405, 436 (1975).

*Guidelines* could tend to do by throwing out the good along with the bad. There is an indication of such intention in the Court's summary affirmance of the District Court judgment in *National Education Association* v. *South Carolina*,[78] although it is difficult to tell what the Court was deciding since it did not hear oral argument or write an opinion.

The case revolved around South Carolina's use of the National Teachers' Examination in the hiring and classification of teachers. The test was not developed for that purpose, and it worked to screen out far higher percentages of black teacher-candidates than white. In order to demonstrate its appropriateness as a screening device, the state commissioned a validation study by the Educational Testing Service, the company that developed the test. That study was designed to demonstrate the validity of the content of the examination by comparing it with the content of the teacher-training programs in South Carolina.

The District Court found that the study satisfied the employer's burden of proof under Title VII.[79] It cited *Washington* v. *Davis* on two counts: first, as endorsing the use of the academic training program rather than actual job performance as the criterion against which the test was measured; and secondly, as extending parity to the three professionally recognized validation strategies,[80] even though the EEOC *Guidelines* accord only grudging and limited approval to content and construct validation.

The District Court also cited the authority of *General Electric* v. *Gilbert* in pointing out that "to the extent that the EEOC *Guidelines* conflict with well grounded expert opinion and accepted professional standards, they need not be controlling."[81]

In sum, the post-*Albemarle* decisions of the Supreme Court appear to counsel a less dogmatic approach to the question of *methods*, while not in any way retreating from the proposition that tests that have a differential racial impact must be shown to have a manifest relationship to successful performance on the job. The *Guidelines* have not been displaced as the major source of guidance in the question of proof, but their status has been defined as lying within the larger context of professional opinion, and their function has been clarified as the exercise of influence rather than dominion.

---

[78] 46 LW 3452.
[79] *U.S.* v. *South Carolina*, 445 F. Supp. 1094, 1112 (1977).
[80] *Ibid.*, 1113-14.
[81] *Ibid.*, 1113 n. 20.

## TESTS ON TRIAL

When one turns from the Supreme Court to contemplate the variety of lower court opinions, the sense of an emerging legal doctrine of job relatedness disappears. The striking fact is that most of the decisions have ruled against the challenged tests; there are numerous rulings on what evidence will not satisfy, but little to illustrate what will satisfy the employer's obligation to establish a manifest relationship between test and job.

In the early years of testing litigation this was not surprising. Although testing for purposes of employee selection was a well-established and widely used practice by the 1960s,[82] the aura of scientific selection surrounding test use appears in many instances to have had little connection with reality. While a number of large firms had researched testing programs, most employers simply assumed that by using tests they were applying objective standards to build their work force. A survey of employment testing practices in the San Francisco area conducted by the California Fair Employment Commission in 1966 revealed that 70 percent of the firms interviewed had introduced testing programs without the advice of testing professionals and without doing job analyses, although 40 percent reported some professional oversight of the ongoing program. Only 16 percent of the firms had empirical evidence that testing had improved their selection practices (see discussion by Rushmore in *Columbia Law Review* 1968).

Even if an employer had the resources and the interest to build a more sophisticated testing program, adequate professional advice was not always easily obtained. Although industrial psychology was a long established research field, the energies of the profession as a whole were focused elsewhere. The triennial essay on personnel selection in the *Annual Review of Psychology* for 1972 noted that the "discovery" of minority and disadvantaged groups in the late 1960s had changed the complexion of the field. Not only had testers formerly ignored minority groups, but the quality of research in general left much to be desired, in the authors' opinion. In the unaccustomed spotlight of Title VII concerns, it had rapidly become clear that there was little unanimity among personnel psychologists about the proper way to validate a test. The authors expressed the added concern that although the challenge of new civil rights sensibilities was causing many employment practices to be reex-

---

[82] According to Psychological Services, Inc., in *Survey of Hiring Procedures, 1958-1963*, eighty-five percent of firms questioned used personnel tests in 1963 (*Columbia Law Review* 1968).

amined, most researchers had not yet faced up to the criterion problem (that is, the problem of finding a good indicator of job success against which to measure the predictive power of a test in establishing its validity) (Bray and Moses 1972).

For their part, the testing companies were far more likely than now to feel that their role ended with the development of the test. One commentator expressed hope that the testing companies were "waking up to their responsibility" to educate the test user by noting that the 1965 Science Research Associates catalogue suggested that personnel managers might "take a test themselves to evaluate how well it measures the critical behavior required." In 1967 the catalogue warned the test user that a test that predicted success well in one company would not necessarily work elsewhere, even if the job title were the same. Modest though these pedagogical efforts were, the author did not see signs of a corresponding degree of awareness among employers (*Columbia Law Review* 1968:700).[83]

It was in this climate that the case law on testing developed. Even before the Supreme Court decision in *Griggs*, a number of courts had accepted the contention of the Equal Employment Opportunity Commission that an employer must demonstrate a correlation between test scores and the ability to perform on the job. In the case of *Hicks* v. *Crown Zellerbach Corp.* (1970), the court wrote:

Title VII does not permit an employer to engage in unsubstantiated speculation at the expense of Negro workers.[84]

After *Griggs* the tendency was stronger for courts to declare test use unlawful in those instances where the employers had not performed validation studies;[85] other types of evidence such as argument based on the similarity of the content of the test and the work to be performed, were usually found inadequate to carry the employer's burden of proof. The Western Electric Co., for example, had a program of instruction in

---

[83] It should be mentioned that Science Research Associates has the reputation of a responsible test developer; the point is the quality of test use when the courts were first being asked to adjudicate employment discrimination complaints.

[84] 310 F. Supp. 536, 538 (1970).

[85] *Hester* v. *Southern Railway Co.*, 349 F. Supp. 812 (1972), (typing test); *United States* v. *Central Motor Lines, Inc.*, 338 F. Supp. 532 (1971) (traffic and driving knowledge test, federal regulations test); *Officers for Civil Justice* v. *Civil Service Commission of San Francisco*, 371 F. Supp. 1328 (1973) (civil service exam used for police entry).

## The Law of Employment Discrimination

electronics culminating in an electronics test that it used to qualify workers for promotion to higher grades. Using the defense of business necessity, the company argued that the test was essential to the safe and efficient operation of the plant because the more responsible positions required a strong knowledge of electronics. The court replied that, since the test had not been validated as suggested by the EEOC *Guidelines*, there was no way to determine whether or not it was serving an essential function.[86]

While a significant body of precedent has accumulated that some sort of formal validation study is necessary to establish the job relatedness of a test under Title VII,[87] the question of what constitutes a sufficient validation study defies easy answer. Among the deficiencies cited in cases where the employer made an effort to validate the tests used are failure to conduct a differential validity study;[88] an inadequate job analysis;[89] failure to justify the use of a content- or construct-validity strategy by showing the infeasibility of a criterion-related validity study as recom-

---

[86] *Ivey v. Western Electric Co.*, 16 EPD ¶8297, 5550 (1977). But see, *Lewis v. Bethlehem Steel Corp.*, 440 F. Supp. 949 (1977).

[87] The 1978 *Guidelines* have adopted a somewhat more flexible position that presumably will be reflected in the case law. Where the validation techniques described in the *Guidelines* are not technically feasible, the user is to justify the test by some other means "in accord with Federal law." 43 Fed. Reg. 38299, §6B(2). In the "Questions and Answers" on the *Guidelines* that statement is elaborated as follows: ". . . Federal agencies will consider evidence that a selection procedure is necessary for the safe and efficient operation of a business to justify the continued use of a selection procedure." 44 Fed. Reg. 12002, Q. 36. This is the *Griggs* business necessity doctrine.

[88] *Clark v. H. K. Porter Company*, 296 F. Supp. 49 (1968); *U.S. v. Jacksonville Terminal Co.*, 451 F. 2d 418 (1971); *U.S. v. Georgia Power Co.*, 474 F. 2d 906 (1973); *Rogers v. International Paper Co.*, 510 F. 2d 1340 (1975); *Green v. Missouri Pacific Railroad Co.*, 523 F. 2d 1290 (1975); *EEOC v. Detroit Edison Co.*, 515 F. 2d 301 (1975); *U.S. v. City of Chicago*, 549 F. 2d 415 (1977); *Commonwealth v. O'Neill*, 19 FEP Cases 55 (1979).

[89] *Albemarle v. Moody*, 422 U.S. 405 (1975); *Vulcan Society City Fire Dept., Inc. v. Civil Service Com'n of N.Y.*, 490 F. 2d 387 (1973); *Kirkland v. New York State Dept. of Correctional Services*, 374 F. Supp. 1361 (1974); *Walston v. County School Board of Nansemond County*, 492 F. 2d 919 (1974); *Jones v. New York City Human Resources Administration*, 391 F. Supp. 1064 (1975); *Officers for Civil Justice v. Civil Service Com'n of San Francisco*, 395 F. Supp. 378 (1975); *Rogers v. International Paper Co.*, 510 F. 2d 1340 (1975); *Firefighters Institute, Etc., v. St. Louis*, 549 F. 2d 506 (1977); *U.S. v. City of Chicago*, 549 F. 2d 415 (1977); *James v. Stockham Valves and Fittings*, 559 F. 2d 310 (1977); *U.S. v. City of Buffalo*, 457 F. Supp. 612 (1978); *Association Against Discrimination v. City of Bridgeport*, 17 FEP Cases 1308 (1978) (defendants spent 1 and 1/2 years, 2,745 man-hours, and $100,000 developing an examination, which was struck down due to an inadequate job analysis).

mended by the EEOC *Guidelines*;[90] use of unvalidated cutoff scores;[91] failure to validate ranked scores;[92] absence of significant statistical correlation;[93] the use of weak or inappropriate criteria;[94] weaknesses of correspondence between skills tested and the domain of job skills;[95] and inadequate attempt to identify an alternative with less adverse impact.[96]

In *United States v. Georgia Power Co.* (1973), the district court remarked upon the "rather startling evidence offered by the government . . . to the effect that there was no test known to exist or yet devised" that could meet the EEOC standards, and concluded that neither Congress nor the Supreme Court could have intended such a meaningless interpretation of Sec. 703(h) of Title VII.[97] The fact of the matter is that judicial interpretation of Title VII has tended to make it unusual for testing pro-

---

[90] *Douglas v. Hampton*, 512 F. 2d 476 (1978); *Officers for Justice v. Civil Service Com'n of San Francisco*, 371 F. Supp. 1328 (1973); *U.S. v. City of Buffalo*, 457 F. Supp. 612 (1978). But see *Washington v. Davis*, 44 LW 4789 (1976); *Firefighters Institute, Etc., v. St. Louis*, 549 F. 2d 506 (1977). The 1978 *Guidelines* do not continue the EEOC preference for criterion-related validation, but rather counsel using whichever strategy is most appropriate to the situation.

[91] *Boston Chapter, NAACP, v. Beecher*, 504 F. 2d 1017 (1974); *Rogers v. International Paper Co.*, 510 F. 2d 1340 (1975); *EEOC v. Detroit Edison*, 400 F. Supp. 343 (1975); *U.S. v. North Carolina*, 400 F. Supp. 343 (1975); *Association Against Discrimination v. City of Bridgeport*, 17 FEP Cases 1308 (1978); *Allen v. City of Mobile*, 18 FEP Cases 217 (1978).

[92] *Allen v. City of Mobile*, 18 FEP Cases 217 (1978); *Louisville Black Police Officers v. City of Louisville*, 20 FEP Cases 1195 (1979). But see *Detroit Police Officers Assn. v. Young*, 16 FEP Cases 1005 (1978).

[93] *U.S. v. Georgia Power Co.*, 474 F. 2d 906 (1973); *Boston Chapter, NAACP v. Beecher*, 504 F 2d 1017 (1974); *EEOC v. Local 638*, 401 F. Supp. 467 (1975); *Rogers v. International Paper Co.*, 510 F. 2d 1340 (1975); *Ensley Branch, NAACP v. Seibels*, 14 FEP Cases 670 (1977).

[94] *Young v. Edgcomb Steel Co.*, 363 F. Supp. 961 (1973); *Rogers v. International Paper Co.*, 510 F. 2d 1340 (1975); *League of United American Citizens v. Santa Ana*, 410 F. Supp. 873 (1976); *U.S. v. City of Chicago*, 549 F. 2d 415 (1977); *Ensley Branch, NAACP v. Seibels*, 14 FEP Cases 670 (1977).

[95] *Chance v. Board of Examiners*, 458 F. 2d 1167 (1972); *Vulcan Society v. Civil Service Com'n*. 490 F. 2d 387 (1973); *Firefighters Institute, Etc., v. St. Louis*, 549 F. 2d 506 (1977); *Fisher v. Procter & Gamble Mfg. Co.*, 14 EPD ¶7662 (1977); *Guardians Ass'n of N.Y. v. Civil Service Com'n*, 431 F. Supp. 526 (1977).

[96] *Boston Chapter, NAACP v. Beecher*, 504 F. 2d 1017 (1974); *Officers for Justice v. Civil Service Com'n of San Francisco*, 395 F. Supp. 378 (1975); *Allen v. City of Mobile*, 18 FEP Cases 217 (1978). Many courts have cited *Albemarle* in extending the right to suggest alternatives to the plaintiff and leaving it to the employer to disprove the viability of the suggested alternatives. *U.S. v. South Carolina*, 445 F. Supp. 1094 (1977); *Crockett v. Green*, 388 F. Supp. 912 (1975); *Harless v. Duck*, 14 FEP Cases 1616 (1977).

[97] 3 FEP Cases, 787 n. 8 (1973). See also *Henderson v. First National Bank of Montgomery*, 360 F. Supp. 531 (1973) 545.

## The Law of Employment Discrimination

grams to withstand challenge. And it is no longer tests introduced hastily in response to the passing of the Civil Rights Act or "validated" during a half-day visit by an outside expert that are the subject of litigation; such relatively carefully constructed and researched tests as the PACE examination[98] and the Sears and Roebuck testing program[99] have also been challenged.

There is variability among the circuits. The Fifth Circuit, which reversed the district court in the *Georgia Power* case, has ruled that the EEOC *Guidelines* have the force of law;[100] the Second Circuit has been less rigid in its interpretation of an employer's obligation under the *Guidelines*. In reviewing the lower court opinion in a case involving the New York City fire fighters entrance examination, the circuit judge said of the *Guidelines* that while not binding on the courts, they "have been relied on as a helpful summary of professional testing standards in both §1983 and Title VII cases."[101] The appellate decision also commended the trial judge's approach to validation requirements:

> As we read his opinion, the judge developed a sliding scale for evaluating the examination, wherein the poorer the quality of the test preparation, the greater must be the showing that the examination was properly job related, and vice versa. . . . A principle of this sort is useful in lessening the burden of judicial examination-reading and the risk that a court will fall into error in umpiring a battle of experts who speak a language it does not fully understand.[102]

In this and other cases, the Second Circuit has developed the line of reasoning that careful test preparation (judged by the qualifications of the test developers, techniques of job analysis, sources of test items, etc.) gives rise to the presumption that the burden of proof has been satisfied,

---

[98] *Luevano* v. *Cambell*, #79-0271 (D.C.D.C., Jan. 29, 1979). The PACE, the major screening device for entry into federal professional and administrative positions, will be apparently phased out over the next 3 years according to a consent decree filed on February 24, 1981, and accepted by the court in November 1981.

[99] EEOC brought suit against Sears in several jurisdictions. Three of four suits were dismissed, and the EEOC and Sears reached an overall settlement on racial discrimination issues in June 1981 (*The Washington Post*, June 1, 1981 A-1).

[100] *Pettway* v. *American Cast Iron Pipe Co.*, 494 F. 2d 211 (1974). But see *Smith* v. *Olin Chemical Corp.*, 555 F. 2d 1283 (1977) in which the Fifth Circuit took the view that there is a narrow class of job criteria that are so clearly job-related that they don't necessitate any evidentiary showing. The case involved a physical requirement, not a paper-and-pencil test, but EEOC would interpret the standard to fall within the *Guidelines*.

[101] *Vulcan Soc. of N.Y. City Fire Dept., Inc.* v. *Civil Serv. Com'n*, 490 F. 2d 387, 394 n. 8 (1973).

[102] *Ibid.*, 396.

thus lessening the need for the court to get involved in the intricacies of test validation.[103]

In addition, the nature of the position for which a test or other selection standard is being used seems to influence the amount of deference accorded the *Guidelines*. The courts have imposed a lighter burden of proof on employers, for example, when the challenge involved selection standards for airplane pilots:

> When a job requires a small amount of skill and training and the consequences of hiring an unqualified applicant are insignificant, the courts should examine closely any pre-employment standard or criteria which discriminates against minorities. . . . On the other hand, when the job clearly requires a high degree of skill and the economic and human risks involved in hiring an unqualified applicant are great, the employer bears a correspondingly lighter burden to show that his employment criteria are job-related.[104]

In a slightly different vein, a number of courts have sustained tests where it was shown that the content of the test paralleled the duties of the job. This has been particularly true of craft jobs where the test is a work sample.[105]

The general thrust of judicial rulings, however, has been to eliminate tests and other selection standards (e.g., requiring a high school diploma) where there is adverse impact. This will probably continue to be the case so long as courts are faced with selection statistics like those presented in the New York State Troopers case (recently decided at the district court level), no matter what the arguments for ranking and competitive selection might be. The suit, a pattern or practice case brought by the Justice Department, involved New York civil service laws, which prescribe competitive examinations, the ranking of candidates according to test scores, and selection strictly by numerical order.

The court showed sensitivity to the complexity of the issues involved

---

[103] *Kirkland* v. *N.Y. Dept. of Correctional Serv.*, 520 F. 2d 420 (1975).

[104] *Spurlock* v. *United Airlines*, 475 F. 2d 216, 219 (1972). *Spurlock* upheld a college degree requirement. See also *Boyd* v. *Ozark Airlines*, 15 EPD ¶7863 (1977); *Johnson* v. *U. of Pittsburgh*, 435 F. Supp. 1328 (1977) (factors determining professional success of college professor too subtle for empirical data to be determinative). But see *Townsend* v. *Nassau County Medical Center*, 11 EPD 1078 (1975) (medical technologists); *Payne* v. *Travenol Lab.*, 416 F. Supp. 248 (1976) (systems and traffic analyst); *Liberles* v. *Daniels*, 20 FEP Cases 1480 (1979) (case worker/social worker), in which a college degree requirement was struck down.

[105] *Lewis* v. *Bethlehem Steel Corp.*, 440 F. Supp. 949 (1977) (electrician); *Henderson* v. *First National Bank of Montgomery*, 360 F. Supp. 531 (1973) (typist); *Coopersmith* v. *Rondebush*, 517 F. 2d 818 (1975) (attorney).

## The Law of Employment Discrimination

in the case and to the limited nature of solutions offered by judicial application of constitutional and statutory principles to the moral, social, and economic problems of a changing society:

> In an action such as this it is hard to escape the feeling that a court will be hopelessly entangled in the formulation of social policy and professional standards outside its field of expertise.[106]

The opinion noted as well that the federal government was unable to present a united stance, divided as it is on the contradictory claims of statutorily established merit systems and adverse impact principles.

> Even the most casual reader of this decision could not help but notice the friction and conflict between the United States Department of Justice and the United States Civil Service Commission. . . . No one could blame the state defendants if they feel misled by the federal government because of the conflicting positions of the employees of these two agencies.[107]

The Court weighed these contrary interests in light of the need to make up for "the lengthy and tragic history of our society's treatment of the Negro." The judge rejected the civil service examination because its justification was based on a content validity strategy not in compliance with professional standards and federal guidelines and ruled that the procedure was shown statistically to be unlawfully discriminatory.

> Less than 1% of the sworn personnel of the New York State Police were Negro, Spanish-surnamed American, or female when this action was commenced in 1977. Yet these groups of individuals comprise about 10.80%, 3.36%, and 38.60%, respectively, of the relevant labor market for entry-level position of trooper. These are startling and eye-catching statistics for a State that aspires to be in the forefront in its endeavors to correct racial employment wrongs of the past.[108]

Seldom will a court find otherwise.

### CONCLUSIONS

Employment tests are being subjected to a degree of governmental scrutiny that very few human contrivances could bear. Whatever interests may be served by testing—efficiency or productivity, the sense of fairness that results from cloaking the allocation of scarce positions with the

---

[106] *United States* v. *State of New York*, slip opinion #77-CV-343, Sept. 6, 1979, 6. See also *Association Against Discrimination* v. *City of Bridgeport*, 20 FEP Cases 985 (1979).
[107] *Ibid.*, 7.
[108] *Ibid.*, 12.

mantle of objective selection, better matching of people and jobs—they are not at present strong enough to compete with the governmental commitment to bringing blacks and other disadvantaged minorities into the mainstream of economic life.

To the extent that this pressure has reduced such test abuse as the unwarranted use of so-called intelligence tests in the selection of unskilled and semiskilled laborers, it has furthered the goal of equal employment opportunity without damage to other legitimate interests. Many employers have been willing to devote more resources to their testing programs and other selection procedures, a development the industrial psychologists often attribute to federal EEO policies (Bray and Moses 1972).

But there have been costs. The extension of the legal meaning of discrimination beyond conscious actions to unintended and perhaps unavoidable consequences of a selection system has strained the sense of fairness that gave birth to the Civil Rights Act of 1964. Employers, no matter what their motives or how great their efforts to attract qualified minority and female candidates, are placed in the position of appearing to discriminate on the basis of race, sex, or national origin by differential selection statistics. The Equal Employment Opportunity Commission and the courts usually treat such statistics as evidence that unlawful discrimination has taken place, because they have acted on the premise that all social groups embody the same spread of talent and abilities and share the same occupational preferences, no matter what degree of poverty, abuse, and social marginality some of those groups have suffered. This situation puts a good deal of pressure on employers to institute what amounts to a quiet quota system to protect themselves against litigation. The recent decision in *Kaiser Aluminum v. Weber*,[109] however, gives some promise that a voluntary, racially conscious affirmative action program involving training to upgrade employees' skills can pass judicial muster.

The combination of the rhetoric of equal treatment under the law with an apparent policy of preferential treatment for those who cannot compete successfully on the basis of test scores, educational attainments, or other common predictors has led to an uneasiness among citizens of both majority and minority status. It is disingenuous to define a fair test as one on which deprived minorities perform as well as the average majority candidate; yet this is the logical impasse we have reached during a decade and a half of administrative and legal interpretation of Title VII. Tests cannot, for the most part, circumvent the effects of deprivation, nor is

---

[109] 47 LW 4851.

the concept of discrimination adequate to address the problem of black or female economic disadvantage. It is time to focus on other methods of combatting economic disadvantage and to let employment testing contribute what it can to business efficiency.

## REFERENCES

American Psychological Association, American Educational Research Association, and National Council on Measurement in Education (1966) *Standards for Educational and Psychological Tests and Manuals.* Washington, D.C.: American Psychological Association.

American Psychological Association, American Educational Research Association, and National Council on Measurement in Education (1974) *Standards for Educational and Psychological Tests.* Washington, D.C.: American Psychological Association.

Balog, R. P. (1976) Note. *Notre Dame Lawyer* 52:95-108.

Bray, D. W., and Moses, J. L. (1972) Personnel selection. *Annual Review of Psychology* 23:545-576.

Bureau of National Affairs (1976) *Daily Labor Report,* June 22.

Columbia Law Review (1968) Notes: legal implications of the use of standardized tests in employment and eduction. *Columbia Law Review* 68:691-744.

Division of Industrial-Organizational Psychology (1974) *Principles for the Validation and Use of Personnel Selection Procedures.* Washington, D.C.: American Psychological Association.

Equal Employment Opportunity Commission (1966) Guidelines on employment testing procedures. *Federal Register* 31:6414.

Harvard Law Review (1971) Developments in the law: employment discrimination and Title VII of the Civil Rights Act of 1964. *Harvard Law Review* 84:1111-1166.

Hay, H. (1978) The use of statistics to disprove employment discrimination. *Labor Law Journal* 29(July):430-440.

Larson, A. (1977) *Employment Discrimination: Race,* Vol. I. New York: Matthew Bender.

Robertson, P. C. (1976) A Staff Analysis of the History of EEOC Guidelines on Employee Selection Procedures. Unpublished document submitted to the General Accounting Office, August 29. Equal Employment Opportunity Commission, Washington, D.C.

Schlei, B. L., and Grossman, P. (1976) *Employment Discrimination Law.* Washington, D.C.: Bureau of National Affairs.

Schlei, B. L., and Grossman, P. (1979) *Employment Discrimination Law: 1979 Supplement.* Washington, D.C.: Bureau of National Affairs.

Shoben, E. (1977) Probing the discriminatory effects of employee selection procedures with disparate impact analysis under Title VII. *Texas Law Review* 56(December):1-45.

Shoben, E. (1978) Differential pass-fail rates in employment testing: statistical proof under Title VII. *Harvard Law Review* 91:793-813.

MELVIN NOVICK
# Ability Testing: Federal Guidelines and Professional Standards

**PARTICIPANTS AND ISSUES**

Ability testing involves and significantly affects individuals (students, teachers, and educational administrators, job applicants, employees, supervisors, and executives), institutions (schools, colleges, businesses, industry and government agencies), and the larger society, which is served by these individuals and institutions. Individuals and institutions benefit when testing helps them achieve their defined goals. Society benefits when the achievement of individual and institutional goals contributes to the general good.

Many difficulties in assessing beneficial ability testing practice arise from the conflicts among what is perceived as good for the individual, the institution, or the society. An unemployed high school dropout benefits from being employed, a prospective employer may regard this person's employment as less than beneficial because of low expected productivity, but society may benefit from modest productivity as compared with the cost of unemployment compensation. In such a situation, testing, as a component of employment, will also be perceived from three different vantages.

Often the multiple objectives of persons, institutions, and society conflict with each other. Persons desire high financial reward, status, and

---

I am indebted to Alexandra Wigdor for constructive criticism of early drafts of this paper.

## Federal Guidelines and Professional Standards

pleasant working conditions. Employers want high productivity, a stable and cooperative workforce, and flexibility to meet the needs of a changing environment. Industry, however, also needs a favorable economic environment with a high level of employment and concomitant consumer purchasing power in which to market its product. Schools and colleges want the best students, but they also want to serve those whom they can serve best and those who can gain the most from their service, including the previously disadvantaged.

The interests of institutions and examinees are sometimes congruent and sometimes not. When a test is given for guidance purposes in a school or for job placement in a factory, the interests of the individual and the institution coincide. However, an applicant for law school or for a widely sought job who takes a test seeks selection, regardless of the *relative* qualifications of interest to an admissions officer or an employer.

Individual federal agencies have responsibilities and goals delegated by the executive and legislative branches of government, monitored by the judicial branch, and ultimately specified by the incumbent agency management. While these agencies share concern for benefits to society as a whole, they tend to focus attention on their own particular mandates, and for this reason often view testing and other issues quite differently. In fact, it is not uncommon for government agencies to be on opposite sides in litigation involving tests, for employers to receive conflicting directives from different government agencies, and for employees to find that their test scores are considered in the light of widely varying objectives by employers and government agency representatives.

There are generally three participants in the ability testing process: the institution or *test user*, who requires the test for some decision-making purpose; the *test producer*, who develops, markets, and/or administers and scores the test; and the *test taker*, who takes the test by choice, direction, or necessity. And in the background, society as a whole sets the context for the participants through its value systems and sets the rules for their interaction through its governmental and professional institutions. Ability testing policies and practices have historically been dominated by the user institutions prescribing the test. The test producing organizations, because of technical expertise, also exert great influence on the testing process, but the common perception that testing organizations set employment and educational policy is inaccurate. They have some influence through exhortation, but it is limited, and they are often reluctant to use it.

The relationship between individual institutions and testing organizations is often mediated by a board or council made up of representatives of user institutions, which develops testing programs through negotiation with the test producer. Typical of these is the College Entrance Examination Board, which sets policy and practice for the construction, administration, scoring, and reporting of the Scholastic Aptitude Test (SAT). Similar entities exist for graduate and professional schools and for the institutions involved in the American College Testing Program. These relationships between producer and user board resemble those of individual professionals providing services to a client for a fee.

The test taker has historically exercised almost no influence on the process. In fact, prior to 1958, the test taker did not directly receive a score report in one major testing program (the College Board SAT program). It was sent to the test taker's high school counselor for transmission and interpretation.

The last two decades, however, have witnessed an increasing change in the relationship between test users and producers, on the one hand, and test takers, on the other. It would be easy to attribute this change to student activism in the late sixties and lower enrollments in the seventies, but the fact is that much change began in the fifties. For example, the American College Testing Program has, since its inception in 1960, described itself as an "inviolate public trust" and has emphasized service to students, no doubt reflecting the posture of the public institutions that dominate its corporate body.

In 1970 the Commission on Tests of the College Board issued a *Report of the Commission on Tests*, consisting of Part I: "Righting the Balance" and Part II: "Briefs." Most widely discussed of the papers in Part II was James S. Coleman's, in which he argued that an asymmetry between institutions and students existed and that this should be rectified by providing more information to students, allowing students to present a broader picture of their competencies, and modifying the College Board governance structure to embody a symmetry of college and applicant interests.

In October 1978 the College Board added two student representatives to each of its seven major national councils and committees. A *Report on Student Involvement in the College Board* (Brouder 1978) outlines other steps taken by the College Board to increase student participation in its deliberations and decision-making process. The Educational Testing Service has established the Office of Program Planning specifically for interaction with student groups through an external advisory group that includes three student representatives. Literature from the American College Testing program (ACT) emphasizes early and continuing involvement of student representatives in organizational policy making.

The significance of these steps should be neither under- nor overvalued. The presence of students on major committees and the interaction with student organizations will certainly provide a forum for the student point

## Federal Guidelines and Professional Standards 73

of view, and this has led and will lead to change. However, it must be noted that the relationship between the student leaders and the constituency they ostensibly represent on these committees may sometimes be distant or transient and thus not always directly representative of the constituency.

An imperfect parallel may be drawn with employment selection in the form of recent interaction between labor unions and employers regarding testing practices. However, labor unions are more directly representative of current employees than they are of job applicants, and there is little reason to believe that the interests of job applicants and current employees necessarily coincide. In the educational setting the de facto representation of applicant interests by students involves fewer conflicts, but it must still be recognized that these representatives are not accountable to the applicant constituency.

Another influence in the conflict is the special status accorded by our society to educational institutions through substantial financial support from federal and state governments and favored tax status with respect to their other income and contributions. This preferred status of American educational institutions is certainly justified by the public function they serve—a public function that devolves, in part, to educational testing organizations and is clearly accepted as such by them.

The relationships among test users, producers, and takers are greatly affected by the technical expertise of the individual testing organizations. While institutions and their representative bodies are free to contract for service with numerous testing organizations, in fact, relatively few producers can offer the facilities and technical expertise necessary to serve larger programs. Competition in the testing industry is intense in some areas but very limited in others. In addition, institutional boards do not always have the independent technical staffs needed for careful scrutiny of producer testing proposals. Adversary interactions between the taker and the producer are completely one-sided because of the technical resources and expertise of the typical producer. It might be noted that a test taker confronting a testing organization would not naturally look to a student organization for help. Generally, test takers are not organized and have varied interests.

The issues arising from the interaction between testing organizations, decision-making users, and those employees, students, and applicants affected by the decisions bear much resemblance to the issues arising in other spheres in which there is an imbalance in expertise and power among the interacting parties. Examinees are unable to judge the quality or appropriateness of the tests they take, just as recipients of medical or legal services are often unable to judge the quality of such services. Both the medical and legal professions have developed ethical standards to protect those they serve. Furthermore, much state and federal legislation has been enacted for the protection of individuals; federal agencies have been created for the special purpose of consumer protection; the Uniform Commercial Code with its section on unconscionability is an important legal tool for the protection of consumers. The approach of the Federal Drug Administration is often mentioned as a model for regulation of testing problems. In general, consumerism has developed rapidly during the past two decades, and persons with experience in this movement have entered the debate on testing issues.

The issues involved in testing, however, may be more complex than those in other areas of consumer and professional client protection. While a physician or a lawyer serves the individual client's interests only, test producers and users may have divided loyalties—some would claim that the interests of the taker are rarely paramount. Consider also that, while a consumer might be able to make a relatively sound judgment as to the quality of a product such as an automobile, the evaluation of the quality of an ability test is much less easy. Beyond this, however, are complicated issues of equity and fairness to individuals that may often appear to conflict with the attainment of institutional goals. Because the examinee is the least powerful participant in the testing and decision-making process, some strengthening of this participant's position would seem inevitable. And indeed, there has been perceptible change in the relative power of the three participants in recent years, but it is difficult, at this time, to evaluate the extent of that change.

The issues of product quality and competing interests of the participants would be enough to guarantee controversy in ability testing, even in a society of relative economic and social homogeneity. Ours, however, is not yet such a society, though those who think we compare unfavorably with other countries might find supporting evidence elusive.

The fact is that massive attempts to eliminate an historic pattern of discrimination because of race, color, religion, sex, age, national origin, and socioeconomic status have not been wholly successful. Even if all such discrimination were to vanish instantaneously, the effects on individuals would linger for generations, and the American ethic of equality of opportunity could not be attained immediately. Education has always been viewed as the primary avenue of upward social and economic mobility, and the reality of that view is one of this country's great strengths. This means, however, that the American educational system bears a heavy burden and, as acknowledged gatekeepers, with the means to open gates as well as to close them, the educational testing industry is often viewed as the fulcrum on which this load balances. It is of interest to note that

## Federal Guidelines and Professional Standards 75

for more than three decades tests were widely accepted as a means of access to higher education for the socioeconomically disadvantaged, a viewpoint widely questioned today.

In our society, conflicts and imbalances between individual and institutional goals are resolved through the legal and political processes. In the field of ability testing, progress has been made through evolution of practices adopted by testing organizations, educational institutions, and major corporate employers, as guided by government agency guidelines, professional standards, and federal and state legislation. The legislative and judicial background is discussed in other sections of this report. In this chapter, the role of federal guidelines and professional standards in resolving conflicts and imbalances associated with the use of ability tests will be examined. We shall focus on the issues of product quality, conflicts in goals among participants, and fairness and due process, survey the various approaches to the solution of these problems, and indicate what remains to be accomplished.

### FEDERAL GUIDELINES

The primary concern of the federal government regarding ability testing has been in the area of discrimination against and/or adverse impact on the selection of minority persons and women. Title VII of the Civil Rights Act of 1964 required nondiscrimination in employment by reason of race, color, religion, sex, or national origin. At the same time, the Tower Amendment stipulated that it was permissible "to give and to act upon the results of any professionally developed ability test provided that such test, its administration or action upon the results is not designed, intended, or used to discriminate because of race, color, religion, sex, or national origin." The Act also established the Equal Employment Opportunity Commission (EEOC) and charged it with broad responsibility for enforcing this requirement.

The authority of the EEOC and other equal employment opportunity enforcement agencies was subsequently strengthened and broadened through executive action. The first EEOC *Guidelines on Employment Testing Procedures* were published in 1966 (EEOC 1966). In 1968 the Labor Department's Office of Federal Contract Compliance (OFCC) published an order on the "Validation of Employment Tests" in support of its efforts against discrimination in work on federal contracts. In 1969 Executive Order 11478 required equal employment opportunity in the federal government and gave this responsibility to the Civil Service Commission (CSC), which subsequently published guidelines of its own. In 1970 the EEOC issued its *Guidelines on Employment Selection Proce-*

*dures* (EEOC 1970), which remained in effect until the adoption of the *Uniform Guidelines* in 1978 (EEOC 1978). In 1971 OFCC published a parallel document (U.S. Department of Labor 1971). Thus, through most of the 1970s, three separate federal agencies had responsibility for eliminating employment discrimination, each with its own policies and guidelines or orders and areas of authority. In addition, the Justice Department served as the legal arm of each of these agencies.

## 1970 EEOC Guidelines

During most of the seventies, this document was of greatest influence in these matters. It stated (EEOC 1970:12333) as a general principle that "properly validated and standardized employee selection procedures . . . contribute to the implementation of nondiscriminatory personnel policies as required by Title VII." The most important statements of the 1970 *Guidelines* for our purposes follow in selective quotation (12333-12335):[1]

*Discrimination defined*:
  5) The use of any test which adversely affects hiring, promotion, transfer or any other employment or membership opportunity of classes protected by Title VII constitutes discrimination unless: (a) the test has been validated and evidences a high degree of utility as hereinafter described, and (b) the person giving or acting upon the results of the particular test can demonstrate that alternative suitable hiring, transfer or promotion procedures are unavailable for his use.

---

[1] The following selected quotations from the EEOC *Guidelines* (1970:1233) complete a general description:
  1) The guidelines are based on the belief that properly validated and standardized employee selection procedures can significantly contribute to the implementation of nondiscriminatory personnel policies, as required by Title VII.
  2) An examination of charges of discrimination filed with the Commission . . . has revealed a decided increase in total test usage and a marked increase in doubtful testing practices which, based on our experience, tend to have discriminatory effects . . . with the result that candidates are selected or rejected on the basis of a single test score. Where tests are so used, minority candidates frequently experience disproportionately high rates of rejection by failing to attain score levels that have been established as minimum standards for qualification.
  3) It has also become clear that in many instances persons are using tests as the basis for employment decisions without evidence that they are valid predictors of employee job performance. . . . A test lacking demonstrated validity . . . and yielding lower scores for classes protected by Title VII may result in the rejection of many who have necessary qualifications for successful work performance.
  4) For the purpose of the guidelines in this part, the term "test" is defined as any paper-and-pencil or performance measure used as a basis for any employment decision.
  11) A test which is differentially valid may be used in groups for which it is valid but not for those in which it is not valid.

## Federal Guidelines and Professional Standards

*Evidence of validity:*

6) Each person using tests to select from among candidates for a position or for membership shall have available for inspection evidence [of validity]. . . . Where technically feasible, a test should be validated for each minority group with which it is used; that is, any differential rejection rates that may exist, based on a test, must be relevant to performance on the jobs in question.

7) Evidence of a test's validity should consist of empirical data demonstrating that the test is predictive of or significantly correlated with important elements of work behavior which comprise or are relevant to the job or jobs for which candidates are being evaluated.

If the job progression structures and seniority provisions are so established that new employees will probably, within a reasonable period of time and in a great majority of cases, progress to a higher level, it may be considered that candidates are being evaluated for jobs at that higher level.

*Validation standards:*

8) For the purpose of satisfying the requirements of this part, empirical evidence in support of a test's validity must be based on studies employing generally accepted procedures for determining criterion-related validity, such as those described in "Standards for Educational and Psychological Tests and Manuals" published by American Psychological Association.

9) Evidence of content or construct validity, as defined in that publication (see (8) above), may also be appropriate where criterion-related validity is not feasible. However, evidence for content or construct validity should be accompanied by sufficient information from job analyses to demonstrate the relevance of the content (in the case of job knowledge or proficiency tests) or the construct (in the case of trait measures).

10) Differential validity. Data must be generated and results separately reported for minority and nonminority groups wherever technically feasible.

12) In cases where the validity of a test cannot be determined . . . evidence from validity studies conducted in other organizations, such as that reported in test manuals and professional literature, may be considered acceptable when: (a) The studies pertain to jobs which are comparable . . . and (b) there are no major differences in contextual variables or sample composition which are likely to significantly affect validity. Any person citing evidence from other validity studies as evidence of test validity for his own jobs must substantiate in detail job comparability and must demonstrate the absence of contextual or sample differences cited in paragraphs (a) and (b) of this section.

Statement (5) required employers to demonstrate that no equally valid test with lesser adverse impact existed. This requirement to prove a negative could never be satisfied and, in fact, was modified in *Albemarle* v. *Moody* by the Supreme Court, which had earlier indicated that "great deference" should be paid to the *Guidelines*. Note that, as used here, the term discrimination does not necessarily imply intent, only adverse impact.

Statements (6) and (10) were based on the then current belief that tests typically had different (differential) validity, so that a test might be valid for prediction in a white group but not in a black group. The concept of differential prediction by race now enjoys little professional support.

Statement (9) opened the possibility of validation by methods other than through direct association with job performance, but in fact the requirements that followed and the interpretations of these requirements in the field made content and construct validation impossible for any but the largest test users. Such validation in the case of civil service examinations was the subject of litigation that resulted in a confrontation between the Justice Department and the Civil Service Commission (now Office of Personnel Management, OPM).

Statement (12) concerning validity transportability or validity generalization proved to be impossible to satisfy as interpreted in the field, partly because there was again a need to prove a negative.

In general, the 1970 EEOC *Guidelines* was a vaguely worded document that, in the process of the resultant litigation, acquired more precise meaning through case law, including several Supreme Court cases.

**Federal Executive Agency Guidelines (1976)**

In an effort to improve the implementation of its purposes, the Equal Employment Opportunity Act of 1972 created the Equal Employment Opportunity Coordinating Council (EEOCC), consisting of representatives from the Labor and Justice Departments, the Civil Service Commission, and the EEOC, with a mandate to produce a set of uniform guidelines for all agencies involved. In spite of much drafting and redrafting, extensive public hearings, and review by the Committee on Psychological Tests and Assessments of the American Psychological Association, agreement was not reached. Finally in 1976, new *Federal Executive Agency Guidelines* were published by the Justice and Labor Departments and the Civil Service Commission (CSC) (see U.S. Department of Justice et al. 1976), while the EEOC republished its 1970 guidelines.

The *Federal Executive Agency Guidelines* of 1976 had much in common as to purpose and coverage with the EEOC *Guidelines*. Both emphasized the requirement for validation, recognized three validation strategies, and provided for generalized validity studies, though the wording of the *FEA Guidelines* seemed more consistent with professional standards. Similar positions were also taken on entry-level testing, alternatives to validation, cutoff scores, disparate treatment, and affirmative action. The *FEA Guidelines*, however, gave parity to content, construct, and

## Federal Guidelines and Professional Standards

empirical validation procedures, whereas the earlier EEOC *Guidelines* had strongly emphasized empirical validation.

There were several major areas in which the two differed. The EEOC *Guidelines* had no definition or standard on adverse impact. The *FEA Guidelines* defined adverse impact in terms of the whole selection process (the bottom line), as a situation in which a particular race, sex, or ethnic group is selected at less than 80 percent of the rate of the most successful group.

Under the *FEA Guidelines*, when equally valid alternate selection procedures were available, use of the one demonstrated to have lesser adverse impact was required. However, an employer was not required to prove that no alternate valid procedures with less adverse impact existed. In addition, while the EEOC *Guidelines* did not specify particular documentation requirements for validation studies, the *FEA Guidelines* were quite specific in this regard.

## 1978 GAO Report

The failure to reach agreement in 1976 on uniform guidelines was discussed at length in a Government Accounting Office Report (GAO 1978:17-20). According to the report:

> . . . the agencies have had longstanding disagreements about guidelines requirements. This is because their views have differed on the legal and technical standards for judging the proper use of tests; also, the agencies perceive their mandates differently and have pursued different operating responsibilities. No agency has been willing to adopt uniform guidelines which it believed would seriously impair its ability to operate and meet program goals. EEOC, Labor, and CSC each had its own rationale for developing its particular set of guidelines and its own approach to putting them into practice and evaluating the results achieved. . . .

The report then described the EEOC mandate in the following way:

> The main task of EEOC is to enforce the mandate of Title VII to eliminate employment discrimination against individuals and groups. Finding the selection process responsible for more discrimination than perhaps any other area of employment practices, EEOC developed its guidelines on testing to help correct this.
>
> The overall goal of the 1970 EEOC guidelines was to get employers to use selection devices and procedures which met their business or operational needs and yet had the least adverse impact because of race, sex, religion, or national origin. The short-term goal was to eliminate the use of unvalidated tests which had adverse effects. If, in the long run, tests were validated but still had adverse effects, then the goal was to see if employers could develop alternate means of selection which satisfied their needs but lessened the impact.

The CSC mandate was described as follows:

> The merit system laws and selection procedures under which CSC and many state and local governments operate were not designed and have not been administered to achieve a representative work force in terms of race, sex, or ethnicity.
>
> The Civil Service Act of 1883, which established CSC, called for bringing the most qualified individuals into public service by ranking candidates on the basis of evaluated ability and fitness and use of a selection process that honors this ranking. . . .

The GAO report includes a quotation from the *Civil Service Journal*, which states in part:

> A test can fairly and accurately provide equal opportunity for individuals to demonstrate ability to perform a job. What the psychological measurement cannot do is provide a valid procedure that assures equal probability of success for members of groups based on characteristics unrelated to performance ability, when real ability levels differ among members of the groups.

In this obvious conflict between the concept of group parity as articulated by EEOC and selection based on merit as conceived by CSC, the central unresolved issues are whether or not the tests are biased and whether or not true differences in ability exist among the various groups. Some people consider the evidence on these issues to be compelling one way or another. Others find the evidence inconclusive.

It has been widely contended that, under the 1970 EEOC *Guidelines*, few employers were able to show the validity of any of their selection procedures and that the risk of their being held unlawful was, therefore, high. Since not only tests but all other procedures had to be validated, the thrust of the guidelines was to place almost all test users in a position of noncompliance; to give great discretion to enforcement personnel to determine who should be prosecuted; and to force employers to abandon objective selection procedures in favor of numerical hiring. Industry representatives have repeatedly argued that employers were and are being forced to satisfy quotas because of inability to satisfy overly stringent validation requirements.

## Uniform Guidelines of 1978

Despite the conflict between the federal agencies, draft uniform guidelines were issued on December 30, 1977, and opened to intensive professional review and public hearings. It would seem that some of the comments received during the professional review process were carefully considered, for substantial changes were made in the final publication

(August 25, 1978, see EEOC 1978), particularly in the sections on construct validity, documentation, the bottom line concept, and the definition of work behaviors. Testimony given at the public hearings seems to have had less effect. With respect to the troublesome question of the examination of alternative strategies, the wording of the December draft was retained, but a cautionary paragraph from the statement of the Committee on Psychological Tests and Assessments (1978) of the American Psychological Association (APA) was quoted. This statement included the comment that "rigid enforcement of these sections, particularly for smaller employers, would impose a substantial and expensive burden. . . ." This issue was discussed in the Questions and Answers[2] of March 2, 1979 (EEOC 1979), but it remained unclear how the guidelines would apply.

How successful the 1978 *Uniform Guidelines* would be in fostering the goals of Title VII, in maintaining an efficient and productive work force, and in avoiding an undue and costly administrative burden on employers trying to maintain such a work force remained to be seen. Much would depend on the interpretation of EEOC and Labor Department field personnel as to several critical sections of the document.

Leaving aside the possible difficulties in interpretation, two general reactions to the *Guidelines* seem valid. The APA Testing Committee commented, "these Guidelines represent a major step forward and with careful interpretation can provide a sound basis for concerned professional work" (Committee on Psychological Tests and Assessments 1978:1). That same statement included a comment on several sections of the *Guidelines* indicating what proper interpretation might be. The APA Division of Industrial and Organizational Psychology (Division 14) (1978) described the original December draft as "superior" in terms of congruence with professional standards to "most previous orders and guidelines. . . ."

The strategy in the construction of the *Uniform Guidelines* was to make specific statements in most sections, in contrast to the more general statements of the 1970 *Guidelines*. This enabled closer adherence to APA Test Standards, but some key sections remained ambiguous and thus subject to varying interpretations. Much depended as well on how rigidly the documentation section was to be interpreted. Taken to one extreme, compliance would be impossible. Taken to the other extreme, the *Uniform Guidelines* would be ineffective. At present, they continue to evolve through the issuance of Questions and Answers. Though ostensibly intended to clarify, they have in fact provided revision of points on which

---

[2] Questions and Answers is the formal process by which the EEOC issues extended explanations of the *Uniform Guidelines*.

agreement has been obtained. Considering all of the inherent and fundamental conflicts and practical difficulties, it would be unrealistic to expect resolution of most major issues in the near future. What may reasonably be expected is a continuing refinement of positions on issues and a cumulative resolution of components of these issues.

## PROFESSIONAL STANDARDS

Ability testing is a highly technical activity, in which effective practice depends on the availability of suitably trained persons. Most work in this field has been done by persons with doctoral degrees in psychology, psychometrics, education, or statistics. A substantial body of theory in support of testing practices has been developed over more than three-quarters of a century. Several professional societies and journals are devoted wholly or largely to testing and related fields of educational and psychological measurement. In this sense, ability testing can be considered a profession in its own right.

Professional society involvement in ability testing began in 1895, when the American Psychological Association formed its first committee on mental measurement for the purpose of investigating the feasibility of standardizing the collection of mental and physical measurement. In 1906 an APA committee on measurements was appointed, whose purpose was to standardize testing techniques. In 1916 and 1921 symposia with leading psychologists published in the *Journal of Educational Psychology* (1916, 1921) questioned the extensive uses to which "mental" testing was being put and stressed the need for cautious interpretation of intelligence tests and attention to the definition of intelligence. It should be noted that, while the level of attention within APA remained high during the early twenties as a result of vigorous criticism of testing, no concrete action to monitor, limit, or review individual professional activity resulted.

In 1923 an APA committee recommended certification and monitoring of nonpsychologists' use of tests. The membership defeated the motion. In the 1940s the Subcommittee of Test Use of the APA Committee on Standards of Ethics recognized the involvement of those other than psychologists in testing, and the *American Psychologist* (1946) surveyed three test publishers with regard to their criteria for purchasers of tests, but no restrictive action was recommended or taken. (For further details on the early history of testing, see Britell (1980).)

In 1938, the desire of many psychologists and others involved in testing to improve both safeguards and quality in the field of ability testing was given substance through the efforts of Professor Oscar K. Buros of the

College of Education of Rutgers University. Buros' (1938) publication of the *1938 Mental Measurements Yearbook* attempted to provide a clearinghouse of information on the availability and evaluation of published tests in order to help users choose more effective tests. At the same time, the *Yearbook* encouraged higher standards on the part of test reviewers and producers as an additional means of protecting consumers against test misuse. This landmark effort was followed over the years by seven more yearbooks and has been published since Buros' death by the University of Nebraska.

## 1954 Technical Recommendations

The first formal presentation by professional organizations of technical recommendations and standards for tests occurred with the publication by APA et al. (1954) of the *Technical Recommendations for Psychological Tests and Diagnostic Techniques*. It was prepared by a joint committee of the American Psychological Association, the American Educational Research Association, and the National Council on Measurement in Education and was followed by publication by the National Education Association of *Technical Recommendations for Achievement Tests* (1955). In part, the first document responded to a rule in the APA code of ethics that it was improper to publish a test without adequate supporting research. It was understood that a psychologist who violated this standard would be subject to sanctions including expulsion from the association (personal communication from L. J. Cronbach). A particular motivation for the recommendations, however, was the overuse of personality testing for employment selection.

The 1954 *Technical Recommendations* focused primarily on "standards of reporting information about tests." It was the outcome of an attempt to survey the possible types of information that test producers might make available, to weigh the importance of these, and to refine the responsibilities inherent to test preparation and publication, and it asserted (p. 2) that

The essential principle that sets the tone of this document is that a test manual should carry information sufficient to enable any qualified user to make sound judgments regarding the usefulness and interpretation of the test.

It was suggested (p. 6) that the recommendations might provide test users working in either psychology or education with "a kind of check list of factors to consider in designing standardization and validation studies," for the "ultimate responsibility for improvement of testing rests on the shoulders of test users. . . ."

An important feature of the recommendations was the insistence that they applied, in carefully specified ways, to projective techniques. The inclusion of examples of the relevance of these recommendations to such devices undoubtedly had a profound effect on the further development and evaluation of such diagnostic techniques. It seems evident that the controversy surrounding the use of such instruments was an important incentive for the *Technical Recommendations* project.

The general topics covered were (A) dissemination of information, (B) interpretation, (C) validity, (D) reliability, (E) administration, and (F) scales and norms. Individual recommendations were labeled: essential, very desirable, or desirable.

The "essential" label was intended to be the consensus of thinking as to what was *normally required* for operational use of a test. When essential information was not available, it was considered adequate to clearly state what research has and has not been done and to discuss the test so that the reader fully understands what is known about it. The category "very desirable" was used to draw attention to information that would "contribute greatly to the user's understanding of the test," but which could not be considered essential. The category "desirable" was used to classify information that would be helpful but less so than essential or very desirable information.

In the area of dissemination of information (A), the recommendations labeled as essential the requirement that, when a test is published for operational use, it should be accompanied by a manual that takes cognizance of the detailed recommendations in this document and this manual should be revised at appropriate intervals as new information becomes available.

In the area of interpretation (B) (p. 10), the recommendations labeled essential the requirement that

Insofar as possible, the test, the manual, record forms, and other accompanying material should assist users to make correct interpretations of the test results . . . [making explicit] . . . the purposes and applications for which the test is recommended. . . .

In the area of validity (C), a whole new terminology was codified and discussed separately with regard to application for ability tests, personality inventories, interest inventories, projective techniques, and related clinical methods. In this area the recommendations defined the concepts of concurrent, predictive, content, and construct validity and included the following points among those labeled essential (p. 18-19):

When validity is reported, the manual should indicate clearly what type of validity is referred to. . . . The manual should report the validity of each type of inference

# Federal Guidelines and Professional Standards

for which a test is recommended. If validity of some recommended interpretation has not been tested, that fact should be made clear. . . .

In the area of reliability (D), the recommendations focused on the concepts of internal consistency, equivalence, and stability and included the following among those points labeled essential (p. 30-31):

In reports of reliability, procedures and sample should be described sufficiently for the reader to judge whether the evidence applies to the persons and problem with which he is concerned. . . . If two forms of a test are made available, with both forms intended for possible use with the same subjects, the correlation between forms and information as to the equivalence of scores on the two forms should be reported. . . . If the manual suggests that a score is a measure of a generalized, homogeneous trait, evidence of internal consistency should be reported. . . . The manual should indicate what degree of stability of scores may be expected if a test is repeated after time has elapsed.

In the areas of administration and scoring (E) and scales and norms (F), the recommendations included the following essential points (p. 33-37):

The directions for the administration should be presented with sufficient clarity that the test user can duplicate the administrative conditions under which the norms and data on reliability and validity were obtained. . . . Where subjective processes enter into the scoring of the test, evidence on degree of agreement between independent scorings should be presented. . . . Norms should report the distribution of scores in an appropriately defined and clearly described reference group or groups. . . . These populations should be the groups to whom users of the test will ordinarily wish to compare the persons tested.

The 1954 *Technical Recommendations* were, by any measure, a monumental achievement. Their influence on test reviews, textbooks, test manuals, and published research was pervasive. And although few published manuals soon conformed to even their essential requirements, users had at least the beginnings of some standards by which to judge the fitness of a particular test for a particular application. At the same time, the document was a somewhat tentative, almost defensive statement that clearly was presented as an aid to, rather than a monitor of, professional activity. "The drafting committee was opposed from the outset to the idea of dividing tests into classes of acceptable and unacceptable tests and was greatly concerned lest a perfectionist approach would inhibit the development of tests" (personal communication from L. J. Cronbach).

## 1966 Standards for Educational and Psychological Tests and Manuals

This document paralleled the 1954 *Technical Recommendations* in many respects, with identical section titles, of which A, B, E, and F were only moderately refined. Section C on validity and section D on reliability, however, were reconstructed, in that the concepts of concurrent and predictive validity were combined as criterion-related validity, and the concept of domain of reference to which a reliability or validity statement could be generalized became the dominant issue underlying most of the standards.

In a greatly expanded theoretical base, the following three sentences (APA et al. 1966:12-25) effectively described the questions to which content, criterion-related, and construct validity applied:

1) The test user wishes to determine how an individual performs at present in a universe of situations that the test situation is claimed to represent.

2) The test user wishes to forecast an individual's future standing or to estimate an individual's present standing on some variable of particular significance that is different from the test.

3) The test user wishes to infer the degree to which the individual possesses some hypothetical trait or quality (construct) presumed to be reflected in the test performance.

And reliability theory was changed in the assertion that:

different methods of determining the reliability coefficient take account of different sources of error. . . . Hence, "reliability coefficient" is a generic term referring to various types of evidence; each type of evidence suggests a different meaning. It is essential that the method used to derive any reliability coefficient should be clearly described. The estimation of clearly labeled components of error variance is the most informative outcome of a reliability study.

Compare the following items from the 1966 *Standards* (APA et al. 1966:15-28) with corresponding items from 1954 *Recommendations* presented earlier.

On content validity:

If a test performance is to be interpreted as a sample of performance or a definition of performance in some universe of situations, the manual should indicate clearly what universe is represented and how adequate is the sampling.

On criterion-related validity:

All measures of criteria should be described completely and accurately. The manual should comment on the adequacy of the criterion. Whenever feasible, it should draw attention to significant aspects of performance that the criterion measure does not reflect and to irrelevant factors that are likely to affect it. The sample employed in a validity study and the conditions under which testing is done should be consistent with the recommendations made in the manual. They should be described sufficiently for the user to judge whether the reported validity is pertinent to his situation.

On construct validity:

If the author proposes to interpret the test as a measure of a theoretical variable (ability, trait, or attitude), the proposed interpretation should be fully stated. The interpretation of the theoretical construct should be distinguished from interpretations arising under other theories.

On reliability:

In the test manual reports on reliability or error of measurement, procedures, and samples should be described sufficiently to permit a user to judge to what extent the evidence is applicable to the person and problems with which he is concerned.

The new theoretical basis for reliability and validity increased the usefulness of the 1966 *Standards* for the design of data-gathering activities and the interpretation of data from these activities, with a resulting effect on test reviews, textbooks, test manuals, and published research. Although the authors did not view their revisions as basic or extensive, their reformulation of the technical sections brought about an important synthesis of generalizability theory for the *Standards*.

## 1974 Standards

The *Standards for Educational and Psychological Tests and Manuals* (APA et al. 1974) progressed from the 1966 statement of test producer obligations to one concerning competency in testing practice. In retrospect, it may seem strange that three-quarters of a century of continuous expansion in the practice of testing elapsed before the psychological and educational professions developed their first standards for test use. Even then, it might not have happened, had it not been for the emergence of the social questions to which the EEOC *Guidelines* clearly responded and the concomitant civil rights pressure of numerous advocacy groups.

Such a rationale for the 1974 *Standards* is confirmed in the introduction, which claims concern about such problems as invasion of privacy or discrimination against minority groups and women. It cites specific examples of test misuse (such as use of tests for one group that have been standardized on another or using heavily verbal tests for jobs in which physical and manipulative abilities are the main requirements), concedes that a "test score describes but does not explain a level of performance," and goes on to list the many environmental and situational factors that can influence level of performance. The *Standards'* many similarities to the 1970 EEOC *Guidelines* are quite obvious, for example, in the new material under reliability and validity, which states in part (APA et al. 1974:43):

A test user should investigate the possibility of bias in tests or in test items. Wherever possible, there should be an investigation of possible differences in criterion-related validity for ethnic, sex, or other subsamples that can be identified when the test is given. The manual or research report should give the results for each subsample separately or report that no differences were found.

While it agreed that some unfairness could be built into a test, nonetheless the introduction stated that many of the social ills attributed to testing seemed more a result of the ways in which tests had been used than of the characteristics of the tests themselves. Such misuse might include: failure to consider the appropriateness of normative data, use of incorrect assumptions about the causes of a low or deviant test score, or administrative rigidity in using test scores for making decisions. Accordingly, a new section on Standards for the Use of Tests was incorporated, which covered (G) qualifications and concerns of users, (H) choice or development of test or method, (I) administration and scoring, and (J) interpretation of scores. The following excerpts illustrate both the importance and the weaknesses of the 1974 *Standards* (pp. 58-68).

> G2 A test user should know and understand the literature relevant to the tests he uses and the testing problems with which he deals.
> G4 Test users should seek to avoid bias in selection, administration, and interpretation; they should try to avoid even the appearance of discriminating practice.
> H3 In choosing an existing test, a test user should relate its history of research and development to his intended use of the instrument.
> I4 If specific cutting scores are to be used as a basis for decisions, a test user should have a rationale, justification, or explanation of the cutting scores adopted.
> J1 A test score should be interpreted as an estimate of performance under a given set of circumstances. It should not be interpreted as some absolute characteristic of the examinee or as something permanent and generalizable to other circumstances.
> J2 Test scores should ordinarily be reported only to people who are qualified to interpret them. If scores are reported, they should be accompanied by explanations sufficient for the recipient to interpret them correctly.

In sum, the 1974 *Standards* must be viewed as a long overdue first step toward professional monitoring of test use. They were created at a time when the social needs that prompted them were as yet largely undefined, which clearly compounded the difficulties inherent in setting standards for test use. Thus, many of the new standards (see, especially G2, G4, and H3) lack the behavioral referents that would make it possible to judge whether or not they were being satisfied.

## OTHER SOURCES OF GUIDELINES AND STANDARDS

The evolution of guidelines and standards for testing practice has been furthered by the contributions of special interest groups and professional organizations. In the light of its own professional obligation, each such group determined that the general statements of federal guidelines and professional standards were not completely adequate for its purposes. An additional objective for these efforts was to provide workable procedures in cases where an unfortunate interpretation of the more global documents might unnecessarily infringe on what was viewed as good professional practice. Two of the resultant documents are the *Division 14 Principles* and the *ETS Principles, Policies, and Procedural Guidelines*.

### Division 14 Principles

The Division (14) of Industrial and Organizational Psychology, American Psychological Association, issued its *Principles For the Validation and Use of Personnel Selection Procedures* in 1975. This action was directed to the need for a professional statement specific to good practice in the use of standardized tests and other employee selection procedures. While the authors felt that the 1974 APA *Standards* were too broad in their coverage and too limited in their discussion of test use to address the specific problems of personnel selection, they intended that the *Principles* be consistent with the *Standards*.

Underlying the stated principles of good practice in the choice, development, and evaluation of personnel selection procedures were the assumptions that: (1) individuals differ in many ways; (2) individual differences in personal characteristics and backgrounds are often related to individual differences in behavior and satisfaction on the job; (3) information about such relevant differences between people can be developed and used in assigning people to jobs.

On the question of fairness, the *Principles* assume ". . . [that the] interests of employers, applicants, and the public at large are best served when selection is made by the most valid means available," and that ". . . bias in the use of employment procedures is ineffective for reaching both employer and job applicant objectives" (Division of Industrial-Organizational Psychology 1975:2). The *Principles* do not directly discuss adverse impact or the use of selection procedures that, with optimum validity, minimize adverse impact.

In line with a basic assertion that evidence must be accumulated to establish relationships between decisions based on assessments made as part of a selection procedure and subsequent criteria, such as job performance, training performance, permanence, advancement, and other job behavior, the document provides:

1) principles upon which personnel research could be based,
2) guidance for practitioners conducting validation, and
3) principles for use of valid selection procedures.

The Division 14 *Principles* go beyond the *Standards* in their discussion of such technical issues as sample sizes, criterion reliability, and panels of experts. The document takes a strong position in support of a wide variety of validation procedures—a position at variance with that taken in the 1970 EEOC *Guidelines*, with which it also differs on the issue of predictors with maximum validity and minimum adverse impact. A generally recognized objective of the *Principles* was to provide professional support for specific procedures that might be challenged by federal agencies—a purpose it undoubtedly has served.[3]

## Educational Testing Service Guidelines

The full title of this ETS document is *Principles, Policies and Procedural Guidelines Regarding ETS Products and Services*. It was published in February 1979 with the stated objective (ETS 1979:ii-iii):

. . . to codify standards used in various ETS programs and services that should be considered for more general application and more formal articulation. . . .

However, it is noted that

. . . Because of their origin and purposes, the Guidelines cannot generally or usefully be applied to organizations whose practices, programs or services differ from those of ETS. . . .

and that

. . . ETS does not have complete responsibility or authority, of course, to determine how the Guidelines will be implemented in ETS programs for which policy is substantially established by a sponsoring group other than ETS. ETS has, however, taken steps to encourage and assist those groups to implement the Guidelines as their activities relate to ETS. New activities ETS enters into will be held to this same expectation. . . .

Despite these restrictions on the enforceability of the *Guidelines*, they

---

[3] A revised second edition of the *Principles* has been published but it was not available in time for review in this paper (Division of Industrial-Organizational Psychology 1980).

## Federal Guidelines and Professional Standards

will inevitably have a beneficial effect on ETS programs and, like the Division 14 *Principles*, will affect the subsequent development of new federal guidelines and professional standards as well. Indeed, the ETS Guidelines provide some of the detail and necessary behavioral referents lacking in the 1974 *Standards*. They are organized under the following headings: accountability, confidentiality of data, product accuracy and timeliness, research and development, tests and measurements, technical quality of tests, test use, and technical assistance, advice, and instruction. Under technical quality of tests there are the following subsections: test development, test administration, test reliability, scale definition, equating, score interpretation, and test validity.

Each section begins with a broadly stated principle followed by general policy statements and then by procedural guidelines that provide detailed specifications of what should and should not be done. For example, under *test use*, the following principle is stated (ETS 1979:47-49): "Proper and fair use of ETS tests is essential to the social utility and professional acceptance of ETS work." This principle leads to the following policies: (a) ETS will set forth clearly to sponsors, institutional or agency users, and examinees the principles of proper use of tests and interpretation of test results; (b) ETS will establish procedures by which fair and appropriate test use can be promoted and misuse can be discouraged or eliminated. Four procedural guidelines are then presented. The most significant is the fourth: In cases where a clear misuse is brought to its attention, ETS should inform the sponsor and the institutional or agency user of its opinion as to the misuse and seek voluntary correction of the misuse. If reasonable efforts to seek voluntary correction are not successful, ETS, in conjunction with the sponsor, should take steps to determine whether to continue supplying tests or reporting scores to the institutional or agency user.

This may be the most important item on the ETS *Guidelines*, for it is the first instance in which a testing organization established, *as a matter of principle*, that it has a responsibility to discourage or eliminate test misuse. The mere acceptance and codification of this responsibility is enough to substantially alter the relationships between test developers, test users, and test takers. It has opened the door, but only a crack.

While this procedural guideline implies that circumstances exist that would lead to withdrawal of testing services, it gives no indication of how flagrant a misuse must be to trigger such action. Obviously, codifying guidelines at this level of detail without extensive experience and professional analysis of significant cases raises many difficulties.

It must also be noted that the ETS procedural guideline states that the steps taken should be "in conjunction with the sponsor." Left unclarified is what, if anything, could be done in a case of a conflict of interest among a sponsoring board, individual members of that board, test takers, and the testing organizations. Any testing organization operates on a fee-for-service basis, and therefore has a subordinate position to its *institutional* client, the test user, or board representing test users. There also remains a question of external acceptance of monitoring arrangements that depend for their enforcement on parties that have individual interests in how conflicts of interest are resolved. Much work remains to be done.

## Standards Review

A decade of activity by testing professionals culminated in the May 1978 recommendation of the joint AERA, APA, NCME Committee to Review the Test Standards that the 1974 *Standards* be revised. The following are major points in these recommendations (AERA et al. 1978:12-13):

1. The new *Standards* should be a statement of technical requirements for sound professional practice and not a social action prescription. While committee members agree that the *Standards* must be responsive to current social, legal, and political concerns, they also believe that the *Standards* should focus on the professional practice of testing in these areas and on the documentation necessary to assess the soundness of such testing.
2. The new *Standards* should provide specific rules by which to determine the technical adequacy of a published test, the appropriateness and propriety of given applications of the test, and the reasonableness of inferences based on given uses of the test.
3. The *Standard* should embody a strong ethical imperative. It is understood that the *Standards* cannot enforce an ethical imperative. Nevertheless, a clear statement in explicit behavioral terms of professional requirements in the *Standards* should make it easier for professional associations, government enforcement agencies, and the courts to enforce the *Standards* to the extent that seems desirable. It should also make it easier for concerned professional workers to conform to the spirit and intent of the *Standards*.
4. The revision committee should recognize that all standards will not be uniformly applicable across a wide range of applications, users, test instruments, and procedures. Different standards will be required for different classes of test users, depending upon the intended domain of application. Different standards may be required for different types of instruments (e.g., simulations, interviews).

The Review Committee supplemented these recommendations with a brief discussion of testing areas treated inadequately in the 1974 *Standards*. These included the use of adaptive testing, latent trait models, decision-theoretic models, criterion-referenced and domain-referenced measurement, and newer methods of content, construct, and criterion-

## Federal Guidelines and Professional Standards

referenced validation. Also mentioned were problems associated with minimum competency testing, coaching schools, professional licensing, and the retention or forced retirement of older employees.

The review committee held that the testing profession ought to provide the primary mechanism for making the scientific monitoring of the quality of testing procedures possible. This does not rule out the possibility or even the desirability of some controls on testing by federal and state governments or by federal agency guidelines. It does suggest, however, that the goals sought through those efforts may be more readily attainable if the scientific issues are carefully codified in professional standards.

### CAN THESE ISSUES BE RESOLVED?

We have indicated that three major classes of issues are relevant to our discussion of federal guidelines and professional standards. Having reviewed the issues of product quality and conflicts in goals among participants, we turn to the third, fairness and due process, and will then consider ways in which all three might be resolved.

Fairness in selection has been discussed at length in the educational measurement literature (see, for example, *Journal of Educational Measurement* 1976). It seems to be widely accepted that there are no psychometric solutions to questions of fairness to individuals or groups and that only a consensus of value judgments can solve these problems. Just how the trade-off between quality of employee performance and equality of opportunity for the disadvantaged will be determined has not been resolved. Certainly there has been a greater willingness to provide increased opportunities for the disadvantaged in educational selection than in employment selection. Absent massive government programs to subsidize the employment of less skillful disadvantaged persons, the educational community will continue to be the avenue for upward social and financial mobility. Much will depend on the level of governmental support for all forms of education.

Testing has a limited role in the search for equality of opportunity. Contrary to accepted belief in some circles, it provides less biased evaluation than any other current measure of ability and any bias in testing is more easily studied than the more subjective biases in other procedures. On a more negative note is the fact that test results can be, and have been, misused to track into dead-end programs students who lack developed skills but are capable of developing them. Professional standards can help to prescribe proper usage of tests in these areas, but it seems likely that a final resolution of this problem will be found in the courtroom, perhaps based on a clearer statement of professional standards.

The question of the relationship between the test taker, on the one hand, and the test producer and test user, on the other, has been a major issue behind the consideration and passage of federal and state testing legislation. We have argued that the test taker's position is decidedly inferior in the event of a controversy with either producer or user. For example, a taker's scores are sometimes suspect because of testing irregularity (possibly involving an allegation of cheating). The testing organizations' solution to this problem for many years was to require retesting whenever a suspicion arose. Indeed, a case has been reported in which ETS was awarded damages from a coaching school because of its use of purloined test items. The test takers were required to retake the test even though they were innocent of any wrongdoing. No one sought damages on their behalf. It is to be hoped that a more sophisticated response will be evolved.

Until recently there was no established due process by which a test taker could argue that his or her obtained score was valid when these scores were challenged by a producer or a user. In recent years substantial progress in providing such procedures for examinees has been made by both ACT and ETS. Their approaches differ substantially and each is, arguably, improvable. Beyond the efforts of these two testing organizations, however, no other attempts have been made (see Buss and Novick 1980).

It may seem surprising that the establishment of examinee rights of due process has lagged. This is understandable, however, because of the absence of a continuing relationship between the parties in conflict. Students and employees are part of their respective schools, colleges, industries, or business committees. School, college, and job applicants are not. Lacking the base for action that a permanent relationship would foster, test takers would seem to require assistance from other sources. One approach comes from recently adopted state legislation and recently considered federal legislation. There seems to be a consensus at present that these legislative alternatives would benefit from revision, and it is arguable that professional standards might address this methodological problem.

Despite the past efforts of federal and state legislation, the regulations and guidelines of federal agencies, and the testing standards set by professional groups, the thorny questions of product quality, goal conflict between participants, and fairness and due process remain largely unresolved. Since legislation, regulation, and professional standards provide the only known avenues for resolution, it may be useful to consider the possibilities for future progress.

At its best, federal and state legislation provides an impetus for change

## Federal Guidelines and Professional Standards

and a broad prescription for what should be required. The Civil Rights Act of 1964 is a good example. But after 16 years, the questions raised by that legislation have not been answered despite the intensive effort of several federal agencies. Furthermore, we have seen that, in regard to crucial issues, EEOC *Guidelines* have frequently referenced the professional *Standards* and that the courts (e.g., the South Carolina case) have also leaned heavily on them. This suggests that these *Standards* may play a very important role in solving testing problems. On the other hand, the deference of the federal agencies to the *Standards* is limited, having to do only with psychometric rather than policy or legal issues. Federal agencies have tried to make the *Guidelines* "consistent" with the *Standards*, but when a choice had to be made between consistency and the attainment of agency goals, consistency was not given first priority. This approach is not at all inappropriate, and it should be noted that consistency continues to be sought through Question and Answer (Q and A) refinement of the *Guidelines*.

Despite these facts, the question might arise as to the possibility of settling these issues by *Standards* revision alone. The answer is immediate and negative. First, as indicated above, many of the issues involve value judgments rather than questions of the psychometric properties of tests or procedures of administration and reporting. Second, none of the organizations associated with test standards has chosen to attempt any meaningful enforcement of these *Standards*.

This conclusion does not lessen the importance of test standards or professional standards revision. Professional standards could be, and have been, adopted in whole or part by reference in legislative or governmental agency guidelines and could become a model of acceptable professional practice. In some civil actions alleging testing abuse, the *Standards* have been introduced as evidence of the gauge by which both user and producer should be judged. Indeed, when this has happened, it has sometimes been argued that the *Standards* should be interpreted literally, especially in connection with the term essential requirements. This, however, conflicts with the following statement appearing in the 1974 *Standards*:

A final caveat is necessary in view of the prominence of testing issues in litigation. This document is prepared as a technical guide for those within the sponsoring professions; it is *not* written as law. What is intended is a set of standards to be used, in part, for self-evaluation by test developers and test users. An evaluation of their competence does not rest on the literal satisfaction of every relevant provision of this document. The individual standards are statements of ideals or goals, some having priority over others. Instead, an evaluation of competence depends on the degree to which the content of this document has been satisfied by the test developer or user (APA 1974:8).

The Standards Review Committee has recommended that a somewhat stronger posture be taken in the new standards. This seems appropriate; however, the concerns that troubled earlier standards committees are no less valid today. Attempts to develop standards that provide highly specific, absolute requirements would be unrealistic because there are typically a variety of ways to do acceptable professional work, and they would be undesirable because they would tend to stifle the development of improved techniques. Undoubtedly the 1974 *Standards* were insufficiently specific. It is important that the new standards not err in the opposite direction.

Since 1970, the history of the interaction between professional standards, government guidelines, and federal and state legislation has been one of interdependence and, to some extent, competition. The 1970 *Guidelines* referenced the 1965 *Standards*. The 1974 *Standards* drew heavily on the 1970 *Guidelines*. The 1976 and 1978 *Guidelines*, in part, incorporated the 1974 *Standards* by reference. The 1980 *Division 14* (draft) *Principles* expand the 1974 *Standards* and attempt to preempt the force of the 1978 *Guidelines* in litigation.

In general, this interaction and competition has been beneficial, but progress has been slow and tortuous. For example, many observers now view the recent New York State law on "Truth in Testing" as a step backward. Nevertheless, the majority of the steps have been forward. The following developments should be a source of encouragement. As early as 1974, there was communication between the APA Committee on Psychological Tests and Assessment and the federal agencies responsible for the drafting of selection guidelines. Prior to their publication, the 1976 *Federal Executive Agency Guidelines* (see U.S. Department of Justice et al. 1976) were reviewed with respect to consistency with their test *Standards* by the APA Committee, resulting in some useful modification in the final document. A similar interaction took place prior to the issuance of the *Uniform Guidelines*.

Following the issuance of the *Uniform Guidelines* and the first set of Questions and Answers, the federal agencies on May 15, 1979, requested a review of the *Guidelines* with respect to their consistency with the *Standards*. In response, the APA Committee on Psychological Tests and Assessments reiterated a statement made in an earlier review in February 1978:

These guidelines represent a major step forward and with careful interpretation can provide a sound basis for concerned professional work. . . . In saying this we are not unaware that many of the statements made in these *Guidelines* were subject to varying interpretations, and it is possible that certain crucial sentences

# Federal Guidelines and Professional Standards

could be interpreted in ways which might not be consistent with what we believe to be sound professional practice.

The committee then noted, with favor, changes in the *Guidelines* resulting from its February 1978 commentary. It also reaffirmed its concern regarding several major sections of the *Guidelines* that seemed to be in conflict with the *Standards*. In response, on January 17, 1980, the federal agencies proposed three supplemental Questions and Answers (91-3) and requested that these be reviewed by the APA Committee.

The first dealt with the question of what constitutes a reasonable investigation of alternatives with lesser adverse impact. As indicated earlier in this chapter, the apparent federal requirement to prove a negative, that there exist no equally valid alternatives having lesser adverse impact, has been a point of controversy throughout the 1970s.

The second Q and A dealt with the question of the necessity of inference of criterion bias based solely on significant differences between races, sexes, or ethnic groups and rejected that necessity.

The third Q and A dealt with the issue of validation with respect to only one or two job duties and provided an affirmative response.

In each of these three cases, the position taken by the federal agency in the Q and A was responsive to the concerns of the APA Testing Committee and the profession at large. All three were reviewed positively by the APA Test Committee on February 11, 1980, though the committee found it necessary to specify in great detail how it believed specific statements should be interpreted. When the three Questions and Answers were adopted and published in the federal register, it was with reference to the letter from the APA Testing Committee.

## REFERENCES

American Educational Research Association, American Psychological Association, and National Council on Measurement in Education (1978) *Report of the Joint AERA, APA, and NCME Committee for Review of the Standards for Educational and Psychological Tests.* Washington, D.C.: American Educational Research Association.

American Psychological Association, American Educational Research Association, and National Council on Measurement in Education (1954) *Technical Recommendations for Psychological Tests and Diagnostic Techniques.* Washington, D.C.: American Psychological Association.

American Psychological Association, American Educational Research Association, and National Council on Measurement in Education (1966 and 1974) *Standards for Educational and Psychological Tests and Manuals.* Washington, D.C.: American Psychological Association.

*American Psychologist* (1946) Checking the qualifications of purchasers of tests. *American Psychologist* 1:353-357.

Britell, J. K. (1980) Never Quite a Public Dalogue: The Discussions of Testing in American Education, 1897-1964. Unpublished doctoral dissertation, Columbia University.

Brouder, K. (1978) *Report on Student Involvement in the College Board*. New York: College Entrance Examination Board.

Buros, O. K. (1938) *1938 Mental Measurements Yearbook*. New Brunswick, N.J.: Rutgers University Press.

Buss, W., and Novick, M. R. (1980) The detection of cheating on standaridzed tests: statistical and legal analysis. *Journal of Law and Education* 9:1-64.

Commission on Tests (1970) *Report of the Commission on Tests*. New York: College Entrance Examination Board.

Committee on Psychological Tests and Assessments (1978) Statement on the Uniform Guidelines on Employee Selection Procedures. Unpublished communication to the Equal Employment Opportunity Commission, February 17. American Psychological Association, Washington, D.C.

Division of Industrial-Organizational Psychology (1978) Comments on the Proposed Uniform Guidelines on Employee Selection Procedures. Unpublished communication, March 17. American Psychological Association, Washington, D.C.

Division of Industrial-Organizational Psychology (1980) *Principles for the Validation and Use of Personnel Selection Procedures*, 2nd ed. Washington, D.C.: American Psychological Association.

Educational Testing Service (1979) *Principles, Policies, and Procedural Guidelines Regarding ETS Products and Services*. Princeton, N.J.: Educational Testing Service.

Equal Employment Opportunity Commission (1966) *Guidelines on Employment Testing Procedures*. 35 U.S.L.W. 2137.

Equal Employment Opportunity Commission (1970) Guidelines on employment selection procedures. *Federal Register* 35:12333.

Equal Employment Opportunity Commission (1978) Uniform guidelines on employment selection procedures. *Federal Register* 43:38290.

Equal Employment Opportunity Commission (1979) Questions and answers. *Federal Register* 44:11996.

*Journal of Educational Measurement* (1976) Special Issue: On Bias in Selection. *Journal of Educational Measurement* 13(1).

*Journal of Educational Psychology* (1916) Mentality tests: a symposium. *Journal of Educational Psychology* 7:229-240, 278-286, 358-360.

*Journal of Educational Psychology* (1921) Intelligence and its measurements: a symposium. *Journal of Educational Psychology* 12:123-147, 195-216.

National Education Association (1955) *Technical Recommendations for Achievement Tests*. Washington, D.C.: National Education Association.

U.S. Department of Justice, U.S. Department of Labor, and U.S. Civil Service Commission (1976) *Federal Executive Agency Guidelines*. Washington, D.C.: U.S. Department of Labor.

U.S. Department of Labor (1971) *Testing and Selection Order*. Office of Federal Contract Compliance. Washington, D.C.: U.S. Department of Labor.

U.S. General Accounting Office (1978) *Report to the Congress by the Comptroller General of the U.S.: Problems with the Federal Equal Employment Opportunity Guidelines on Employee Selection Procedures Need to be Resolved*. Washington, D.C.: U.S. General Accounting Office.

TOBY FRIEDMAN and E. BELVIN WILLIAMS
# Current Use of Tests for Employment

## INTRODUCTION

The usefulness of tests for employment, as demonstrated first by the federal government and later, conclusively, by the military during two world wars, gave impetus to their widespread adoption by business, industry, and local and state governments. Today tests are used not only to assist with hiring decisions, but for many other personnel decisions as well, including placement, assignment to training programs, entry into union journeyman status, promotion, retention, licensing, and certification.

As tests have affected the lives of more and more people, they have become the subject of increased scrutiny by the public and government alike. Indeed, with the passage of the Civil Rights Act of 1964 and the issuance of various drafts of the federal guidelines on employee selection procedures—culminating in the *Uniform Guidelines* of August 1978—selection procedures of all types have come under increasing challenge. The *Uniform Guidelines* of 1978 left no doubt that this greatly broadened concept of selection procedures has extended to "the full range of as-

---

The authors wish to thank a number of their colleagues at Educational Testing Service for their assistance: Audre A. Griffiths and Robert F. Boldt contributed to the writing of the study; Albert P. Maslow, Benjamin Shimberg, Ronald L. Flaugher, and Joel T. Campbell reviewed the manuscript; Jacqueline Pellaton provided editorial advice; Monica L. Thatcher conducted a literature search and provided secretarial support.

sessment techniques from traditional paper-and-pencil tests, performance tests, training programs or probationary periods, and physical, educational, and work experience requirements through informal or casual interviews and unscored application forms" (Equal Employment Opportunity Commission 1978:38308). All are required to meet guidelines standards of job relevance and validity.

This paper seeks to gain a perspective on the present status of test usage in occupational assessment through an examination of the three major employment sectors—private, civilian government, and military. Because of the paucity of adequate descriptive data, the examination of each sector will also draw on review of nonquantitative literature, meetings, and discussion with knowledgeable people in the field.

## PRIVATE SECTOR

The private sector is by far the largest of the three sectors to be examined in this paper. Given this tremendous size, as well as its amorphous and diverse nature, it is not surprising that it has also proved to be the sector in which it is most difficult to discover the extent and impact of testing today.

### Description of Private Sector Work Force

As of 1976, according to the Bureau of the Census, more than 62 million Americans were employed in the private sector (excluding self-employed people and farm, railroad, and domestic service workers). About two-thirds of these employees worked in three fields: manufacturing, retail trade, and service occupations. The complete breakdown by major industry group can be seen in Table 1.

Supplemental data indicate that within the major industry groups, health services is by far the largest single category at more than 4 million employees. Other categories with more than 2 million employees each are wholesale trade-durable goods, eating and drinking places, and business services.

U.S. workers are employed at over 4 million single business locations or establishments, most of which are very small. According to Figure 1, also based on 1976 census data, 88.1 percent of these establishments employed fewer than twenty people, for a total of 16.7 million people, whereas only .1 percent of the over 4 million establishments employed more than 1,000 people, for a total of 9.3 million. In this regard, it is of particular interest to note that the 1978 *Uniform Guidelines for Employee*

## Current Use of Tests for Employment

TABLE 1  Breakdown of Private Sector by Major Industry Group (1976)

| Major Industry Group | Number of Establishments | Number of Employees |
|---|---|---|
| Agricultural services, forestry, fisheries | 42,699 | 227,505 |
| Mining | 25,436 | 763,017 |
| Contract construction | 394,963 | 3,433,764 |
| Manufacturing | 310,633 | 18,965,344 |
| Transportation and other public utilities | 155,219 | 3,967,341 |
| Wholesale trade | 357,653 | 4,455,120 |
| Retail trade | 1,215,654 | 12,972,278 |
| Finance, insurance, and real estate | 392,819 | 4,400,206 |
| Services (business, health, membership, legal, educational, social, etc.) | 1,164,782 | 13,340,684 |
| Nonclassifiable | 89,951 | 112,621 |
| TOTAL | 4,142,809 | 62,647,846 |

SOURCE: Bureau of the Census (1975/1976).

*Selection Procedures* do not apply to any establishments that employ fewer than fifteen people.

A breakdown of workers by occupational group within the private sector only is not available. However, data from the Bureau of Labor Statistics (see Table 2) provides a breakdown including civilian government workers, self-employed individuals, farm workers, etc., which enables some useful comparisons.

Clerical workers constitute both the largest and the fastest growing occupational group within a total work force that is itself expanding. Employment in these occupations (secretaries, bookkeepers, cashiers, typists, etc.) is expected to increase by about 29 percent between 1976 and 1985, rising from 15.6 million to 20 million workers.

### Test Use in Private Sector

We know that the use of tests, or systematic use of a variety of measures of ability or of various processes that are weighted or scored on some overall grading system, is scattered throughout the private sector to help in making decisions on selection, placement, training, promotion, and retention of personnel. Employers also utilize other procedures for decision making, some of which may include tests, e.g., the certification

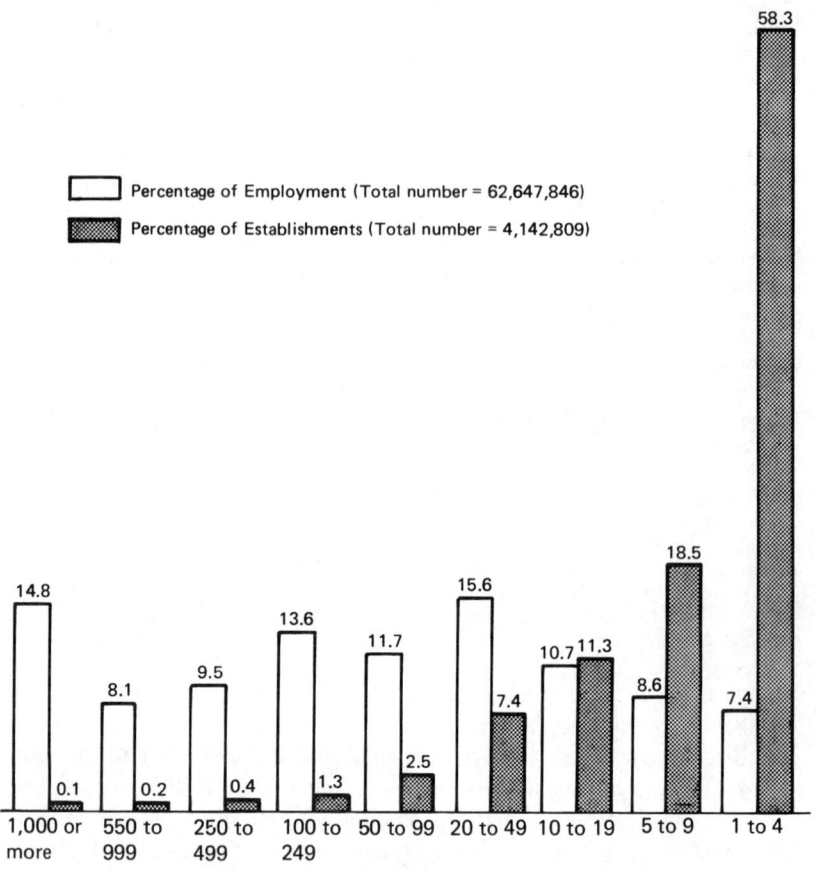

**FIGURE 1** Percent distribution of employment and establishments by employment-size class: 1976. SOURCE: Bureau of the Census (1975/1976).

processes of special agencies or schools, which credential individuals as being competent to practice a given occupation at a certain level of skill.

There is no way at present, however, to ascertain exactly how many employment tests are used, in what ways they are used, how well they are chosen for a given use, or what their overall effect is. Such information is simply not available, at least not in any systematic form.

This lack of information represents an important detriment to the effective use of tests for employment. Policy makers in particular need to understand the nature and scope of testing in the private sector in order to develop and implement legislative policies and guidelines that are realistic for the employer and fair to the job seeker or employee. Em-

## Current Use of Tests for Employment

TABLE 2  Breakdown of Workers by Occupational Group (1976)

| Occupational Group | Workers (millions) | Percent of Total Civilian Work Force |
|---|---|---|
| Clerical workers | 15.6 | 17.8 |
| Operatives (assemblers, packers, machine operators, etc.) | 13.4 | 15.3 |
| Professional and technical | 13.3 | 15.2 |
| Craft (construction workers, mechanics, etc.) | 11.3 | 12.9 |
| Service workers, except private household | 12.0 | 13.7 |
| Managers and administrators, except farm | 9.3 | 10.6 |
| Sales workers | 5.5 | 6.3 |
| Nonfarm laborers | 4.3 | 4.9 |
| Farm workers | 2.8 | 3.3 |
| Total civilian work force | 87.5 | |

NOTE: The current population survey by the Bureau of the Census on the day of the census in April 1980 estimated the employed civilian labor force, including private and governmental, as 97.2 million.
SOURCE: Bureau of Labor Statistics (1978/1978).

ployers as well need to know the answers to some of these questions, because, as a practical matter of personnel management, they confront a variety of selection procedures of unequal relevance and quality. Without this necessary information, it is difficult to make prudent choice of the most appropriate selection methods.

A number of surveys of test use were conducted during the 1970s, and they provide the best available information on employment testing overall. In general, the questions in these surveys did not elicit the kind of specific information that would be of greatest use for this report. They tended to focus on numbers of firms rather than numbers of people and to use general descriptive terms rather than specific test titles, occupational groups, and job levels. The discussion of the use of tests in the private sector that follows is based mainly on the 1975 survey conducted jointly by Prentice-Hall (P-H) and the American Society for Personnel Administration (ASPA) and the one in 1976 conducted by the Bureau of National Affairs (BNA).

Data based on survey research have certain limitations. For example, sometimes the number of questionnaires distributed is reported, but not the number completed and returned. Results may be affected by self-selection among respondents and by the self-report nature of the instrument; there is no way to be sure whether what is reported represents actual practice or stated company policy. The use of percentages, with differences in the base populations, may easily result in misleading or incorrect interpretations.

The problem of survey data is further compounded by differences in how respondents interpret the term "test," how they categorize different types of tests, and what they mean by "test use." For example, some companies may consider a performance test of typing (for speed and accuracy) a "clerical" test, and there are differences among companies as to what constitutes a test of verbal ability. Again, some companies use tests with some, but not all, prospective employees in a given category; others may test all applicants. Gross differences exist in passing standards (Byham and Spitzer 1971:149). Such differences remain elusive and present difficulties in attempting to generalize from the results of a single survey or in making comparisons across results of two or more surveys. Despite these difficulties, the surveys provide some useful clues about the magnitude of test use among various types and sizes of private employers.

*Prentice-Hall/American Society for Personnel Administrators Survey (P-H/ASPA)*

Although the major purpose of the P-H/ASPA survey was to ascertain how ASPA member companies were dealing with test validation questions during the period when the federal guidelines on employee selection procedures were in a state of flux, it yielded considerable general information about company testing policies and practices.

The survey instrument was sent to personnel officers in 2,000 member companies, of whom 1,339 responded. Analysis concentrated on company size and type of business. Table 3 shows the number and percent of total organizations responding by P-H category. A comparison with Bureau of Census data in Table 1 shows that the three largest industry groups, which accounted for 71 percent of employees in 1975 and 1976, comprised more than half of the P-H respondents.

Overall, the P-H/ASPA survey showed that: (1) practically no company relies on just one method for hiring or promotion (almost two-thirds of all respondents reported some use of written testing for selection or promotion, but fewer than 20 percent of those who test said they disqualified candidates on the basis of test scores alone); (2) written test usage was declining; of those that were tested, clerical candidates were the most heavily tested group; (3) there seemed to be a relationship between firm size and incidence of test use for hiring (large companies tended to use

*Current Use of Tests for Employment*

TABLE 3  Breakdown of Responding Organizations in P-H Survey

| P-H Category | Number Responding | Percent of 1,339 Total Responses |
|---|---|---|
| Manufacturers | 592 | 44.2 |
| Bank | 142 | 10.6 |
| Insurance | 111 | 8.3 |
| Other office | 52 | 3.9 |
| Retail store | 80 | 6.0 |
| Public utility | 67 | 5.0 |
| Transportation and communication | 49 | 3.7 |
| Hospitals | 101 | 7.5 |
| Other | 145 | 10.8 |

SOURCE: Prentice-Hall, Inc. (1975).

tests more and to conduct validity studies on their tests more often than smaller companies).

Table 4 shows the incidence of testing for hiring and promotion for all employer size categories, while Table 5 indicates the incidence of testing by various categories of employers.

(1) Few companies relied on any one selection method for hiring or promotion. Practice usually involved a number of different steps in various combinations—what respondents referred to as "nontest" selection procedures—although the survey warned readers that these could in fact be considered "tests":

As a group, companies in the P-H Survey voted interview the most important of these procedures. Previous experience in related jobs was considered second in importance; personal references, third; educational background, fourth; and the candidates's credit rating was deemed least important, with only a handful of firms bothering to check it at all (Prentice-Hall, Inc. 1975:4).

(2) The survey also reported signs that test usage was declining. Although data were not reported by size of establishment, 74.7 percent of the respondents stated that they had cut back on their employment testing programs during the past 5 years, and 13.7 percent said they would probably eliminate most of their testing some time in the future.

At the same time, 9.4 percent were planning to redesign their testing program to conform to government regulations, 19.2 percent were waiting for new guidelines before proceeding, and 35.1 percent were already working on test refinements and anticipated few changes:

Signs that the scope of employee testing is waning were evident in the survey

TABLE 4 P-H Chart 3: Incidence of Testing for Hiring and Promotion (by Size of Employer)[a]

|  | Fewer than 100 Employees | 100 to 449 Employees | 500 to 999 Employees | 1,000 to 4,999 Employees | 5,000 to 9,999 Employees | 10,000 to 25,000 Employees | More than 25,000 Employees | All Respondents |
|---|---|---|---|---|---|---|---|---|
| Test for hiring | 30.4% | 43.4% | 46.8% | 55.4% | 62.7% | 54.9% | 57.1% | 49.1% |
| Test for promotion | 17.9 | 17.3 | 24.0 | 29.3 | 27.4 | 32.7 | 32.4 | 24.0 |
| Don't test | 61.0 | 49.2 | 45.1 | 40.4 | 32.9 | 38.4 | 39.6 | 36.5 |

[a]Percentages total more than 100% because some respondents test for both hiring and promotion.
SOURCE: Prentice-Hall, Inc. (1975:658).

TABLE 5 P-H Chart 2: Incidence of Testing for Hiring and Promotion (by Employer Category)[a]

|  | Manufacturers | Public Utilities | Hospitals | Banks | Insurance | Other Offices | Retail Stores | Transportation and Communications | Other | All Respondents |
|---|---|---|---|---|---|---|---|---|---|---|
| Test for hiring | 41.2% | 59.1% | 41.8% | 47.5% | 67.9% | 69.2% | 44.2% | 75.5% | 55.1% | 49.1% |
| Test for promotion | 24.9 | 49.2 | 17.4 | 16.0 | 25.5 | 19.7 | 22.5 | 42.2 | 19.7 | 24.0 |
| Don't test | 42.3 | 22.4 | 46.6 | 36.5 | 21.8 | 25.0 | 42.5 | 18.3 | 33.8 | 36.5 |

[a]Percentages total more than 100% because some respondents test for both hiring and promotion.
SOURCE: Prentice-Hall, Inc. (1975:658).

## Current Use of Tests for Employment

responses. Does this represent a permanent shift in emphasis away from testing as an employee selection tool? Or are personnel managers just retrenching in their battle for accurate, nondiscriminatory selection methods? According to many employers, only more time and more guidance from the federal government will tell (Prentice-Hall, Inc. 1975:9).

Table 6 shows the types of tests used by various categories of business

TABLE 6   P-H Charts 4-13

P-H Chart 4: Testing of Candidates for Hourly Job Entry (Unskilled)

|  | Manufacturers | Public Utilities | Retail Stores | Insurance | Other Offices |
|---|---|---|---|---|---|
| General aptitude test | 3.3% | 9.3% | 3.4% | 6.1% | 2.7% |
| Clerical achievement test | 0.7 | — | 3.4 | 6.1 | 8.1 |
| Mechanical knowledge test | 2.9 | 1.9 | 1.7 | — | 2.7 |
| Work sample | 2.0 | — | 3.4 | 3.0 | 8.1 |
| Other test | 3.5 | — | 6.7 | 4.5 | 2.7 |
| Two or more tests | 7.6 | 25.9 | 10.2 | 7.6 | 10.8 |
| Don't test these candidates | 80.0 | 62.9 | 71.2 | 72.7 | 64.9 |

P-H Chart 5: Testing of Candidates for Hourly Job Promotion (Unskilled)

|  | Manufacturers | Hospitals | Public Utilities | Transportation and Communications | Other Offices |
|---|---|---|---|---|---|
| General aptitude test | 1.6% | 2.9% | 4.3% | 7.9% | — |
| Mechanical knowledge test | 2.3 | 2.3 | 2.1 | — | — |
| Work sample | 1.9 | 1.5 | 2.1 | — | 6.1% |
| Other test | 2.2 | 3.6 | 2.2 | 7.9 | — |
| Two or more tests | 4.9 | 1.5 | 17.0 | 7.9 | 3.0 |
| Don't test these candidates | 87.1 | 88.2 | 72.3 | 76.3 | 90.9 |

P-H Chart 6: Testing of Candidates for Hourly Job Entry (Skilled)

|  | Manufacturers | Public Utilities | Other Offices | Retail Stores | Transportation and Communications |
|---|---|---|---|---|---|
| General aptitude test | 1.8% | 2.9% | — | 3.4% | 2.4% |
| Clerical achievement test | — | 4.4 | 2.7% | 5.2 | 4.9 |
| Mechanical knowledge test | 10.9 | 2.9 | 2.7 | — | 12.2 |
| Work sample | 6.7 | 1.9 | 10.8 | 3.4 | 2.4 |
| Other test | 3.7 | 3.2 | 2.7 | 3.5 | 7.4 |
| Two or more tests | 13.7 | 42.3 | 21.6 | 20.7 | 31.7 |
| Don't test these candidates | 63.2 | 42.3 | 59.5 | 63.8 | 39.0 |

TABLE 6  *Continued*

P-H Chart 7: Testing of Candidates for Hourly Job Promotion (Skilled)

|  | Manufacturers | Public Utilities | Retail Stores | Transportation and Communications | Hospitals |
|---|---|---|---|---|---|
| General aptitude test | 0.9% | 4.3% | 3.8% | 2.6% | 1.4% |
| Mechanical knowledge test | 7.4 | 6.5 | — | 7.9 | 2.9 |
| Other test of achievement or knowledge | 0.9 | 2.2 | — | 2.6 | 1.4 |
| Work sample | 5.3 | 4.3 | 1.9 | — | 2.9 |
| Other test | 2.0 | 4.5 | 2.0 | 10.6 | 3.0 |
| Two or more tests | 12.6 | 23.9 | 9.6 | 10.5 | 7.2 |
| Don't test these candidates | 70.9 | 54.3 | 82.7 | 65.8 | 81.2 |

P-H Chart 8: Testing of Candidates for Clerical Jobs

|  | Manufacturers | Banks | Insurance | Other Offices | Other |
|---|---|---|---|---|---|
| General aptitude test | 1.8% | 0.9% | 10.0% | 2.1% | 2.8% |
| Clerical achievement test | 21.9 | 16.2 | 33.0 | 10.6 | 25.7 |
| Work sample | 19.7 | 17.1 | 14.0 | 19.1 | 20.2 |
| Other test | 1.8 | 6.4 | 4.0 | 4.4 | 4.5 |
| Two or more tests | 15.8 | 26.1 | 19.0 | 34.0 | 21.1 |
| Don't test these candidates | 39.0 | 33.3 | 20.0 | 29.8 | 25.7 |

P-H Chart 9: Testing of Candidates for Technical and Professional Positions

|  | Banks | Public Utilities | Insurance | Other Offices | Transportation and Communications |
|---|---|---|---|---|---|
| General aptitude test | 4.6% | 13.5% | 11.7% | 5.1% | 5.4% |
| Other test of achievement or knowledge | 1.9 | 1.9 | 6.5 | 2.6 | — |
| Personality test | 2.3 | 5.8 | 2.6 | — | — |
| Work sample | 3.4 | — | 3.9 | 5.1 | 2.7 |
| Other test | 3.9 | 1.9 | 5.2 | 2.6 | 5.4 |
| Two or more tests | 16.1 | 23.1 | 10.4 | 20.5 | 24.3 |
| Don't test these candidates | 67.8 | 53.8 | 59.7 | 64.1 | 62.2 |

P-H Chart 10: Testing of Candidates for Supervisory Jobs

|  | Manufacturers | Public Utilities | Insurance | Other Offices | Transportation and Communications |
|---|---|---|---|---|---|
| General aptitude test | 2.4% | 7.8% | 8.0% | 2.5% | 10.5% |
| Personality test | 3.1 | 3.8 | 2.7 | — | 2.6 |
| Company-devised test | 1.4 | — | 4.0 | — | — |
| Other test | 2.1 | — | 2.0 | — | — |
| Two or more tests | 16.5 | 19.2 | 14.7 | 15.0 | 23.7 |
| Don't test these candidates | 74.5 | 69.2 | 69.3 | 82.5 | 63.2 |

## Current Use of Tests for Employment

### TABLE 6  Continued

P-H Chart 11: Testing of Candidates for Managerial Jobs (Entry)

|  | Manufacturers | Banks | Insurance | Other Offices | Retail Stores |
|---|---|---|---|---|---|
| General aptitude test | 3.3% | 2.3% | 6.7% | 2.4% | 7.4% |
| Other test of achievement or knowledge | 0.9 | 1.1 | 5.3 | — | — |
| Personality test | 3.3 | 2.3 | 2.7 | — | 1.9 |
| Company-devised test | 1.4 | 1.1 | 4.0 | — | 3.7 |
| Other test | 1.2 | 1.2 | 1.3 | — | — |
| Two or more tests | 15.3 | 20.7 | 13.3 | 17.1 | 29.6 |
| Don't test these candidates | 74.6 | 71.3 | 66.7 | 80.5 | 57.4 |

P-H Chart 12: Testing of Candidates for Managerial Jobs (Promotion)

|  | Public Utilities | Retail Stores | Transportation and Communications | Other Offices | Other |
|---|---|---|---|---|---|
| General aptitude test | 4.1% | 2.0% | 2.8% | — | 4.3% |
| Personality test | 2.0 | — | 11.1 | — | 2.2 |
| Company-devised test | — | — | — | — | 2.2 |
| Other test | — | — | 2.8 | — | 1.0 |
| Two or more tests | 6.1 | 19.2 | 13.9 | 10.5% | 9.7 |
| Don't test these candidates | 87.8 | 78.8 | 69.4 | 89.5 | 80.6 |

P-H Chart 13: Testing of Candidates for Sales Jobs

|  | Manufacturers | Insurance | Other Offices | Retail Stores | Other |
|---|---|---|---|---|---|
| General aptitude test | 3.3% | 6.1% | — | 4.2% | 3.6% |
| Personality test | 3.3 | 7.6 | 2.9% | — | 4.8 |
| Company-devised test | 1.8 | 6.1 | — | 8.3 | 2.4 |
| Other test | 2.4 | 2.9 | — | 8.3 | 2.3 |
| Two or more tests | 13.6 | 12.1 | 11.8 | 4.2 | 14.3 |
| Don't test these candidates | 75.6 | 65.2 | 85.3 | 75.0 | 72.6 |

SOURCE: Prentice-Hall, Inc. (1975:660-663).

for hiring and promotion of different types of workers (ranging from unskilled hourly job candidates to managerial, technical, and professional staff). It does not contain any information on the numbers of people tested. Clerical workers were the most extensively tested worker type. Between 61 and 80 percent of test users across all business categories reported testing to fill clerical openings, and more than 25 percent of them said these were the only employment tests they used. Testing was most widespread at transportation and communication companies, followed by insurance companies and public utilities. Although two-thirds of manufacturing companies did not test any job candidates, those that did tended to test in eight of the ten job categories surveyed and to administer more than one test per candidate. While hospitals did the least testing of any employer group, they tended to rely on professional certification and licensing in selection.

(3) The P-H analysis indicated that size seemed to be a determining factor in many aspects of test usage by employers. Fewer than half of the establishments employing 1,000 or less reported that they used tests, while among those employing more than 1,000 test use for hiring was consistently over 50 percent. Decisions to purchase or to develop their own tests seemed to relate to a company's size as well since small companies were not so apt to employ for the positions that standardized tests were designed for, while large companies could often afford to produce tests, tailored to their own needs. Only among the smallest companies (under 100 employees) did a significant proportion (60.9 percent) report that they relied exclusively on company devised tests. Exclusive reliance on tests designed and marketed by test publishers was heaviest among medium-sized companies, employing 100 to 25,000 employees (40 to 50 percent). Combinations of company-devised and published tests were favored by 42 percent of companies with more than 25,000 employees, 30 to 39 percent of medium-sized companies and 21.7 percent of companies with fewer than 100 employees.

More than three-fourths of all respondents reported dependence on either in-house or consulting professionals. Larger companies tended to have more job categories and were more apt to employ in-house psychologists to handle test development and administration (55.6 percent of firms with more than 25,000 employees). Smaller companies with fewer testing needs managed with the work of a personnel officer (44.4 percent of companies with fewer than 100 employees) or a consulting psychologist (33.3 percent).

The P-H Survey results indicated that size would also appear to be related to the conduct of validity studies on tests used for selection and promotion. There is no indication as to how many of the 1,339 respondents answered the validation questions in the P-H Survey, but the answers of those who did revealed that the larger the firm surveyed, the more likely it was to validate its tests. Two-thirds of the responding firms employing more than 25,000 said they had conducted validity studies. These firms reported validity studies in every job category, and 50 to 60 percent of them conducted validity studies for clerical and hourly workers. About 17 percent of companies employing fewer than 100 employees had conducted validity studies. In all size categories, most companies that validated their test or nontest selection procedures spent less than $5,000

## Current Use of Tests for Employment

per job studied, and differential validation research for members of minority groups was rare.

### Other Survey Studies

Other studies conducted during the 1970s with much smaller groups have confirmed that the state of flux caused by developing federal regulations was prompting frequent changes in testing procedures (Miner 1976) and decline in use of employment tests (Petersen 1974).

In the Miner survey of 160 personnel executives, 60 percent reported one or more changes in selection procedures designed to implement equal employment opportunity goals. Of the companies reporting changes, the most frequent changes involved use of tests (39 percent) and job qualifications (31 percent). Other changes included those affecting application forms (20 percent), recruiting techniques (19 percent), interviewing procedures (7 percent), and other (23 percent). Testing changes included: elimination of all testing; elimination of all tests except skill tests (e.g., typing, steno, and keypunching); elimination of unvalidated testing programs; modification and validation of test programs to ensure job relatedness.

Petersen surveyed 185 companies in a variety of industries to investigate the impact of the 1971 *Griggs* v. *Duke Power* decision on testing, validation, and selection procedures. Of sixty usable responses to the questionnaire (from firms employing 780 to more than 500,000 employees), fifty-three firms had been conducting testing programs at the factory, clerical, or managerial/professional levels prior to the Duke Power decision. After the decision, eight (15.1 percent) of the fifty-three companies dropped tests altogether, all of them among the smallest surveyed. Rates of test use for clerical workers, while declining, remained highest of three categories surveyed by Petersen, however.

### Bureau of National Affairs (BNA)

This survey (Miner 1976b) sought information about selection practices and policies from members of the 1975-1976 panel of BNA's Personnel Policies Forum (PPF). Responses were obtained from 196 personnel executives. The respondents were not categorized as to type of industry, as in the P-H/ASPA survey. Instead, they were categorized as manufacturing, nonmanufacturing, and nonbusiness. Categories were further characterized as to size and geographic location (see Table 7).

The nonmanufacturing category included financial institutions, retail stores, and public utilities, and nonbusiness enterprises included edu-

TABLE 7 BNA Survey: Sample Composition by Industry, by Size, and by Geographic Location

| Industry | | | Size | | Geographic Location | | | |
|---|---|---|---|---|---|---|---|---|
| Mfg. | Non-mfg. | Non-bus. | Large | Small | Northeast | South | North Central | West |
| N  106 | 53 | 37 | 100 | 96 | 45 | 67 | 47 | 37 |
| %   54 | 27 | 19 | 51 | 49 | 23 | 34 | 24 | 19 |
| Total N = 196 | | | | | | | | |

SOURCE: Miner (1976b).

cational institutions, hospitals, and government agencies. Companies employing 1,000 or more persons were classified as large, while all others were characterized as small.

The BNA Survey defined psychological tests as "measures of skill, ability, intelligence or personality." Results indicated that:

—42 percent of the responding companies used such tests in 1976, compared to 55 percent in a 1971 ASPA-BNA survey (ASPA No. 12) and 90 percent in a 1963 BNA survey (PPF No. 70).

—Tests were used much more frequently in nonmanufacturing companies (62 percent) than in manufacturing (35 percent) or in nonbusiness organizations (38 percent).

—A larger percentage of large companies (51 percent) tended to use such tests more often than small ones (34 percent).

—Of companies that used tests:
- more than 80 percent used them for office/clerical positions (60 to 80 percent, in the P-H Study);
- 20 percent used them for production or maintenance jobs;
- 14 percent used them for data processing jobs; and
- less than 10 percent used them for sales or service jobs (14 to 35 percent, in the P-H Study).

Other types of jobs for which tests were used included actuarial trainees, truck drivers, police officers and firemen, and various professional positions. A few personnel executives indicated that tests were used for all or nearly all nonmanagement jobs. Although management selection procedures were not specifically covered by this survey, several respondents noted that tests were used to select management trainees and candidates for supervisory or foreman jobs.

## Current Use of Tests for Employment

The BNA Survey indicated that validity studies of the tests had been conducted by slightly more than half of the companies using tests, by a larger percentage of large companies than small ones, and by seven out of ten nonbusiness organizations compared to half of the business firms (both manufacturing and nonmanufacturing).

An interesting point of agreement between findings in the BNA and P-H surveys was that interviews were considered to have the strongest impact on the hiring decision. They were considered the most important aspect of the selection procedure in 56 percent of the responding companies in the BNA Survey, and to have equal weight with test results and other selection techniques in 35 percent. Four respondents (2 percent) had conducted validation studies on interviewing.

The survey also found that nearly all employers checked out previous employment records, but only about half checked educational records and even fewer checked personal references. Preemployment physical examinations were given to employees in three-fourths of the companies, and 4 percent required polygraph tests for certain kinds of jobs.

### Information Science Incorporated (InSci)

This survey, reported in *InSci Bulletin* (Client Services Group 1978), was conducted by telephone. The report indicates that respondents were InSci Human Resource Systems clients. Neither the sample size nor the number of respondents was given. It was reported, however, that 60 percent of the companies were engaged in manufacturing, while 40 percent were nonmanufacturing firms. All the companies had more than 1,000 employees and 63 percent had 5,000 or more. The results are presented in Table 8.

The InSci Survey results indicated that fewer "paper-and-pencil" tests were being used for management, technical, sales, office and clerical, craft, labor, and service jobs in 1978 than in 1970. The sole exception was the operative category, which remained unchanged at 14 percent.

It is noteworthy that, despite a decrease in usage for office and clerical jobs (from 84 percent to 77 percent), general test use remained high for this category. This finding is consistent with those of the P-H, BNA, and Petersen surveys.

The results showed that, while a decreasing percentage of respondents were using selection tests in 1978 as compared to 1970, more of these tests were validated. However, the data representing anticipated usage and validation are confusing, given the lack of additional information.

TABLE 8  InSci Survey: Test Usage, Past, Present, and Future

| Job Category | Percent of Respondents Who Used Selection Tests in 1970 | Percent of the 1970 Selection Tests That Were Validated | Percent of Respondents Currently Using Selection Tests | Percent of Currently Used Selection Tests That Are Validated | Percent of Respondents Who Expect To Use Selection Tests in 1986 | Percent of Selections Tests Expected To Be Used in 1986 That Will be Validated |
|---|---|---|---|---|---|---|
| Management | 38 | 21 | 21 | 44 | 29 | 17 |
| Technical | 46 | 24 | 28 | 50 | 43 | 28 |
| Sales | 22 | 38 | 19 | 50 | 24 | 100 |
| Office/clerical | 84 | 26 | 77 | 45 | 76 | 66 |
| Craft | 41 | 20 | 33 | 57 | 29 | 83 |
| Operative | 14 | 40 | 14 | 50 | 9 | 75 |
| Labor (unskilled) | 19 | 29 | 12 | 80 | 9 | 100 |
| Service | 11 | 25 | 9 | 50 | 5 | 100 |

SOURCE: Client Services Group (1978:2).

## Evaluation and Discussion

The review here of the surveys of test use makes it apparent that there are great gaps in the data and disparities in the methods of data presentation. The data on the numbers and kinds of tests used in any industry in the private sector are insufficient to allow conclusions as to the impact of tests on selection or promotion. There is no solid information on what percentage of jobs is filled via testing in any job category or in any industry. Where tests are used, there is no evidence or reason to believe that there is any regularity in the setting of passing scores, in the weighting of the test within the selection or promotion process, or in the use of comparable tests for comparable jobs, from company to company, or within companies. There is no way to identify the tests as "achievement" or "aptitude," i.e., to ascertain whether they are measures of what a person has learned or measures of what a person can learn. Job analyses, the detailed statements of work behavior and other information relevant to the job, are not mentioned in the surveys. Companies presently report performing validation studies, but the monies expended on the studies are often so small that the studies cannot be extensive. Even when there is considerable expenditure of funds, validation studies may not be comparable because of differences in what they study, how terms are defined, and methods used. Companies report an interest in cooperative studies, but results cannot be generalized where standardization does not exist.

Considering the size and complexity of U.S. industry, it is doubtful that the use of tests can be uniform; companies will continue to adapt tests to their changing employment needs and to the available labor market. Nevertheless, a far more adequate data base than is presently available could be generated by the establishment of a clearinghouse and guidelines for conducting surveys. Such a clearinghouse could work toward achieving more precise interpretation of existing standards and uniformity in definitions for job analysis, validation studies, and other methods of data collection. Upon such a base, a group of comparable studies could be conducted to provide for analysis of cumulative data, thereby achieving the necessary information while eliminating waste.

There is of course the danger that established requirements would be so comprehensive as to preclude realistic fulfillment. For example, there is no way to professionally validate existing tests and other selection procedures because there are simply not enough professionally competent individuals available for such a task. Also, as with test use, validation cannot be permanent and fixed, in a changing labor market with changing jobs and requirements. Employers who have had tests developed or have purchased tests have managed to get by thus far with the use of a single test form. However, the amount of test maintenance and validation required, as the various demands of "truth in testing" burgeon, is likely to jar the system considerably, if not shatter it completely. Some means of systematically dealing with these practical, fundamental considerations must be devised.

The questions of who prepares, administers, and validates the tests that are being used for selection and promotion in the private sector, and how well they are trained to do so, are crucial to the issues being explored in this report. Both the P-H and the BNA surveys indicated that a considerable amount of test development, administration, and validation is performed by company staff. The P-H Survey indicated that the size of the company was an important determinant of who is involved in the testing program: "The smaller the company, the more it's apt to depend on non-psychologists in its personnel department to administer all phases of its program" (Prentice-Hall, Inc. 1975:20).

The 1971 and 1976 BNA studies listed tests used by PPF member companies that are available from commercial test publishers (along with indications of validity studies). The 1971 survey listed fifty-two psychological tests and twenty-one publishers. The 1976 survey listed fifty-four psychological tests and seventeen publishers. The BNA surveys do not specifically indicate who administers, interprets, and validates these tests.

In their study of the testing industry, Holmen and Docter (1972) listed close to 100 testing and scoring organizations and provided brief descriptions of the organizations' activities. It is clear that most of these organizations feature written tests, although some also produce performance tests. Except for a few consulting organizations, however, they do not deal with the entire range of selection activities. Indeed, many of the organizations or individuals listed provide only one test.

While Holmen and Docter did not give estimates of what portion of all tests used are supplied by testing organizations, they did estimate that the six largest testing companies, California Test Bureau, Educational Testing Service, Harcourt Brace Jovanovich, Inc., Houghton Mifflin Co., The Psychological Corporation (now merged with Harcourt Brace Jovanovich, Inc.), and Science Research Associates account for at least three-quarters or more of all written tests sold. (This figure is confusing because it included educational tests as well as employment tests, and the authors did not indicate whether educational and employment tests were equally represented in the three-quarters of all tests sold. Some of the testing companies mentioned above do not really work in the private sector except for certification tests. Also, tests are produced by the private sector itself.) Holmen and Docter also estimated that test development, standardization, and revision probably account for three-fourths or more of the total professional activity within these testing organizations. Two of the characteristics shared by the six large organizations are: "they provide extensive services to test customers" and "the organizations employ many individuals who are well trained in testing and who are leaders in professional organizations involved with testing; further, these persons are in the top management of the company or are influential in company management" (Holmen and Docter 1972:33).

Most of the medium-sized testing organizations (twenty-two were listed by Holmen and Docter) are primarily in the testing business rather than in some other field with testing only an adjunctive activity. They account for about 5 percent of the sales made by the testing industry.

Moving from those who develop tests to those who use tests, Holmen and Docter (1972:165) offered an interesting comment:

There is considerable reason to believe that employment selection tests are often used improperly, that far too many test users are inadequately trained for the responsibilities they have accepted and that job related validity data are typically not available at all. Not surprisingly, therefore, as estimated 20% of all complaints filed with EEOC involve testing in some way. For some years this has represented about 1,000 cases annually. [This in 1972!]

We have concluded that the central problem of testing and discriminatory employment practice lies not in the use of "bad tests", but rather in the discrepancy between professional testing standards and the actual testing procedures of many personnel departments. Major changes are needed in the level of professional competence and training required of personnel responsible for the use of tests which contribute to employment decision making.

Concern about the competence of test users has been echoed by others. The ASPA *Handbook* (Stone and Ruch 1974:122) states:

Experience has made it abundantly clear that not every personnel administrator can choose, validate, and interpret tests. In most cases it is better not to use tests without professional assistance. Because of the problems associated with testing, a prime consideration in personnel policy is whether or not the organization will conduct a professionally competent selection and placement program.

### Certification—Credentials to Practice

Increasingly more and more individuals are undergoing job competency testing before they enter the personnel office. Some of these individuals will have been examined in conjunction with statutorily based licensing or certification programs (see below, p. 143), while others will have been tested and certified by nongovernmental agencies, such as professional associations.

Both the governmental and nongovernmental agencies that issue credentials attesting to an individual's competence have predetermined qualifications, which may include: graduation from an accredited or approved program; acceptable performance on a qualifying examination; and/or completion of a given amount of work experience.

Occupational and professional testing for certification has increased considerably in the last 10 years for a variety of reasons including: the 1978 *Uniform Guidelines*; consumer demand for professional accountability; and knowledge expansion leading to more and more specialization.

A 1976 survey by Nafziger and Hiscox estimated that "over 2,000 occupations have licensing or certification procedures of some sort, but only a fraction of these involve demonstration of the applicant's competency through examination" (1976:7). No figures were given to support the estimate. A November 11, 1979, article in *The New York Times* by Nancy Rubin (1979, Education Supplement:8), addressing the topic of occupational tests, noted that "the most dramatic example of growing specialization and, as a result, standardized assessment tests, has been in the health fields. . . . There are now 5.1 million people employed in 717 job categories in the health field, with 2.5 million of them in allied health occupations." No test usage figures were given to support the statement.

The exact volume of voluntary certification tests given each year by nongovernmental agencies is not known. In the health fields a group of certification agencies recently formed the National Commission for Health Certifying Agencies (NCHA). This Commission, concerned with standards and definitions, has begun the process of gathering information on its member agencies' test volume. In other fields, the information could be obtained by establishing and maintaining contact with each voluntary certification agency. While fewer tests are given for certification than for other purposes in the private sector, some estimate of test program size and range can be gained from the following figures: in 1979 certification tests were administered to approximately 75,000 automobile mechanics (one of the largest volume test programs), 12,000 respiratory therapists/technologists, 4,000 shorthand reporters, 600 placement counselors, 450 computer programmers, and 150 preventive medicine physicians (one of the smallest volume test programs).

Because of increasing concern over the continued competence of occupational and professional workers, the concept of recertification, at intervals ranging from 2 to 6 years, is gaining support, especially in the health fields. At present, most recertification programs are based on the acquisition of specified amounts of continuing education credit.

Recently, interest has developed in the use of tests to serve the recer-

## Current Use of Tests for Employment

tification function, as uncertainty has grown concerning the notion that participation in a continuing education course automatically ensures an individual's continued competence. For example, in addition to its requirement for continuing education, the American Board of Family Practice requires practitioners in this medical specialty to undergo a reassessment process every 6 years. The process includes an objective test of medical knowledge, several patient management problems, which require the practitioner to apply his or her knowledge and skill to the solution of a simulated medical situation, and a chart audit of the physician's records.

It is clear that tests cannot provide all the answers to assessment of continued competence, however. The issues are complex and have not been clearly delineated. Are practitioners only supposed to keep up with the state-of-the-art in their profession? Are they supposed to maintain entry-level generalist skills, when in fact they have specialized during the course of their practice? If specialties are to be assessed, rather than general skills, how many specialties must be tested? How many tests will be needed to cover a profession or occupation that is changing? These questions and others need to be answered before effective assessment strategies can be implemented.

### Evaluation and Discussion

Tests for voluntary certification purposes are prepared and administered rather differently than those used for selection and promotion purposes. They are typically job-related achievement tests used to determine if the individual meets standards of job knowledge set by a nongovernmental certification agency. Some tests are developed and administered by the certifying agency. Others are conducted by professional testing organizations on behalf of the certifying agencies. In these cases the professional testing agencies work closely with practitioners and educators from all over the country.

Tests are generally administered under standardized conditions, and consideration is given to item statistics, test statistics, pass/fail scores, and the weighting of the test with other elements in the certification process. As changes occur in the practice of the occupation or profession, the test is usually changed as well.

Voluntary certification tests are subject to some of the same criticism as has been leveled at selection and promotion tests. It cites such issues as inadequacy of the job analyses used for test development, failure of some tests to meet professional standards of validation, inadequate training of many certifying agencies in measurement principles, lack of accountability, etc. The recent formation of the National Commission for Health Certifying Agencies is a cooperative attempt in the health fields to remedy some of these concerns.

At present, voluntary, nongovernmental certification agencies do not need to conform to the *Uniform Guidelines* as long as their certification is not required by law. If an employer relies upon such certification in making an employment decision, however, the employer must conform to the requirements of the *Uniform Guidelines*.

## Trends in Private Sector Testing

Because of the difficulty of detecting trends from available data, the following discussion utilizes a variety of other sources in addition to the surveys discussed, including: nonquantitative professional literature; discussion with colleagues; proceedings of professional meetings.

—A major current trend is the increased sensitivity of private sector employers with respect to their hiring practices and to charges of discrimination and unfairness. In an attempt to reduce their vulnerability, many employers chose to abandon or sharply reduce the use of paper-and-pencil tests, which are the primary focus of the *Uniform Guidelines* proscriptions. The resulting decline in test use is clearly documented in all of the survey data.

The matter is complicated, however, by the fact that the *Uniform Guidelines*, while phrased primarily in terms of testing, also apply to any selection procedure that creates adverse impact. This means that simply abandoning tests is no solution for employers attempting to avoid the scrutiny of the Equal Employment Opportunity Commission (EEOC), because as long as any selection at all is performed, the vulnerability remains, if adverse impact is found. The *Uniform Guidelines* require extremely elaborate validation and documentation procedures for any selection procedure having adverse impact. Compared to alternative procedures such as interviewing, written tests can more easily be brought into compliance with these requirements. It may be that we are seeing, therefore, a cautious return by employers to the use of written tests in their selection procedures.

Consideration of such a return is likely to be influenced by recent studies by Frank L. Schmidt of the U.S. Office of Personnel Management and his colleagues (Schmidt et al. 1979). Schmidt studied the apparent abandonment of written selection tests during the period when EEOC influence was spreading. Schmidt believes this hasty abandonment was because most personnel psychologists did not realize the great impact of

## Current Use of Tests for Employment

valid selection procedures on work force productivity. Briefly, his studies attempted to express in dollar amounts the loss in productivity that occurs when valid selection procedures are abandoned in favor of less valid ones, selection procedures that often produce little more than random selection. He estimates that hundreds of millions of dollars in productivity are at stake in the choice of selection procedures. Generalization of these findings depends, of course, on the adequacy of the methods used to determine the dollar value of productivity.

—In contrast to the decline in the use of written selection tests, test use for certification purposes has increased. While individuals in the occupations and professions subject to certification have not typically applied for jobs in which selection tests are used, it may be possible that this increased use of certification tests accounts for some of the decrease in selection tests; if so, the extent cannot be determined.

—Written tests are reported to be used most heavily for clerical workers, as in the past. Interviews, however, are relied on most often for all types of workers.

—The professional literature reports a move toward multiassessment strategies. The ASPA *Handbook* suggests the use of a professionally developed and validated battery of selection procedures tailored to a company's objective, including screening of applicants, review of application blanks, checking of references, testing, employment interviews, and physical examinations. The P-H Survey would seem to support this approach with its finding that no company relies on a single selection procedure, although it did not report the use of a professionally developed or validated battery.

—The professional literature also discusses the need to tighten selection procedures—to develop weighted application blanks, to use structured interviews, to use professionally developed psychological tests, and to standardize administration. The ASPA *Handbook,* Holmen and Docter, and others all speak to this need.

—The surveys all reported an increase in validation studies. There was not much discussion of details, however. The surveys also reported an interest in cooperative studies on the part of their member companies.

—In certification testing, there is a movement toward development of criterion-referenced tests, an expression of the feeling that this type of test best fits the concept of a standard of job competence that must be met before an individual can be allowed to practice.

—In addition to the use of criterion-referenced tests in certification testing, there is a trend toward proficiency testing, i.e., allowing individuals who have not completed their training at an accredited institution to demonstrate that they can perform up to predetermined standards by passing a job-related test. The concept has met with concern from some professional groups who believe that passing a test is not sufficient evidence of competent performance and that graduation from an approved school is necessary as well.

—A variety of job-related testing techniques are being utilized in order to assess more accurately those abilities or qualities that are hard to test for. Written simulations of situations that attempt to assess decision-making and information-gathering behavior are being used in credentialing tests, e.g., respiratory therapist certification tests. Assessment center strategies that attempt to identify supervisory, management, and technical potential by evaluating such dimensions as leadership, decision-making ability, oral and written skills, energy, forcefulness, and dependence on others are being used as well. Assessment centers use such techniques as leaderless group discussions, in-basket exercises, written assignments, and interviews. One reverse trend: paper-and-pencil personality tests are on the decrease once again.

—A concern for standards and the need to assess competence has led to more research on pass/fail scores. Different methods of arriving at pass/fail scores (judgmental and empirical) are being investigated and tried out. Particular attention is being paid to analysis of the score area immediately surrounding the pass/fail score point, as clients ask for more information on candidates who score in that "gray zone," to help them in the difficult pass/fail decision-making process.

—Diagnostic feedback is becoming more of a concern to test makers in recognition of their responsibility to give precise information on areas of weakness to individuals who fail a test. Recent state legislation has spurred this trend. In addition to feedback on operational tests, there is an increasing demand for self-assessment tests in certain occupations and professions. These tests provide diagnostic feedback to individuals to help them discover the areas in which they are weak and, subsequently, to plan continuing education programs to serve their needs. Two national concerns stimulated by recent federal legislation will undoubtedly require the support of diagnostic tests to make them effective: employment of the handicapped and employment of the elderly.

## CIVILIAN GOVERNMENT SECTOR

Federal, state, and local governments are involved in testing primarily as employers and educators. They also use tests in the process of licensing for certain professions and occupations. More recently governments have assumed the role of test regulator as well, especially in connection with administration of the mandates of the equal employment opportunity legislation.

## Current Use of Tests for Employment

The focus here will be on employment tests used by civilian governments, particularly: the federal government as an employer and as a provider of guidance and placement services for job seekers; state and local governments as employers; and all three as protectors of public interest. In these different roles, the governments assign responsibility for testing to various agencies. As employers, governments tend to assign responsibility for implementation of the merit system to personnel agencies, which conduct examinations for applicants, using testing among other means. These personnel agencies vary in size of staff and in the nature of staff technical background. If a merit system is not in force, in those cases where examinations are conducted, administration of procedures is even more diversified. When government acts as a licensing agent, it assigns examination authority to licensing boards. The disparate nature of these many groups responsible for testing in civilian government leads to tremendously varied processes and methods of testing.

### Description of Federal Government Work Force

The civilian work force of the executive branch of the federal government comprises about 2.8 million employees, more than 90 percent of whom are employed under some form of merit system. About 80 percent of them hold white-collar positions. The other 20 percent are in blue-collar trades and labor occupations (U.S. Office of Personnel Management 1977a,b). Figures 2 and 3 show that in 1977 the largest single employer of both blue-collar and white-collar employees was the Department of

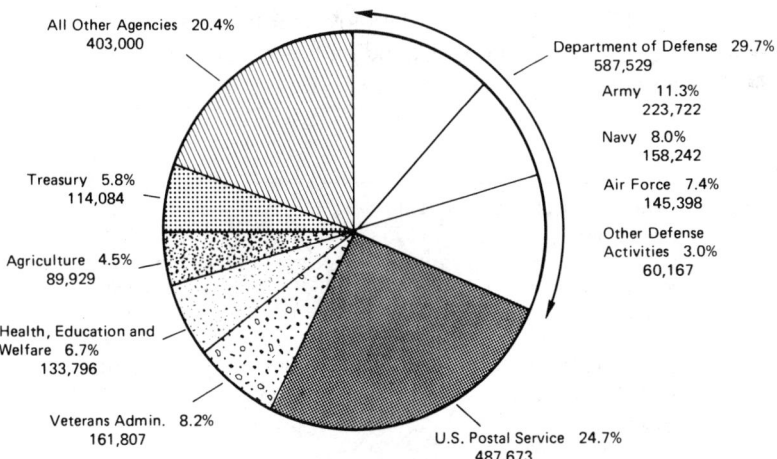

**FIGURE 2** Full-time white-collar employment by department and selected agency (1977). SOURCE: U.S. Office of Personnel Management (1977b).

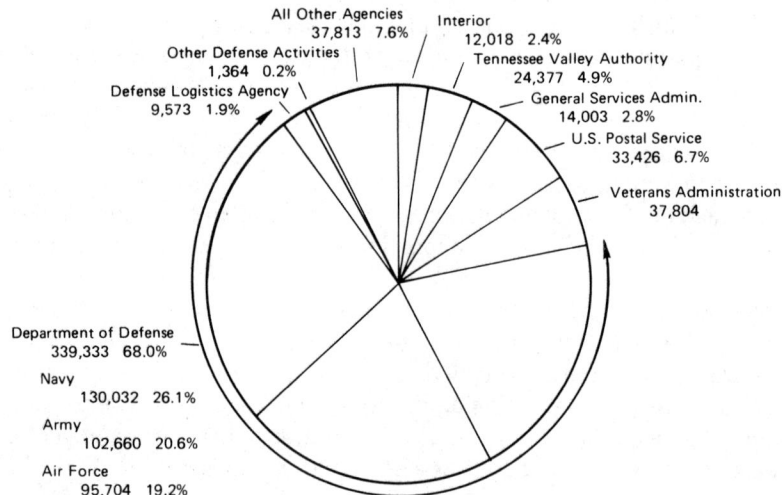

**FIGURE 3**  Blue-collar employment by department and selected agency (1977). SOURCE: U.S. Office of Personnel Management (1977a).

Defense. The second largest employer of white-collar workers was the U.S. Postal Service. (The Postal Service is now an independent agency.)

The two largest blue-collar occupational groups work in mobile industrial equipment operation and maintenance or manual labor (more than 50,000 employees each). The two largest white-collar occupational groups are general administrative-clerical and postal operations, which

TABLE 9  White-Collar Employment in the Ten Largest Occupations (Excluding Postal Service Employees) October 31, 1977

| Title | 1977 Employment |
|---|---|
| General clerical and administrative | 146,622 |
| Clerk-typist | 69,349 |
| Secretary | 63,420 |
| Nursing assistant | 38,568 |
| Nurse | 32,918 |
| Supply clerk and technician | 31,109 |
| Clerk-stenographer and reporter | 30,321 |
| Air traffic controller | 27,284 |
| Engineering technician | 26,003 |
| Electronic technician | 23,939 |
| TOTAL | 489,533 |

SOURCE: U.S. Office of Personnel Management (1977b).

## Current Use of Tests for Employment

TABLE 10 White-Collar Employment in Largest Occupations in Postal Service

| Title | 1977 Employment |
|---|---|
| Other postal distribution | 174,357 |
| Postal collection and delivery | 158,166 |
| Distribution window and miscellaneous | 46,733 |

SOURCE: U.S. Office of Personnel Management (1977b).

in 1977 numbered close to 500,000 employees each. Tables 9 and 10 show respectively the amount of white-collar employment in the ten largest occupations, excluding Postal Service, and the three largest occupations within the Postal Service.

## Test Use in Federal Government

### Use of Tests for Selection

The involvement of the federal government in employment testing had its beginnings in 1883 when Congress created the U.S. Civil Service Commission. Under the Civil Service Reform Act of 1978 (CSRA), the Office of Personnel Management (OPM) succeeded to the duties of the Civil Service Commission (CSC) in January 1979. There are more than 1,000 types of jobs for which OPM establishes standards for job classification, competitive examination procedures for filling job openings, and personnel policies. Until 1979, CSC, and then OPM, had examining jurisdiction over a competitive service covering some 1.7 million workers. Some federal agencies have always been exempted from this competitive service and may use their own tests. For example, the Department of State uses its own standardized tests for such occupations as foreign service officer. More than 1 million civilian positions are in this "excepted service," including 700,000 in the independent U.S. Postal Service. Since 1979, OPM has moved to delegate a substantial part of its examining procedures to individual agencies. It is too early to assess the impact of this large-scale attempt at decentralization.

The information on federal government test usage presented in Table 11 summarizes the OPM/CSC examination system in operation until 1979. Excluded are tests used for civilian positions in the excepted service; tests used in blue-collar examining, although OPM is responsible for examining blue-collar positions; and tests for in-service placement or merit promotion. Despite these exclusions, the information that is available provides a useful impression of the kinds of jobs that are tested for and in what numbers.

TABLE 11 Workload Report for Federal Examinations: Number of Applications, Selections, and Veterans Selected

| Time Period | Examinations Requiring Written Tests: | | | | | | All Six | All Federal Exams |
|---|---|---|---|---|---|---|---|---|
| | Steno-typist | Other Clerical | Summer Employment | Technical Assistant[a] | PACE[b] | Air Traffic Controllers | | |
| FY 74 | | | | | | | | |
| Applications | 275,201 | 184,213 | 60,788 | 69,630 | 187,569 | 23,898 | 801,299 | 1,620,798 |
| Selections | 49,650 | 32,593 | 11,315 | 5,198 | 12,457 | 1,809 | 113,022 | 237,278 |
| Veterans selected | 1,747 | 2,953 | 334 | 1,486 | 3,988 | 1,407 | 11,915 | 70,644 |
| FY 75 | | | | | | | | |
| Applications | 283,675 | 173,821 | 80,053 | 96,824 | 219,947 | 15,794 | 870,114 | 1,682,046 |
| Selections | 42,707 | 24,639 | 11,085 | 10,274 | 12,562 | 2,423 | 103,690 | 192,818 |
| Veterans selected | 1,609 | 2,191 | 303 | 3,186 | 4,174 | 1,812 | 13,275 | 56,378 |
| FY 76 | | | | | | | | |
| Applications | 260,613 | 163,248 | 72,523 | 56,819 | 235,333 | 14,686 | 931,519 | 1,676,936 |
| Selections | 36,823 | 23,343 | 8,967 | 5,147 | 9,304 | 1,853 | 85,437 | 156,534 |
| Veterans selected | 1,541 | 2,405 | 199 | 1,565 | 2,619 | 1,304 | 9,633 | 42,948 |

|  | | | | | | | |
|---|---|---|---|---|---|---|---|
| Transition quarter 76[c] | | | | | | | |
| Applications | 60,051 | 43,784 | 1,563 | 12,920 | 23,361 | 4,933 | 146,612 | 348,547 |
| Selections | 9,090 | 4,746 | 3,798 | 1,351 | 2,303 | 390 | 21,678 | 39,491 |
| Veterans Selected | 460 | 587 | 54 | | 744 | 316 | 2,568 | 11,039 |
| FY 77 | | | | | | | |
| Applications | 256,789 | 175,382 | 65,430 | 56,236 | 219,210 | 18,229 | 791,276 | 1,671,119 |
| Selections | 34,455 | 18,724 | 7,860 | 5,085 | 6,748 | 1,728 | 74,600 | 151,614 |
| Veterans selected | 1,672 | 2,177 | 151 | 1,394 | 2,095 | 1,213 | 8,702 | 44,781 |
| FY 78 | | | | | | | |
| Applications | 253,159 | 176,520 | 45,111 | 34,380 | 166,440 | 13,055 | 688,665 | 1,616,178 |
| Selections | 37,208 | 21,591 | [d] | 5,221 | 7,587 | 2,294 | 73,935 | 152,771 |
| Veterans selected | 1,853 | 2,480 | [d] | 1,435 | 2,072 | 1,615 | 9,455 | 41,610 |

[a]Fiscal Years 1976-1978 Technical Assistant data are estimated.
[b]Figures for Fiscal Year 1974 are from the predecessor FSEE.
[c]Fiscal Year 1976 ended June 30, 1976. Fiscal Year 1977 began October 1, 1976.
[d]Data not available.

SOURCE: Data from U.S. Office of Personnel Management; see also Campbell (1979:18).

In federal examining practice, the word "examination" refers to the complete set of procedures by which assessment and ranking of candidates for employment are made. "Test" refers to a written test, which may or may not be a part of any given examination. The examining process may include as well preemployment interviews; physical, experience, education, or training requirements; determinations of suitability based on personal history; and a probationary period.

A report on the status of test usage by the CSC (Wing 1977) indicated that sixty-three different standardized tests were used, singly or in combination, to fill entry-level federal positions in approximately 300 occupations. Data from this study are presented in Table 11 for six major examinations, all of which used written tests for clerical and lower-level occupations and for entry-level professional and administrative occupations. About half of the total number of applicants for federal positions seek the jobs covered by these examinations. In May 1979, Alan K. Campbell, Director of OPM, supplied 1978 figures in a statement to a U.S. House of Representatives hearing on the Professional and Administrative Career Examination (PACE). In that year, out of some 1.6 million applications, almost 700,000 applicants were given written tests, a ratio that is consistent with the earlier years (see Table 11). Of the sixty-three standardized tests, Campbell (1979:18-19) said:

OPM's written tests are used mainly for selecting persons for entry level positions, in which extensive experience is neither expected nor required. The tests are mostly designed to predict an untrained applicant's ability to function on the job after being hired. As a result, the majority of the tests measure cognitive abilities such as the ability to read and comprehend material which is similar to that for the target job, quantitative reasoning, and abstract reasoning. A few tests, such as the librarian equivalency tests, measure specific knowledge required for entry into a particular job. Still others measure specific skills such as typing speed and accuracy, which are measured directly by performance tests.

*Use of Tests for Guidance and Placement*

Another aspect of federal involvement in testing is the cooperative development and validation of guidance tests with state employment agencies under the auspices of the U.S. Employment Service (USES), a division of the Department of Labor's Employment and Training Administration. The tests are used primarily by some 2,400 local offices of state employment service agencies to provide vocational guidance and counseling to persons seeking employment. The tests are also used for job referrals and for recommendations for training program participation. Most well-known is the General Aptitude Test Battery (GATB), but USES also pro-

## Current Use of Tests for Employment

vides tests of proficiency in dictation, typing, and spelling and a series of Oral Trade Questions.

State employment services have been using the GATB since 1947 to help place workers in suitable jobs. Local schools sometimes arrange for the state employment service to give this test to students for counseling purposes. The GATB consists of twelve tests and provides scores in the following aptitudes: verbal, numerical, spatial, form perception, clerical perception, motor coordination, finger dexterity, and manual dexterity. The last two tests are apparatus tests; the others are written tests. Scores are compared with patterns of workers' scores in twenty-three different occupations covering about 600 different jobs.

## Evaluation and Discussion

Until recently, OPM has had major responsibility for test development, administration, and interpretation for two-thirds of the civilian work force of the federal government. Three organizational units of OPM, all in the Staffing Service Group, deal with examining. Job analysis information, collected by the Standards Development Center, is one input for the psychologists in the Personnel Research and Development Center (PRDC). With a staff of about seventy psychologists and support personnel, PRDC provides technical support for OPM examination programs and guidance to other agencies. An annual budget of $2 million supports test development, research, and scientifically based support for personnel policies, standards, and practices. The Division of Staffing, which is responsible for the operational examining system, develops and administers most examinations (McKillip et al. 1980). The tests used are generally "broadband," i.e., a single test that can be used as a selection device for a number of jobs. Therefore, they contain job-relevant, but not job-specific, content.

Under the provisions of the 1978 Civil Service Reform Act, however, the Director of OPM is empowered to delegate, in whole or in part, authority for competitive examinations to the heads of agencies in the executive branch and other agencies employing persons in the competitive service. With some exceptions, OPM may not delegate examining authority with respect to positions that have requirements common to a number of agencies in the federal government. A considerable amount of delegation is under way. OPM will, in general, retain responsibility for the administration and scoring of written tests. At the same time, PRDC and OPM generally are giving special attention to a variety of alternative selection procedures.

In response to criticism of the Federal Service Entrance Examination

(FSEE superseded by PACE) in the early 1970s (e.g., Sadacca and Brackett 1971) and the impact of the federal guidelines, OPM chose a construct validation strategy for PACE and has pursued a number of criterion-related studies as well. It has also examined issues of differential validity and validity generalization. Responding to recent charges of adverse impact, i.e., different passing ratios of minorities and women as compared to whites and males, OPM cited these studies and reported that it has pursued alternate means of entry as a solution. According to Campbell (1979:35) at present:

... the majority of employees in the 118 occupations covered by PACE are selected through means other than the competitive examination. Our estimate of the relative percentages is about 65% non-PACE entry as opposed to 35% through PACE.

This statement points to an interesting trend that surfaces in the data on civilian government test use. While it is often true that an individual must pass a test in order to become eligible for a job, there is no evidence that tests are the only, or even the most favored, device in a complex selection process, which will become more complex under the Civil Service Reform Act. As long ago as 1971, when the FSEE was a requirement for eligibility for job appointment, Sadacca and Brackett (1971:2) stated:

Passing the FSEE does not insure the appointment of an applicant. . . . As appropriate vacancies develop in the various federal agencies, the FSEE scores, education, and job experience of the applicants are appraised against the requirements of the agency positions. The emphasis placed on the FSEE in the final appraisal of an applicant varies from agency to agency and within each agency . . . across the job spectrum. However, in general, the higher the FSEE score, the greater the probability an applicant will receive an appointment.

Since no data were presented to support the last sentence, it is difficult to tell whether the statement is true, or only a widely shared impression. With the advent of alternate pathways, the fragmentation of the examining process under the Civil Service Reform Act, and the continuing lack of complete records on selection, it may become even more difficult to determine the impact of tests in the federal government selection process. OPM has not kept sufficient records to make such a determination. Even though the federal guidelines now require that records be kept on applicant race, sex, and ethnicity, OPM in 1979 admitted to major problems in meeting this requirement (Campbell 1979:7):

Where we do not have automated certification historical records kept—the usual case—the tracking of applicants to the point of hire is difficult and requires

## Current Use of Tests for Employment

significant resources. If a tracking system should be set up for all modes of entry, it would cost about $1 million. In our current system for tracking Federal employees, we have no records concerning how people were considered for any position, nor how many people were considered for the positions.

OPM plans, however, "to collect these data on high priority examinations which have a likelihood for high adverse impact and on high volume examinations" (Campbell 1979:7).

As stated earlier, OPM has had responsibility for two-thirds of the federal civilian work force. Information on the other one-third is not readily available. Given this lack of information and the limited information on the selection process itself in examinations where tests are used, it is difficult to draw conclusions as to the impact of tests on the selection process. No data at all were found on use of testing in the promotion process.

### Description of State and Local Government Work Force

The pattern established by the federal government for selection and promotion, based on education and experience requirements and objective examinations, has been variously adopted by the states in an effort to base government employment decisions on merit rather than patronage. States employ some 2 million people through their civil service systems. In addition, there are an unknown number of employees in the nonmerit system portion of the fourteen states that do not have a merit system throughout their jurisdictions. Thousands of agencies at the local level engage in employment testing or other selection procedures for the more than 9 million employees of local governments. The larger local governments typically have a merit system. The personnel needs of this combined population of close to 13 million full- and part-time employees are managed by a much more diverse group of agencies than that of the considerably smaller federal government system.

A principal reason for the difference in size derives from the provision of educational services, which account for about half of all jobs in state and local goverment—more than 6.5 million jobs in all, over 5 million of them at the local level. The next largest field of employment is health services at 1.3 million jobs, evenly split between state and local levels. More than 500,000 people work in street and highway construction and maintenance, more than half of them at the local level. More than 600,000 people are engaged in police protection, most of them at the local level, and almost 300,000 people are engaged in fire protection, all of them at the local level. Close to 400,000 people work in public welfare activities, more than half of them at the local level. An additional 1 million people work in sanitation, parks, natural resources, and financial administration areas. Other miscellaneous activities involve some 2 million employees, three-fourths of them at the local level.

A survey of occupational areas based on reports from state governments and a sample of county, municipal, township, and special jurisdictions is presented in Table 12. Excluded are educational services and part-time employees.

## Test Use in State and Local Government

### Use of Tests for Selection

Given the massive and diverse nature of state and local government systems, a complete picture of their test use would necessitate surveys specifically focused on test development, use, and validation procedures.

In the absence of such specific studies, four surveys that contain elements of the necessary information are reported here: two OPM (CSC) Annual Statistical Reports on State and Local Personnel Systems (1975 and 1979); a 1970 *Survey of Current Personnel Systems in State and Local Governments*, conducted by the National Civil Service League (Rutstein 1971); and an *Analysis of Baseline Data Survey on Personnel Practices for States, Counties, Cities*, conducted by OPM and the Council of State Governments (CSG) (1979).

The OPM *State and Local Personnel Systems, 1978 Annual Statistical Report* (U.S. Office of Personnel Management 1979) indicated that 220 state and local merit system personnel agencies (serving 2.9 million employees) received more than 4.5 million applications for open competitive

TABLE 12   State and Local Government in 1977: Employment by Occupational Area

| Occupation | No. of Full-Time Employees |
|---|---|
| Officials/administrators | 227,000 |
| Professionals | 778,000 |
| Technicians | 436,000 |
| Protective service | 615,000 |
| Paraprofessionals | 360,000 |
| Office/clerical | 826,000 |
| Skilled craft | 382,000 |
| Service/maintenance | 791,000 |
| TOTAL | 4,415,000 |

SOURCE: Bureau of the Census (1979).

## Current Use of Tests for Employment

selection and promotional examinations in 1977 and again in 1978. In 1978 more than 3 million of these applications (fewer than in 1977) were made to state agencies and more than 1.3 million (more than in 1977) to local agencies.

The same report also provided information on more than 3,000 state and local grant-aided agencies covered by the intergovernmental Merit System Standards (see Standards 1979), which employed an additional 600,000 people. Some 69 percent of the jobs in these state agencies were filled competitively, as were 47 to 79 percent of the jobs in local agencies.

The earlier 1974 CSC report (U.S. Civil Service Commission 1975) sheds some light on the question of how many of these job examinations required written tests, although it does not indicate how many written tests were actually administered. In FY 1974, some 2.6 million applications were received by state agencies and 800,000 by local agencies. Open competitive examinations were held for 18,010 state classes ("class" indicates both job and job level, e.g., Typist I) and 6,872 local classes. Of those totals, 62 percent of the state examinations (11,077) and 41 percent of the local examinations (2,820) relied heavily on a single selection device (in addition to an initial interview and a minimum education or experience requirement), but no information was provided to indicate which selection device was most favored. In the remaining 38 percent of state examinations and 59 percent of local examinations, a variety of selection devices were used, written tests most frequent. Table 13 summarizes the types of selection devices and the number of classes for which each was used.

In addition to the tests used for the job classes described in the OPM report, many state and local agencies examine for job classes not covered by the Intergovernmental Merit System Standards. Written tests are used in some of these examinations. While comprehensive data on the number of tests used do not exist, it is known, for example, that in 1978 the International Personnel Management Association supplied requesting jurisdictions with close to 100,000 tests for several levels of police officers and firefighters.

In 1970 a *National Civil Service League Survey* (Rutstein 1971) was sent to more than 500 state, county, and municipal governments (only those governments employing over 500 employees, exclusive of educational and institutional staff). Responses were received from 45 state units, 110 county units, and 202 municipal units, representing "coverage of over 2.5 million public employees, or about 55 percent of all state and local public workers, outside of educational organizations in the United States as of February, 1970" (Rutstein 1971:1).

TABLE 13 State and Local Personnel Selection (FY 1974)

| State Personnel Systems | Number of Classes Using Various Selection Devices | | | | | | |
|---|---|---|---|---|---|---|---|
| | Rating of Training and Experience | Written | Performance | Oral | | Following Directions | Other |
| | | | | Group | Individuals | | |
| All | 8,371 | 9,171 | 838 | 54 | 1,387 | 18 | 329 |
| Jurisdiction-wide | 6,126 | 6,651 | 635 | 16 | 1,077 | 10 | 219 |
| Cooperative | 2,115 | 2,108 | 163 | 34 | 285 | 3 | 11 |
| Single agency | 130 | 412 | 40 | 4 | 25 | 5 | 99 |
| Local personnel systems | 3,797 | 4,716 | 947 | 39 | 3,702 | 114 | 175 |

SOURCE: U.S. Civil Service Commission (1975:6).

## Current Use of Tests for Employment

The report's findings indicated the following:

—Eight out of ten public employees were merit system employees. (This conclusion may be unjustified, however, since a greater proportion of states (88.2 percent) responded than of counties (53.9 percent) or cities (64.5 percent). It is likely that states have a greater proportion of employees under a merit system than do counties and cities.)

—More than three-quarters of a million state and local government job opportunities developed each year—exclusive of positions in educational institutions (extrapolated figures).

—For hiring of unskilled workers: 35 percent of respondents used written tests; 37 percent, oral tests; and 27 percent, performance (or "hands on") tests. Local governments made less use of written tests than states, but more use of oral and performance tests. Experience, education, good character, and residence requirements might also be included.

—For hiring of skilled workers: 66 percent of respondents used written tests; 41 percent, oral tests; and 46 percent, performance tests. Local governments made more use of all three methods than states.

—For hiring the entry-level office worker: 88 percent of respondents used written tests; 33 percent, oral tests; and 77 percent, performance tests. Local governments made less use of written and performance tests than states, but more use of oral tests.

—For hiring the entry-level administrative, professional, and technical workers: 65 percent of respondents used written tests; 58 percent, oral tests; and 13 percent, performance tests. Local governments made less use of written tests than states, but more use of oral and performance tests.

### Analysis of Baseline Data Survey on Personnel Practices for States, Counties, Cities

In 1977, the National League of Cities, the National Association of Counties and the Council of State Governments, in cooperation with OPM (CSC), surveyed the governments of 50 states, 2,100 cities, and 1,201 counties (U.S. Office of Personnel Management and Council of State Governments 1979). Responses were received from 48 states, 372 cities, and 165 counties, of which a sample of 48 states, 101 cities, and 140 counties were selected as a representative basis for reporting information. Issues of interest here include use of selection procedures, job analysis, validation procedures, and criteria for promotion.

Selection procedures were reported for states only. Tables 14 and 15 indicate use of written tests, performance tests, ratings of training and

TABLE 14 State Selection Procedures: Number and Percent of States Using Each Procedure, by Occupation (1977)

| Occupations | Written Test | Performance Test | Rating of Training and Experience | Assessment Center | Interviewer | Other |
|---|---|---|---|---|---|---|
| Clerical | 43 states 89.6% | 38 states 79.2% | 12 states 25% | None — | 17 states 35.4% | None — |
| Trades and labor | 25 states 52.1% | 6 states 12.5% | 34 states 70.8% | None — | 16 states 33.3% | 3 states 6.3% |
| Professional | 38 states 79.2% | 1 state 2.1% | 42 states 87.5% | 2 states 4.2% | 34 states 70.8% | 4 states 8.3% |
| Technical | 40 states 83.3% | 6 states 12.5% | 37 states 77.1% | None — | 26 states 54.8% | 3 states 6.3% |
| Management and administrative | 28 states 58.3% | None — | 40 states 83.3% | 5 states 10.4% | 32 states 66.7% | 5 states 10.4% |

SOURCE: U.S. Office of Personnel Management and Council of State Governments (1979:11).

TABLE 15 State Selection Procedures: Prevalence of Use in Occupations (1977)

| Exam Method | Highest Use for: | Used, but Used Least for: |
|---|---|---|
| Written test | Clerical | Trades/labor |
| Performance test | Clerical | Professional |
| Ratings of training and experience | Professional | Clerical |
| Assessment center | Managerial/administrative | Professional |
| Interviews | Professional | Trades/labor |

SOURCE: U.S. Office of Personnel Management and Council of State Governments (1979:11).

experience, assessment centers, interviews, and other methods. Written tests are used for all occupations surveyed by more than half the states, but, as is the case in private sector employment, they are used most often for clerical occupations.

Job analysis was considered by the report to be "the process of obtaining and analyzing job-related information." It was not defined at all in the actual questionnaire, which asked only if job analysis were used in development of class specifications and in development and revision of selection procedures. Table 16 compares the findings for states, counties, and cities. Two key findings of the report were that 39 percent of the cities and 24 percent of the counties did not use job analysis in developing class specifications and that 29 percent of the cities and 22 percent of the counties did not use job analysis in developing or revising selection procedures.

The OPM-CSG questionnaire did not succeed in eliciting accurate

TABLE 16 Use of Job Analysis in States, Counties, Cities (1977)

| | Class Specifications | | | Selection Procedures | | |
|---|---|---|---|---|---|---|
| | Yes | No | N/R | Yes | No | N/R |
| States | 75% | 21% | 4% | 90% | 2% | 8% |
| Cities | 53% | 39% | 8% | 70% | 29% | 1% |
| Counties | 53% | 24% | 23% | 67% | 22% | 11% |

N/R = No response.
SOURCE: U.S. Office of Personnel Management and Council of State Governments (1979).

information on what percentage of examinations were validated and by what means because there was some confusion on the part of the respondents concerning the question, "Do you have written procedures for conducting 1) content validity studies? 2) criterion-related studies? 3) construct validity studies? If yes, show %." Percentage of what was not clear, especially since the question referred to procedures. The report concluded that the percentages reported might have been of total validity studies, of all examinations, or most likely, of written examinations. Any hope for accuracy was further clouded by the fact that respondents may have purchased tests which had already been validated and therefore did not report them, as well as by the fact that the survey reported results differently by state, county, and city. Nonetheless, the survey makes clear that content validity studies were used most often by all three governmental systems: 33 states (68 percent), 18 cities (17.8 percent), and 17 counties (12 percent) had written procedures for conducting content validity studies. Written procedures for criterion-related validity studies were reported by only 16 states (33 percent), 9 cities (9.3 percent), and 7 counties (5 percent), and written procedures for construct validity studies were reported by 4 states (8.5 percent), 4 cities (4.3 percent), and 6 counties (4.3 percent).

A small portion of the cities had been using personnel measurement consultants. Twelve cities had used them for development of written tests, five for the development of other selection procedures, thirteen for validation of selection procedures, and three for other purposes. Thirty-three counties indicated that they were using outside consultants to develop written tests, develop other selection procedures, and validate selection procedures presently being used.

In response to the OPM-CSG question, "Of the following issues, which five will be most important to your jurisdiction in the next two years?", improvement and validation of selection procedures was the most frequently cited issue for states (36 states or 76.6 percent), sixth most frequently cited issue for cities (50 cities or 50 percent), and third most frequently cited issue for counties (80 counties or 57 percent). In response to the question "With which of the major personnel issues, if any, will you need outside assistance during the next two years?", improvement and validation of selection procedures was the most frequently cited issue for all governments. From whom would the states, cities, and counties be most likely to seek assistance? Two organizations were identified by all three levels of government as being among the top five sources of assistance: OPM and the International Personnel Management Association. Private consultants, as a group, were among the top five preferred sources for both states and cities, and tied for sixth place with the counties.

Holmen and Docter (1972:63) point out that state and local govern-

## Current Use of Tests for Employment

ments adapt to special conditions that are not faced by private employers. One major problem is the difficulty in maintaining confidentiality of test questions. The exposure of test questions limits not only reuse of the tests but the cost effectiveness of efforts to validate them as well. As a result, these employers depend more on the development of job-knowledge tests based on expert judgment.

*Use of Tests for Promotion*

Only two of the surveys discussed above reported information in regard to the use of tests in the promotion process, and much of that was ambiguous.

The National Civil Service League study (Rutstein 1971) reported the following: for unskilled workers, written test results ranked sixth after performance in present job, general experience, seniority, supervisory evaluation, and trial in new job; for skilled workers, written test results ranked third after performance in present position and general experience; for office work employees, written tests ranked second after performance; for entry-level administrative, professional, or technical employees, they Because the questionnaire was not included in the study report, it is diffcult to determine whether respondents used all the promotion procedures described above or whether single procedures were used by some and combinations were used by others. In the case of combinations, there was no mention of the weighting of each procedure.

The OPM-CSG (1979) survey indicated only that written tests were used for promotions to fill most vacancies in 33.3 percent of the states surveyed. Criteria such as training, experience, and supervisor's ratings are used in making promotion decisions in 81.3 percent of the states (see Table 17).

## Discussion and Evaluation

The 220 state and local merit system personnel agencies, which serve fewer than one-fourth of the state and local government personnel, employ some 11,000 persons, more than half of them administrative, technical, and professional staff. The latest OPM-CSG survey (1979) calculated ratios of the number of personnel employees to that of all general government employees covered by the personnel system. The resultant comparisons are as follows:

States—1 personnel employee to 151.4 general government employees;

TABLE 17   Promotions in States (1977)

| | |
|---|---|
| No formal, written procedure exists. | 7 states 14.6% |
| Qualified employees are automatically considered for promotions without having to apply. | 1 state 2.1% |
| There are written tests for promotion to fill most vacancies. | 16 states 33.3% |
| Only qualified employees who apply are considered for promotions. | 38 states 79.2% |
| Criteria such as training, experience, and supervisors' ratings are used in making promotion decisions. | 39 states 81.3% |
| Promotions are often made on a noncompetitive basis. | 22 states 45.8% |

SOURCE: U.S. Office of Personnel Management and Council of State Governments (1979).

Cities—1 personnel employee to 279.3 general government employees;
Counties—1 personnel employee to 141.3 general government employees.

Office of Personnel Management annual report data (U.S. Civil Service Commission 1975) reviewed above indicate that these agencies use a variety of sources for their written tests:

—Primary sources of written tests for state merit system agencies included merit system staff, staff of other in-state agencies, OPM, and the International Personnel Management Association (IPMA). Other sources include consultants, the Professional Examination Service (PES), commercially available tests, and agencies in other states.

—Primary sources of written tests for local merit system agencies included merit system staff, staff of other in-state agencies, and IPMA. Other sources included commercially available tests, consultants, PES, and OPM.

The OPM-CSG (1979) survey also indicated that OPM, IPMA, and private consultants would be primary sources for future assistance in improving and validating selection procedures. From these surveys, it appears that the quality of tests varies considerably because of the great number of state and local agencies engaged in testing, the variety of test sources used, and the use by many agencies of the services of their own staff to prepare and administer tests. Holmen and Docter (1972:68) commented as follows about written tests used by both state and local governments:

Tests used for employment by state and local governments generally are part of a system oriented selection-and-placement process; further, all elements are generally under the control of a single person or agency. Although these organizations tend to lump all similar jobs together, they do study the job requirements more thoroughly than is the case in industrial personnel selection. At the federal and state level, test development is usually competently done by professionals in personnel testing. At the local level, there is much more emphasis on test items than on tests; in fact, tests are most often simply assembled from previously used items which appear useful for a job or job family. New items are developed to test for any unique aspects (such as geography or specialized equipment) of the job for which the test is being developed.

Such single-use tests are difficult to evaluate. It must be assumed that the fragmentation in this method of test development contributes to the wide variance in test quality. However, important questions are being asked in a systematic manner by the state and local government system itself, as pressure from legislation, *Uniform Guidelines*, and other sources mounts.

Growing concern over the lack of job analysis data and the need for improvement and validation of selection procedures is evidenced in the OPM-CSG survey reported above, especially about county reports of infrequent classification and compensation review and tests based on job specifications that are not themselves based on job analysis. This concern relates to the impact of the Kirkland case (U.S. Office of Personnel Management and Council of State Governments 1979:58).

The 1974 Kirkland case was a class action suit challenging the constitutionality of the New York State Civil Service Commission's promotional examination for correctional sergeants. The examination was based partly upon information gained from a job audit, which contained skill, knowledge, and ability statements. The court ruled the job audit inappropriate because it was outdated (2 years old) and developed for salary purposes rather than for examination preparation. Furthermore, the job audit did not indicate the relative importance of the skills and tasks or the competency required. Moreover, the persons who prepared the audit did not participate in the construction of the examination, nor was their competency to conduct the audit established by the record. Under such conditions the court found the class specification useless, which meant it could not form the basis for the examination.

This case provides a statement of the changes that have come to employment testing, also reflected in the following statement about cities, from the U.S. Office of Personnel Management and Council of State Governments report (1979:38):

The cities may have been in a very vulnerable position from two viewpoints. One, do their examinations screen for necessary-at-entry job related knowledge, skills and abilities? And, two, without documentation of examination validity they are open to lawsuits that their tests are based upon criteria which dscriminate against minorities and are not job related.

The OPM-CSG survey report (1972:12) made an observation about another selection procedure as well:

Chart 5, Selection Methods, showed a heavy reliance by the states on ratings of training and experience (commonly called T & E's) as a selection device. It is very likely that most of these T & E's have not been validated. Additionally, reliability is difficult to establish for T & E's: reliability from rater to rater and of the same rater over time. Generally written tests, which are especially used for large population classes at the entry level, have had first priority in validity efforts. However, the fact remains that a vast amount of work remains in establishing validity and reliability for T & E's which impact upon many applicants for a broad range (variety) of classes.

In sum, the surveys reviewed here reveal a rather incomplete picture of the role of written tests in the state and local employment selection processes. Early data (U.S. Civil Service Commission 1975) indicated that, when used with other selection procedures, written tests were the most frequently used procedure, but no information was provided on the weight assigned to test scores in the selection process, nor on which procedure was most favored in examinations where only one selection procedure was used. Nor did the National Civil Service League data (Rutstein 1971) indicate what weight was assigned to tests in the selection process. This survey did report that the selection process is complicated by the fact that some agencies may select any qualified applicant, while others may select only one of the top three or five applicants and that procedures varied within agencies, depending on the type of job being selected for. The latest OPM-CSG survey (1979) indicated that there is no longer a single selection procedure for any one occupational group. Written tests were used most often for clerical and technical occupations, but performance tests, ratings of training and experience, and interviews were also used for these occupational groups. Again, no information was provided on the weight assigned to test scores, but the following statement (U.S. Office of Personnel Management and Council of State Governments 1979:36), made as part of a discussion on the importance of recruitment

## Current Use of Tests for Employment

in the selection process, puts the process itself and the role of tests in an appropriate perspective:

It is difficult to ascertain where recruiting ends and the screening process begins. It can be said that the screening process involves 1) finding (learning about) job vacancies and 2) filling out an application acceptably, passing one or more kinds of tests (written, performance, etc.), interviewing well and completing the probationary period.

### Occupational and Professional Licensing

The right to practice a given occupation may be restricted by law where such action is decreed necessary to protect the public health, safety, or welfare. Occupational licensing in the United States is based for the most part on state legislation, although some licensing is authorized by local ordinance or federal legislation. Since the enactment of laws regulating physicians during the latter part of the nineteenth century, there has been an enormous proliferation of state licensure laws. A recent survey of state licensing by the U.S. Department of Labor (Greene and Gay 1980) estimates that at least 800 different occupations are regulated by law in one or more states and that, in perhaps 500 of these, passing a written test is required, in addition to such other requirements as those relating to education, training, experience, citizenship, residence, and good moral character.

The number of regulated occupations varies greatly from state to state. Readily available examples of the extent of licensing are provided in listings of the occupations that come under the jurisdiction of the California Department of Consumer Affairs, the New York Department of Professional Regulation, and the Florida Department of Professional and Occupational Regulation (see Tables 18, 19, and 20). Missing from some of these lists are such occupations as real estate or life insurance salesmen and brokers. These occupations, too, are regulated, but by other departments of state government. These tables indicate that, for the occupations listed, there were 110,000 new examinees in California in 1978-1979 and 55,473 in New York. Halstead (1974) reported that in Florida well over 27,000 new examinations were given each year by twenty-seven examining and licensing boards, which oversee a total of about 250,000 practitioners.

*Test Use in Licensing*

Consolidated figures on test use for licensing are not generally available. However, one state report, *Fair Employment Implications of Licensing*

TABLE 18  California's Licensing Boards and Examinees, 1979

| Independent Boards and Agencies | Total No. of Licensees | No. of Examinees 1978-1979 | Passing Percent 1978-1979 |
|---|---|---|---|
| Board of Accountancy | 31,668 | 10,876 | 47 |
| Board of Architectural Examiners | 10,000 | 3,900 | 60 |
| Board of Barber Examiners | 29,876 | 1,316 | 85 |
| Board of Cosmetology | 190,680 | 15,196 | 84 |
| Board of Behavioral Science Examiners | 19,017 | 2,497 | 84 |
| Cemetery Board | 1,810 | 291 | 89 |
| Contractors State License Board | 155,043 | 15,730 | 83 |
| Board of Dental Examiners | 34,163 | 6,302 | 60 |
| Board of Registration for Professional Engineers | 84,870 | 6,993 | 82 |
| Board of Fabric Care | 13,971 | 890 | 53 |
| Board of Funeral Directors and Embalmers | 3,931 | 189 | 79 |
| Board of Registration for Geologists and Geophysicists | 4,711 | 145 | 58 |
| Board of Guide Dogs for the Blind | 311 | 0 | 0 |
| Board of Landscape Architects | 1,371 | 330 | 50 |
| Board of Medical Quality Assurance | 73,311 | 2,844 | 73 |
| Acupuncture Committee | 879 | 55 | 75 |
| Hearing Aid Committee | 1,149 | 143 | 67 |
| Physicians Assistants | 1,490 | 0 | N/A |
| Physical Therapy Committee | 7,083 | 517 | 88 |
| Psychology Committee | 4,803 | 779 | 57 |
| Podiatry Examining Committee | 1,606 | 7 | 86 |
| Speech Pathology and Audiology Committee | 4,139 | N/A | N/A |
| Board of Registered Nursing | 187,182 | 10,146 | 88 |
| Board of Examiners of Nursing Home Administrators | 2,344 | 247 | 80 |
| Board of Optometry | 6,222 | 1,391 | 91 |
| Board of Pharmacy | 24,235 | 1,159 | 83 |
| Board of Certified Shorthand Reporters | 3,387 | 1,148 | 28 |
| Structural Pest Control Board | 7,343 | 4,119 | 25 |
| Board of Examiners in Veterinary Medicine | 4,888 | 515 | 53 |
| Board of Vocational Nurse and Psychiatric Technician Examiners | 79,171 | 8,232 | (66/59)[a] |
| Athletic Commission | 2,228 | 100 | 98 |

| Nonindependent Licensing Arms of the Department of Consumer Affairs | | | |
|---|---|---|---|
| Bureau of Automotive Repair | 97,821 | 10,947 | 69 |
| Bureau of Collection and Investigative Services | 200,000 | 2,294 | 59 |
| Bureau of Electronic and Appliance Repair | 9,179 | N/A | N/A |
| Bureau of Employment Agencies | 1,382 | 529 | 74 |
| Bureau of Home Furnishings | 21,432 | N/A | N/A |
| Tax Preparer Program | 12,627 | N/A | N/A |

[a] 6,933 Voc. Nurses were examined, 66% passed; 1,299 Psych. Techs were examined, 59% passed.
N/A = Not available.
SOURCE: Provided by the California Department of Consumer Affairs.

## Current Use of Tests for Employment

TABLE 19  New York's Licensees and Examinees, 1979

| Occupations | Total No. of Licensees | No. of Examinees (1979) |
|---|---|---|
| Public accountants | 4,113 | — |
| Certified Public Accountants | 22,543 | 13,582 |
| Acupuncturists | 32 | — |
| Architects | 6,907 | 1,524 |
| Chiropractors | 1,729 | 113 |
| Dentists | 14,560 | 11 |
| Dental hygienists | 6,929 | 339 |
| Engineers | 22,412 | 2,626 |
| Landscape architects | 455 | 42 |
| Land surveyors | 1,591 | 112 |
| Massagers | 1,268 | 168 |
| Occupational therapists | 1,570 | N/A |
| Occupational therapy assistants | 488 | N/A |
| Opthalmic dispensers | 2,201 | 909 |
| Optometrists | 1,903 | 124 |
| Registered nurses | 187,837 | 19,836 |
| Practical nurses | 64,744 | 8,404 |
| Pharmacists | 15,983 | 2,002 |
| Physical therapists | 3,373 | 571 |
| Physicians | 51,008 | 1,992 |
| Physician's assistants | 939 | N/A |
| Specialist's assistants | 9 | N/A |
| Podiatrists | 1,452 | 149 |
| Psychologists | 4,632 | 446 |
| Certified shorthand reporters | 314 | 70 |
| Certified social workers | 15,025 | 2,005 |
| Speech pathologists | 2,000 | N/A |
| Audiologists | 384 | N/A |
| Veterinarians | 1,779 | 161 |
| Animal health technicians | 421 | 287 |

N/A—Not available.
SOURCE: Personal communication from the New York State Education Department, Division of Professional Licensing Services.

*and Certification Standards* (State of California 1975:73) stated that "Written examinations are by far the most commonly used technique for assessing candidate competency among licensing boards in California. In fact, approximately 90 percent of the boards surveyed use some form of a written examination in the licensing process." More than thirty licensing boards were surveyed in this report.

Most of the tests produced for licensing purposes are job-related achievement tests used to determine if the individual would-be practi-

TABLE 20 Florida's Professional and Occupational Examining Boards and Examinees from 1969 to 1972

| Division of Professions | No. of Examinees 1969-1972 | Passing Percent 1969-1972 |
|---|---|---|
| Board of Accountancy | — | — |
| Board of Architecture | — | — |
| Board of Chiropractic Examiners | 445 | 73.7 |
| Board of Dentistry | 1,204 | 65.4 |
| Board of Professional Engineers and Land Surveyors | 2,876 | 80.6 |
| Board of Registration for Foresters | | |
| Board of Funeral Directors and Embalmers | 353 | 92.3 |
| Board of Examiners of Landscape Architects | 91 | 33.0 |
| Board of Medical Examiners | 6,965 | 69.8 |
| Board of Nursing | 6,879 | 69.4 |
| Board of Examiners of Nursing Home Administrators | — | — |
| Board of Optometry | 180 | 69.4 |
| Board of Osteopathic Medical Examiners | 1,250 | 90.4 |
| Board of Pharmacy | 1,442 | 93.3 |
| Board of Podiatry Examiners | 373 | 49.0 |
| Board of Examiners of Psychology | — | — |
| Board of Veterinary Medicine | 406 | 65.7 |
| Barber's Sanitary Commission | 2,389 | 82.0 |
| Construction Industry Licensing Board | 5,771 | 46.2 |
| Board of Cosmetology | 13,835 | 58.0 |
| Board of Electrical Contractors Licensing Board | — | — |
| Board of Massage | — | — |
| Board of Naturopathic Examiners | — | — |
| Board of Dispensing Opticians | — | — |
| Real Estate Commission | 36,475 | 80.6 |
| Sanitarian's Registration Board | 91 | 87.9 |
| Florida Watchmakers' Commission | — | — |
| AVERAGE | | 70.13 |

SOURCE: Halsted (1974).

tioner meets the standards of job knowledge and skills set by the responsible state licensing board. These tests may be used along with other elements of the licensing process, e.g., proof of completion of required courses, clinical training, or apprenticeship requirements. They can be used at different points in the process: early on as a screening device, or later, after other requirements have been met.

## Current Use of Tests for Employment

*Evaluation and Discussion*

Licensing tests are developed by a variety of people and groups ranging from state board members to professional testing agencies engaged by state boards or associations of the state boards. Most occupational licensing examinations are prepared by board members, who are usually practitioners in the licensed occupation or profession. Some occupations and professions use national examinations prepared by professional testing agencies working in close cooperation with state regulatory officials, practitioners, and educators from all parts of the country.

Locally prepared examinations have tended to vary in quality. A report entitled *Improving Occupational Regulation* (Shimberg 1976:39-40) summarized the views expressed by nearly one hundred licensing officials in thirty states who participated in four regional conferences.

> Locally prepared exams had few defenders among licensing administrators or other state officials. It was observed that such exams were frequently of inferior quality. They were seldom based on an up to date job analysis; questions were often ambiguously worded; there was a tendency to measure obscure parts; and both the content and difficulty of the test often fluctuated from one administration to the next. . . .

Locally prepared examinations are also criticized as being easier to misuse than are national examinations, an allegation given some support by Rayack and Stevens (n.d.). They studied passing rates on licensing examinations for twelve skilled occupations in four New England states and found that in every occupation, when the rate of unemployment was low, the passing rate on the licensing examination for that occupation tended to be high. When the rate of unemployment increased, however, the passing rate decreased. They also found statistical evidence that in ten out of the twelve occupations, this fluctuation was not a chance phenomenon. They concluded that boards use the examination system as a restrictive device, to reduce competition for scarce jobs, although they emphasized that other factors affect failure rates as well. Of course, this situation could obtain even with a national test, since states set their own passing scores for national as well as local tests.

In most professions, state licensing boards use national examinations when available. Officials from several states often form an association and then contract with a professional testing agency to develop, administer, and score the examination. In addition, some professional groups have established their own testing agencies (e.g., physicians and nurses), which develop national examinations for use by the states.

National tests are generally conceded to have certain advantages over locally prepared tests. Shimberg (1976:41-42) says:

> The quality of the tests is usually higher. What is to be covered by the test is usually considered on the basis of a careful job analysis. Questions are written by experts, reviewed by other experts, and subjected to item analysis. Security arrangements are generally good, as is the quality of scoring and reporting services.

However, he adds that:

> . . . the fact that an exam is offered for national use doesn't guarantee that it will be of high quality. It's up to the board to satisfy itself on these points before it adopts the exam; and it should check periodically to make sure that quality has been maintained.

There have been some differences of opinion as to whether or not licensing tests must conform to the provisions of the *Uniform Guidelines*. One aspect of the issue relates to the question of who is the "user" of a test and thus, who is responsible for its validity. The 1978 *Uniform Guidelines on Employee Selection Procedures* asserts, in its section on definition of a user (EEOC 1978:38308, Section 16, W) that:

> Whenever an employer, labor organization or employment agency is required by law to restrict recruitment for any occupation to those applicants who have met licensing or certification requirements, the licensing or certifying authority, to the extent it may be covered by Federal equal opportunity law, will be considered the user with respect to those licensing or certification requirements.

Thus the issue really hinges on the underlying legal statutes. National organizations representing the licensed professions, such as the Federation of Associations of Health Regulatory Boards, point out that neither Title VII of the Civil Rights Act of 1964 nor subsequent amendments to that act specifically mention licensing or certification agencies as falling within its scope. In several suits by individuals against state licensing agencies, federal courts have held generally that state licensing agencies are neither employers nor employment agencies under Title VII. Therefore licensing activities of state agencies, including examination requirements have been held not to be employment practices (see, for example, *Tyler v. Vickery, Parrish v. Board of Commissioners of Alabama State Bar*, and *Richardson v. McFadden*). There are a handful of lower federal court decisions apparently to the contrary (e.g., *Puntolillo v. New Hampshire Racing Commission, Sibley Memorial v. Wilson*), but the cases are factually distinguishable, insofar as licensure depended on considerations other than the assessment of competency.

## Current Use of Tests for Employment

Although this dispute must await resolution by Congress or the Supreme Court, licensing agencies are beginning to show some concern that their tests conform to guideline requirements. At least one state has acted to remove doubt that the *Uniform Guidelines* apply to licensing. The California legislature passed the Dixon Law (AB 1495) in its 1978-1979 session, making licensing examinations that fall under the California Department of Consumer Affairs subject to demonstration of job relatedness if they have an adverse impact.

**Trends**

Despite notable gaps in the information available, civilian government employment practices can be perceived as exhibiting similar trends to those already noted in the private sector.

—There is increased sensitivity to the challenges to hiring practices. The federal government is especially vulnerable to charges of discrimination and unfairness since OPM's predecessor, the Civil Service Commission, was a signatory of the *Uniform Guidelines*. Test fairness studies, validation studies, and alternate pathway studies are proceeding, but the use of written tests is not increasing in the federal government. Some believe the federal government may be adopting a more flexible procedure for appraising an individual's competence to fill a specific position. Policies of accepting proficiency based on experience records and other nontesting means of making employment decisions that heretofore required PACE or other examinations are cited as examples of this trend. If true, this may be an extension of longstanding policies regarding evaluation for promotion and appointment to higher level positions, where evidence of job performance, work-history information, etc., have been used instead of aptitude tests for many years. This trend is consistent with the policy of broader delegation of examining authority to agencies for selection and promotion.

—At all levels of government written tests appear to be used most heavily for clerical workers and other entry-level office workers. At local levels, written tests are also used heavily for police officers and firefighters.

—All levels seem to rely increasingly on multiassessment strategies rather than on one assessment device. It is not clear, however, whether multiassessment strategies use multiple cutoffs, a compensatory model, or a mixture.

—In state testing for selection and licensing, there is a trend toward a cooperative approach to testing in order to maximize resources. The Southern Regional Test Development Center provides an example of states cooperating to develop tests for various government job categories. In licensing, an example is the use of national tests developed by professional testing agencies that work closely with many states. Within states there is a trend toward state provision of technical assistance to licensing boards to help upgrade the quality of tests. New York State has for many years required all board tests to undergo review by testing specialists in the New York State Department of Education. Other states, including Illinois, Michigan, and Pennsylvania, have offered consultation services and other types of assistance to licensing boards. A number of states regularly monitor the licensing activities of their regulatory boards; most recently a 1979 Florida law authorized the Department of Occupational and Professional Regulation to carry on such monitoring. The secretary of the department can intervene if it is found that a test does not adequately measure the applicant's competence to practice.

—In licensing there is a trend toward periodic reassessment of competence for licensure. At present, many states are requiring, or considering requiring, practitioners to show evidence of participation in continuing education courses related to practice, in order to be allowed to continue to practice. As the correlation of continuing education to competence has come to be questioned, tests are being considered as a means of verifying an individual's continued competence. One example of a preliminary attempt is the decision by California to offer a test as an alternative to compilation of a specified number of continuing education credits required for nurse relicensure, with the individual nurse to make the decision on which route to take.

—Innovative testing techniques are being developed. OPM's recent interest in computerized, tailored testing, which provides individual examinees with only those questions appropriate to their particular level of ability, is an example. Examinees sit at a computer terminal with a keyboard and video display screen. Test items appear on the video screen, and as the examinee responds to each question, the computer makes a revised estimate of the candidate's ability. The test is terminated when a prespecified level of reliability is reached. In 1978, OPM stated that "computerized tailored testing offers improved accuracy of measurement at reduced costs, and a strong psychometric base for selection decision" (McKillip et al. 1980:17). While OPM is no longer able to fund this testing technique, the Department of Defense is moving ahead with it, and others are considering it. Elsewhere, written simulations, video presentations of tests, performance tests, oral examinations, and other techniques are being used in licensing for physicians, dentists, dental hygienists, etc.

# Current Use of Tests for Employment

## Other Considerations

A pertinent question that has not been discussed concerns the differences between occupation or job-specific tests, e.g., licensing tests, and what might be called construct based tests, e.g., PACE. The job-specific tests, while phrasing questions in terms of the job, are often broad-band tests in the sense that some of them sample the skills necessary to an entire occupation or profession. The construct based tests are broad-band in that they assess people for a number of occupations that require similar broad skills, and test questions may be job relevant but are not job specific. Both kinds of tests have been used. There are insufficient data about the advantages, disadvantages, and resulting utility of each in the selection process.

## MILITARY SECTOR

While the military is the smallest of the three sectors examined in this report, it has a vast, systematic testing program that includes the largest volume employment test in the nation. In addition to aptitude tests used to select applicants for enlisted duty in the armed services and for eligibility for officer and flight training, hundreds of job-specific tests are currently in use.

This report concentrates on the major tests in order to describe and evaluate military test usage and to determine trends.

## Description of Military Sector Work Force

At the end of FY 1978, the total number of military personnel on active duty was 2,062,404, the lowest since 1950. Table 21 (U.S. Department of Defense 1979) shows a manpower overview of total military strength, including national guard, reserves, and officer trainees, in addition to active duty personnel. Civilian employees are also shown but will not be discussed in this section, since they were included in the federal civilian government sector.

Table 21 also shows a breakdown of military personnel into officer, enlisted, and academy cadets by branch of service. It is to be noted that individuals enrolled in "in-service" officer training, i.e., Army Officer Candidate School (OCS), Air Force Officer Training School (OTS), and Marine Officer Candidate Corps (OCC), are not included in the academy cadet category. They are included in the enlisted category instead.

TABLE 21 Department of Defense Military/Civilian Personnel, September 30, 1978

| Type of Personnel | Total | Army | Navy | Marine Corps | Air Force | Other Defense Activities |
|---|---|---|---|---|---|---|
| Total active duty military | 2,062,404 | 771,624 | 530,253 | 190,815 | 569,712 | N/A |
| Officer | 274,275 | 97,785 | 62,639 | 18,388 | 95,463 | |
| Enlisted | 1,775,021 | 669,515 | 463,217 | 172,427 | 469,862 | |
| Academy cadets | 13,108 | 4,324 | 4,397 | — | 4,387 | |
| Total national guard and reserves | 2,118,394 | 1,177,956 | 337,395 | 97,531 | 505,512 | N/A |
| (in paid status) | (787,767) | (526,749) | (82,765) | (32,695) | (145,558) | |
| National guard | 441,516 | 349,615 | — | — | 91,901 | |
| (in paid status) | (432,670) | (340,996) | — | — | (91,674) | |
| Reserves | 1,676,878 | 828,341 | 337,395 | 97,531 | 413,611 | |
| (in paid status) | (355,097) | (185,753) | (82,765) | (32,695) | (53,844) | |
| Officer training in colleges[a] | 79,665[b] | 57,910 | 7,095 | — | 14,660 | N/A |
| Total civilian personnel[c] | 1,061,361 | 408,494 | 320,256[d] | — | 254,249 | 78,362 |
| Direct hire | 980,313 | 353,203 | 309,880 | — | 240,182 | 77,048 |
| Indirect hire | 81,048 | 55,291 | 10,376 | — | 14,067 | 1,314 |

[a] As of May 1978.
[b] Excludes 155,849 in Junior Division, Military Schools and National Defense Cadets Corps.
[c] Includes Civil Functions Employment of 34,563 Army and Air Force; also includes Disadvantaged Youth Employees.
[d] Includes Marine Corps personnel.

SOURCE: U.S. Department of Defense (1979).

## Current Use of Tests for Employment 153

### Test Use in the Military Sector

*Use of Tests for Selection-Classification*

A first view of the major armed services selection and classification tests can be bewildering. Many of the acronyms are similar, and some tests are composites (weighted scores of two or more tests from the same battery). Table 22 offers an outline of these selection and classification tests. Numbers and letters in the outline will be used to designate corresponding test descriptions in the text.

Although some of the tests outlined are used for school admissions, they are included in this report because they actually serve as employment tests, in that they are used to select for further training, guidance, and placement, after an applicant has entered the organization.

### Enlisted Personnel Eligibility Tests

*ASVAB—Armed Services Vocational Aptitude Battery*

A variety of aptitude tests have been used for military selection since World War I. In the mid-1970s, validated subtests from the various service test batteries were consolidated to form the ASVAB so that there would be a single test battery for use throughout the Department of Defense. The ASVAB was implemented as such in January 1976. Currently, one of three parallel forms is administered to applicants for military service to determine their eligibility to enlist and subsequently to classify successful applicants into the various military occupations. Further, a fourth form of ASVAB, similar in content, is administered as part of the department's high school testing program. Its results are provided to high school officials for counseling and to military recruiters for use in identifying high school graduates for potential enlistment, technical training, and employment in the armed services.

The ASVAB battery subtests include paragraph comprehension, numerical operations, coding speed, word knowledge, arithmetic reasoning, mathematical knowledge, electronics information, mechanical comprehension, general science, automotive and shop information.

The history of development of the ASVAB forms is interesting. In the late 1960s the first ASVAB (Form 1) was constructed from items in the files of the various services. It was used only in the DoD High School Testing Program to aid in recruiting qualified applicants. Two subsequent forms were constructed in the early 1970s by Army psychologists. Form 2 was used in the High School Testing Program. Form 3 was used by the Air Force and Marine Corps to replace their classification batteries. A fourth version was constructed for high school testing but was never used.

By 1975, three new versions of ASVAB (Forms 5, 6, and 7) were developed under the direction of the Air Force Human Resources Laboratory. In January 1976, Forms 6 and 7 were used by all services as the common DoD enlisted selection and classification test. Form 5, identical to Forms 6 and 7, except for the deletion of a noncognitive subtest included in Forms 6 and 7, was used in the High School Testing Program beginning in the fall of 1976. In October 1980, three new versions of ASVAB (Forms 8, 9, and 10) were introduced for operational use. Form 5 continued to be used in high schools.

Policies regarding the development, maintenance, and use of ASVAB are established by a committee of general officers representing all the services. Technical direction of ASVAB is accomplished by a working group of civilian and military test researchers and test policy staffers from each service. Research on the program is accomplished by the personnel research laboratories of the services, the Office of the Secretary of Defense, and the Military Enlistment Processing Command (MEPCOM), which is interservice in nature and includes both civilian professionals and military specialists. The test battery is used in military procurement by MEPCOM and operationally administered at Armed Forces Examining and Entrance Stations (AFEES), mobile testing sites, and high schools across the country.

In 1978, the ASVAB was administered to 601,782 applicants for military service. In addition, 965,409 students took the ASVAB during school year 1978-1979. Thus it is the largest volume employment test in the nation today. Only two other tests come close to matching ASVAB in volume—the SAT and the ACT, which are used primarily for admission to institutions of higher education.

*AFQT—Armed Forces Qualification Test*

The AFQT was originally developed to meet the requirement set by Congress for procedures to screen selective service registrants for military trainability. Since 1950, the AFQT has been the primary selection test used by all military services to determine enlistment eligibility.

With the implementation of the ASVAB, the AFQT became a composite of three of the ASVAB subtests and is no longer a separate screening test. Since October 1980, there have been four subtests that form the AFQT composite: word knowledge, paragraph comprehension, arithmetic reasoning, and numerical operations. In addition to AFQT, separate service composite aptitude scores are also developed for determining job assignments.

## Current Use of Tests for Employment

TABLE 22  Military Selection and Classification Tests

A. *Enlisted Personnel Eligibility Tests*
Armed Services Vocational Aptitude Battery (ASVAB)
The single DoD test battery. One version is given to applicants for military enlistment and another version is given to high school students.

Armed Forces Qualification Test (AFQT)
The primary test for enlistment screening. Used by all services. Now obtained as a composite from ASVAB.

B. *Officer Eligibility Tests*
   (1) Service Academies
       Scholastic Aptitude Test (SAT) or American College Test (ACT)

   (2) Reserve Officer Training Corps (ROTC)
       Army and Navy: SAT/ACT. Army may also use Cadet Evaluation Battery (CEB).

       Air Force: SAT/ACT scores if candidates have already taken them. If not, the Air Force Officer Qualifying Test (AFOQT) is used.

   (3) Officer Candidate Schools
       Army: CEB. For those who scored low on ASVAB, the Officer Candidate Test (OCT) is administered first, then the CEB.

       Navy: Officer Aptitude Rating (OAR). This is a composite formed from the Academic Qualification Test (AQT) and the Mechanical Comprehension Test of the Navy and Marine Corps Aviation Selection Test.

       Air Force: Officer Quality Composite of AFOQT

C. *Flying Training Program Eligibility Tests*
Army: Flight Aptitude Selection Tests (FAST)

Navy and Marine Corps: AQT and Flight Aptitude Rating (FAR)—both from Navy and Marine Corps Aviation Selection Test.

Air Force: Pilot and Navigator-Technical composites of AFOQT

D. *Other Widely Used Tests*
Defense Language Aptitude Test
Qualification for foreign language training

---

The AFQT has five categories or ranges of scores. Individuals scoring in the lowest 9 percent of a standard reference group are placed in Category V (commonly called Cat V). Individuals scoring from the 10th to 30th percentile are placed in Category IV. The 31st to 64th percentile comprises Category III, the 65th to 92nd percentile, Category II, and the 93rd to 100th percentile, Category I. Unless directed otherwise by the Secretary of Defense or by legislation, the services establish their own minimum standards for selection and assignment. Since its introduction, various minimum AFQT standards have been applied by the services, and, on the occasion of rapid personnel build-up of the active forces, by the Secretary of Defense. According to the Selective Service Act of 1958, in time of war the services must accept AFQT Category IV and above. They can accept Category V personnel, but traditionally they do not. Current entrance minimums are as follows:

—the Army requires a score at the 16th percentile for high school graduates and the 31st percentile for nongraduates;

—the Navy and Marine Corps require a score at the 21st percentile or higher to qualify for enlistment;

—the Air Force requires a score at the 21st percentile for high school graduates and the 65th percentile for nongraduates.

A DoD information release states that:

Determination of AFQT and Service composite score minimums are based upon two major considerations: (1) the ability levels considered necessary for successful performance in training and general adjustment to military service; and (2) supply and demand considerations in meeting accession and training quotas. Service aptitude composite minimums are changed when required to meet increased attrition in technical training and/or changes in training content.

**Officer Eligibility Tests**

There are three major types of officer education/training programs, completion of which leads to commissioned status: the U.S. Service Academies, Reserve Officer Training Corps (ROTC) programs, and Officer Candidate Schools. Written tests are an integral part of the selection process for each program, but are not the sole selection device for any of them.

*Service Academies*

Since the service academies offer academic programs similar to those of other colleges (as well as leadership training), they use either the Scholastic Aptitude Test (SAT) or the American College Test (ACT) in their selection processes. Both tests are college entrance examinations designed to measure general verbal and mathematical comprehension, the two cognitive abilities considered most predictive of success in academic work, and as such, felt to be of greatest use in admitting the most promising candidates to the academies. The SAT is developed by Educational

## Current Use of Tests for Employment

Testing Service for the College Entrance Examination Board, and ACT is developed by the American College Testing Program. It should be noted, however, that test scores are only one of several factors (e.g., high school grades, class rank, recommendations of teachers, participation in extracurricular activities) considered in making academy selections.

### Reserve Officer Training Corps (ROTC) Programs

Reserve officer training is offered at participating universities by the Army, Navy, and Air Force. Students take the training along with regular college courses and on successfully completing it are commissioned into their chosen service. Exceptionally well-qualified individuals are awarded ROTC scholarships. Except for the scholarship programs, screening for entry into ROTC occurs just prior to the junior year. Selections are based on the probability of success in the combined course work.

The Army and the Navy use the SAT/ACT for selection into ROTC. The Army also uses the Cadet Evaluation Battery (CEB) for admission to advanced ROTC programs. The Air Force uses SAT/ACT for applicants who have previously taken them and have readily available scores. If they have not, they are given a service developed and validated test, the Air Force Officer Qualifying Test (AFOQT).

*AFOQT—Air Force Officer Qualifying Test* The AFOQT is designed to evaluate aptitudes considered important for a variety of Air Force commissioned officer training programs. For example, one of the composites, officer quality, is one of the measures used in selecting individuals for the junior and senior years of ROTC college programs, AFROTC scholarships, and also for Officer Training School. The aptitude composites may also be used for counseling in order to help officer candidates find suitable military occupations.

Actually a test battery, it was developed by the Air Force Human Resources Laboratory and includes subtests on such subjects as math knowledge, data interpretation, reading comprehension, background for current events, electrical maze, mechanical comprehension, aerial landmarks, general science, and instrument comprehension. The subtests are combined to produce five composites: pilot, navigator-technical, officer quality, verbal, and quantitative. AFOQT is administered on a monthly basis to approximately 12,000 AFROTC scholarship and professional officer course applicants and 18,000 officer training school applicants each year.

*CEB—Cadet Evaluation Battery* The CEB is prepared by the U.S. Army Research Institute for the Behavioral and Social Sciences. It is designed to assist in assessing a cadet's leadership potential and career motivation. This battery was based on data collected in the course of administering situational tests at officer evaluation centers.

The battery consists of the cadet evaluation inventory and the cadet evaluation test. It includes seven subtests in such areas as combat leadership and technical-managerial leadership, which are combined to form three composite scores. It is administered on campuses to between 10,000 and 12,000 ROTC cadets each year and used for advanced ROTC program admissions or for counseling students about such programs.

## Officer Candidate Schools

A third source of commissioned officers are the officer candidate schools of the various branches of the service, for which only college graduates are eligible. All tests used in the selection process for these programs are service developed and validated.

The Army uses the Cadet Evaluation Battery (CEB) to screen applicants. Those enlisted personnel who had scored below 115 on the general technical composite of the ASVAB (word knowledge and arithmetic reasoning) are first given the Officer Candidate Test (OCT), and, if they attain a score of 115 or better, are permitted to proceed to the CEB. Two forms of OCT, introduced in 1967 and 1968, are currently in use. There are no plans to introduce new forms and no information on the number of candidates now being tested.

The Navy and the Marine Corps use the Officer Aptitude Rating (OAR) for their officer candidate school selections. The OAR is a composite formed from two tests of the U.S. Navy and Marine Corps Aviation Selection Test battery. The battery contains four tests which yield three scores. The tests are the Academic Qualification Test, the Mechanical Comprehension Test, the Spatial Apperception Test, and the Biographical Inventory. The three scores are: the Academic Qualification Test (AQT); the Flight Aptitude Rating (FAR), a composite of the Mechanical Comprehension test, the Spatial Apperception test, and the Biographical Inventory; and the Officer Aptitude Rating (OAR), a composite of the AQT and the Mechanical Comprehension Test.

Despite the name of the battery, the scores derived are used for selection for both aviation and nonaviation programs. The AQT and FAR are used as part of the screening for naval flight training. The OAR is used for officer candidate school selection, as noted. There are two forms of each test, with new forms introduced at approximately 10-year intervals.

## Current Use of Tests for Employment

Tests are administered almost on a daily basis to between 33,000 and 35,000 applicants each year.

The Air Force uses the officer quality composite of the AFOQT as one of several factors that are considered in selecting applicants for officer candidate school.

The composites used by the services for officer candidate school selection have been validated against a criterion of performance in the officer commissioning programs.

### Flying Training Program Eligibility Tests

In the Army, officer personnel volunteering for aviation training in rotary wing aircraft, as well as civilians and enlisted personnel volunteering for warrant officer flight training, must take the Flight Aptitude Selection Tests (FAST), which consist of five tests covering biographical information, mechanical principles, flight orientation, instrument comprehension, visualization of maneuvers, and helicopter knowledge. The scores are summed to provide a composite score, which is the basis for ranking applicants with scores above a pass/fail point. The FAST has been validated against the criterion of performance in rotary wing training. Enlisted personnel are also scored on an examining board interview.

In the Navy and the Marine Corps, composites from the U.S. Navy and Marine Corps Aviation Selection Test—the AQT measuring academic performance and validated using the criterion of performance in pre-flight ground school, and the FAR measuring abilities closely related to flying an airplane and validated against the criterion of passing flight training—are used to determine eligibility for all personnel.

In the Air Force, the pilot and navigator-technical composite scores from the Air Force Officer Qualifying Test are used to select candidates for these two types of training. Both composite tests have been validated against passing scores in the training courses.

### Other Widely Used Tests

The *Defense Language Aptitude Test* is used for determining qualifications of personnel for foreign language training. All officers and all enlisted personnel who score higher than 100 on the ASVAB general technical composite are eligible for the test. Two forms are in use.

Personnel who have completed training in a foreign language or who claim to possess a fair to fluent knowledge of a foreign language are eligible for a *Defense Language Proficiency Test* in any of thirty-four languages and dialects. Two tests in listening comprehension and reading comprehension yield scores, which are combined with a numerical code from a language proficiency questionnaire given to the test takers to produce proficiency ratings in listening and reading.

*Use of Tests for Promotion in the Military*

Each branch of the military service conducts its own extensive examination program for enlisted personnel promotion. These programs include written tests, which were administered to over 800,000 enlisted personnel in 1979. While systematic promotion programs also exist for officers, they do not include written tests.

*Army Enlisted Promotion Tests* Until recently the Army used the Military Occupational Specialty (MOS) test, a norm-referenced written test, as a proficiency indicator for promotion. In 1977 MOS tests were phased out and replaced by the Skill Qualification Tests (SQT) program, a criterion-referenced, performance-based testing system, which includes both hands-on and written components. SQT results are used by training personnel for the assessment of strengths and weaknesses, as well as by management personnel for promotion decisions. By the end of FY 1981, there will be over 900 separate tests, one for each occupational speciality and skill level through pay grade 7, and it is expected that all active enlisted personnel in pay grades 1-7 will have been tested by that time. Similar testing of the Army Reserve will be concluded by the end of FY 1982. In FY 1979, over 207,000 soldiers were tested.

*Navy Enlisted Advancement* This program is composed of three elements, each worth about one-third of the total score:

—Display of technical knowledge by taking a 150-item, multiple-choice, job knowledge test.
—Demonstration of job performance by review of supervisory rating evaluations.
—Experience factors, including time in pay grade, total time in Navy, bonus points for previously taking and passing the test, and certain combat and noncombat medals and awards (each factor worth 5 to 13 percent).

Written tests are based on job content from several sources including task analyses, Navy occupational standards manuals, and other technical, training, and administrative manuals. For enlisted personnel there are seventy basic occupations and 1,000 specialty classifications, some of which cut across occupations.

## Current Use of Tests for Employment

The Navy has nine enlisted pay grades:

—Tests are administered semiannually to pay grades 4, 5, and 6. These are unique tests for each occupation at each pay grade, in addition to subtests within occupations, which means that about eighty-five tests are administered at each of the three pay grades. Thus, over 250 tests may be administered to as many as 100,000 candidates every 6 months.

—Tests are administered annually to pay grades, 7, 8 and 9. About fifty tests are administered at each pay grade. Thus, about 150 tests are administered to as many as fifty to sixty thousand candidates every year.

For grades 4, 5, and 6, a composite score is generated from the written test, the supervisory ratings, and the experience factors, and individuals are put on an advancement list in rank order of score. Selection for advancement is made from these lists as needed. The lists are produced after each testing period, so if an individual has not been selected for advancement during one such period, he or she must take the test again in order to be put back on the list.

For grades 7, 8, and 9, a composite score is generated from the written test and performance ratings. Individuals are rank ordered, and the top half of the candidates are sent to selection boards for final selection. These individuals must also take the test again if not selected. Because there are fewer jobs available in these pay grades and job competition is keen, many candidates for advancement take the test several times.

*Marine Corps Enlisted Promotion* This program does not have a testing prerequisite for promotion. Local screening boards at the command level determine qualification for promotion to the ranks of grades 2 through 4, based on eligibility criteria established by Headquarters Marine Corps. Selection for promotion to grades 5 through 9 is accomplished by screening boards convened at Headquarters Marine Corps, based on eligibility criteria established by the commandant of the Marine Corps.

*Air Force Enlisted Promotion Tests* The Weighted Airman Promotion System (WAPS) is used for pay grades 5, 6, and 7. WAPS consists of the following elements, which generate a composite score used to rank order eligible personnel within each specialty classification:

—Specialty Knowledge Tests (SKT). This test is designed to discriminate among incumbents of an Air Force specialty. The SKT was initially developed in 1951 to support the skill-upgrading program under the airman classification system and has been used as a component of WAPS since

September 1969. Two levels are developed for each Air Force specialty. A journeyman level SKT is administered to grade 5, and the other, supervisory level SKT, is administered to grades 6 and 7.

—Promotion Fitness Examination (PFE). This test is designed to measure Air Force knowledge in areas other than technical skills, e.g., leadership, management, military justice, and other military subjects. It covers the knowledge areas specified in the Military Training Standard for the rank in which the individual is competing for promotion. The PFE has been in use since September 1969. Three levels of the examination are developed for administration to grades 5, 6, and 7. The PFE for grade 5 has two forms in use.

—Airman performance reports.

—Experience factors including time in service, time in grade, and decorations.

For pay grades 8 and 9, the USAF Supervisory Examination (USAFSE) was developed in 1960 to measure supervisory and managerial knowledge. It covers those areas of responsibility desired of senior Air Force noncommissioned officers. Combined with airman performance reports, decorations, time in grade, time in service, and professional military education, USAFSE scores are used in conjunction with a central evaluation board score to rank order eligible candidates within each specialty classification for pay grades 8 and 9.

With the exception of grade 4 promotion tests, which are administered twice a year, all tests are administered annually. During 1979, this amounted to approximately 165,000 SKTs, 175,000 PFEs, and 18,500 USAFSEs.

### Evaluation and Discussion

Military tests are far too numerous to permit discussion of them individually. There are similarities, however, in the administrative arrangements of the various branches of service that allow some general characterizations. Each service supports a personnel research organization to conduct test development, validation, and maintenance. These research organizations share a common philosophy in their approach to testing programs, although their actual work may differ somewhat. Research results are supplied to operational military units, who work out the details of test use, typically in cooperation with the research organizations.

The service's approach to test development is empirical. Careful attention is given to validity issues as well as to details of test development. For example: subtests are chosen on the basis of their contribution to validity; when forms of tests are changed, care is taken to retain the same meaning for scores on the new forms; careful attention is given to both item statistics and test statistics; when available test scores or other variables (such as high school grades) are used to make decisions for which they are not specifically intended, there is usually an attempt to validate such use.

Validation is usually accomplished by relating test scores, or other measures used, to a criterion of final grades in training programs. Performance tests, or what the military calls job proficiency tests, have also been used as a criterion, and use of these tests may increase. At various times in the past, supervisor performance ratings have served as validation criteria. When these ratings have been used along with training criteria in differential classification systems (the systematic assignment of people to jobs), they have tended to differentiate less sharply among specialties than do the training criteria. This result is due perhaps to the fact that job performance involves such factors as individual motivation and environmental context in addition to technicalities of the specialties. In the case of officers, performance in training and some form of performance rating have traditionally been used. The validation work that has been reported appears to be reasonably well done, but more studies need to be reported.

The most frequently used military test is the Armed Services Vocational Aptitude Battery. Like many tests in other sectors of our society, ASVAB is used to assess applicants for employment. Unlike test users in other sectors, however, the military can request the government to change the character of the manpower pool through conscription, should it decide that it does not have a sufficient number of competent volunteers. Data based on the administration of ASVAB could be among the factors leading to the government's decision to exercise this power. The issue of volunteer armed forces, and the quality of the volunteers, is a matter of current national concern, which was expressed during recent testimony on military manpower plans before the Senate Armed Services Committee (March 21, 27, 1979). ASVAB-based statistics contributed a part of this testimony. The issue has also been widely discussed in the media and was the subject of a segment of the television show, *Prime Time Saturday*, on March 15, 1980. Once again, ASVAB was prominently featured. It is particularly important, therefore, that the assessment of the manpower pool and ASVAB's ability to detect applicant potential for service be accurate.

It is possible that the present use of ASVAB scores leads to an understatement of the adequacy of the manpower pool in two, perhaps three, ways: (1) the choice of pass/fail scores used to define eligibility; (2) the use of multiple hurdles for training requirements; and (3) the choice of ASVAB composites.

(1) The choice of pass/fail scores used to define eligibility. An applicant who is disqualified from some particular type of training because his or her score isn't high enough may merely be the victim of a misplaced pass/fail cutoff. Indeed it may have been placed so high that few are selected for training, thus creating an apparent manpower shortage. But if the pass/fail cutoff were lowered in order to obtain, over a suitable period of time, sufficient applicants for training, the average competence of the trainees would be lowered and the cost of training would increase. Training personnel have attested to such training difficulties and increased costs, but the more important questions concern the quality of manpower supplied. Seen in this light, disqualification of the applicant in the situation above should be based on the knowledge either that his or her scores forecast the high probability of an unsatisfactory performance in any military unit to which he or she would be assigned, or that military units in which test scores average around the level of his or her score perform unsatisfactorily. Development of this "knowledge" must be based on adequate research and the formulation of a definition of "satisfactory unit performance" translated into meaningful test scores.

(2) The use of multiple hurdles for training requirements. Pass/fail cutoff scores on two or more ASVAB composites are used for admission to training in the large majority of enlisted jobs in all branches of the service. By virtue of its role in selection, one of the composites is the Armed Forces Qualification Test, and for many jobs two or more others are used, e.g., Bureau of Personnel Instruction BUPERSINST 1236.4A, Subject: Criteria for selection of recruits for formal school training, 1978. This procedure is contrary to the recommended best practice of using a single, most valid composite for selecting people with the best potential for a job, unless special conditions obtain (see Lord 1962). The reason the multiple hurdles approach is chosen rather than a single most valid composite is not clear. Research evidence supporting its continued use is needed.

(3) The choice of ASVAB composites. The best composites are those that predict performance with greatest validity. In selection of several composites (one each for several jobs), professional measurement specialists recommend choosing a set of composites with minimum intercorrelation and maximum validity. This approach has not been uniformly followed. Sims (Sims and Mifflin 1978) produced data to show that the system of composites used at one time by the Army intercorrelated so highly as to indicate that they all measured essentially the same thing. In a later study Sims (1978) was able to choose another set of composites that had satisfactory validity and much lower intercorrelation. Application

## Current Use of Tests for Employment

of the Army composites might therefore lead to an underevaluation of the manpower pool.

Each of the services uses different composites. If all the services were to use the same system of assessing the manpower pool, ASVAB composites could constitute a valuable management tool for assessing the distribution of manpower quality across services.

Improved alternatives to the AFQT, both for screening personnel and for describing the manpower pool, are desirable. AFQT is valid for some jobs, but is often not the best choice. The validity studies do not support the choice of pass/fail cutoff scores, because validity assesses the relative ordering of performance and composite scores, but not their levels. As for describing the manpower pool, several properly constructed classification composites, as described above, might be suitable.

### Trends

Review of employment testing in the military sector reveals several trends similar to those in the private and civilian government sectors.

—The military sector has long been a leader in the development of job analysis techniques, such as the Comprehensive Occupational Development and Analysis Program (CODAP) and is presently engaged in holding seminars on CODAP applications for federal, state, and local government staff.

—DoD is seriously interested in possible applications of tailored testing for the selection and classification of military personnel. Pursuant to this, the DoD has formed a joint services committee, charged with evaluating the feasibility of computer-based adaptive testing and developing the capability to implement it. The committee is in the early stages of a 4-year R&D program, building on the pioneering work of the Personnel Research and Development Center (PRDC) and with continuing assistance from that organization. Implementation of a computer-based system is tentatively scheduled for October 1983, subject to a satisfactory evaluation.

—There is an increased use of "interest" tests. The Strong-Campbell Interest Inventory is being used for the Naval Academy. The Vocational Occupational Interest Career Examination (VOICE), developed by the Air Force against a criterion of job satisfaction, is currently being considered for joint service use within the next 2 years.

—There is some use of criterion-referenced tests for promotion purposes, for example, the Army skill qualification tests.

—There is an increased interest in the use of on-the-job performance as a validation measure. The Office of the Secretary of Defense, in conjunction with the military services, has initiated a research and development program of several years' duration. This program will develop criteria for job and military unit performance and validate ASVAB against them. Plans are under way to establish a DoD advisory committee on enlistment testing, to be composed of nationally recognized experts in personnel testing. This committee will review the research programs of the various services and make recommendations to DoD regarding future directions.

## REFERENCES

ASPA-BNA Survey (1971) Personnel testing. ASPA Survey No. 12. In *Bulletin to Management* (BNA Policy and Practice Series) (September). Washington, D.C.: Bureau of National Affairs.

BNA Survey (1963) *Employee Selection Procedures.* Personnel Policies Forum Survey No. 70. Washington, D.C.: Bureau of National Affairs.

Bayroff, A. G., and Fuchs, E. F. (1970) *The Armed Services Vocational Aptitude Battery.* Technical Research Report No. 1161. Arlington, Va.: U.S. Army Behavior and Systems Research Laboratory.

Bureau of Labor Statistics (1978/1978) *Occupational Outlook Handbook,* Bulletin 1955. Washington, D.C.: U.S. Department of Labor.

Bureau of the Census (1979) *Statistical Abstract of the United States.* Washington, D.C.: U.S. Department of Commerce.

Bureau of the Census (1975/1976) *County Business Patterns.* Washington, D.C.: U.S. Department of Commerce.

Byham, W. C., and Spitzer, M. E. (1971) *The Law and Personnel Testing.* New York: American Management Association.

Campbell, A. K. (1979) Statement for Hearing on the PACE before the Subcommittee on Civil Service, Committee on Post Office and Civil Service, U.S. House of Representatives. May 15, Washington, D.C.

Client Services Group (1978) *Information Science Bulletin,* Issue #2. Washington, D.C.: Information Science, Inc.

Equal Employment Opportunity Commission (1978) *Uniform Guidelines on Employee Selection Procedures. Federal Register,* vol. 43, no. 166.

Greene, K., and Gay, R. (1980) *Occupational Regulations in the U.S.* Monograph, Employment and Training Administration. Washington, D.C.: U.S. Department of Labor.

Griggs v. Duke Power, 401 U.S. 424, 1971.

Halstead, J. P. (1974) *At the Cross Roads: Public Policy for Professional and Occupational Licensing and Examining in Florida.* Tallahassee: Florida House of Representatives, Committee on Commerce.

Hawley, J. K., Mullins, C. J., and Weeks, J. (1977) *Jet Engine Mechanic - AFSC 426X2: Experimental Job Performance Tests.* AFHRL-TR-77-73. Brooks Air Force Base, Tex.: U.S. Air Force Human Resources Laboratory.

Holmen, M. G., and Docter, R. F. (1972) *Educational and Psychological Testing: A Study of the Industry and its Practices.* New York: Russell Sage Foundation.

Jensen, H. E., Massey, I. H., and Valentine, L. D. (1976) *Armed Services Vocational Aptitude Battery Development (ASVAB Forms 5, 6, and 7)*. AFHRL-TR-76-87. Brooks Air Force Base, Tex.: U.S. Air Force Human Resources Laboratory.

Jensen, H. E., and Valentine, L. D. (1976) *Validation of ASVAB-2 Against Civilian Vocational-Technical High School Criteria*. AFHRL-TR-76-16. Brooks Air Force Base, Tex.: U.S. Air Force Human Resources Laboratory.

Kettner, N. (1976) *Armed Services Vocational Aptitude Battery (ASVAB Form 5): Comparison with GATB and DAT Tests*. AFHRL-TR-76-78. Brooks Air Force Base, Texas: U.S. Air Force Human Resources Laboratory. Also published in December 1977 Technical Research Report 77-1 by the Directorate of Testing, U.S. Military Enlistment Processing Command, Ft. Sheridan, Ill.

Kroeker, L. P. (March 2, 1979) *CLASP (Classification and Assignment Within PRIDE)*. Unpublished paper. San Diego, Calif.: Naval Personnel Research and Development Center.

Lord, F. M. (1962) Cutting scores and errors of measurement. *Psychometrica*, 27:19-30.

Maier, M. H., and Fuchs, E. F. (1972) *Development and Evaluation of A New ACB and Aptitude Area System*. Technical Research Note 239. Arlington, Va.: U.S. Army Behavior and Systems Research Laboratory.

Maier, M. H. (1971) *Effects of General Ability, Education, and Racial Group on Aptitude Test Performance*. Technical Research Note 228. Arlington, Va.: U.S. Army Behavior and Systems Research Laboratory.

Maier, M. H., and Fuchs, E. F. Differential Validity of the Army Classification Battery for Blacks and Whites. Unpublished technical paper, no date.

Maier, M. H., and Fuchs, E. F. (1973) *Effectiveness of Selection and Classification Testing*. Research Report 1179. Arlington, Va.: U.S. Army Research Institute for the Behavioral and Social Sciences.

McKillip, R. H., O'Leary, B. S., and Clark, C. L. (1980) Employment Testing for Federal Government Agencies. Paper presented to an open meeting of the Committee on Ability Testing of the National Research Council. Pp. 80-82. U.S. Office of Personnel Management, Personnel Research and Development Center.

Miner, M. G. (1976a) *Equal Employment Opportunity: Programs and Results*. Personnel Policies Forum Survey No. 112. Washington, D.C.: Bureau of National Affairs.

Miner, M. G. (1976b) *Selection Procedures and Personnel Records*. Personnel Policies Forum Survey No. 114. Washington, D.C.: Bureau of National Affairs.

Nafziger, D. G., and Hiscox, N. D. (1976) A Survey of Occupational Licensing and Certification Procedures. Paper presented at National Council on Measurement in Education Annual Meeting, San Francisco, Calif.

Navy Personnel Research and Development Center (January 1979) *Validation of NROTC Selection Procedures*. NPRDC SR 79-12. San Diego, Calif.: Navy Personnel Research and Development Center.

Neumann, I., and Abrahams, N. (June 1976) *Empirical Weighting of Predictors for The Naval Academy Selection Program*. NPRDC TR 76-37. San Diego, Calif.: Naval Personnel Development and Research Center.

*Parrish v. Board of Commissioners of Alabama State Bar*, 533 F.2d 942, 949 (5th Cir. 1976).

Petersen, D. J. (1974) The impact of Duke Power on testing. *Personnel* 51:30-37.

Prentice-Hall, Inc. (1975) *P-H Survey: Employee Testing and Selection Procedures—Where Are They Headed?* Englewood Cliffs, N.J.: Prentice-Hall, Inc.

*Puntolillo v. New Hampshire Racing Commission*, 390 F. Supp. 231 (D.N.H. 1975).

Rayack, E., and Stevens, R. (n.d.) *An Economic Analysis of Occupational Licensure*. Final

Report to U.S. Department of Labor under Grant No. 98-02-6851. Washington, D.C.: U.S. Department of Labor.

*Richardson v. McFadden*, 540 F.2d 744, 747 (4th Cir. 1976).

Rubin, N. (1979) Consumer and Government Forces Pushing for Job-Competency Tests. *The New York Times*, November 11, p. 8 in Education Supplement.

Rutstein, J. J. (1971) Survey of current personnel systems in state and local governments. *Good Government* 87:1-28.

Sadacca, R., and Brackett, J. (1971) *The Validity and Discriminatory Impact of the Federal Service Entrance Examination.* Washington, D.C.: The Urban Institute.

Schmidt, F. L., Hunter, J. E., McKenzie, R. C., and Muldrow, T. W. (1979) Impact of valid selection procedures on work force productivity. *Journal of Applied Psychology* 64(6):609-626.

Seeley, L. C. (September 1977) *Preparation of the ASVAB Information Pamphlet.* Research Memorandum 77-14. Arlington, Va.: U.S. Army Research Institute for the Behavioral and Social Sciences.

Shimberg, B. (1976) *Improving Occupational Regulation.* Final Report to Employment and Training Administration, U.S. Department of Labor, under Grant No. 21-34-75-12. Princeton, N.J.: Educational Testing Service.

*Sibley Memorial v. Wilson*, 488 F.2d 1338 (D.C. Cir. 1973).

Sims, W. H. (1978) *An Application of Factor Analysis to the Construction of Improved Classification Composites from the Armed Services Vocational Aptitude Battery (ASVAB) Forms 6 and 7.* (CNA) 78-3094. Arlington, Va.: Center for Naval Analyses.

Sims, W. H., and Mifflin, T. L. (1978) *A Factor Analysis of the Armed Services Vocational Battery (ASVAB) Forms 6 and 7.* (CNA) 78-3092. Arlington, Va.: Center for Naval Analyses.

Standards for a Merit System of Personnel Administration (1979) *Federal Register*, vol. 44, no. 34, Friday, February 16, 1979.

State of California (1975) *The Fair Employment Implications of Licensing and Certification Standards in the State of California.* Department of Consumer Affairs. Sacramento, Calif.: Selection Consulting Center.

Stone, C. H., and Ruch, F. L. (1974) Selection, interviewing, and testing. Pp. 117-158 in D. C. Yoder and H. G. Heneman, eds., *Staffing Policies and Strategies; American Society for Personnel Administration Handbook of Personnel and Industrial Relations.* Washington, D.C.: Bureau of National Affairs.

Swanson, L. (June 1978) *Armed Services Vocational Aptitude Battery Forms 6 and 7: Validation Against School Performance—Interim Report.* NPRDC TR 78-24. San Diego, Calif.: Naval Personnel Research and Development Center.

*Tyler v. Vickery*, 517 F.2d 1089 (5th Cir. 1975).

U.S. Army Research Institute for the Behavioral and Social Sciences (January 1976, reprinted November 1976) *Psychological Testing Programs in the U.S. Army.* Arlington, Va.: U.S. Army Research Institute for the Behavioral and Social Sciences.

U.S. Civil Service Commission (1975) *State and Local Personnel Systems, Annual Statistical Report. Statistical Indicators for Self Evaluation.* Bureau of Intergovernmental Personnel Programs. Washington, D.C.: U.S. Government Printing Office.

U.S. Department of Defense (1979) *Selected Manpower Statistics.* Washington Headquarter Services, Directorate for Information, Operations and Reports. Washington, D.C.: U.S. Department of Defense.

U.S. Office of Personnel Management (1979) *State and Local Personnel Systems, 1978 Annual Statistical Report. Statistical Indicators for Self Evaluation.* Office of Intergovernmental Personnel Programs. Washington, D.C.: U.S. Government Printing Office.

U.S. Office of Personnel Management and the Council of State Governments (1979) *Analysis of Baseline Data Survey on Personnel Practices for States, Counties, Cities.* Washington, D.C.: U.S. Government Printing Office.

U.S. Office of Personnel Management (1977a) *Federal Civilian Work Force Statistics. Occupations of Federal Blue Collar Workers.* Agency Compliance and Evaluation. SM 59-11. Washington, D.C.: U.S. Government Printing Office.

U.S. Office of Personnel Management (1977b) *Federal Civilian Work Force Statistics. Occupations of Federal White Collar Workers.* Agency Compliance and Evaluation. SM 56-13. Washington, D.C.: U.S. Government Printing Office.

Vitola, B. M., and Alley, W. (September 1968) *Development and Standardization of Air Force Composites for the Armed Services Vocational Aptitude Battery.* AFHRL-TR-68-110. Brooks Air Force Base, Tex.: U.S. Air Force Human Resources Laboratory.

Vitola, B. M., Mullins, C. J., and Croll, P. R. (July 1973) *Validity of Armed Services Vocational Aptitude Battery, Form 1, to Predict Technical School Success.* AFHRL-TR-73-7. Brooks Air Force Base, Tex.: U.S. Air Force Human Resources Laboratory.

Weeks, J. L., Mullins, C. J., and Vitola, B. M. (December 1975) *Airman Classification Batteries from 1948 to 1975: A Review and Evaluation.* AFHRL-TR-75-78. Brooks Air Force Base, Tex.: U.S. Air Force Human Resources Laboratory.

Wing, H. (1977) *Status of Test Usage in FY 77.* Personnel Research and Development Center, Test Services Section. Technical Note 77-2. Washington, D.C.: U.S. Civil Service Commission.

# Educational
# Testing

Daniel Resnick
# History of Educational Testing

## OVERVIEW

Educational testing has played an important role in American education for more than 70 years. In no other Western nation does it occupy so large a place in the processes of schooling. Selection, guidance, placement, credentialing, and program evaluation, which all tend to be dealt with in other ways in other nations, are closely tied in our society to standardized testing.

Our historical analysis indicates that the significant place presently occupied by testing in dealing with these functions is the result of interrelated developments in the past century in the concerns of psychology, the structure of the schools, and the capabilities of educational publishers. Through the interaction of psychologists, school administrators, and publishers, relatively low-cost methods have been developed for dealing with the needs of a rapidly growing system of mass education. These have been introduced in a society which, by present count, still has more than 15,000 local school systems and functions without central administrative control.

Controversy has surrounded the use of standardized tests from the first localized trial in the 1840s to the comparative studies of spelling performance a half century later. The introduction of group intelligence tests in World War I, moreover, further enlarged the public debate. Nonetheless, the legitimacy that educational testing has enjoyed is the result of the deep rooting of this technology in American social and institutional development. Standardized testing enjoys the support not only of the organized groups which have fostered its development—psychologists, school administrators, and publishers alike—but of public agencies, state and federal, and of taxpayers, whose contributions help to support our localized school systems. Public support for testing has grown out of a desire to keep our schools accountable for their costs and their educational quality. At the same time, testing has met a variety of other needs in the organization of schools and their interface with colleges and universities. The present waves of controversy would have to wash very high to erode a base of use and support that has grown considerably in size and character over the past three-quarters of a century.

## MAIN CURRENTS IN AMERICAN PSYCHOLOGY (1880-1914)

### Individual Differences

The first generation of American psychologists, working from the 1880s on in American and European institutions, had no difficulty accepting the widespread view in our culture that the distribution of talent was far from even and that, in education, those with different levels of ability ought to be treated differently. Charles W. Eliot, president of Harvard, like President Benjamin Ide Wheeler of the University of California, argued this position. In the preceding century, Thomas Jefferson in *Notes on Virginia* (1795) had taken a similar stance.

The dominant intellectual tradition in nineteenth century American life was still that of British empiricism and its leading seventeenth century spokesman, John Locke. An educator, he argued in *Some Thoughts Concerning Education* (Locke (1705) 1968, Kandel 1936:162), could not afford to treat all in the same way:

God has stamp'd certain Characters upon Mens Minds, which like their shapes, may perhaps be a little mended; but can hardly be totally alter'd and transform'd into the contrary. He therefore, that is about Children, should well study their Natures and Aptitudes, and see, by often trials, what turn they easily take, and what becomes them; observe what their Native Stock is, how it may be improved, and what it is fit for. He should consider, what they want; whether they be capable of having it wrought into them by industry, and incorporated there by Practice; and whether it be worth while to endeavor it. . . . Everyone's Natural Genius should be carried as far as it could. . . .

In the popular biological imagery of the latter half of the nineteenth century, influenced by social applications of Darwinian theory, the individuals, races, and nations who dominated did so because of their natural superiority. Thus, any theory of individual differences inherited

## History of Educational Testing

from an earlier Lockean tradition was overlaid in the late nineteenth century by theories of race, class, and cultural dominance (Cravens 1978, Kamin 1974). The theory of underlying individual differences offered, nonetheless, a useful model to the generation of psychologists who emerged in the 1880s. Some, like Lester Ward, did not accept the dominant racial theories, and others rejected them after a serious early commitment (Brigham 1923, 1930). But not until the late 1920s did the theory of individual differences stand largely free in both America and England of its overlay of a racial mentality.

### Measurement

The leading figure in the training of American psychologists in measurement was Wilhelm Wundt at the University of Leipzig. He ran a renowned laboratory for psychophysical measurement and was Europe's most important experimentalist. Mainly interested in physical tests, Wundt had focused on phenomena like sensation, perception, and reaction time. Among the Americans who studied with Wundt were G. Stanley Hall and James McKeen Cattell. It was Cattell who first coined the term "mental tests" in an article published in 1890. Later, in 1895, he chaired the first American Psychological Association Committee on Mental and Physical Tests. Although Wundt had developed tests for activities like recall in his experiments, he was not very supportive of Cattell's larger focus on the independent interest of mental measures (Boring 1950).

In England, however, at the time that Cattell was working with Wundt, two major developments were in progress, which gave even more direct encouragement to the development of mental tests. Sir Francis Galton, who some 25 years earlier had published a study of the hereditary transmission of traits of genius in leading British families (Galton 1869), had opened for the public in 1882 at South Kensington Museum an anthropometric measurement lab. In it, he tested hearing, energy levels, and sensation. Memory and reaction time were tested in parallel with weight, height, and other body measures. Relationships between and among such variables became the subject for statistical investigation. Working with Spearman and Pearson, Galton provided for psychology a mathematical theory of statistical significance. This was to make it possible to place the search for individual differences on a more sophisticated plane, one that would involve the correlation and integration of traits of difference along a complex scale of mental abilities (Cooley and Lohnes 1976:45-51).

In France, there was a long tradition of mental measurement tied directly to the diagnosis and treatment of the feebleminded. This work can be traced back to the early nineteenth century, when the "wild boy of the Aveyron" was taken in charge by J. M. Itard (1962 [1801], Lane 1976). Exercises to train perception and coordination were developed by Itard and his student Seguin. The work of Itard and Seguin, like that of their compatriot Esquirol, however, centered on those with the largest and most obvious deficits—only a small portion of the group that would be considered "feebleminded" at the end of the century. They worked largely with those who would later be classified by Alfred Binet (1857-1911) as idiots—those with a mental age of seven or less.

Binet began working with the diagnosis of mentally retarded children in the late 1890s, assisted by Theodore Simon (Wolf 1973). A few years later, in a study for a commission of the Ministry of Public Instruction, begun in 1904, he developed ways of predicting which children would be unable to succeed in elementary school. His scale of normal behavior at specified ages was established by observations and testing of children who attended primary schools. Of major interest was the 8-13 age group.

Binet's conception of intelligence as tied to school success was first presented to the public in 1905 in his journal, *L'Année Psychologique*. In his landmark article, he found in the capacity for abstract thinking a yardstick for the ability to succeed in school. A scale of thirty questions was developed, each of increasing difficulty. Idiots were those who could not go beyond the sixth item, and imbeciles were stymied after the twelfth. Morons were found able to deal with the first twenty-three questions. They were able to do the memory tests and arrange lines and weights in a series, but not more. In his work, Binet drew on the kinds of questions devised by Ebbinghaus for Breslau school children 8 years earlier (Peterson 1925).

The test of thirty items, published in 1905, was designed as an examination to remove from the mainstream of schooling, and place in newly developed special classes for the retarded, those who would be unable to follow the normal prescribed curriculum. As such, it was a test for selection, removing from normal instruction those with the lowest level of ability. Binet argued, however, that the treatment the children would receive in the special classes would be more suited to their learning needs. The testing, therefore, was to promote more effective and appropriate instruction. To this end, Binet argued for the special training needs of teachers in classes for the retarded and the importance of testing activity when linked to pedagogy (Wolf 1973).

Within 6 years of the development of this scale, the eminent laboratory director and educational reformer was dead at the age of 54. He had finished his career without the distinction of a university chair and with very few disciples. Among them, however, were three American psychologists—Henry Goddard, Edmund Huey, and Lewis Terman. Goddard published the first American revision of Binet's scale before Binet's death. Huey, who had worked with Binet in Paris, encouraged Lewis Terman, shortly after his arrival at Stanford in 1910, to revise the Binet scale specifically for use with American school children. The product of that labor was published 4 years later as the Stanford-Binet. Binet's work was closely followed in the pages of the *Pedagogical Seminary*, founded and edited by G. Stanley Hall. In turn, articles published in the journal Binet edited were indexed in the *American Psychologist*.

At a practical level, Binet's scale quickly entered the mainstream of American psychological practice. Of eighty-three surveyed American cities with psychological clinics in 1912, seventy-one were found to use the Binet scale to identify the "feebleminded" and "backward" (Wallin 1914). Although many of the clinics were in institutions for the criminal, the insane, and the retarded, most were in public school systems, universities, normal schools, and medical facilities, where they could be used for the screening of children.

## THE AMERICAN SCHOOLS, 1880-1914: A DEMAND FOR TESTING

The interest in establishing the aptitude of young people for school, which prompted Binet's research on the intelligence scale, was at a high level in the United States by the turn of the century. The need to identify, particularly those children who had the least probability of being able to carry on normal work for their age, was stimulated by a demographic explosion, which enlarged very quickly the rolls of the schools (Trow 1961). Immigration and natural population growth in the period 1880-1910 were the main contributors to this expansion. Another factor was the decision of students to stay in school longer, even before they were forced to by a growing wave of compulsory and enforceable school attendance and child labor laws (Landes and Solmon 1972). During that period, the proportion of the age group in the secondary schools increased fivefold and the costs of public schooling tripled. To avoid placing pupils in classes where they could not function, efforts were undertaken to increase attention to individual differences by small group instruction within larger classes, flexible promotion schemes, and increasingly tracked programs (Chapman 1979).

During the Progressive era (1900-1917), schools that did not have adaptive educational programs came to appear as increasingly inefficient.

The Procrustean bed of a common educational program in each grade, rigid standards, and high failure rates had the inevitable result of creating classes where a high proportion of the pupils were older than their classmates. Products of one or more failures, which obliged them to repeat the work of a grade, they were unlikely to complete the elementary program, much less move beyond it.

"Retardation" was the label given to this condition. Those who were "retarded" were behind their peers for a variety of reasons that had little to do with disease or heredity. The problem was dramatized by a former school superintendent, Leonard Ayres, in a study for the Russell Sage Foundation. His work, Laggards in the Schools (1909), appeared to describe a major social and instructional problem of American school systems. One in six might fail in first grade, and in a typical eighth grade class, more than half would lag behind their age group.

The movement for cost-efficiency (Callahan 1962), which began with school expansion in the 1890s, identified school failure as a common and unacceptable practice. External evaluations of school systems called, among other recommendations, for the regular use of achievement tests to monitor school performance. A Cleveland survey called on the city to "at once set up the administrative machinery for making constant, exhaustive studies of non-promotions and of other problems of a similar nature" (Ayres 1917:12). Better grouping practices in tracked programs seemed the way to increase school success (Cubberley 1919). Test administration to improve the placement of pupils in homogeneous classes was recommended by several surveys undertaken before World War I. In one city after another, beginning with Montclair, East Orange, and Baltimore in 1911, but most visibly with New York City in 1912, school surveys issued their reports (Sears 1950). The recommendation of the survey group was, invariably, that research bureaus be set up within the schools and funded on an ongoing basis to continuously evaluate the effectiveness of schooling.

Close to sixty research bureaus were set up in the years 1912-1922 (Martens 1934, Deffenbaugh 1923, Resnick and Schumacher 1980, Resnick 1980). By the end of that decade, nine of the twelve largest cities in the country had their research and measurement bureaus in place. In some cases, the school-based research bureaus, like the external survey team, had to devise tests of their own because none was available. In many instances, however, they drew on an already commercially available set of achievement measures, which claimed to be standardized.

## THE TRADITION OF STANDARDIZED ACHIEVEMENT TESTS, 1848-1917

Standardization generally meant, even before World War I, that information would be provided by the publisher on the distribution of performance in one or more trial populations. That information would be used to suggest an expected distribution of performance to future users. Thus, users of standardized tests would be able to establish how well student populations in their school systems were doing in comparison with students elsewhere.

Standardization, however, did not always mean the norm referencing of tests. Nor was it general practice to have items increase in difficulty along an interval scale or to remove and add items to create certain distributional effects. Standardization did mean that the tests were published, that directions were given for administration, that the exam could be answered in consistent and easily graded ways, and that there would be instructions on the interpretation of the results. Even within this pattern, there was considerable variation.

The interest in comparative norm-referenced standardized tests can be traced to the mid-nineteenth century. The first reported use of a written examination in the United States to monitor the effectiveness of schools citywide occurred in Massachusetts in the 1840s, when public instruction was largely free, although not compulsory. The annual committee of the school trustees in the city of Boston, after some harassment by the State Superintendent of Instruction about the shortcomings of its schools, decided in 1845, "to adopt, in addition to the usual mode of oral examination, the plan of submitting to the scholars a series of printed questions on all the subjects studied in the schools" (Caldwell and Courtis 1971:6). The reasons given for this decision involved the pressure of numbers—seven thousand children in nineteen schools had become too many to survey by oral examination. The test of thirty questions on the subjects scheduled for study during the year was given to about half the eighth grade, one thousand students. Even within the grade, it was not a fair sample of the students, since the schoolmasters were free to choose who would take the test.

The results, reported by school as well as individually, indicated a large number of failures. The findings, however, appear to have been more immediately useful to the first Superintendent of Instruction in the Commonwealth of Massachusetts than they were to teachers and principals. Although the tests showed that there were deficiencies of instruction, and perhaps excessive difficulty in the curriculum, the results were not intended primarily as helpful advice for teachers. The most important reported result, an unintended one from the standpoint of the school committee, was to make city teachers and principals accountable to supervisory authority at the state level. The Superintendent of Instruction, reportedly "gleeful" at the mode of examination, the performance of certain schools, and the public reporting of the results, had found in the common written examination a means of keeping the schools within his jurisdiction accountable to common standards of student and teacher performance.

A standard short-answer examination, such as the one given in Boston in the mid-1840s, became quickly identified with the needs of school administrators and supervisors to judge the effectiveness of personnel and programs. The most common instrument for this purpose, until shortly before World War I, was the high school entrance examination. Although only a minority of students, those wishing to enter the high school, took such tests, performance on a high school entrance examination could function, within the larger communities, to compare the performance of classes from different feeder schools. Such examinations also served the supervisory needs of central administration for better control of teachers.

By the 1870s, a leader of the National Education Association, Emerson White, was arguing that results of these examinations "should not be used to compare schools and teachers" (Tyack 1974:49)—suggesting thereby that the practice of using examination results for this purpose was already established.

Examinations generated locally, or administered within the boundaries of a state, might receive little national notice. But those which compared performance across states and among different municipal school systems were quickly noted by educators and school reformers. The leader of the movement to reform educational practices through the administration of subject matter tests, beginning in the primary grades, was the talented medical doctor and publicist, Joseph Mayer Rice. The first report of his testing activities in *The Forum* (1896-1897) brought his work to public attention (Graham 1966, Noble 1970, Venezky 1980).

Rice, whom Leonard Ayres (1918) has called "the real inventor of the comparative test" began work in 1892 to test the efficiency of the uses of instructional time, focusing first on spelling. In one study, he looked at the instructional time given to spelling in two different school systems and found that it varied from 15 to 30 minutes per day at different grade levels. Tests of student performance on a common list of words revealed that the extra 15 minutes a day made no difference in demonstrated spelling ability. Here, too, the achievement test was used to hold teachers and school administrators accountable for the appropriateness of the curriculum, the effectiveness of teaching, and the uses of school time.

There was considerable teacher opposition to testing, and support for comparative testing grew first among school administrators.

In 1907, the National Education Association Committee on the Education of Exceptional Children, chaired by Calvin Kendall, Minneapolis Superintendent of Schools, called for some standardized measurement, and interest in measuring achievement began to become more widespread within the association by 1910. Rice, who had tried unsuccessfully to get NEA support for evaluation through standardized testing when his articles appeared in *The Forum*, finally achieved a limited success some 17 years later. The Department of Superintendence within the NEA adopted in 1914 the recommendation of its Committee on Tests and Standards, supporting evaluation activities of the kind that Rice had outlined (Buckingham 1925).

By the time that America entered World War I, more than two hundred achievement tests were available for use in the primary and secondary schools. A study of the market by Walter Monroe (National Society for the Study of Education), published in 1918, indicated that there were eleven available in arithmetic alone. These tests, which began to appear around 1908 in fields that ranged from geography to handwriting, came from a number of different publishing houses, many of which were already strong competitors in the school textbook market. Among the publishers that have maintained in some form a continuing influence in the field are Houghton-Mifflin and World Book Company.

Different tests met different criteria for standardization. Within the field of arithmetic, the Cleveland Survey and Courtis Standard had stated times for completion and offered median scores from different test populations. In two others, items were arranged by order of increasing difficulty. There was as yet no common pattern. Scaling, which created norms of performance appropriate to a particular grade level, had been attempted by a number of test developers, drawing on the work of Binet and Simon on intelligence. Early pioneers in the development of scaled achievement tests were Edward L. Thorndike and his students at Columbia University. Six scaled achievement tests for arithmetic, reading, handwriting, and other subjects were developed in the years 1908-1916 (Peterson 1925, Joncich 1968).

The test perceived as closest to a general ability test likely to predict success in school and later life was handwriting. Handwriting was a major concern of the testers, for handwriting was believed to reveal character by many more psychologists of that period than currently hold to such a position. It was thought possible to offer consistent and uniform judgments about the quality of handwriting through the use of writing specimens. At least ten different published tests of handwriting were then available.

All involved a dictated passage in which all words had to be spelled out within a specified time period. Scales then rated handwriting according to certain characteristics. Edward Thorndike's scale, as one example, used beauty, legibility, and general merit, with specimens offered for each level of performance on a scale that ranged from 4 to 18. Johnson and Stone's scale also used legibility, and Ayres rated test takers on speed and quality.

## THE INTRODUCTION OF GROUP INTELLIGENCE TESTS: WORLD WAR I AS WATERSHED

A strong competitor to the standardized achievement test, perhaps dominant in the school market for a few years after World War I, was the intelligence test. Before the war, it had been available only as an examination individually administered by a specially trained psychologist— either the translation of the Binet-Simon or one of the American revisions. The Stanford Revision, published in 1916 by Louis Terman, was already becoming the most widely used, when one of Terman's graduate students at Stanford, Arthur Otis, succeeded in developing a pencil-and-paper group test that, Terman reported to a colleague early in 1917, "gives almost exactly the same scores as we get in individual testing."[1] Norming was then proceeding on selected school populations, and it was in the schools that the intelligence test would eventually have its largest market. Before the group intelligence test was marketed to the schools, however, it had a large-scale trial with almost two million recruits in 1917-1918 (Kevles 1968, Yerkes 1921).

The successful placement in appropriate jobs of the 1.7 million army recruits mobilized in 1917-1918 proved an enormous challenge. Robert Yerkes, President of the American Psychological Association, offered to help, and the group of psychologists he brought to Vineland, New Jersey, generated in a matter of two weeks a pencil-and-paper group intelligence test to classify the recruits. They were helped in this effort by Arthur Otis's pioneering efforts.

The performance of recruits on this test, Army Alpha (the Beta Scale was used with illiterates) was registered by scores that were converted into letter grades and then "mental age," based on the correlation of Alpha performance with that on the Stanford-Binet. The norming had been done for a small California school population. Within the Army, these scores were found to be useful in the selection of officers and for

---

[1] Terman to Walter Bingham, May 2, 1917, Bingham Papers, Carnegie-Mellon Archives.

a variety of classification purposes. In the society at large, reports of army test score results sparked a debate about the mental age of Americans, their limited potential for higher education, and the failings of our schools (Cremin 1964).

That wartime experience had also created at least two networks with an interest in testing. One, under Walter Dill Scott and Walter Bingham, would later find some of its people heavily involved in the problems of recruiting, identifying, and training personnel for industry. The other, under Robert M. Yerkes and with the leadership of Lewis Terman, would make its postwar contribution most directly to education. Of the war years, Terman later wrote that their "most important aspect . . . was in the opportunity they gave me to become acquainted with all the leading psychologists of America. . . ."[2] Not all of the psychologists called into national service to deal with classification of recruits continued thereafter to have an interest in testing, nor were the two concerns of industry and education mutually exclusive, but two such networks, each with a different set of predominant interests, were created during the war years.

At the close of the war, close to three hundred psychologists involved in wartime testing were ready to seek civilian employment, and many headed for the schools. Aiding this movement was Philander P. Claxton, U.S. Commissioner of Education, who circularized school superintendents throughout the country about the reserve of trained people that could be tapped for the needs of the schools. He wrote enthusiastically about the "unusual opportunity for city schools to obtain the services of competent men. . . ." Among the services they could render was "discovering defective children and children of superior intelligence. . . ."[3]

The postwar entry of the group intelligence test in American school systems was also facilitated by the earlier use of the individually administered IQ tests to identify, as Binet had, students who did not have the ability to successfully maintain themselves in a class for normal children. There were numerous complaints in school systems, in the course of current surveys, about feebleminded children receiving no special treatment. A great many school systems, nonetheless, had made special provision for either separate classes for the feebleminded or their institutionalization (Wallin 1914). Intelligence testing had also been used to identify the most able students for special educational opportunities. These opportunities were then generally defined by faster "tracks" and accelera-

---

[2] Quoted from Terman's autobiographical contribution in Murchison (1930:325).
[3] P. Claxton, *School and Society*, II, no. 216, February 1919. Cited in Paul Chapman's excellent dissertation, *Lewis M. Terman and the Intelligence Testing Movement*, Stanford University, 1979. Chapman's research has been of great assistance to the author.

tion. School systems that maintained promotions on a semester basis, and expected to fail a substantial portion of each class, naturally found themselves with at least two tracks at each grade level. Various school districts—Batavia, Winnetka, St. Louis, Cambridge—gave their names to plans that would allow the acceleration of the gifted (Bureau of Education 1926).

There was, however, in the early 1920s, a great deal of discontent with acceleration as a means of dealing with the gifted. Leaders of the child study movement argued that it was socially detrimental to accelerate young people. The child should enjoy the companionship of his or her own age group. For this reason, but also because of growing administrative complexities in the practice of twice-yearly promotions, larger school systems, particularly, were looking with favor on the notion of creating planned and separate programs for the most able students.

The very bright students, a target for much of the testing research because of the early focus of Anglo-American psychologists on traits of genius, were also of interest because they appeared to be increasingly displaced within the schools. The school environment of the gifted had been altered by the changing and broadening character of the high school. In 1900, about 11 percent of the age group 14-17 was in the high schools, and the dominant academic program was geared to college entrance. Three decades later, more than half of the age group was in the high schools, and the precollege student was no longer the center of school attention.

It was typical by the mid-twenties to find high schools divided vertically into programs for commercial, general, and academic students with a vocational-technical component existing as a fourth track in many areas. The primary function of group intelligence tests under such conditions was to facilitate or legitimate the placement of students in these programs, a process that began in elementary schools.

When, between 1919 and 1923, Lewis Terman introduced the National Intelligence Tests for grades three to eight, and the Terman Group Test, for grades seven to twelve, he found the schools, many with research and measurement bureaus already in place, eager to use the new instruments. A survey conducted by the Bureau of Education in 1925 detailed the major uses of intelligence tests in the schools (Deffenbaugh 1926). All cities of 10,000 or more population were surveyed, some 600 in number, and responses were received from the superintendents' offices in about a third of the systems.

The single most important reported use of the tests was for placement of pupils in homogeneous groups. Sixty-four percent of the reporting cities used group intelligence tests for this purpose in elementary schools, 56 percent in junior high schools, and 41 percent in high schools. Enthusiasm for the use of testing systemwide for this purpose was at a high level. In 1923, Terman's group test for grades seven to thirteen sold more than a half-million copies. Terman's publisher, Caspar W. Hodgson of World Book Company, had developed very effective strategies for reaching out to the school market (Chapman 1979:111).

## GROWTH AND CHANGE IN TESTING BETWEEN THE WARS: ADAPTATION TO NEW USES

Guidance initially involved the selection of a job or career to be pursued on leaving school. As secondary schooling became more prolonged, however, it involved helping students to make a choice among colleges, or to choose between continued education and immediate employment. For vocational or educational guidance, testing—whether of aptitudes, interests, or skills—became a useful tool to the emerging corps of professional guidance counselors.

The most important guidance project of the interwar period, made possible through testing on a scale not previously attempted, was the Pennsylvania Study, sponsored by the Carnegie Foundation in the years 1928-1932.[4] About 90 percent of the high school seniors in the state, some 27,000, were tested in 1928, along with about half of the private school seniors. Those who went on to colleges in the state were then tested again in 1930 and 1932. The widely reported results of the study, carried out by William S. Learned and Ben Wood (1938), indicated that a large portion of the intellectually able were not going on to college, that college administered grades were not functionally equivalent—the highest scorers in some colleges did more poorly on some achievement tests than the lowest scorers in other colleges—and that the students who were choosing to, and did, go on to teachers' colleges, scored more poorly in areas like science than the high school students they would have to teach.[5]

One outcome of the Pennsylvania Study was to encourage high schools and colleges to keep cumulative records of their students for use in advising them about their educational careers. Ben Wood, Director of the Educational Records Bureau at Columbia, got the American Council on

---

[4] For a review of the Pennsylvania study, see Kandel (1936:133-140).
[5] For Wood, concern about the quality of teachers led him, at the end of the decade, to promote and develop with the support of the Carnegie Foundation, the National Teacher Examinations. See Downey (1965:57-64).

Education to adopt in 1928 a standard record form for this purpose, with about one-fifth of the space allocated to information not derived from test scores. He hoped in this way to turn the educational testing movement to a concern with the continuous development of the individual. On this issue, he shared many of the views of the Progressive Education Association, whose Eight-Year Study he followed with interest and to which he gave service as a technical consultant.

The Eight-Year Study of 1933-1941, for which Ralph Tyler directed the Evaluation Project (Smith and Tyler 1942), was undertaken to explore the effects on student performance at the college level of secondary school programs that were not conventionally college preparatory, that is to say, that did not follow the prescribed program of Carnegie units, adopted in 1909.

Some thirty preparatory schools, private and public, participated in the experiment, which was sanctioned by more than 300 colleges and universities, who agreed to waive their normal admissions requirements for students from the schools participating in the experiment. The results confirmed the value of freeing secondary schools from rigid college preparatory requirements, but they also confirmed the importance of following student progress on a continuous basis, recording data drawn from standardized tests, as well as other kinds of achievement. Without conventional course requirements, there would be a need for more monitoring of student performance, and not less.

A third study of the period, the Regents' Inquiry, confirmed more directly the need for better guidance in the high schools. For this study, a commission investigated the knowledge, work orientation, and level of satisfaction of all those who left secondary school in New York State before, at, or after graduation in 1936-1937. The results of the study, directed by Luther Gulick, were published in eleven volumes in the late 1930s. Among its conclusions was that "the guidance program for pupils in the schools was decidedly inadequate" (Gulick 1938:129).

The Regents' examinations, introduced in 1865 and used since 1878 to establish and maintain a set of standards for high school graduation, had become increasingly dominant in shaping classroom objectives. With respect to curriculum and instruction, the Inquiry indicated that there was too much teaching to the Regents' tests in the academic program and not enough inventiveness in the program otherwise. In the name of more effective programs and better "vocational and social adjustment," a plea was made that "each school ought not merely to keep a systematic record of its pupils' school work and to use all its information as to pupils' out-of-school circumstances and interests, but it ought thoroughly to test its pupils' capacity to learn."⁶ The problem of teaching to tests was recognized, but there was also an affirmation of the need for more and better monitoring of student capabilities. "Evaluating, recording and reporting are inextricably interwoven in the whole fabric of education" (Eckert and Marshall 1938:31)

## THE ARTICULATION OF SCHOOL AND COLLEGE, 1900-1980

The crucial take-off period in American secondary education had been in the years 1870-1910. In 1870, there were about 500 high schools; in 1910 there were 10,000. In 1870, there were about 80,000 students in those schools, most of them in private institutions. By 1910, there were 900,000 students in secondary schools, about 90 percent in public institutions. This phenomenal growth had placed an intolerable strain on the older system of establishing admission to the colleges.

College selections had formerly been carried out in a variety of ways (Schudson 1972). The private Eastern colleges in the nineteenth century generally administered a written examination on their own campuses. Secondary schools and tutors had to prepare students for examinations that would differ from college to college. In the Midwest, two methods were commonly used. Universities, like Michigan, sent faculty to inspect a high school and to certify its programs. Graduates of certified secondary schools were then admitted. In other cases, the larger schools would judge an applicant by the record of other graduates from the same secondary school who had already matriculated. It was generally agreed by the end of the century that these methods of screening applicants were too costly and uncoordinated. Responding to these needs in admissions procedures, the Association of Colleges and Secondary Schools of the Middle States and Maryland approved in 1899, on the recommendation of a committee chaired by President Nicholas Murray Butler of Columbia University, a College Entrance Examination Board. Its role would be to establish, administer, and evaluate examinations in defined subject areas for entrance to participating colleges. Only a dozen colleges and universities were then members. Ten years after its creation, it was "still, at most, a service agency to a few Eastern colleges" (Schudson 1972:46). The number of participating institutions grew throughout the interwar period, and test users increased in numbers.

---

⁶ From Francis T. Spaulding (1938), *High School and Life*, a supporting volume in the series, cited in Raubinger et al. (1969:292).

The perceived success of aptitude testing in World War I for classifying soldiers for different positions and tasks encouraged the application of group intelligence testing to the needs of education. Many colleges had been persuaded by the results of army classification that a measure of general intelligence would be a useful addition to the other entrance requirements. At Columbia University, Ben Wood and Herbert Hawkins introduced the Thorndike intelligence test into the screening process. Later, in the years 1918-1926, when Columbia wished to impose a quota on its largest minority, an effort was made to do so through the use of intelligence tests that would screen out Jews (Wechsler 1977). The Eastern European Jews, like other Eastern and Southern European immigrants and American blacks from the deep south, had scored poorly on Army Alpha in World War I (Brigham 1923). Sometimes with malice, at other times in the name of better prediction, intelligence testing entered the screening process of our colleges. These efforts by individual colleges, and the perceived success of World War I army screening, encouraged Carl Brigham of the Psychology Department at Princeton University to begin work on the Scholastic Aptitude Test (SAT) for the College Board.

Until 1926, the College Board administered only essay-type achievement tests. In that year, the Board first introduced the SAT with the characteristic new-type questions, each with a multiple-choice answer. It maintained, however, the alternative of an essay-type achievement examination. By 1937-1940, the multiple-choice aptitude test became the preferred instrument for helping to select students at the more elite colleges. When World War II conditions prevented examination readers from coming to central locations, and pressures developed to have students enter college sooner, the Board, in 1942, dropped the essay-type achievement examination for application to college. Not until the Advanced Placement (AP) tests were introduced in the 1950s were readers again convoked to read examinations.

The old achievement examinations administered by the Board were based on a preparatory school curriculum that was available only in the more traditional and elite secondary schools. Thus the SAT, which did not depend as heavily on a fixed curriculum, appeared to be a more equitable selection instrument. Greater social equity was also associated with the aptitude tests in Great Britain, where many of the scholarship applicants for the grammar schools in the 1920s had not had the benefit of a rich preparatory curriculum. Advocates of a broader base of social recruitment for elite schools favored the use of an aptitude test in the screening of applicants (Burt 1924). During the postwar reform period, and supported by the same kind of reasoning, an aptitude section became part of the eleven-plus examinations.

SAT use after World War II grew more rapidly than college enrollments. Either the SAT or the ACT (American College Testing Program) is presently required of applicants by all but a small fraction of our 2,500 colleges and universities. In 1970, one million students took the SAT; in 1980, one million and a half, a number roughly equal to the number of freshmen who actually entered colleges and universities. In serving the interests of the members of the College Board, and other nonmember colleges and universities, the SATs have played an important role in directing the flow of students into higher education, but they have not staunched it.

## THE BURGEONING OF MULTIPLE ASSESSMENT TESTING SINCE 1935

The early intelligence tests, like Army Alpha, were often single-score batteries and rarely offered assessment on more than two dimensions—verbal and mathematical. Efforts were made, however, by L. L. Thurstone at Chicago and others to extend the range of mental abilities being measured (Carroll 1978). At the same time, in Iowa, testing programs under the direction of E. F. Lindquist moved openly to explore a broad range of abilities for purposes of educational guidance (Lindquist 1970). Tests that might play a diagnostic and monitoring function for the primary and secondary schools were developed under his direction. The Iowa Test of Basic Skills (ITBS), for grades three to eight, was developed in the years 1935-1940. By 1942, the Iowa Test of Educational Development (ITED) was under way for the high schools. Administrators and teachers were encouraged to give the tests in the fall, so that the work of the school year could be adapted to the strengths and deficits of the individual student. Spinoffs from ITED included an achievement measure for the armed services in World War II, the Qualifying Tests for the National Merit Scholarship in 1957, and the American College Testing Program (ACT).

ACT generally served state universities, municipal colleges, and small private institutions not using the services of the College Entrance Examination Board (CEEB). Its tests were avowedly for purposes of guidance. In 1960, ACT split off from Iowa's Measurement Research Center to become an independent, nonprofit corporation. With the Educational Testing Service (ETS) of the College Entrance Examination Board, it is the leading provider of tests to college applicants.

The most widely used of the multidimensional tests in the secondary schools is the Differential Aptitude Test (DAT), developed by the Psychological Corporation. The earlier forms of the DAT reported scores as linguistic and mathematical, but for most of its history the test has been able to offer nine separate scores under headings that range from abstract reasoning to clerical speed and accuracy (Buros 1953-1979, Carroll 1978). There has been some debate over whether the aptitudes are truly differential, but the appeal to school administrators and teachers of a measure that offers more than one score is unquestioned. The drift toward this type of reporting in the name of more effective guidance can be seen in the transformation of former single-score mental ability tests into broader school ability measures.

The postwar acceleration of testing activity was certainly deepened by the commitment to guidance developed in wartime service by leading figures in the profession. Among the many psychologists who deserve mention for this service is John Flanagan, who turned from successful work with pilot training programs in wartime to multifactor aptitude tests for high school students, launching Project Talent (Flanagan 1962).

A critical contribution to the increased use of tests after the war for guidance and other purposes was made by changes in the technology of processing the tests, which reduced the expense of test administration to a small fraction of its former cost, making it an even more modest investment on a per capita basis for school systems. As early as 1928, Ben Wood had had conversations with Thomas Watson of IBM about the possibility of introducing an electronic data processor to handle the large volume of tests that had been generated in inquiries like the Pennsylvania Study. As a result of many collaborative efforts, the IBM 805 was introduced in 1935 (Downey 1965). The effect was astounding—the cost, for example, of administering the Strong Inventory of Vocational Interests, introduced in 1927, dropped from $5.00 to 50¢. Inexpensive detachable forms could be used, and test booklets became reusable. A second major technological breakthrough occurred in the early 1950s, when optical scanning replaced electro-mechanical processing. For a few dollars per pupil, it became possible to have an annual program of systemwide testing.

Such relatively low-cost programs are marketed by a half dozen major companies. The leaders are Harcourt Brace Jovanovich (which acquired both World Book Company and Psychological Corporation), Houghton-Mifflin, California Test Bureau (now part of McGraw-Hill), Science Research Associates (now part of IBM), Educational Testing Service (which integrated with Cooperative Testing Service in 1947), and American Council on Testing (Holmen and Docter 1972).

For leaders in the industry, the last 30 years have been years of growth.[7]

---

[7] Reports of steadily rising sales by publishers can be found, from 1946 on, in *Bowker Annual of Library and Booktrade Information*, New York: Bowker Company, 1972-1979. Retrospective data is provided to 1946 only.

## History of Educational Testing

The movement to multidimensional testing has added new markets at the same time that achievement test sales to the schools have continued to grow. Even in the area of mental aptitude testing, which has been under review by the courts and public agencies, the movement toward multi-score ability tests seems to assure a substantial place for some version of the intelligence test.

### REFLECTIONS ON THE FUTURE

Reports of the demise of standardized national testing would seem premature, for the three major agents in the growth of this enterprise—applied psychology, school administration, and the publishing industry—still contribute to its continuing life, and support has appeared, as well, from other quarters. Despite the present controversy, this newfound backing has emerged over the past 20 years in the public sector. At both the state and federal level, interest in testing as a means of establishing equity in school finance and eligibility for federal education appropriations has been developing in the judicial and legislative branches of government.

Testing, moreover, continues to perform functions in the schools that are important to public confidence. In other societies, these may be handled by a corps of school inspectors, a regularly defined curriculum, or demanding entrance examinations. In our own society, the American public has come to rely on standardized testing to help establish the quality and cost-efficiency of the educational system and is likely to call for even more testing when confidence in the school system is shaken.

Testing initiatives at the national level, through the Elementary and Secondary Education Act and the National Assessment of Educational Progress have maintained in different ways some of Joseph M. Rice's concern with comparative data. It is not yet clear, however, that the Minimum Competency Movement (MCT), which in some form has now touched two-thirds of our states, belongs in the mainstream of American educational development. For about a third of the states that have put this legislation on their books, a primary goal is to certify the high school diploma. MCT's attention to exit-level skills, rather than the continuous monitoring of skill growth through the primary and secondary grades, places it outside the general direction of testing activity since the 1930s.

The launching of MCT, however, like the earlier accountability movement discussed in this chapter, reflects a sense of crisis in our schools (Resnick 1980). Present concern reaches out to subject matter, instructional skill, and the very organization of our system. As a result of the first surge of testing activity, the comprehensive high school, with its diversified but tracked 4-year program, was put securely in place. The problems of that structure are now apparent, but it is not yet clear what form the resolution will take. In the first instance, testing was an agent of reform for the creation of an adaptive educational program, though not a fully successful one. What proposals for the restructuring of our schools will come out of the present surge of testing activity are yet to be seen.

## REFERENCES

Ayres, L. P. (1970) *The Cleveland School Survey: Summary Volume.* Reprint of the Survey Committee of the Cleveland Foundation, 1917. New York: Arno Press.

Ayres, L. P. (1918) History and present status of educational measurements. *Seventeenth Yearbook of the National Society for the Study of Education.* Bloomington, Ind.: Public School Publishing Company.

Ayres, L. P. (1909) *Laggards in Our Schools: A Study of Retardation and Elimination in City School Systems.* New York: Russell Sage Foundation.

Binet, A., and Simon, T. (1905) Méthodes nouvelles pour le diagnostic du niveau intellectuel des anormaux, *L'Année Psychologique* XI:191-244.

Bingham, W. (n.d.) Collected papers. Carnegie-Mellon University Archives.

Brigham, C. (1923) *A Study of American Intelligence.* Princeton, N.J.: Princeton University Press.

Brigham, C. (1930) Intelligence tests of immigrant groups. *Psychological Review* XXXVII:158-165.

Boring, E. G. (1950) *A History of Experimental Psychology.* 2nd ed. New York: Appleton-Century-Crofts.

Buckingham, B. R. (1925) Our first twenty-five years. *Addresses and Proceedings of the National Education Association,* LXIII:805-811. Washington, D.C.: National Education Association.

Bureau of Education (1926) *Cities Reporting the Use of Homogeneous Grouping and of the Winnetka Technique and the Dalton Plan.* City School Leaflet No. 22. Washington, D.C.: U.S. Department of the Interior.

Buros, O. (1953-1979) *Mental Measurement Yearbook,* editions of 1953, 1959, 1965, 1972, 1979. Highland Park, N.J.: The Gryphon Press.

Burt, C. (1924) *Report of the Consultative Committee (Board of Education) on Psychological Tests of Educable Capacity and Their Possible Use in the Public System of Education.* London: H. M. Stationer's Office. Reprinted in 1971 by Arno Press, New York.

Caldwell, O. W., and Courtis, S. A. (1971) *Then & Now in Education, 1845:1923.* Copyright 1923. New York: Arno Press.

Callahan, R. (1962) *Education and the Cult of Efficiency.* Chicago: University of Chicago Press.

Carroll, J. B. (1978) On the theory-practice interface in the measurement of intellectual abilities. In Patrick Suppes, ed., *Impact of Research on Education: Some Case Studies.* Washington, D.C.: National Academy of Education.

Cattell, J. M. (1980) Mental tests and measurements. *Mind* XV:373-381.

Chapman, P. (1979) Lewis M. Terman and the Intelligence Testing Movement, 1890-1930. Unpublished Ph.D. dissertation, Stanford University.

Cooley, W. R., and Lohnes, P. R. (1976) *Evaluation Research in Education: Theory, Principles and Practice.* New York: Irving Publishers.

Cravens, H. (1978) *The Triumph of Evolution: American Scientists and the Heredity-Environment Controversy, 1900-1941.* Philadelphia: University of Pennsylvania Press.

Cremin, L. (1964) *Transformation of the School: Progressivism in American Education, 1876-1957.* New York: Random House.

Cubberley, E. P. (1919) *Public School Administration in the United States: A Study and Interpretation of American Educational History.* Boston: Houghton Mifflin Co.

Deffenbaugh, W. S. (1923) *Research Bureaus in City School Systems.* Washington, D.C.: U.S. Department of the Interior.

Deffenbaugh, W. S. (1926) *Uses of Intelligence and Achievement Tests in 215 Cities.* U.S. Bureau of Education, City School Leaflet No. 20. Washington, D.C.: U.S. Department of the Interior.

Downey, M. T. (1965) *Ben D. Wood, Educational Reformer.* Princeton, N.J.: Educational Testing Service.

Eckert, R., and Marshall, T. (1938) *When Youth Leave School.* New York: McGraw-Hill.

Flanagan, J. C. (1962) *A Survey and Follow-up of Educational Plans and Decisions in Relationship to Aptitude Patterns: Studies of the American High School.* Pittsburgh: U.S. Office of Education and the University of Pittsburgh.

Galton, F. (1869) *Hereditary Genius: An Inquiry Into its Laws and Consequences.* London: Macmillan and Company.

Graham, P. (1966) Joseph Mayer Rice as a founder of the progressive education movement. *Journal of Educational Measurement* III:129-133.

Gulick, L. H. (1938) *Education for American Life.* New York: McGraw-Hill.

Holmen, M. G., and Docter, R. (1972) *Educational and Psychological Testing: A Study of the Industry and its Practices.* New York: Russell Sage Foundation.

Itard, J. M. G. (1801) *De l'éducation d'un homme sauvage ou des premiers développements physiques et moraux du jeune sauvage de l'Aveyron.* Paris: Gaujon. Translated by G. Humphrey and M. Humphrey (1962) *The Wild Boy of the Aveyron.* New York: Appleton-Century-Crofts.

Jefferson, T. *Notes on Virginia.* Pp. 1-261 in A. E. Bergh, ed., (1905) *The Writings of Thomas Jefferson,* Vol. I. Washington, D.C.: The Thomas Jefferson Memorial Association.

Joncich, G. (1968) *The Sane Positivist: A Biography of Edward L. Thorndike.* Middletown, Conn.: Wesleyan University Press.

Kamin, L. J. (1974) *The Science and Politics of I.Q.* New York: Halsted Press.

Kandel, I. L. (1936) *Examinations and Their Substitutes in the United States, Bulletin No. 28.* New York: The Carnegie Foundation for the Advancement of Teaching.

Kevles, D. J. (1968) Testing the army's intelligence: Psychologists and the military in World War I. *Journal of American History* LV(December):565-581.

Landes, W., and Solmon, L. (1972) Compulsory schooling legislation: An economic analysis of law and social changes in the nineteenth century. *Journal of Economic History* XXXII:54-91.

Lane, H. (1976) *The Wild Boy of Aveyron.* Cambridge: Harvard University Press.

Learned, W. S., and Wood, B. D. (1938) *The Student and his Knowledge; A Report to the Carnegie Foundation on Results of the High School and College Examinations of 1928, 1930 and 1932.* New York: The Carnegie Foundation for the Advancement of Teaching.

Lindquist, E. F. (1970) The Iowa testing program: A retrospective view. *Education* LXXXI:7-23.

Locke, J. (1968) *Some Thoughts Concerning Education.* Pp. 114-325 in J. L. Axtell, ed., *The Educational Writings of John Locke: A Critical Edition With Introduction and Notes.* London: Cambridge University Press.

Martens, E. H. (1934) *Organization of Research Bureaus in City School Systems.* U.S. Bureau of Education, City School Leaflet No. 14. Washington, D.C.: U.S. Department of the Interior.

Monroe, W. S. (1918) Existing tests and standards. *Seventeenth Yearbook of the National Society for the Study of Education,* Part 2. Bloomington, Ind.: Public School Publishing Company.

Murchison, C., ed. (1930) *A History of Psychology in Autobiography,* Vol. II. London: Oxford University Press.

Noble, G. L. (1970) Joseph Mayer Rice: Critic of the Public Schools and Pioneer in Educational Measurement. Unpublished Ph.D. dissertation, S.U.N.Y. at Buffalo. Dissertation Abstracts Vol. 31, 4503A.

Peterson, J. (1925) *Early Conceptions and Tests of Intelligence.* Yonkers-on-Hudson, N.Y.: World Book.

Raubinger, F. M., Rowe, H. G., Piper, D. L., and West, C. K., eds. (1969) *The Development of Secondary Education.* New York: The Macmillan Co.

Resnick, D. (1980) Minimum competency testing historically considered. *Review of Research in Education,* VIII:3-29.

Resnick, D., and Schumacher, C. (1980) The Pittsburgh Research and Measurement Bureau, 1918-1939. Unpublished paper presented at AERA conference, Boston, April 8.

Schudson, M. S. (1972) Organizing the 'meritocracy': A history of the College Entrance Examination Board. *Harvard Educational Review* XLII (February):34-69.

Sears, J. B. (1950) School surveys. Pp. 1126-1131 in W. S. Monroe, ed., *Encyclopedia of Educational Research,* 2nd ed. New York: Macmillan.

Smith, E. R., and Tyler, R. W., and the Evaluation Staff (1942) *Appraising and Recording Student Progress.* New York and London: Harper and Brothers.

Spaulding, F. T. (1938) *High School and Life.* New York: McGraw-Hill.

Trow, M. (1966) The second transformation of American secondary education. *The International Journal of Comparative Sociology* II:144-166. Reprinted in R. Bendix and S. M. Lipset, eds., (1966) *Class, Status and Power,* 2nd ed. New York: Free Press.

Tyack, D. (1974) *The One Best System: A History of American Urban Education.* Cambridge: Harvard University Press.

Venezky, R. (1980) From Webster to Rice to Roosevelt: The formative years for spelling instruction and spelling reform in the USA. Pp. 10-30 in U. Frith, ed., *Cognitive Processes in Spelling.* New York: Academic Press.

Wallin, J. E. W. (1914) *Mental Health of the School Child.* New Haven, Conn.: Yale University Press.

Wechsler, H. (1977) *The Qualified Student: A History of Selective College Admissions in America.* New York: John Wiley & Sons.

Wolf, T. H. (1973) *Alfred Binet.* Chicago: University of Chicago Press.

Yerkes, R., ed. (1921) *Psychological Examining in the United States Army.* Memoirs of the National Academy of Sciences, XL, Part 2. Washington, D.C.: U.S. Government Printing Office.

Patricia Hollander
# Legal Context of Educational Testing

## INTRODUCTION

Traditionally, standardized ability and achievement tests have been used in schools to assess how much students *could* learn and how much they actually *have* learned. This assessment process has intended generally to assist schools in reaching their educational goals and to provide access to education for all students. Increasingly, however, it has been claimed that not all standardized tests are actually of benefit to all student test takers in achieving these goals. Many such claims have become the subjects of recent litigation, and this paper examines the legal standards of fairness and equity that have been applied by the courts in deciding cases involving educational ability and achievement testing.

Legal standards are relied upon by schools and by students as bases for educational opportunities that are equitable for heterogeneous populations. Where state action is involved, as occurs when public school officials administer standardized tests, constitutional guarantees of equal protection or due process may apply. In other circumstances, where federal financial aid is received by private or public schools, the guarantees may be statutory. Notable examples would include Title VI of the Civil Rights Act of 1964,[1] Section 504 of the Rehabilitation Act of 1973,[2]

---

[1] Title VI of the Civil Rights Act of 1964, 42 U.S.C. §2000d. Regulations at 45 C.F.R. §121 (1977).
[2] Section 504 of the Rehabilitation Act of 1973, 29 U.S.C. §794. Regulations at 45 C.F.R. §84 (1977).

and the Education for All Handicapped Children Act of 1975.[3] The common purpose of both constitutional and statutory guarantees may be said to be to assure fair treatment in assessing educational ability and achievement, and in the subsequent decisions regarding appropriate education.

Standardized tests have numerous educational purposes: to classify students as having normal or retarded ability with resulting differential treatment; to ascertain whether students have or have not mastered a particular subject matter; to determine which high school students are to receive regular diplomas rather than certificates of completion; and to help evaluate students for admission to undergraduate, graduate, or professional schools.

The classification of students by the use of standardized testing has been widespread. It was originally accepted as a more objective, scientific means of grouping students and an improvement in practice over former reliance on the subjective evaluations of teachers and administrators and on prior educational performance. Testing was also considered to be a way to provide a larger number of able students with educational opportunities. The search for talent was thought to be more effective and less biased when tests were used to identify capable students from obscure schools or students who had been misjudged by teachers.

Beginning in the 1960s, however, a series of legal challenges indicated that the balance of public opinion had begun to shift away from this generally positive view of standardized testing. Voices were heard in court criticizing testing as a principal factor in fostering unacceptable educational policies and practices. Among the alleged effects of testing were the misclassification of normal children as retarded,[4] exclusion of physically or mentally handicapped children from schooling,[5] denial to blacks of education of the same quality as that offered whites,[6] unequal educational opportunity for females,[7] denial of equal educational opportunities to whites,[8] and denial of regular high school diplomas to students who failed minimum competency tests.[9] In all the situations just cited, litigation challenging testing was successful.

---

[3] Education for All Handicapped Children Act, 20 U.S.C. §1401, et seq., Public Law 94-192. Regulations at 45 C.F R. §121 (1977).

[4] *Larry P. v. Riles*, 343 F. Supp. 1306 (N.D. Cal. 1972); 502 F.2d 963 (CA 9, Aug. 16, 1974); Civil No. C-71-2270 RFP (N.D. Cal. Oct. 11, 1979), 48 U.S.L.W. 2298 (1979).

[5] *Diana v. State Board of Education*, Civil No. C-70-37 RFR (N.D. Cal. Jan. 7, 1970 and June 18, 1973).

[6] *Hobson v. Hansen*, 269 F. Supp. 401 (D.D.C. 1967).

[7] *Bray v. Lee*, Civ. No. 70-2002-C (D. Mass. Aug. 27, 1971).

[8] *Regents of the University of California v. Bakke*, 57 L.Ed. 2d 750 (1978).

[9] *Debra P. v. Turlington*, Case No. 78-892-Civ-T-C (M.D. Fla. 1979).

## Legal Context of Educational Testing

By the end of the 1970s, many uses of standardized testing had been linked, whether rightly or wrongly, with the notion of unfair treatment in the educational setting. In this atmosphere of ever increasing heavy judicial scrutiny, the survival of testing as a factor in educational decision making has come to depend on its compliance with an extremely complex body of law being adjudicated in courts throughout the country.

### LEGAL STANDARDS RELEVANT TO TESTING

The legal standards courts apply to ascertain the fairness of tests and testing procedures emanate from both constitutional and statutory guarantees. When state action, e.g., standardized testing in a public school, is alleged to be a violation of the Constitution, there must be proof of discriminatory intent or purpose, as well as discriminatory effect. However, when a statutory violation is alleged, there must be proof of effect, but not necessarily intent.

### Constitutional Standards

The Equal Protection Clause of the Fourteenth Amendment to the Constitution protects against intentional unjustifiable classification by government. A statute that results in state action classifying people by means of testing is subject to "minimal scrutiny" and is permitted so long as the classification is justified, that is, the test is rationally related to the purpose for which it is used. Generally, courts presume the validity of a statute where a rational relationship is apparent. The major exception to this presumption occurs when classification under a statute adversely and intentionally affects a suspect class of persons, that is, a class based on race or national origin, and when other methods of classification may be available. In such circumstances, a court will subject the statute to "strict scrutiny," which requires the demonstration of a compelling state interest. In addition, an "intermediate" standard of review is possible. Litigation in this regard was exemplified in a significant public school testing case in California known as *Larry P. v. Riles* (1979)[10] (see below).

Due process, required under the Fourteenth Amendment, is another constitutional standard applied in public school testing cases. Testing litigation has raised the issue of fairness and equity under this mandated ordering of legal process chiefly in connection with appropriate notice

---

[10] See note 4.

and hearing vis-à-vis testing requirements (see below, *Debra P. v. Turlington* (1979)).[11]

## Statutory and Regulatory Standards

In addition to constitutionally based standards, legal standards are derived from statutes and their implementing regulations. These may affect both private and public schools and colleges, because the statutes cover all recipients of federal financial assistance.

Title VI of the Civil Rights Act of 1964[12] provides that no person shall, on the grounds of race, color, or national origin, be denied the benefits of, or be subject to discrimination under, any program or activity receiving federal financial assistance. This law focuses on effects, rather than intent, in most cases.

The major Title VI Supreme Court decision was *Lau v. Nichols* (1974) (described below),[13] in which the "effects tests" under Title VI bars discrimination that defeats or substantially impairs accomplishment of the objectives of a federally funded program, even though no purposeful design is present.

Public Law 94-142, the Education for All Handicapped Children Act (EHA) of 1975,[14] states:

It is the purpose of this Act to assure that all handicapped children have available to them, within the time period specified, a free, appropriate public education which emphasizes special education and related services designed to meet their unique needs [Sec. 3, C].

The policy expressed in this law is that no child is uneducable. All can learn to some degree. Its aims are to assess and meet individual needs and to "mainstream" students by placing them in regular classes as much as possible. The EHA will affect all children, of course, though it is meant to assist handicapped children in particular.

EHA regulations, 45 C.F.R. §84.35(b), mandate that tests and other evaluation materials not be culturally discriminatory; that such materials and procedures are to be in the child's native language or mode of communication; that no single test or procedure is to serve as the sole criterion for determining the appropriate educational program for a child;

---

[11] See note 9.
[12] See note 1.
[13] *Lau v. Nichols*, 414 U.S. 563 (1974).
[14] See note 3.

## Legal Context of Educational Testing

and that the test materials are to be *validated for the specific purpose used* (emphasis added).

The use of standardized tests and procedures is not viewed as bad practice per se but only if the tests are constructed or employed in an inappropriate fashion. Indeed, testing is bound to increase as these new laws are implemented. Under the EHA regulations, each handicapped child is to be provided with an individualized education program (IEP). The program will involve standardized testing and other assessment techniques. These instruments and techniques will require modification depending upon the various disabilities of students to be tested. For instance, blind children cannot take tests utilizing pictures or colors; deaf children cannot be tested by the use of sounds.

Accurate assessment of educational ability and need, therefore, has become essential in carrying out that part of public educational policy that requires an appropriate education. Public policy may be said, now, to provide students with the right to accurate assessment, in order that they may be placed in appropriate tracks, special classes, or even residential settings.

Section 504 of the Rehabilitation Act of 1973[15] provides that:

... no otherwise qualified handicapped individual ... shall, solely by reason of his handicap, be excluded from the participation in, be denied the benefits of, or be subjected to discrimination under any program or activity receiving federal assistance from HEW.

The term "handicapped" includes physical or mental impairment that substantially limits, or is perceived to limit, one or more major life activities. Included are conditions such as cancer, cerebral palsy, deafness or hearing impairment, diabetes, emotional illness, epilepsy, heart disease, mental retardation, multiple sclerosis, muscular dystrophy, orthopedic impairment, speech or visual impairment, and such perceptual handicaps as dyslexia, minimal brain dysfunction, and developmental aphasia. Alcoholism and drug addiction are included; however, institutions may take into account the actual behavior of such individuals in deciding whether they are qualified.

By definition, "qualified" handicapped individuals are those capable of learning, or being employed, with reasonable accommodation to the handicap. Under Section 504 regulations, preschool, elementary, secondary, and adult students are entitled to a free, appropriate education in the most normal setting possible; evaluation procedures must be im-

---

[15] See note 2.

proved to avoid inappropriate education resulting from misclassification; due process procedures must be provided to resolve disputes over placement of students; and if a handicapped student is so disruptive that the education of other students in the classroom is seriously impaired, the student can be reassigned.

Further Section 504 regulations specifically pertain to tests. They provide that tests, including admissions tests, must be selected and administered so that the test results of handicapped students are not unfavorably distorted; tests are to measure the student's aptitude or achievement level, not the disability; the director of the Office for Civil Rights of HEW has the responsiblity of identifying alternate tests; auxiliary aids must be provided, such as readers, tape records, and Braille materials; and tests must be given in places that are physically accessible to handicapped persons.

Postsecondary students who are qualified but handicapped must be recruited, admitted, and treated in a fashion that is as normal as possible. Preadmission inquiries about handicaps generally are not permitted.

The 1979 Supreme Court decision in *Southeastern Community College v. Davis*[16] held that Section 504 does not require colleges and universities to lower their admission requirements. To be admitted, applicants must be qualified "in spite of" their handicaps. In the *Davis* case, a severely deaf candidate was refused admission to the college's registered nursing program. The Court upheld the refusal because evidence regarding Davis' inability to safely perform tasks related to the care of patients convinced the Court that she was not "otherwise qualified" for the specific professional clinical training program involved.

On the other hand, deafness need not disqualify students. In *Barnes v. Converse* (1977),[17] a private college was ordered to provide the services of an interpreter for a deaf person who was attending updating classes in education so as to remain certified as a teacher, a job she was already performing and so was assumed to be qualified in spite of her handicap.

The "effects test" under both Section 504 and the EHA provides that when a violation of one of these statutes is alleged, discriminatory or adverse impact, but not necessarily discriminatory intent, must be shown. Generally a complainant may prove a *prima facie* case of adverse impact by statistics. Thereafter, the burden of proof shifts to the alleged discriminatory decision maker to show that the decision was made for some reason other than that prohibited by the statute. Successful proof here

---

[16] *Southeastern Community College* v. *Davis*, 574 F.2d 1158 (1978); 47 U.S.L.W. 4689 (1979).
[17] *Barnes* v. *Converse College*, 436 F. Supp. 635 (D.S.C. 1977).

## Legal Context of Educational Testing

will shift the burden of proof once again back to the alleged victim of discriminatory effect to show there was some other alternative method available to assist in making the decision.

Title IX of the 1972 Education Amendments[18] prohibits impact discrimination on the basis of sex in any education program or activity which receives federal financial assistance. Exceptions are made for certain religious and military institutions. Title IX is quite similar to Title VI in operation, but for sex rather than race bias.

The Age Discrimination Act of 1975[19] prohibits impact discrimination on the basis of age. Its regulations were effective only in mid-1979, so its effect is unknown as yet. Age bias in standardized testing is one of its targets.

The Family Educational Rights and Privacy Act of 1974,[20] also known as the Buckley Amendment, requires that educational institutions receiving federal financial assistance provide access by students (or parents or guardians) to their academic files. It also mandates the confidentiality of these files. Test scores related to academic skills should be in such files and disclosed to students by institutions. Testing organizations are not covered by this statute.

So-called sunshine laws provide that public decisions be made in open meetings and that public records be open. Such laws may give access to test scores if a particular state sunshine statute is interpreted as requiring that admissions meetings be open to the public. The federal sunshine law covers educational institutions run by the federal government, such as armed forces schools.

Human Subjects Research Regulations[21] usually require informed consent of subjects taking part in test research projects funded by HEW.

Truth-in-testing laws are contemplated in several states. New York has already enacted such laws,[22] providing for disclosure of test scores to test takers, along with the filing of certain tests and research studies. Hearings on proposed federal truth-in-testing laws[23] have been held before the

---

[18] Title IX, Education Amendments of 1972, 20 U.S.C. §1681. Regulations at 45 C.F.R. Part 86 (1975). Amended 1976.
[19] Age Discrimination Act of 1975, Public Law 94-135, 42 U.S.C. §6101. Final Rules in *Federal Register*, June 12, 1979.
[20] Family Educational Rights and Privacy Act of 1974 (Buckley Amendment), 20 U.S.C. §1232g. Regulations at 45 C.F.R. §99.
[21] Human Rights Research Regulations, 45 C.F.R. §46, July 1, 1974.
[22] New York State Standardized Testing Law (1979).
[23] U.S. House of Representatives, Proposed H.R. 3564 (Gibbons Bill) and H.R. 4949 (Weiss Bill), 96th Cong., 1st Sess., 1979.

House Subcommittee on Primary, Secondary, and Vocational Education over the past year.

The Education Amendments of 1976 (Student Consumer Information),[24] mandate that applicants for student loans be given anonymous information about test scores of admittees at a particular institution.

The 1871 Civil Rights Act[25] provides a basis for recourse in situations where a public official may deprive someone of federal constitutional or statutory rights. Hypothetically, federal constitutionally or statutorily impermissible testing causing injury may result in a suit for damages or declaratory or injunctive relief (*Maine* v. *Thiboutot* (1980)).[26]

Federal funding statutes, in general, prohibit discriminatory practices. One example would be the Equal Educational Opportunity Act of 1974,[27] which provides, in part, that

> No state shall deny equal educational opportunity to an individual on account of his or her race, color, sex, or national origin, by . . . the failure by an educational agency to take appropriate action to overcome language barriers that impede equal participation by its students in its instructional programs.

## An Overview

Most of the constitutional and statutory protection afforded test takers by law relates to individuals who are members of groups considered vulnerable to discriminatory practices based on race, ethnic origin, sex, age, or handicap. Other test takers who feel unfairly treated have had less success in securing legal rights and remedies, but the demand for fair and accurate educational assessment will continue, especially at critical junctures in life, such as initial entrance in school and entry into higher or professional education. If such decisions are to involve some use of testing, careful provision must be made for equal protection and procedural due process, where applicable, as well as strict compliance with statutory regulations, such as the EHA and Section 504 of the Rehabilitation Act, most especially in regard to the administration of tests by trained personnel in conformance with the instructions provided by the producer and the validation of tests for the specific purpose for which they are used.

---

[24] Education Amendments of 1976 (Student Consumer Information, 20 U.S.C. §1070, Public Law 94-482).
[25] 1866 Civil Rights Act, 42 U.S.C. §1981; 1871 Civil Rights Act, 42 U.S.C. §1983; 1871 Civil Rights Act, 42 U.S.C. §1985(3).
[26] *Maine* v. *Thiboutot*, 48 U.S.L.W. (U.S.S.Ct. June 25, 1980).
[27] Equal Educational Opportunity Act of 1974, 20 U.S.C. §1703.

# Legal Context of Educational Testing

## REVIEW OF CASES ILLUSTRATIVE OF THE ALLEGATIONS AGAINST EDUCATIONAL TESTING

### Cultural Bias

Cultural bias occurs when tests have been found to be inaccurate because they were validated with students from a culture different from that of the students to whom they were administered.

Three U.S. District Court cases are discussed here. In two of them, the court found sufficient evidence that the tests used were culturally biased and moved on to focus primarily on the proper legal standards for evaluating compliance with federal law. The third court found insufficient evidence that the tests, or their use, were culturally biased. It found that the misclassification was due to improper interpretation of the tests by school psychologists and did not go forward to discuss legal standards for evaluating compliance with federal law.

*Hobson v. Hansen* (1967),[28] a case against the District of Columbia public schools, involved a charge that the use of IQ tests resulted in an ability tracking system that placed disproportionate numbers of disadvantaged students, primarily black, in lower tracks. The Court found that this process had an outright segregatory purpose

> ... because these tests are standardized primarily on and are relevant to a white middle-class group of students (and produce) inaccurate and misleading test scores when given to lower-class and Negro students [269 F. Supp. 401, at 514].

The Court found from the evidence that the scholastic aptitude and standardized achievement tests did not measure innate abilities accurately, but instead often reflected environmental, psychological, and socioeconomic factors, and resulted in student misclassification. The Court abolished tracking as then practiced in the District of Columbia. A later decision, *Smuck v. Hansen* (1969),[29] relating to this case emphasized that this order was not to be read as a total ban on ability grouping, but only as an attack on tracking systems with serious format deficiencies. Beginning in the fall of 1978, use of both criterion- and norm-referenced achievement tests was resumed in District of Columbia schools in grades one through nine, largely for diagnostic purposes.

*Larry P. v. Riles*[30] proved to be a landmark case on the issue of racial bias. In 1972, a preliminary injunction was sought and issued, restraining

---

[28] See note 6.
[29] *Smuck v. Hansen*, 408 F.2d 175 (D.D.C. 1969).
[30] See note 4.

the Unified San Francisco School District (USFSD) from administering IQ tests as a basis for determining whether black students should be assigned to special educable mentally retarded (EMR) classes. The complaint was that such use of IQ tests was a violation of the Fourteenth Amendment. The injunction was to prevent further harm to black children pending a trial on the merits of the case and in 1974 was expanded to apply to black students in the rest of the state. In January 1975, the State of California voluntarily discontinued the use of IQ testing for EMR placement of all children, regardless of race. In October 1977 the trial on the merits began and the decision was rendered in October 1979, continuing the injunction. In view of the 1979 opinion, it is likely that the total ban on IQ testing for EMR placement in California will remain in effect until the Court removes it.

The following discussion describes the issues raised in the original 1972 hearing seeking a preliminary injunction and in the 1979 decision on the merits of the case that kept the injunction in place.

### 1972—Larry P. v. Riles

In 1972 the plaintiffs were black elementary school children who had been placed in educable mentally retarded (EMR) classes because they scored below 75 on the USFSD's tests. They claimed they were not retarded and supported the claim with affidavits indicating that, when given the same IQ tests by psychologists from the Bay Area Association of Black Psychologists, they scored significantly above 75. The black psychologists, it was said, were able to establish rapport with the children, to overcome their low self-esteem and to reduce distraction, to reword the test items in terms consonant with the children's cultural background, and to count as correct certain answers that were not correct according to the manual but were intelligent responses in light of the children's background.

In this case, the plaintiffs sought to shift the burden of proof so that the USFSD would have to justify the use of IQ tests. The basis for their complaints was statistical evidence showing disproportionate numbers of minority children in the district's EMR classes.

As the defendant, the USFSD responded in the first instance by contending that the racial imbalance was not due to the IQ tests. However, the second line of argument was that, even if it were, the tests were rationally related to the purpose for which they were being used because they were the best means of classification currently available.

After hearing the evidence, the U.S. District Court found first that there was racial imbalance in the EMR classes, in these words:

## Legal Context of Educational Testing

The fact of racial imbalance is demonstrated by plaintiffs' undisputed statistics, which indicate that while blacks constitute 28.5 percent of all students in the San Francisco United School District, 66 percent of all students in San Francisco's EMR program are black. Statewide, the disproportion is similar. Blacks comprise 9.1 percent of all school children in California, but 27.5 percent of all school children in EMR classes. Certainly these statistics indicate that there is a significant disproportion of blacks in EMR classes in San Francisco and in California [at 343 F. Supp. 1311].

Next, the Court ascertained from the evidence that the result of an IQ test formed the principal basis for a decision to place a student in an EMR class. The Court took care to point out that IQ tests were not the only type of psychological assessment required by Section 6902.085 of the California Education Code. An IQ test was the initial requirement after a student had been referred to a counselor by his teacher because he or she had demonstrated "a general pattern of low academic achievement, maladaptive or immature behavior, poor social relationships, and consistently low standardized test scores" [at 1311]. The school psychologist was to explain the nature and purpose of IQ tests and secure parental consent prior to administering the test. Even then, no such placement was to be made unless

. . . a complete psychological examination by a credentialed school psychologist investiating such factors as developmental history, cultural background, and school achievement substantiates the retarded intellectual development indicated by the . . . individual test scores. This examination shall include estimates of adaptive behavior. Until adaptive behavior scales are normal and approved by the State Board of Education, such adaptability testing shall include, but is not limited to, a visit, with the consent of the parent or guardian, to the minor's home by the school psychologist or a person designated by the chief adminstrator of the district, upon the recommendation of the school psychologist, and interviews of members of the minor's family at their home" [at 1311].

(The Code goes on to require that, when the recommendation was for placement in an EMR class, the parent or guardian was to be given an exact description of the special education program and be informed that it was for pupils who have retarded intellectual development. Only if the parent or guardian gave consent was the child to be transferred to an EMR class.)

On the basis of these two findings, the burden of proof did indeed shift to the defendants to show a rational relationship between the use of IQ tests and the classification of students as mentally retarded.

The plaintiffs presented other evidence substantiating the operational importance of the IQ test scores. For instance, evidence was offered that IQ test scores influence teacher evaluation of pupils, and subsequently, tracking decisions. This evidence included references to such psychological studies as the 1968 Rosenthal and Jacobson book called *Pygmalion in the Classroom*.[31] In an experiment with teachers, it was demonstrated that teachers' expectations of student performance are influenced by knowledge of a student's IQ test score. Evidence regarding work challenging these findings apparently was not offered to the Court. Another source of evidence presented was the Examiner's Manual for the Lorge-Thorndike Group test, used in most California schools, which explains the various ways a student's expected level of performance may affect a teacher's judgments or actions.

The plaintiffs also produced two affidavits to support similar notions from psychologists who served as expert witnesses for the plaintiffs [at 1313]. The Court referred to an earlier Washington, D.C., case, *Hobson v. Hansen* (1967),[32] which also had found heavy emphasis on IQ test scores and had referred particularly to Dr. Kenneth B. Clark's expert testimony that:

> When a child from a deprived background is treated as if he is uneducable because he has a low test score, he becomes uneducable and the low test score is therefore reinforced . . . [269 F. Supp. at 484].

The defendants contended that the racial imbalance in EMR classes was not the result of IQ test scores because parental consent was necessary prior to placement. Although the Court appeared to feel that fully informed consent would be a defense, it pointed out that parents, too, were likely to be influenced by "scientific-sounding pronouncements about IQ," [at 1313], and, if so, the parents' decisions, too, would be determined largely by IQ test scores. The Court further said that "if the IQ tests are found in fact to be biased against the culture and experience of black children, any consent which is obtained from the parents of such children absent communication of full information to that effect is not effective enough" [at 1313].

Clearly, the Court was not persuaded by the evidence produced by the defendants to justify the use of IQ tests as a means of classification. The Court said:

> Defendants do not seem to dispute the evidence amassed by plaintiffs to demonstrate that the IQ tests in fact are culturally biased. Indeed, defendants have stated that they are merely awaiting the development of what they expect will

---

[31] Rosenthal, R. and Jacobson, L. (1968) *Pygmalion in the Classroom*. New York: Holt, Rinehart & Winston.

[32] See note 6.

## Legal Context of Educational Testing

be a minimally biased test. This test currently is being standardized; but the final product is not expected to be available for more than a year [at 1313].

Significantly, the defendants did not argue the issue of bias said to be inherent in the IQ tests. Instead, they held to their contentions that the tests were not the cause of the racial imbalance in EMR classes or, if they were, the tests were rationally related to the purpose for which they were used because they were said to be the best means of classification available at the time. The defendants also claimed that the racial imbalance was the result of the location of EMR classes in predominantly black schools prior to the desegration of the USFSD, or the fact that more white than black parents placed their "mentally retarded" children in private schools. The Court found that the defendants had not been able to substantiate these claims for the record.

The Court was also unimpressed by the defendants' argument that the IQ test, though racially biased, was necessary because of lack of alternatives. It pointed out that

... the absence of any rational means of identifying children in need of such treatment can hardly render acceptable an otherwise concededly irrational means, such as the IQ test as it is presently administered to black students [at 1313].

The Court found that ". . . there exist alternatives which seem to the Court to be at least as useful to defendants in addressing this need" [at 1313]. Four alternatives were discussed by the Court. Two examples were presented by the plaintiffs of school systems which had attempted to minimize the importance of IQ tests.

At the time of the 1972 *Larry P.* hearing, IQ tests had been banned in New York City, and heavy use was being made of achievement test results and teacher evaluations. This information was supplied by the plaintiffs in a letter dated February 9, 1972, from Vera A. Paster, Director of the Washington Heights-West Harlem-Inwood Mental Health Council, to Harold E. Dent, Ph.D. And again, the "Massachusetts Regulations Pertaining to Education of Certain Children," dated October 27, 1971, required "psychological assessment" of potential EMR students, but did not specify IQ tests as part of the assessment. Massachusetts had also instituted an elaborate due process system for revising decisions to place students in such classes.

The other two alternatives mentioned by the Court were: to administer the IQ tests to black children in the same manner as had been used with the plaintiffs by the Bay Area Association of Black Psychologists; or to set up requirements to get fully informed consent from parents, as suggested in an affidavit from Dr. Edward Opton, a local clinical psychologist.

After a review of the plaintiffs' and defendants' evidence, the Court concluded that the defendants had not sustained their burden of demonstrating that the IQ tests were rationally related to the purpose of segregating students according to their ability, at least insofar as these tests are applied to black students.

The Court also concluded that the plaintiffs therefore had established the prerequisites to issuance of a preliminary injunction and found that the plaintiffs would suffer irreparable injury if relief were not granted. In addition, the Court held that the plaintiffs were likely to be able to establish that they had been deprived of their rights to equal protection of the law and that they would likely succeed on the merits of the case. Furthermore, the Court found that the defendants had not substantiated their contention that no alternatives existed to primary use of IQ tests for placing students in EMR classes. By implication, it found that the defendants would not suffer irreparable harm if a preliminary injunction were granted.

The plaintiffs had asked the Court for the following remedies:

1. Elimination of all culturally biased tests.
2. Immediate evaluation of black students already in EMR classes.
3. A mandatory injunction requiring the USFSD to supplement the education of those students who were wrongfully placed in EMR classes in the past in order to compensate them for any harm they may already have suffered.
4. That state and city defendants be required to hire minority group psychologists and consultants "to make concerted efforts that psychological assessment of black school children be conducted and interpreted by persons adequately prepared to consider the cultural background of the child, preferably a person of similar ethnic background as the child being encountered" [at 1314].
5. That the Court establish a ratio by which the percentage of black students in EMR classes could exceed the percentage of black students in the school district as a whole by no more than 15 percent. This was requested as an attempt to avoid racial bias in whatever methods the defendants utilized in place of IQ tests.

No black student may be placed in an EMR class on the basis of criteria which place primary reliance on the results of IQ tests as they are currently administered, if the consequence of use of such criteria is racial imbalance in the composition of such classes [at 1315].

## Legal Context of Educational Testing

The plaintiffs' requests for remedies were successful only in part. The Court pointed out that it would deal only with future testing and future evaluation.

1. The Court's order virtually eliminated the use of IQ tests for the time being.
2. The Court did not order immediate evaluation of black students already in EMR classes.
3. No compensatory supplemental education was ordered for students who had been wrongfully placed in EMR classes in the past.
4. As to future hiring of minority group psychologists and consultants, the Court could be said to have supported this concept at least indirectly. It did prohibit primary reliance on IQ tests as currently administered. The Court also said that the yearly reevaluations of black children in EMR classes must be conducted by means that do not deprive them of the equal protection of the laws. In carrying out the Court's order, the defendants possibly would find helpful the hiring of minority group psychologists and consultants.
5. The Court refused to establish the requested ratio, believing that it would leave the needs of retarded black students at the mercy of white parents, who might decline to place their retarded children in EMR classes and thereby reduce the number of retarded black children placed there.

In general, because it was clear that there were several alternative classification plans that could be used by the defendants, the Court provided as much flexibility as possible for formulating systems that met Constitutional requirements.

### 1979—Larry P. v. Riles

The full trial on the merits of this case began on October 11, 1977. It lasted for some 5 months and involved detailed testimony from expert witnesses on IQ tests. On October 11, 1979, 2 years after the trial began, Chief Justice Peckham of the U.S. District Court in San Francisco signed the opinion in this mammoth, nonjury case. By the time the trial on the merits began, the initial Fourteenth Amendment complaint had been amended to include alleged violations of three statutes: Title VI of the Civil Rights Act of 1964, the Education for All Handicapped Children Act of 1975 (EHA), and Section 504 of the Rehabilitation Act of 1973. Ultimately, the evidence supported a decision that both the constitutional and statutory claims had been proved by plaintiffs. This was the first federal case to apply validation criteria to tests used for EMR placement.

There was no disagreement between the parties about two facts. First, EMR classes are "dead-end" classes for children thought to be incapable of learning the material in regular classes; the emphasis is on social adjustment and economic usefulness, not academic skills, and the placement generally is permanent. EMR classes are not remedial or compensatory; mildly retarded students are not expected to be able to participate in academic classes, so are not prepared to return to such classes. Second, black children were found in EMR classes in numbers grossly disproportionate to their representation in the student population. Black children represented only 10 percent of the general student population in California, but provided some 25 percent of the population enrolled in EMR classes.

Evidence was presented regarding three basic reasons for the disparity in the IQ scores of blacks and whites. The first was the genetic argument, described as based on the notion that natural selection has resulted in black persons having a "gene pool" that dooms them as a group to less intelligence. The second was the socioeconomic argument, that IQ tests were biased against poor students, both black and white, not because of inferior genes or divergent cultures, but because of inferior home and neighborhood environments. Neither of these arguments was convincing to the judge. The third argument was that the tests were culturally biased, and Judge Peckham found the evidence for this argument the most worthy.

Cultural bias was proved by inferential evidence that the tests were never designed to try to eliminate biases against black children. It was assumed that black children were less intelligent than whites. Yet, developer of the Wechsler Test, Dr. David Wechsler, said in 1944 that the test's norms could not be used for the "colored" population of the United States as it was standardized and developed on an all-white population. Later, according to the evidence, several tests were restandardized on mixed populations; but the test items remained substantially the same, so the tests remained inappropriate. The famous "fight item" on the Wechsler Intelligence Scale for Children (WISC) tests was used as an illustration. The question is what should you do if struck by a smaller child of the same sex. The "correct" answer is that it is wrong to hit back. Black 6- and 7-year-old children gave "wrong" answers more than twice as often as whites. The difference was attributed to a cultural variation at that age. Only one of the defendants' experts felt there were no cultural differences between blacks and whites. Otherwise there was general agreement by all sides on the inevitable effect of cultural differences on IQ scores.

Judge Peckham next faced the matter of the relevance of cultural bias to the disparity in the IQ scores of blacks and whites. He commented

## Legal Context of Educational Testing

that the evidence indicated that IQ tests could not give a simple number corresponding to an innate trait called intelligence. Instead, he said, the tests give a statistically correlated score indicating the current performance of children on the items chosen and utilized by test designers. Since the tests had been standardized on middle-class white children, their validity for measuring skills and potential of such children could be assumed. The same could not be assumed for blacks. For, the judge said, to the extent that a "black culture" exists and translates into skills and knowledge untested by the standardized IQ tests, those tests cannot measure the capabilities of black children.

Title VI of the 1964 Civil Rights Act[33] was the first of the statutes addressed by Judge Peckham in the legal analysis. Intent was not considered here, though the Bakke decision[34] suggested it might be at some future time. Judge Peckham found that the plaintiffs had established a *prima facie* case by proving that the mechanisms in use had placed grossly disproportionate numbers of black children in EMR classes, and this had the discriminatory effect of excluding them from a normal education.

The next legal issue was whether the adverse impact alone dictated a decision for the plaintiffs under Title VI. The judge indicated that the *prima facie* case could have been rebutted if the defendants had been able to prove either that there was in fact more mild mental retardation in black children, or that the IQ tests had been "validated for the purpose of EMR placement of black children."

The Rehabilitation Act of 1973[35] and the Education for All Handicapped Children Act of 1975 (EHA)[36] were considered next. They represent an educational philosophy unlike that which had formerly characterized California's treatment of EMR pupils, in terms of the classification of children and mainstreaming, as well as provisions that tests and other evaluation materials be properly validated.

The Court said that, based on the evidence, the validation had been assumed, not established, with regard to mental retardation for blacks. California had failed to take the steps necessary to ensure the tests' validity. Whether or not the tests do in fact what they are supposed to do, the law requires California to *show* that they have been validated for each minority group with which they are used.

Even if the tests had been proved rationally related to the placement

---

[33] See note 1.
[34] See note 8.
[35] See note 2.
[36] See note 3.

process, the Court asserted that the plaintiffs still would have prevailed because they showed that alternative devices for EMR placement exist.

Regarding the defendants' claim that the IQ tests had predictive validity, the evidence persuaded the Court that it was apparent that the tests were differentially valid as to blacks and whites and therefore not reliable.

Judge Peckham said his decision could rest on the federal statutory claims, but that it would be inappropriate to conclude the analysis there. He then took up the original claim, that of invidious discrimination under the Equal Protection Clause of the Fourteenth Amendment. The strict scrutiny applied to racial classifications is no longer triggered by disproportionate impact alone but by reactions that are deemed to be intentional (*Washington v. Davis* (1976)).[37] Ascertaining that intent is not a simple matter.

In the *Larry P.* decisions, the Court discussed a recent Supreme Court decision that it found helpful in ascertaining intent (*Personnel Administration of Massachusetts v. Feeney* (1979)).[38] The Supreme Court held there that the Massachusetts veterans' preference resulted in a very substantial overrepresentation of men in the Massachusetts civil service. On this point, the Supreme Court indicated that "inevitability of foreseeability of consequences" can permit "a strong inference that the adverse effects were desired," but "an inference is a working tool, not a synonym for proof." The presumption-of-intent analysis is therefore not necessarily precluded, but it cannot be utilized mechanistically to reject probative evidence and find a subjective intent grounded solely on discriminatory impact. The situation "demands a sensitive inquiry into such circumstantial and direct evidence of intent as may be available" (*Village of Arlington Heights v. Metropolitan Housing Development Corp* (1976)).[39] The Supreme Court let stand another relevant decision that stated:

When such actions have the "natural, probable, and foreseeable result of increasing or perpetuating segregation," a presumption of segregative purpose is created. The burden of proof then shifts to defendant officials to show that the pattern of actions taken by those officials can be explained in a manner consistent with the absence of segregative intent (*Arthur v. Nyquist* (1978)).[40]

Judge Peckham also returned to *Brown v. Board of Education* (1954)[41]

---

[37] *Washington v. Davis*, 426 U.S. 229 (1976).
[38] *Personnel Administrator of Massachusetts v. Feeney*, 47 U.S.L.W. 4924 (June 26, 1974).
[39] *Village of Arlington Heights v. Metropolitan Housing Development Corp.*, 429 U.S. 254 (1976).
[40] *Arthur v. Nyquist*, 573 F.2d 134, 142-43 (2d Cir. 1978), cert. denied, 99 S.Ct. 179.
[41] *Brown v. Board of Education*, 347 U.S. 483 (1954), 349 U.S. 294 (1955).

for help in applying the law to the facts in this case. He noted that, since *Brown*, an intent to segregate minority children in separate schools has sufficed to prove a *prima facie* violation of the Fourteenth Amendment. Even more than segregated schools, he asserted, disproportionate enrollment of minorities in EMR classes stigmatizes those in the classes and serves inevitably to perpetuate invidious stereotypes based on the superiority or inferiority of "racial stocks."

Regarding intent by the defendants, Judge Peckham based his finding on the timing of the State Board of Education's decision in 1969 to mandate EMR placement based on a list of approved IQ tests. This occurred just when the legislature had indicated it wanted, instead, to study the disproportionate enrollment of minorities in EMR classes. Judge Peckham found that this revealed impermissible intent to discriminate. Furthermore, he said, requiring IQ tests had profound discriminatory effects, and racially neutral tests had not been developed, nor were any efforts made to do so. Also, the process of compiling the list of IQ tests in 1969 was characterized as peculiar. Only persons connected with testing companies were consulted, not outside experts. The final decision about which tests would be required (the two Wechslers, the Stanford-Binet, the Leiter) was made on the basis of frequency of use, not validation studies. In short, he said, since the tests could be expected to perpetuate overenrollment of minorities in EMR classes, the inference of discriminatory intent was inescapable.

Accordingly, Judge Peckham held that the plaintiffs had met their burden of proving discriminatory intent. He then found that the defendants had not met their burden under the strict scrutiny test of showing a strong justification or compelling state interest in the use of IQ tests or in the maintenance of EMR classes that were overwhelmingly black in enrollment. He enjoined California from utilizing, permitting the use of, or approving the use of, any standardized intelligence tests without securing prior approval of the Court. To get approval, the defendants would be required to make a written request stating that the tests were not discriminatory and were validated for the determination of EMR status; they also would be required to supply specific statistics on scores of blacks and whites and certify that an open meeting on the subject had been held.

The defendants also were ordered to monitor and eliminate disproportionate placement of black children in EMR classes. Again, specific provisions were made for reporting information to the Court. In addition, each school district was to be directed to reevaluate every black child currently classified as an EMR pupil. Each child who was found misdiagnosed was to be given an individualized education plan (IEP) to prepare for return to regular classes. Finally, the Court found, regarding the named plaintiffs, that the only relevant evidence in their cases indicated that they were not retarded.

*Parents In Action On Special Education v. Hannon* (1980),[42] a third major case of alleged racial bias, again involved the use of IQ tests for placement of black children in EMR classes. In the *Parents* case, two black Chicago school children had been placed erroneously in EMR classes. Their parents joined in a class action suit against the Chicago school system, alleging that the error in placement was because of cultural bias in the standardized intelligence tests administered to black school children. In contrast to the U.S. District Court for Northern California, the U.S. District Court for Northern Illinois refused to bar the use of the intelligence tests, even though they were part of a classification process that placed a disproportionate number of black children in EMR classes. The Illinois court found fault, not with the tests or their use, but with the interpretations of the test results by the school psychologists.

The Illinois court heard evidence on over 400 test items on the three tests used in Chicago—the Stanford-Binet and two Wechsler (WISC and WISC-R) tests—and upon completion of the testimony concluded that only nine questions might contain cultural bias. (These three tests were among those found racially biased in California.) The court also found that the IQ score was not the only criterion used to place a child in an EMR class; that the numerical test score was interpreted by school psychologists who had at least a master's degree with a minimum of 54 hours of psychology; and that 44 of the 193 school psychologists were black, so there was little likelihood that a black child would be recommended for EMR without the concurrence of at least one black psychologist. Therefore, the possibility that the few biased test items would result in misplacement was said by the court to be practically nonexistent.

The California court in *Larry P.* had focused on determining the proper legal standards for evaluating compliance with federal law, after finding the intelligence tests racially biased, insofar as there was discriminatory intent in violation of constitutional guarantees of equal protection and discriminatory impact in violation of Title VI of the 1964 Civil Rights Act. In the California case, the court had remarked that the threshold issue of the cultural bias of the tests was hardly disputed in the litigation and went on to the issue of what legal standards were to be applied when biased tests were being used. As noted above, the tests in California had been found biased because they had not been validated specifically for the

---

[42] *Parents in Action On Special Education v. Hannon* (USDC NILL: 49 U.S.L.W. 2087, July 7, 1980).

purpose for which they were being used, that is, placement of black school children in EMR classes, according to the validation standards of the regulations of the Education for All Handicapped Children Act and the Rehabilitation Act.

The Illinois federal district court focused on the allegation of racial bias in the tests themselves and in their use for placement of Chicago children in EMR classes. The Illinois court did not go beyond this threshold question to a consideration of legal standards. Indeed, it found there was insufficient evidence presented to prove racial bias in either the tests or their use for placement of children in EMR classes.

In essence, the court in *Parents* found that the misassessment of the two plaintiffs was not due to racial bias of the tests, but that their problems were caused by learning disabilities. The Illinois court said that the test results had been improperly interpreted by the school psychologists. It ruled that the use of these tests, in conjunction with other criteria, did not discriminate against black children in the Chicago schools. Possible liability for injury due to improper interpretation of test results was not discussed.

**Linguistic Bias**

In *Diana v. California State Board of Education* (1970),[43] tests used for placement in EMR classes were challenged as violating the Fourteenth Amendment and Title VI of the 1964 Civil Rights Act. In this case, Stanford-Binet IQ and WISC tests had been individually administered in English to Mexican-American children, whose scores ranged between 68 and 52. When retested by a bilingual psychologist, however, and permitted to answer in either English or Spanish, their scores increased 15 points on the average. As in *Hobson*,[44] evidence was offered in the complaint that the tests used had been standardized on white Anglo-Americans and were biased against Mexican-Americans. This case did not go to trial. A consent agreement was negotiated that stipulated: (1) future testing of non-Anglo children for EMR placement should use both the child's primary language and English; (2) only certain tests or parts thereof could be used, that is, no vocabulary, general information, or other unfair verbal questions could be asked; and (3) state psychologists were to develop and standardize an IQ test appropriate for Mexican-American and other non-English-speaking Californians.

---

[43] See note 5.
[44] See note 6.

The *Diana* case was a turning point of sorts. Very shortly thereafter, the California state legislature acted specifically to prevent overreliance on IQ test scores for EMR placements. It passed legislation in 1970 requiring that test scores had to be substantiated by other techniques, such as a complete evaluation of the child's developmental history, academic achievement, and family and cultural background. Also in 1970, at the federal level, HEW issued a Memorandum, 35 Fed. Reg. 11,595 (1970), to the effect that schools throughout the U.S. should not assign non-English-speaking children to EMR classes on the basis of tests that measure English language skills, as such practice might violate Title VI of the Civil Rights Act of 1964.

In 1972 a similar decision was reached in *Guadalupe Organization Inc. v. Tempe Elementary School District*[45] in Arizona. Again, the complaint was in violation of the Fourteenth Amendment and of Title VI, in which the Court assisted the parties to a negotiated agreement. Students whose principal language was Spanish, not English, had been wrongly placed in classes for the mentally handicapped. The consent agreement provided that all such students would have their placements reevaluated. In the future, appropriate testing and examination would be administered to ensure that language and cultural factors would be taken into account in determining placement.

In implementing the *Guadalupe* agreement, the school set up a system for remedial English. This system was challenged in 1978 in a second, separate suit by parents of Spanish-speaking students, who claimed this form of implementation was a violation of the Fourteenth Amendment and of the Civil Rights Act of 1964, or of the Equal Educational Opportunity Act of 1974. They sought instead a system providing that each child in kindergarten through twelfth grade become competent and functional in reading, writing, and comprehension of their own language as well as English. They argued that an appropriate educational program should offer bilingual and bicultural courses of instruction, instructional materials, and testing procedures, in order to reflect the customs and history of the parents. The Court held that the school district's plan for only remedial English did not violate the Constitution or the statutes specified. This holding was consistent with an earlier 1974 U.S. Supreme Court decision.

In this decision, *Lau v. Nichols* (1974),[46] the Supreme Court found that

---

[45] *Guadalupe Organization, Inc. v. Tempe Elementary School District*, No. 71-435 PHX (D. Ariz., Jan. 24, 1972).
[46] See note 13.

## Legal Context of Educational Testing

a substantial number of Chinese-speaking elementary school children in San Francisco were being taught and tested in English without sufficient training in the language. The Court found this had an adverse impact on a substantial number of children that denied them a meaningful education and held that the school district had violated Title VI of the Civil Rights Act of 1964 and also the 1970 HEW Regulations which, read together, require school districts receiving federal funds to provide equal educational opportunities for all children, including those with linguistic deficiencies [at 567]. The Court did not reach the equal protection agreement but found that, under Title VI, school officials were obligated to provide students, who were non-English-speaking, with the necessary language skills to profit from their school attendance by means of remedial English instruction, bilingual classes, or some other method. The Court left the choice of method to the school district.

In *Serna v. Portales Municipal Schools* (1972 and 1974),[47] a District Court, and later a Court of Appeals, found that a substantial number of Spanish-surnamed students at the elementary school level in New Mexico, who spoke Spanish at home, lived in a Spanish culture, and knew very little English when they entered the school system, were given achievement tests totally in the English language. IQ tests showed that they fell farther behind as they moved from first to fifth grade. The high school dropout rate was high. The schools had provided a bilingual-bicultural program, but it had proved inadequate. The school district neither applied for funds under the federal Bilingual Education Act, 20 U.S.C. Sec. 880b, nor would it accept funds for a similar purpose when offered them by the State of New Mexico.

In *Serna*, the Court of Appeals upheld the District Court, finding that the record established violations of Title VI of the Civil Rights Act of 1964, which prohibits exclusion from participation in, denial of benefits of, and discrimination under federally assisted programs on grounds of race, color, or national origin. The Court of Appeals also held that the District Court could properly establish a program for the elimination of discrimination, to include increased bilingual instruction, a bicultural outlook in as many subject areas as practicable, a special effort to recruit and hire bilingual teachers, and utilization of sources of available funding.

### Inadequate Reevaluation of Test Scores

In these cases against school districts, a court was held not to be the proper forum to seek redress.

---

[47] *Serna v. Portales Municipal Schools*, 351 F. Supp. 1279 (1972); 499 F.2d 1147 (1974).

*Hoffman v. The Board of Education of New York City* (1979)[48] involved an allegation of negligence, which had resulted in a 1976 jury award of $500,000 that was reversed in 1979. The claim was made by a student who had a severe speech defect. He had been tested by a school psychologist in 1956-1957 when he was 6 years old. The test used was the primarily verbal Stanford-Binet Intelligence Test, which showed the child had an IQ of 74, one point below the minimum necessary for admission to regular classes. The psychologist noted the difficulty in assessing the child's mental ability, and suggested he be reevaluated within 2 years.

Nevertheless, as a result of that evaluation he was placed in EMR classes and was not evaluated again until the beginning of the 1969-1970 school year, when he applied for placement in an occupational training center run by the district. It was then discovered he had a "verbal" IQ of 85 and a "performance" IQ of 107 for a "full scale" IQ of 94. He was, in fact, of normal, or slightly above normal, intelligence. He was denied admission to the center. He sued the district for depriving him of 12 years of appropriate learning opportunity, the loss of earning capacity, and the private expenditures for services that the school should have provided.

The student charged the school district with negligence in hiring incompetent personnel, in incorrectly evaluating him, and then neglecting to reevaluate him, in failing to supervise personnel properly, in depriving him of speech therapy, and in misleading his mother as to his true intelligence. This suit was based upon the consideration that more rigorous standards of professional conduct apply in dealing with special education students than with those who remained in regular classes. A school board regulation required "competently administered" individual intelligence tests. The state education code required that the placement be evaluated by an accredited psychologist or psychiatrist. The trial court's instructions to the jury requested a finding of negligence if the jury found that a violation of the state code regarding mentally retarded children was a proximate cause of harm or injury to this plaintiff. The trial court defined educational negligence in special education in terms of the duty of care, relating to the special training received for teaching mentally retarded children, rather than that relating to the training for teaching normal children.

The New York State Court of Appeals reversed this on the principle that courts ought not to interfere with the professional judgment involved

---

[48] *Hoffman v. The Board of Education of New York City*, Index No. 12593/71, Supreme Court of the State of New York Queens County (Oct. 21, 1976); reversed, 424 N.Y.S. 2d 376 (1979).

## Legal Context of Educational Testing

and pointed out that there was a state administrative review procedure available. Three judges dissented because they thought the case involved not "educational malpractice" but "discernible affirmative negligence" in the failure to carry out the reevaluation.

Other educational negligence cases as well have been unsuccessful on appeal. One of these was *Peter Doe v. San Francisco Unified School District* (1976).[49] The parents of a student who graduated from high school with only fifth grade reading ability charged the school district with negligence in not providing the student with basic reading and writing skills, thereby substantially limiting his future income. The matter of routine testing of students for competence in basic skills was not mentioned. The parents' claim failed because the court found no evidence of a direct causal link between the quality of teaching at the school and the student's lack of basic skills. The Court said, "The achievement of literacy in the schools, or its failure, is influenced by a host of factors which affect the pupil subjectively, from outside the formal teaching process, and beyond the control of its ministers."

### Challenges to Minimum Competency Testing

Tests measuring achievement and subject mastery have also been challenged, especially minimum competency tests, which have been adopted by at least thirty-seven states, according to the Education Commission of the States (*The New York Times*, March 19, 1979, p. 1). Litigation concerning these tests shows signs of increasing, and not just for their effects on minority students.

*Debra P. v. Turlington* (1979)[50] was the first federal court decision on minimum competency testing. It was a class action lawsuit brought by ten black twelfth grade public school students in Hillsborough County, Florida, challenging the administration of the Florida Functional Literacy Examination, known as the SSAT II. The plaintiffs had taken the SSAT II as eleventh graders in October 1977 and Spring 1978 and failed to pass it. They took it again as twelfth graders in May 1979, and again failed. Because they had not passed, they would not be awarded regular high school diplomas, but would receive certificates of completion instead. They claimed this would stigmatize them unfairly, since they had not been educated in desegregated schools long enough to overcome the effects of earlier racial discrimination on their education.

---

[49] *Peter Doe v. San Francisco Unified School District*, 60 Cal. App. 3d 814 (1976).
[50] See note 9.

The students made three claims in their lawsuit. First, they said that the SSAT II was racially biased, due partially to past segregation practices, in violation of the Fourteenth Amendment's Equal Protection Clause, of Title VI of the 1964 Civil Rights Act, and the Equal Educational Opportunity Act. Second, they contended that they were denied due process by virtue of not being given adequate notice of the new graduation requirement or adequate time to prepare for it. Third, they asserted that Florida public officials used the SSAT II as a mechanism for resegregating the Florida public schools by separating into remedial classes those students who failed the SSAT II in their junior year.

Florida's Educational Accountability Act had become effective on July 1, 1976. It provided that standards were to be set for minimum performance in the state's public education plan, including, but not limited to, basic skills in reading, writing, and mathematics. Students' progress and achievement in these skills were to be assessed periodically by testing in grades 3, 5, 8, and 11, and testing in other grades and skill areas could be added as specified by the commissioner of education. The State Student Achievement Test (SSAT I) was developed for this ongoing assessment.

In addition, the Act provided that satisfactory performance on an examination of functional literacy (SSAT II) be a requirement for high school graduation by the school year 1978-1979.

Then, in 1978, the Educational Accountability Act was amended to provide that, beginning in 1978-1979, students failing to pass the SSAT II would receive only a certificate of completion, not a regular high school diploma.

The Florida Legislature thereby set three standards for graduation from public high school: that students complete the minimum number of credits set by their local school board; that they show mastery of basic skills, as measured by the ongoing SSAT I; that they demonstrate functional literacy, as measured finally by the SSAT II.

The results of the third SSAT II administration to the plaintiffs in May 1979 were released during the *Debra P.* trial; 20 percent of the black students failed a third time, compared to only 1.9 percent of the white students. The Court noted that the failure rate among black students was about ten times that of the white students. In total numbers, about 5,300 twelfth graders, 3,466 black and 1,342 white students, out of 91,000 seniors, or 5.8 percent, had failed to pass the SSAT II by the end of their senior year.

The Court said that "the denial of a standard diploma based on the failure of the SSAT II triggers a number of economic and academic deprivations." Regarding employment, for example, the Court pointed out

## Legal Context of Educational Testing

that the Florida Career Service Department employed only 10 percent of its labor force from people who did not have high school diplomas. Those in that 10 percent were predominantly in dead end, menial jobs.

Further to the point, a certificate of completion would not be considered a diploma for purposes of employment with the state itself. Regarding educational progress, a high school diploma was required for admission to all but one of the nine universities in Florida; a certificate of completion would not suffice. In the past, some black students in the lowest two deciles of their high school classes who received diplomas had gone on to higher education. Now, the Court noted, there would be an estimated 20-percent decline in black students' college attendance. The Court, therefore, found that the stigma attached to failing the SSAT II was very serious. Indeed, those who failed were often labelled "functionally illiterate."

The Court noted that, prior to the trial, the parties had agreed to the facts that a dual school system had existed in Florida for a period of time, and that, historically, black children had not scored well on standardized tests in Florida schools. Also, the Court took judicial notice that from 1890 to 1967, Florida operated by force of law complete and separate public school systems for black and white students. This went as far as absolute segregation of school faculty on a racial basis and maintenance of segregated professional associations and unions. Black schools were inferior to white schools in physical facilities, size and scope of curricula, libraries, duration of school day and year, supplies, and textbooks. This duality was supported by the Florida Constitution, various state statutes, and policies and practices of local school boards. The Court noted that this state of affairs violated the "separate but equal" doctrine of *Plessy v. Ferguson* (1896).[51]

In addition to the claim in the *Debra P.* case that the SSAT II perpetuated and reemphasized the effects of past purposeful discrimination, the students contended that the test was invalid and not correlated with the public school curriculum; that the test instrument itself was racially biased; and that passage of the test was not required for graduation from Florida private schools. The students also contended that the higher percentage of black twelfth grade failures was the probable and foreseeable consequence of enactment and implementation of the statutory scheme by Florida public officials and that the SSAT II, therefore, violated the Fourteenth Amendment Equal Protection Clause, Title VI, and the Equal Education Opportunity Act.

---

[51] *Plessy v. Ferguson*, 163 U.S. 537 (1896).

The evidence offered by the parties regarding this first claim led the Court to the following findings. The students who brought this lawsuit had begun their education in 1967, and, until 1971, when they finished fourth grade, had attended schools that still were uniformly de facto racially segregated. *Brown v. Board of Education* (1954)[52] had held that such separate facilities were inherently unequal. Therefore, during those 4 years, the dual school systems violated the black student plaintiffs' Fourteenth Amendment equal protection rights.

The Court viewed the evidence as showing that the pervasive racial isolation condemned in *Brown*, along with the inferiority of the black schools, created an atmosphere that was not as conducive to learning as that found in white schools. The Court found this environment a serious impairment to black students' ability to learn, especially in the important early grades.

When fully integrated education began in 1971-1972, in their fifth grade of schooling, they faced many new problems: disparate busing schedules, lingering racial stereotypes, disproportionate terminations of black principles and administrators, and a high incidence of suspensions. The Court said that these conditions made significant academic gains difficult. Moreover, it took note that not until 1977-1978, the eleventh grade of schooling for these black students, was the state beginning to deal with the educational deficits created during the period of segregation. This was the same year that the SSAT II was administered for the first time. The Court found that, although remediation was under way, the effects of past purposeful segregation had not been erased or overcome.

Proof of past intent of the state to discriminate was therefore clear. As to present intent to discriminate, during the trial numerous state Department of Education employees, as well as State Education Commissioner Turlington, testified that they anticipated a high percentage of black failure on the SSAT II. Turlington also admitted that the earlier 4 years of inferior segregated education must have contributed to some portion of the plaintiff's failure.

The plaintiffs did not assert that, in passing this law, the Florida legislature was motivated by racial animus. This would be necessary to prove discriminatory intent, as defined by the Supreme Court in *Personnel Administrator of Massachusetts v. Feeney* (1979):[53]

"Discriminatory purpose" . . . implies more than . . . intent as awareness of consequences. . . . It implies that . . . a state legislature, selected or reaffirmed

---

[52] See note 42.
[53] See note 39.

a particular course of action at least in part "because of," not merely "in spite of," its adverse effects upon an indentifiable group [47 U.S.L.W. at 4656].

The Supreme Court added in Note 25, however, that inevitability or foreseeability of a consequence, where clear and obvious, did have a bearing on the discriminatory intent.

The Florida Court in this case found that both the adverse consequences of the effects of the SSAT II on black school children and the obvious linkage of their poor performance to their early inferior education during segregation, were clear to the State Board of Education at the critical stages of the development and implementation of the SSAT II.

The Court agreed with the defendants that the state had a legitimate interest in implementing a test to evaluate the established statewide educational objectives. But the Court found that the timing of the program had to be questioned and that the proof of present intent was insufficient. However, the Court did find that past purposeful discrimination was perpetuated by the test and the diploma sanction regardless of its neutrality.

Other cases involving literacy tests were referred to by the Court, especially those in which the constitutionality of ability groupings in public schools was considered. In two such cases, ability groupings derived by standardized testing and teacher evaluation resulted in higher concentrations of white students in advanced classes and black students in slower classes (*McNeal v. Tate* (1975)[54] and *United States v. Gadsden County School District* (1978).[55]

*McNeal* focused particularly on the nexus between inferior education in a dual school system and the present ability categorization. That decision held, in effect, that such segregation would be permissible only after the school district had operated as a unitary system long enough to ensure that the underachievement of the slower groups was not due to former educational disparities.

The Florida Court felt that not enough time had elapsed for the effect of past purposeful discrimination to be eliminated in the Florida schools. As further evidence that black schoolchildren still bore the effects of racial isolation and the deprivation of equal educational opportunities, the Court mentioned that these factors were cited again and again by Florida school districts in their applications for federal funds for educational remediation.

This evidence, said the Court, plus the passing ratios for the SSAT II, both numerically and proportionately, indicated that race more than any

---

[54] *McNeal v. Tate*, 508 F.2d 1017 (5th Cir. 1975).
[55] *United States v. Gadsen County School District*, 572 F.2d 1049 (5th Cir. 1978).

other factor, including socioeconomic status, was a predictor of passing the test. The fact that 20 percent of the black students failed the SSAT II compared to only 1.9 percent of the whites persuaded the Florida Court that peer status had not yet been achieved. The Court said further that only when students, regardless of race, were permitted to commence and pursue their education in a unitary school system without the taint of a dual system would a graduation requirement based on a neutral test be permitted. In the meantime, the Court concluded, using the SSAT II as a requirement for a high school diploma was a violation of the Equal Protection Clause of the Fourteenth Amendment, Title VI, and the Equal Educational Opportunity Act. As a remedy, the Court enjoined the use of the SSAT II as a requirement for high school graduation until the 1982-1983 school year.

Regarding the validity of the test itself, the Court was asked to consider the manner in which the SSAT II was developed and whether it was valid, from both a constitutional and professional testing perspective. Evidence showed that development of the test was assigned to the Florida Department of Education. The statute requiring the test was effective July 1, 1976, and the test was to be ready to determine eligibility for graduation in the 1978-1979 school year. In that short period of time, it had to decide upon functional objectives or skills, and then develop or purchase a test that would measure whether students had mastered them. By December 1976, the department had decided that the objectives would be the practical applications of eleven basic reading and writing skills and thirteen mathematical skills from the eleventh grade and contracted with the Educational Testing Service (ETS) to draft test items to match the objectives.

In February 1977, the Department of Education staff decided on a definition of "functional literacy":

. . . the satisfactory application of basic skills in reading, writing and arithmetic, to problems and tasks of a practical nature in everyday life.

In March 1977, ETS and one other company were ready with sample test items, and field testing was carried out in five Florida counties. In October 1977, the SSAT II was administered for the first time, and the plaintiffs failed it. The criterion-referenced test contained 117 questions, covering the twenty-four skill objectives. In early 1978, more test items were developed and field tested. The evidence indicated that the test and the item specifications were kept secure and confidential.

The Court discussed a matter it felt was at the heart of the controversy between the litigants. The test was legislatively created as a functional literacy test. The evidence presented at the trial indicated that there was

## Legal Context of Educational Testing

no one definition of functional literacy. It was clear, however, that the term had a universally negative inference and connotation.

Indeed, the plaintiffs' experts commented that students who failed the test perceived themselves as "global failures." Another of the plaintiffs' experts testified that the biggest flaw in the Florida program was its name. The Court said it was in complete agreement and that the stigma associated with the term "functional illiteracy" was the most substantial harm presented. However, the Court took note of the fact that the State Board of Education had adopted a new name for the test, that is, SSAT II. Also, the Court said that it had to determine the validity of the test according to the definition provided by the state, not that perceived by the public.

The Court asserted that its task was to determine whether the test used met the constitutional due process standard of being related to its purpose as a valid measure for classifying students as to high school graduation. That is, did the test reasonably or arbitrarily evaluate the skill objectives established by the State Board of Education?

The Court found that the domain of the test did not fit all, or even many, definitions of functional literacy, but that it did match the one given by both the Florida Department of Education and the State Board of Education. The evidence presented did persuade the Court that the skill objectives of the test were adequately evaluated by the test items and that the test therefore had adequate content validity. The Court went on to comment that the evidence also indicated that the test had adequate construct validity.

The Court was therefore of the opinion that the test did bear a rational relation to a valid state interest. Students had been divided into two categories, pass and fail, using a test found by the Court to be rationally related to the purpose for which it was designed, despite expert testimony to the contrary.

However, the plaintiffs contended that there was test item bias. The Court found that two testing companies had reviewed the items for possible racial or ethnic bias, and that the Department of Education had analyzed the items for bias with the help of groups of teachers. In addition, the department commissioned a scatter plot analysis of the test to determine bias. The Court said that, while some of the questions did seem to have factual settings unfamiliar to certain racial groups, such distraction was minimal and not pervasive. Therefore, the Court was not convinced that the test or any item should be invalidated for racial or ethnic bias.

Furthermore, the Court rejected the plaintiffs' argument that applying the SSAT II testing program only to public schools, and not to private ones, was a violation of the Equal Protection and Due Process Clauses of the Fourteenth Amendment. Florida required only that private schools register the name and address of the institution, names of administrative offices, enrollment, and number of teachers, and that they keep attendance records. No accreditation was required. The Court found a rational basis for the state's decision that it need not correct all education problems at once, but could decide to ensure effectiveness by beginning with schools it controlled and funded.

The plaintiffs' second claim was that their due process rights were violated because of inadequate notice about the new requirement for receipt of regular high school diplomas, which gave them insufficient time to prepare for the tests. During the summer of 1977, the department distributed the basic skill and functional literacy objectives to all Florida public schools. Thus, public school teachers knew of the literacy objectives 4 months in advance of the first administration of the test, but only 2 months of school time were available for instruction in the application of the skills. Moreover, only 13 months of instructional time intervened from December 1977, when the first test results were released, to April 1979, the date of the final administration. Remediation classes were held in the interim, but the remedial instructional materials prepared by the education department were not immediately available. Remediation programs are still going on and are being funded by the state. The Court found that identification of the skills for graduation was not done in a timely fashion, and that remedial instruction was not adequate to meet the implementation schedule.

The Court was convinced that the plaintiffs, both black and white, had a property right in graduation from high school with a standard diploma, if they had passed the ongoing basic skills tests, known as the SSAT I, and had enough credits. The Court was also of the opinion that the plaintiffs had a liberty interest in being free of the adverse stigma associated with the certificate of completion. The Court asserted that the inadequacy of the notice provided prior to the invocation of the diploma sanction, the objectives, and the test, was a violation of the Due Process Clause. It said:

. . . the Court is loath to interfere in the operations of the Florida public schools. . . . The Defendants had other constitutionally acceptable alternatives such as phased introduction of the objectives in all grades without the diploma sanction and longer term remediation. The Court cannot help but focus on the fact that the present Plaintiffs . . . have been the victims of segregation, social promotion and various other educational ills but have persisted and remained in school and should not now, at this late date, be denied the diplomas they have earned by mastery of the basic skills and completion of the minimum number of academic credits.

In their third claim, the black plaintiffs asserted that the defendants were aware that a substantial number of black twelfth graders would fail the SSAT II, and thus would be placed in compensatory education classes with high proportions of black children and low proportions of whites, resulting in resegregation. The Court found that the evidence showed that blacks moved in and out the compensatory classes and their presence there was not static. This persuaded the Court that remediation was working and that the goal was not resegregation, even though in this transitional phase the compensatory classrooms were disproportionately black.

Despite expert testimony to the contrary, the U.S. District Court ruled that the literacy test itself was valid. But the Court held that the statute violated the Equal Protection Clause of the Fourteenth Amendment as to black twelfth grade students. The Court also held that the schedule for implementation of the literacy requirement violated the Due Process Clause of the Fourteenth Amendment as to *all* twelfth grade public high school students, both black and white. The Court enjoined the use of the literacy test as a requirement for high school graduation only until the 1982-1983 school year. The Court also directed school authorities to issue regular diplomas to students who met the preliteracy test requirements for graduation up until 1982-1983.

In short, the Court in *Debra P.* recognized the *Brown* doctrine that public education plays a seminal role in our society and that it is critical, therefore, to provide and administer education in a manner that comports with our historical and constitutional notions of fairness and equity. The Court granted injunctive relief of a limited duration, only for that period of time necessary to purge the taint of past segregation and inadequate notice. At the end of the injunctive period, the state will be permitted to pursue its educational policies and goals free of intervention.

## Sexual Discrimination

This occurs when the use of test scores is found to show discriminatory purpose on the basis of sex.

In *Bray* v. *Lee* (1971 and 1972),[56] 177 female students took the entrance exam for admission to Boston's two Latin Schools and received scores high enough to entitle them to enter Boys' Latin, but not high enough to meet the more rigorous admissions standards of Girls' Latin. The Latin Schools are among the most prestigious public high schools in the country

---

[56] See note 7.

and send most of their graduates to college. However, Girls' Latin accommodates only half as many students as Boys' Latin. The Court held that the women had been denied equal protection provided by the Fourteenth Amendment and ordered that they be admitted to Boy's Latin without further competitive exams.

### Circumvention of Desegregation Rulings

The judicial review of educational policy regarding the classification of students through the use of ability tests is paralleled generally by the development of legal theories regarding the rights of children to public schooling. The concept of public education as a right rather than a privilege was reconfirmed by the landmark school desegregation decision in *Brown v. Board of Education*[57] in 1954, which extended the concept to include equal protection of the laws under the Fourteenth Amendment of the Constitution. The *Brown* decision held that separate education was inherently unequal.

In 1968, the Supreme Court held in *Green v. County School Board of New Kent County, Virginia*[58] that public school districts had an affirmative duty to overcome segregation. The Court said that where the state created *de jure* segregation, in violation of the Fourteenth Amendment, it must correct it. This case added support to the elimination of dual school systems and the creation of unitary ones.

Black parents claimed schools were using tests to avoid the impact of such desegregation orders. In cases such as *Singleton v. Jackson Muncipal Separate School District* (1970)[59] and *Moses v. Washington Parish School Board* (1972),[60] courts prohibited, on equal protection grounds, an educational policy that used standardized ability and achievement test scores as the basis for assigning black students to homogeneous ability groups, if the result of the policy was segregated classes within the school. These courts recognized that black students previously had been forced to attend inferior schools, which accounted for scores lower than white students on the tests. For example, in *Moses*, the Court held that until the disadvantageous effect of the earlier inferior education received by black stu-

---

[57] See note 42.
[58] *Green v. County School Board of New Kent County, Virginia*, 391 U.S. 430; 88 S.Ct. 1689; 20 L.Ed. 2d 716 (1968).
[59] *Singleton v. Jackson Municipal Separate School District*, 419 F.2d 1211 (CA 5 1969), rev'd in part on other grounds, 396 U.S. 290 (1970).
[60] *Moses v. Washington Parish School Board*, 330 F. Supp. 1340 (E.D. La. 1971), aff'd, 456 F.2d 1285 (CA 5 1972 per curiam); *cert. denied*, 409 U.S. 1013 (1972).

## Legal Context of Educational Testing

dents in a dual school system had been eradicated, heterogeneous classes would have to be maintained. It is noteworthy, however, that in these cases there was no determination per se regarding the validity of the tests used.

### Excluding Children from Schools

Tests have been found to have been used in some cases as a rational basis for a state to exclude children from school. For instance, those with IQ test scores below a certain level were found mentally retarded and, until recently, were refused admission to school.

In *Pennsylvania Association for Retarded Children (PARC) v. Commonwealth of Pennsylvania* (1972),[61] a consent agreement provided that mentally retarded children had the same right to public education as normal children did. The parents of children who had been tested and classified as "uneducable and untrainable" claimed that, under the state law, the children had a right to education, and that, under the Fourteenth Amendment, such education should be available to them on the same basis as provided to other school children, that is, free and appropriate.

A consent agreement was worked out in *PARC*, which provided that the state could not apply any policy that would deny, postpone, or terminate access to a publicly supported education to mentally retarded children. It also provided that by September 1, 1972, every mentally retarded person between the ages of 6 and 21 years was to have access to a free public program of education and training appropriate to his learning capacities. A similar provision was made for preschool programs where they existed. The state was required to give notice and an opportunity for a hearing prior to a change in educational status of any child who is or is thought to be mentally retarded. Regular reevaluation was required as well. In this exclusion case, as in *Mills v. Board of Education of the District of Columbia* (1972),[62] the validity of the tests used apparently was not questioned. The issue was *whether* exceptional children had a right to a public education.

In *Lebanks v. Spears* (1976),[63] a court was asked to rule in a case in which a mentally retarded child was excluded from attending public school. The court ruled that the child had a right to be admitted to school,

---

[61] *Pennsylvania Association for Retarded Children (PARC) v. Commonwealth of Pennsylvania*, 343 F. Supp. 279 (1972).
[62] *Mills v. Board of Education of the District of Columbia*, 348 F. Supp. 866 (D.D.C. 1972).
[63] *Lebanks v. Spears*, 60 F.R.D. 135 (E.D. La. 1973); 417 F. Supp. 169 (E.D. La. 1976).

in a decision similar to that in *PARC* and *Mills*. The Court said that such a right leads to an extension that handicapped children have a right to an appropriate education suited to their conditions and needs. Regarding tests, the court imposed specific requirements concerning the use of tests in placement of the mentally retarded, saying such placements could not be made unless: (1) the IQ, as measured by an individually measured test, is 69 or below; (2) the child's adaptive behavior is subnormal; and (3) the effects of the child's sociocultural background are found not to affect the rating.

Other cases were brought on behalf of retarded children who were enrolled in public schools. They claimed violation of civil rights by denial of equal protection and due process based on an alleged failure by local school district officials and state officials to provide a suitable education for retarded children. For instance, in 1975, in *Fialkowski* v. *Shapp*,[64] retarded children were explicitly denied a public school education and contended that they had been deprived of their civil rights. Here again, the tests used to determine their mental capacity were not questioned per se. However, the case is significant because of the alleged liability of four individual public officials under 42 U.S.C.A. Sec. 1983 in permitting such children to be excluded from school. The court held that two of the public officials were personally involved in the decision and also ruled that there was no absolute immunity defense in a civil rights action against governmental officials exercising discretionary authority.

At least two cases upheld the constitutionality of state laws which excluded certain classifications of children from public school. *Cuyahoga County Association for Retarded Children and Adults* v. *Essex* (1976),[65] upheld the exclusion of mentally retarded school age children with IQs below 80, deemed to be unable to profit substantially from further instruction by virtue of test scores. However, the court found certain state regulations constitutionally deficient in not containing proper provision for notice, availability for review of material used in the proposed classification, opportunity for input by persons affected, and guarantees that all relevant material would be at the disposal of the person charged with the responsibility for the final decision. The other notable case is *Taylor* v. *Maryland School for the Blind* (1976),[66] in which the court ruled that

---

[64] *Fialkowski* v. *Shapp*, 405 F. Supp. 946 (E.D. Pa. 1975).
[65] *Cuyahoga County Association for Retarded Children and Adults* v. *Essex*, 411 F. Supp. 46 (N.D. Ohio 1976).
[66] *Taylor* v. *Maryland School for the Blind*, 409 F. Supp. 148 (D. Md. 1976), aff'd, 542 F.2d 1169 (CA 4 1976).

## Legal Context of Educational Testing

certain mentally retarded blind children could be barred from attending public school. While both of these cases upheld the use of tests to exclude children from public school as constitutionally rational, they emphasized the need for procedural safeguards.

### TRENDS TOWARD INCREASED REGULATION: A FINAL WORD

Access to education remains a major social concern. For young children who are required by law to attend school, the focus of concern is accurate assessment and access to schooling appropriate to their needs. In the case of applicants for admission to higher education, the central concern is being accepted by a postsecondary school of their choice. Standardized testing is employed in decision making in both circumstances. At this time, there appear to be more legal remedies available to those who feel unfairly treated in the first instance than to those in the second. Admissions test takers especially are exerting pressure for truth-in-testing legislation to provide fuller information about tests beforehand and disclosure of the tests after taking them.

Because of these pressures, interest is burgeoning now in the monitoring and regulation of standardized educational testing. For the most part, such regulation has been based on professional standards and guidelines, as exemplified by those of the American Psychological Association.[67] Government regulation of educational testing was relatively limited, but it increased when the implementing rules of both the Education for All Handicapped Children Act of 1975[68] and the Rehabilitation Act of 1973[69] provided that testing and evaluation materials were to be validated for the specific purpose for which they were used. Furthermore, requirements were set out for the challenge and review of decisions made on the basis of test results.

Clearly, more scrutiny will be given to many aspects of educational testing, should truth-in-testing legislation become widespread. In all likelihood, the trend toward regulation of testing will continue rather than subside for both legal and social reasons. At the heart of the matter are questions of test validity, due process, and nondiscrimination.

---

[67] American Psychological Association, American Educational Research Association, and National Council on Measurement in Education (1974) *Standards for Educational and Psychological Tests*. Washington, D.C.: American Psychological Association.
[68] See note 3.
[69] See note 2.

BEVERLY ANDERSON
# Test Use Today in Elementary and Secondary Schools

## INTRODUCTION

In 1975 Houts estimated that in the United States each student receives from six to twelve full batteries of achievement tests during the years from kindergarten through high school (Houts 1975). This estimate did not even take into account specialized achievement testing, locally developed diagnostic tests, testing done through the National Assessment of Educational Progress, or competency tests now in effect in many states. Given a 1978 population of about 48 million 5- to 17-year-olds, the number of tests administered to elementary and secondary school students each year must be in the hundreds of millions.

Despite such widespread use of testing, very little research has been conducted on the overall position of tests and testing in U.S. schools. It would seem, nonetheless, that a notion of the current role of testing in U.S. schools could be developed on the basis of information gathered from the various districts in one region. Such is the intent of this report. As such, it cannot be considered a research report based on systematic data collection, but rather an informed impression gained through the author's more than 6 years of close association with state education departments and local school districts in planning, implementing, and evaluating testing programs.

In her work in the Title I Evaluation Technical Assistance Center for Region VIII and as the present director of the Assessment and Measurement Program for the Northwest Regional Educational Laboratory (NWREL),

## Test Use Today in Elementary and Secondary Schools        233

the author has worked with teachers, district and state special program directors, principals, superintendents, state and district evaluators, and testing specialists in fourteen western states. The range of Alaska, California, Colorado, Hawaii, Idaho, Montana, Nevada, North Dakota, Oregon, Pacific Trust Territories, South Dakota, Utah, Washington, and Wyoming includes all types of school populations and possible testing situations. The viewpoint throughout the report approximates most closely the generalized vantage of a district administrator.

Although some districtwide testing occurs in nearly every district, it is only a part of a student's complete testing experience in a particular school, and it is a rare district office that has full knowledge of the testing program in each individual school. For this reason, questionnaires were distributed in ten districts to school building personnel (usually principals or project coordinators) in an effort to gather actual examples of testing program characteristics. The questions asked in connection with regular testing programs concerned the kinds, purposes, and frequency of achievement and aptitude tests used, how many student hours were involved, and who actually learned results. In the case of testing of students in compensatory and special education classes, narrative answers to twelve questions elicited the same sort of information. Although the twenty questionnaires returned represent testing programs of various sizes and sophistication, they do not comprise a broad enough sample to be considered representative of all western states. On the other hand, the results clearly support the overall impressions of typical testing patterns. Ten typical examples are included here as the Appendix. These general concepts were confirmed and amplified through the review of this report by four NWREL staff members (Dean Nafziger, Nelson Noggle, Roy Gabriel, and Evelyn Brzezinski). It is presented as a basis for formulating future research needs with the goal of optimizing the effectiveness of testing in the educational setting.

### One Testing Administrator's Viewpoint

How would you describe the testing pattern in a typical U.S. school district? One such description was provided in the following interview with Jack (not his real name), test coordinator for 5 years in an upper-middle-class, medium-sized school district in a western state.

INTERVIEWER:
What is the testing experience for the typical student in your district throughout twelve school years?
JACK:
Testing begins in kindergarten, when students take a screening test sometime

during their first two months of school. In our district, we use the Santa Clara Inventory of Developmental Tasks, which is essentially an observation of psychomotor and verbal and other cognitive skills.

Then, in grades one through six, students take a standardized reading and math test each spring. In grades seven, nine, and eleven, they take a language test as well. In grades three through seven and grades nine and eleven, an aptitude test is given along with the achievement battery. The purpose of the aptitude test is to establish expected levels of performance on the achievement test. We do not report scores from the aptitude test. The only other achievement test administered districtwide is a writing test given in grades five, eight, and ten. Each year, testing extends over the better part of a week.

INTERVIEWER:
What about interest and attitude testing?
JACK:
We have developed a 115-item attitude measure that we give in grades five, seven, nine, and eleven as part of our standardized testing. This measure attempts to examine school climate, attitudes towards the principal, librarian, teachers, and others. We report these data at the building level only. Individual data are not reported; we do not consider the measure reliable enough for that.

We do not administer districtwide interest inventories. Instead, interest inventories are given in conjunction with career interest classes as part of career awareness. We want students to understand how their own interests may lead them to be more suited for one career than for another.

INTERVIEWER:
How many hours of testing do you think the typical student experiences?
JACK:
Well, the districtwide testing I mentioned takes about 1.8 hours in the first grade with the amount of time increasing progressively to about 5.8 hours in the fifth grade. From the fifth grade on, it fluctuates between 4.4 and 5.8 hours.

INTERVIEWER:
What are the main reasons for testing in your district?
JACK:
We test for three major purposes: first, quality control and accountability; second, curricular and program evaluation; and third, student evaluation. Student evaluation information is important. It is reported and is kept in student records.

INTERVIEWER:
How are data used to meet these purposes?
JACK:
Each school receives data for its own students only and decides how to present the data to parents, teachers, and the general public. At the district level, we report districtwide data to the school board and public without school-by-school comparisons. We conduct training for teachers or bring them together to discuss needed curricular or programmatic changes for low scoring areas.

INTERVIEWER:
What about students who are having difficulties in certain areas or appear to be in need of special education?

JACK:
Now you have hit on one of the most extensive testing uses. Students with such difficulties are placed in special programs, such as those in Title I, Follow-Through, or bilingual programs. Nearly all these federally or state funded programs require program evaluation, and students are usually tested in both spring and fall for this purpose. We wish the testing could be coordinated with district-wide testing, but an evaluation frequently requires a different test; thus these students have to take at least two extra tests during the year. Furthermore, some programs under Title I require diagnostic testing throughout the year. Students in these programs may experience two or three times as much testing as mainstream students.

INTERVIEWER:
You have identified what is happening at the district level. What additional testing may be going on in the schools?

JACK:
A very good question. Certainly a great deal of testing goes on at the building level which we have neither control over nor awareness of. My guess would be that in many buildings extra reading tests are given in first and second grades. Some teachers happen to like the Gates-McGinitie and have been using it for a long time and continue to do so, even though our district results are available. Perhaps they feel more comfortable with that test or they want to give it at a certain time when our results are not available. Other teachers want to use their own diagnostic tests. We strongly discourage the use of group aptitude tests. Number scores, such as the IQ, are too frequently misinterpreted—people tend to use them as intelligence labels—but I know some schools in the district are still using them. Since a principal's knowledge of, and views on, testing have a strong impact on how much additional testing is done, we are attempting to provide training on correct test use, but it is a big task. Many educators have not been well trained in this area.

Jack's training in, and knowledge of, testing are more extensive than that of many testing coordinators. In many cases, particularly in small districts, people in Jack's position have had limited formal training in testing administration. Moreover, test coordination may be just one of many responsibilities, and as such, it may not receive high priority. Nonetheless, Jack's description touches on the testing practice that is typical of most schools today, as the following more detailed discussion will show.

## TYPES OF TESTS

Our primary focus is on cognitive measures—tests of achievement or aptitude used in the elementary and secondary schools—that have been commercially or locally developed using systematic procedures resulting in indices of validity and reliability.

Teacher-made tests and curriculum-embedded tests, e.g., those that appear at the end of a unit for a textbook, will be excluded. They are typically used to assist in guiding instruction and assigning course grades, a function that varies greatly depending on individual teaching style.

Also excluded are psychomotor tests, except for those used in kindergarten, and such measures of the affective domain as attitude or interest tests. Attitude measures investigate how students feel toward school or particular subjects or teachers within the educational system. While such measures are available from commercial publishers, these tests are frequently developed locally to answer questions about specific programs of interest only to a particular district. They often have low or unknown validity and, even when appropriately used, must be interpreted cautiously and in conjunction with other data. Interest inventories attempt to pinpoint student interests that may be of value in formulating education or career plans. Such measures are sometimes used in conjunction with career awareness classes; generally, they are not given districtwide, but most students, even in small rural schools, respond to a published interest inventory at least once during their high school years. Usually, a guidance counselor or teacher has responsibility for test interpretation.

The principal measures used in today's elementary and secondary schools can be classified under three headings: norm-referenced achievement tests, objective-referenced achievement tests, and aptitude tests.

Achievement tests are designed to measure a specific level of learning accomplishment within a content area such as reading, mathematics, science, or language arts. Aptitude tests, on the other hand, purport to measure cognitive processes, such as verbal and mathematical reasoning. While aptitude tests formerly were thought of as measuring innate unchanging abilities, it is now commonly felt that they measure intellectual skills, which students develop through school and nonschool experiences. These skills are expected to be broadly applicable to learning within any particular course of study.

That the most comprehensive study of teachers' use of norm-referenced standardized test results was done nearly 15 years ago (Goslin 1967) makes the need for new research in this area all too apparent.

**Norm-Referenced Achievement Tests**

A commercially published, norm-referenced achievement test has standardized content and instructions and is nationally normed on a group of students at a particular grade level. Norm-referenced tests are available from commercial publishers for many subject areas, including basic reading and mathematics skills, language arts, social science, and reference skills, but are most commonly used for reading and mathematics. Publishers continue to develop tests in other areas, though few have ventured into areas such as health and science.

A norm-referenced test allows comparison of the performance of one student to that of another student or group of students. Commercially published tests generally provide comparisons to a national or regional referent group. If the publisher's scoring service is used, local or other special norms can often be obtained.

Despite the criticism levied against norm-referenced achievement tests, and the National Education Association's (NEA) call for a moratorium on all such testing, it appears that their use is nearly universal in American public schools. A 1976 survey of Michigan schools (Brzezinski and Womer 1978) revealed that 93 percent of the schools had a regular standardized testing program. And Michigan is not unique.

## Objective-Referenced Achievement Tests

In the early 1970s, a new perspective on achievement testing developed among educators, the underlying principle of which was that test data based on comparison of one student to another were not of basic usefulness to teachers. Rather, to improve instruction, they needed information on how well a given student has learned a particular skill, regardless of how other students performed. Tests that provide this sort of information are known as objective-referenced or criterion-referenced tests. They differ from norm-referenced tests in that comparisons are not made among students. The scoring is based instead on the comparison of a student's performance on a specific skill to a possible or desired level of performance.

Nearly all major test publishers produce objective-referenced tests. In some cases, test publishers have responded to conflicting needs by providing both objective and norm-referenced test interpretation of a given test. Since some of the desired test characteristics of a norm-referenced test are different from those of an objective-referenced test, technical difficulties are likely with this procedure. In addition, increasing numbers of local districts, which employ testing specialists, are developing their own objective-referenced diagnostic tests—either for districtwide testing or for discretionary diagnostic use by teachers. Some western states (e.g., California, Oregon, and Alaska) are also developing objective-referenced tests for statewide assessment purposes.

As objective-referenced tests have gained popularity, so has the idea that such tests could and should be locally developed in order to provide information specific to an individual school's learning needs and objectives. This notion has been encouraged by the development of "item banks" that range from simple shoeboxed collections to sophisticated systems maintained through computer storage. A recent survey conducted by the Northwest Regional Educational Laboratory (Hiscox and Brzezinski 1980) indicated that many districts are attempting to develop item banks.

## Aptitude Tests

Over the last few years criticism of aptitude tests has mounted. Claims of cultural bias and uncertainty of what the tests actually measure have caused reduction in the use of group-administered aptitude tests. Even among the most unsophisticated districts, the impact of this trend is obvious. It is likely that about a third of the districts in the western states seldom or never use group-administered aptitude tests in their regular testing programs. Of the districts that still give these tests, about half probably are responding to public pressure or school board policy, and the results are seldom used.

An exception to this is in the relatively small number of districts where group-administered aptitude tests are given along with achievement tests as a basis for determining expected achievement levels. Students who perform well on an aptitude test are expected to perform well on an achievement test. In effect, this procedure affords a means of judging whether schools or students are performing at the expected level without need for comparison of one school or student to another.

At the present time, individually administered ability tests, such as the Wechsler Intelligence Scale for Children (WISC), continue to be used to identify students who are to receive special education. They are administered by trained personnel and are used with students referred for special testing. However, recent legal challenges have focused both on the nature of the tests and the ways in which the results are used. The most significant legal precedent in aptitude testing flows from a 1979 Federal District Court decision in a California case, *Larry P. v. Riles*, No. C71-2270 RFP (N.D. Cal. Decision 10/16/79). The opinion held that California school officials unlawfully discriminated against black children by using racially and culturally biased intelligence quotient (IQ) tests to classify and place them in classes for the educable mentally retarded (EMR).

The basis for the *Larry P.* court's legal scrutiny of IQ tests and test bias was the disproportionate number of black children placed in EMR classes as a result of IQ testing and the detriment to the education of children misclassified as EMR. The court found that the EMR classes were "conceived of as 'dead-end classes' " for children incapable of learning within the regular curriculum, and children in these classes tended to fall farther

# Test Use Today in Elementary and Secondary Schools 239

and farther behind children in regular classes since they were provided with instruction that deemphasized academic skills in favor of adjustment. The *Larry P.* decision will probably have two major effects: it could curtail even more the use of traditional IQ tests around the nation; and the decision will undoubtedly stimulate further the existing research efforts to develop so-called nondiscriminatory assessment batteries, the results of which will be a more accurate reflection of the cognitive potential of minority children.

## TESTING FUNCTIONS

The tests described above are used for a variety of purposes, all of which are included in three broad decision-making functions: (1) instructional management, (2) entry-exit decisions, and (3) programmatic decisions. Instructional management and entry-exit decisions require test data for each student. Programmatic decisions can be based on group data, collected through testing samples of students rather than every student.

These three categories have been defined according to the author's observations and actual surveys in many schools. Personnel within a given school, however, may not think of testing functions in terms of these categories. In fact, the failure to understand the differentiation of testing functions and the lack of knowledge of the different test characteristics required by each function are major barriers to achieving an effective testing program in many schools.

### Instructional Management

Data from ability tests can help with instructional management decisions in: (1) the diagnosis of individual learner strengths and weaknesses, (2) student placement, and (3) educational and vocational guidance.

#### Diagnosis

Teachers often use objective-referenced tests and other performance indicators very effectively to determine each student's level of development in specific skills, most frequently such basic skills as reading and mathematics. These data assist teachers in deciding when a student has adequately learned a particular skill and is ready to progress to other instruction. Tests used for this purpose measure specific skills and knowledge and are closely linked to course content. Diagnostic tests are not so broad as survey achievement tests, which, incidentally, cannot be effectively used for this purpose.

*Placement*

High quality instructional management requires that students be placed in the instructional environment in which they can learn most readily. Achievement test data, along with grades and records of other course work, can help administrators place students in those programs that will best meet their needs; e.g., placement tests are given to determine which students need compensatory instruction in reading in addition to, or in place of, that provided in the regular classroom program. Placement decisions are typically made only once a year, whereas decisions based on diagnostic tests are made continuously throughout the year. Placement tests usually cover a wider array of skills and knowledge than diagnostic tests, and different types of tests are used for the various placement needs.

Testing is a major, if not *the* major, method used to identify students who would benefit from special programs (e.g., bilingual, remedial reading and mathematics, talented and gifted) or particular educational tracks. Commercially published, norm-referenced achievement tests are perhaps the most frequently used measures for placement in compensatory education programs. In addition to achievement tests, aptitude and psychomotor tests are used to identify students needing special education programs. In general, the results of regularly administered achievement and sometimes aptitude tests, along with measures of special talents (e.g., in art, music, and performance), are used to identify students for talented and gifted programs. In this area, however, there is a serious need for the development of tests more specific to the function.

*Guidance and Counseling*

Tests are also used to give students guidance as to the general program of study they should pursue. Cumulative information gathered over several years can tell students how they stand relative to others and in what subject areas they seem to be particularly strong.

The use of test data for guidance is generally determined by school or district administrators and guidance counselors and is usually a secondary purpose of testing conducted primarily for placement or programmatic decisions.

## Student Entry-Exit Decisions

Tests are also administered in very structured circumstances to assist in making decisions about a student's readiness to enter or exit from a school or major line of study. Such tests would include (1) selection for admission to programs with enrollment limits (e.g., college entrance or trade school) and (2) certification of minimum competencies (e.g., for high school graduation or occupational licensing).

## Selection

The terms "selection" and "placement" are not always clearly differentiated. The term selection means placement following decisions concerning a limited number of entry spaces in an educational program, and entrants are selected on the basis of test predictions as to which ones are the most likely to perform successfully. A test developed for this purpose focuses on those skills and knowledge considered essential for future success. A norm-referenced approach is generally used since comparisons are made among students. College entrance or selection into a particular training course (e.g., airline pilot) are prime examples.

During the K-12 years, the only widespread selection testing is for college entry. Almost all colleges stipulate the particular college entrance examinations that they will recognize, and only students interested in attending college take them. Administration of such tests is carefully controlled. Students register with publishers of the college entrance examinations (either the Scholastic Aptitude Test or the American College Test) to take the test at locations and on the dates they arrange.

## Certification

Tests tailored to a specified domain of knowledge or skills are often used to verify and document required mastery of particular knowledge or skills. For example, the most recent major testing trend is the measuring of minimum competencies, particularly at the high school level and sometimes for high school graduation. Through such testing, students are sorted into those who have achieved certain levels of proficiency and those who have not. And increasingly, districts are offering remedial work for the latter to help them pass during the next round. Little uniformity exists in procedures, however. Some states specify statewide consistency; others give schools great flexibility in deciding which competencies will be measured and how. In general, competencies fall into two categories: basic skills of reading, writing, and mathematics; and life skills—the application of basic skills to such real life tasks as reading maps, completing job applications, computing correct change following a purchase, and writing a letter of complaint. A survey (Connelly and Casserly 1979) conducted by the Council of the Great City Schools indicates that twenty-six of their twenty-nine member school districts have implemented or have developed a minimum competency test program. Of these twenty-six districts, six require passage of the test for graduation, and twenty-one use them for placement in remedial classes. Some districts use a series of tests, some use one test. Often they are developed at a state or district level. The number of testing opportunities allowed a student varies from district to district.

In 1978, Pipho reported that thirty-five states operated state mandated minimum competency testing programs. The growth of these programs was so rapid between 1976 and 1978 that the Education Commission of the States published seven legislative updates on the topic.

**Programmatic Decisions**

A third general use of tests is to assist in making decisions about educational programs. Test data may be helpful in assessing the needs of a group to serve as the basis for developing a new program, allocating resources, or evaluating existing programs. Such testing falls in three categories: (1) survey assessment, (2) formative program evaluation, and (3) summative program evaluation.

*Survey Assessment*

Survey assessment refers to collecting achievement data on groups of students to determine general educational development as a guide to educational planning. Tests for this purpose may be administered to a carefully selected random sample of students in the target population or to the entire group of students. Survey assessment often takes place on a regular cycle, so that trends in student development can be examined over time. Data users include building, district, or state level administrators who allocate resources for special instructional needs or plan educational programs.

Districts most often use commercially published achievement tests for this purpose; occasionally the same tests are used for placement, but increasingly such tests represent a construction specific to state assessment needs. They typically test students at several grade levels each year. The results are used to help local administrators identify general areas that may need more emphasis within a school or in the district as a whole. For example, they may find that students' mathematics scores are declining over the elementary school years. The results often are also used to report to the school board and the public to show that the schools are functioning adequately, as a means of keeping the educational system accountable to those it serves.

About thirty states conduct some type of annual statewide assessment program (Pipho 1978). Many use state-developed rather than commercially published tests. Such assessment is generally based on a statewide sample and involves students at two or three grade levels.

## Formative Evaluation

In formative program evaluation, program administrators and teachers want to discover which instructional components of an ongoing program are functioning as intended and which need further refinement. They may test students on a periodic basis on intermediate and final outcomes of the program to determine what programmatic changes are needed. The formative evaluation function is most often encountered in connection with new programs.

## Summative Evaluation

Summative evaluation seeks to reveal a program's overall merit, thus suggesting whether that program should be continued, terminated, or modified. Tests designed to assess students' performance on final learning outcomes of a program are typically a key part of such an evaluation.

Summative program evaluation has become a major function of testing in recent years, particularly for programs that receive special funding from state and federal agencies. As many as 75 to 95 percent of all students in special programs (such as bilingual or Title I programs) are likely to be tested annually for evaluation purposes—often at both the beginning and the end of the year. For example, Title I evaluations presently require that programs either use a nationally normed test or at least link a nationally normed test to the test being used for evaluation purposes.

## TESTING INITIATORS

Who decides when a test should be given? Conventional wisdom assumes that teachers needing information to improve instruction are the major initiators of testing. But teachers usually play this role only in the case of teacher-made or curriculum-embedded, detailed diagnostic tests (not covered in this paper). The use of most commercially published district or state developed achievement tests is initiated by decision makers at many levels and for purposes sometimes far removed from building and classroom needs.

To illustrate, ten of the survey questionnaires used as supplementary material for this report were selected to represent a range of schools of varying size, grade level (elementary, junior high, and high schools), and location. In ten schools, forty-one tests were used in one year in regular programs. Of these, two tests were selected by a teacher, one by a school principal, one jointly by the school principal and a teacher, one by the guidance counselors, four by district personnel and the school principal jointly, one by the state department of education, and five by colleges (college entrance examinations). The other twenty-six (63 percent) were selected by district personnel. In the case of the many diagnostic tests used within remedial education programs and not included in the regular program, teachers were involved in about 80 percent of the selection decisions.

At the federal level, the primary impetus for testing comes from federally funded special programs, most of which require evaluation, usually via commercially published, norm-referenced achievement testing. Title I of the Elementary and Secondary Act, which provides funding for compensatory education, is a case in point. As the largest single item in the U.S. education budget, Title I is subject to rigorous evaluation to demonstrate its effectiveness. The present Title I evaluation procedures require the programs to use norm-referenced tests or to link a nonnormed test to a normed test. The procedures, however, carefully avoid recommending any specific, commercially available test.

Evaluation is also federally mandated for Title IV-C projects, which provide resources for local development of innovative programs that have potential for adaptation elsewhere. State agencies receive Title IV-C monies as block grants and distribute funds to local districts on a competitive basis.

Title IV-C evaluation, unlike Title I evaluation, lacks uniformity in data collection and reporting. In fact, Title IV-C evaluation often involves tests that differ markedly in content, format, and type. This diversity is understandable, given the range of populations to be tested, for example, bilingual, gifted, and migrant; and the range of content areas to be covered, such as problem solving, creativity, writing, guidance, decision making, and leadership. Evaluators report that the Title IV-C evaluations tend to rely on available, commercially produced tests, regardless of whether or not such tests reflect program goals (Nafziger 1979).

Public Law 94-142, the Education for All Handicapped Children Act, enacted in fall 1977, required that handicapped children be put in the least restrictive environment in which they are capable of functioning and that their instruction be guided by individual educational programs (IEPs). The effectiveness of IEPs depends, of course, on appropriate assessment of student needs and correct placement. The current mandate for evaluation of P.L. 94-142 calls only for descriptive information about services. As a result, program evaluation testing is likely to receive less emphasis than instructional management testing.

The kinds of testing, most commonly initiated at the state level, are statewide assessment testing for accountability, minimum competency, and evaluation of state funded special programs. Who decides that such tests are needed? The answer varies greatly. For example, statewide assessment testing received much attention in the late 1960s. Legislators and state boards of education often initiated it to determine if schools were doing the job for which they were being funded. Educators and others responded with their concerns: Are school or district comparisons to be made? Do teachers want or need individual student data? Are the data to be used primarily for legislative decision making and allocation of funds? Are such tests going to be used for teacher evaluation? (This last question has sparked tremendous controversy between teachers' unions and states.) Consequently, teachers and district personnel are often involved in the design of legislature-initiated, statewide assessment testing programs, but in many states how the data are used is not clear.

The public's newly awakened interest in accountability also gave impetus to the spread of minimum competency testing before high school graduation. As noted earlier, at least thirty-five states have enacted legislation requiring minimum competency testing.

Evaluation of state-funded special programs is a third instance of testing initiated at the state level. Testing requirements in these cases appear very idiosyncratic.

Generally, federal and state regulations allow state and local education agencies considerable latitude in setting their own testing procedures. For example, although Title I evaluation requires the use of, or linking to, commercially published, norm-referenced tests, many tests are available for use. Although state education agencies may put some limitations on test acceptability, the decision is generally made locally.

Most district-initiated testing is conducted for purposes of limited accountability, placement of students in special programs, and program evaluations. Decisions are typically made at the district level about the choice of test to be used for evaluation required by federally and state-funded special programs. District level testing, beyond that required by federal and state regulations, is shaped by multiple forces: public pressure for accountability, teachers' and administrators' demands that tests be more reflective of program goals and content, pressure from teachers' unions against the use of student test results in teacher evaluation, and requests from all concerned to reduce the amount of testing. District administrators and school boards are frequently in a quandary as to how to establish a testing program that responds to these conflicting pressures.

At the building level, the amount of additional testing beyond district requirements varies greatly. Generally, districts allow schools considerable autonomy in this matter. The principal's perspective can be a major influence. A principal who is knowledgeable about testing and its appropriate uses may wisely incorporate additional testing into the existing district testing plan or see ways to accomplish other purposes through the use of existing tests. In cases where principals' technical training and experience are less sophisticated, additional testing may be allowed or required that is unneccessary or nonfunctional.

At the classroom level, teachers as individuals or teams are often free to conduct additional testing at their discretion. Some teachers employ very comprehensive diagnostic systems, particularly in the basic skill areas of reading and mathematics. They may also administer unit tests which accompany textbooks. Student performance may well influence a teacher's decisions about the amount and frequency of diagnostic testing, and because of this, those whose performance is lower tend to be most heavily tested.

The survey of schools (reviewed in the Appendix to this chapter), as well as work with districts throughout the northwest region, have made one aspect of the initiation of school testing very clear: the pattern of testing in a typical organized district program reflects federal, state, and district mandates for evaluation, accountability, placement, and certification far more than it does teacher or local administration-initiated instructional management needs. Tests used to fulfill such mandates can rarely provide the level of detail that a teacher must have to diagnose the specific instructional needs of an individual student. As a consequence, teachers and principals often feel that too much classroom time is spent in giving and taking tests, the results of which are of little service to the most important goal of all, an effective education for each and every student.

One final influence on the initiation of testing programs is that of test publishers. Testing is a multimillion-dollar operation. The competitiveness of test publishers in developing and marketing tests or testing services has had a significant impact on testing programs. How much testing is done in response to expressed need and how much in response to a publisher's desire to sell tests poses a delicate question.

## TYPICAL TESTING PATTERNS

What, then, is the typical testing pattern for a student from kindergarten through twelfth grade? This question must be answered in terms of the three main types of educational programs: the regular (mainstream) program, compensatory education programs, and special education programs. Compensatory programs, of which the Elementary and Secondary Education Act (ESEA), Title I, is the most common, generally are designed to provide extra instruction, often on an individualized basis, for students who are having difficulty learning basic concepts at the rate taught in the regular program. In such programs, students frequently are taken out of the regular classroom for a few hours each week for individualized help on specific reading or mathematics skills. Compensatory education programs are offered at all grade levels but are definitely most widely used in the elementary grades.

Special education programs are designed for mentally or physically handicapped students who cannot function in the regular classroom. Presently, every attempt is being made to keep such students in the regular classroom for as much time as possible, but generally they are in special classrooms for all or part of the day. Special education programs are offered fairly evenly across all grades but, because of dropouts at higher grades, enrollments are higher in the lower grades.

Most schools offer instruction within all three of these programs, for which students are typically tested in a pattern similar to that depicted in Figure 1, which was developed on the basis of survey results, observation, and involvement in northwest schools. Although the various purposes of such a pattern of testing can be clearly differentiated, as we have seen in the discussion above, they are all too often not so clearly differentiated by those who are responsible for testing. In fact, it is highly unlikely that a summary chart like Table 1 could be found in any district or school office. A frequent response to the survey questionnaire sent to schools to gather information for this paper was that school personnel had found it very useful to construct the summary requested. Doing so had provided an overall picture of the testing program in their schools, where heretofore the personnel involved in testing had been aware of only parts of the program.

Because so many parties are involved in shaping testing programs, informed decisions as to when to discontinue certain kinds of testing or when to introduce a new testing program are difficult to make, especially in districts where personnel with testing expertise is limited. The pros and cons of norm-referenced versus objective-referenced tests, the issues surrounding how to structure minimum competency testing, the appropriateness of the use of tests for multiple purposes, and the frequency with which tests need to be administered to serve identified purposes—all are factors apt to be unclear to many people responsible for testing.

From Table 1, certain patterns are evident. Students are tested in kindergarten to determine psychomotor and readiness skills. Every year or

TABLE 1  Typical Student Testing Pattern

| Grade | Testing Areas | Purposes | | | | | | | |
|---|---|---|---|---|---|---|---|---|---|
| | | Instructional Management Decisions | | | Entry-Exit Decisions | | Programmatic Decisions | | |
| | | Diagnosis | Placement | Guidance | Selection | Certification | Survey Assessment | Formative Evaluation | Summative Evaluation |
| K | Psychomotor and readiness skills | | | | | | | | |
| 1 | Basic skills tests | ✓ | ✓ | | | | | | |
| 2 | Basic skills tests | ✓ | ✓ | | | | | | |
| 3 | Basic skills tests | ✓ | ✓ | | | | | | |
| 4 | Basic skills tests | ✓ | ✓ | | | | ✓ | | ✓ |
| | Aptitude tests | | ✓ | ✓ | | | ✓ | | ✓ |
| 5 | Basic skills tests | | ✓ | | | | ✓ | | ✓ |
| 6 | Basic skills tests | ✓ | ✓ | | | | ✓ | | ✓ |
| | Other achievement tests | | | | | | ✓ | | |

| Grade | Test type | | | | | | | | | | |
|---|---|---|---|---|---|---|---|---|---|---|---|
| 7 | Basic skills tests | | | | | > | | | | | |
| | Other achievement tests | | | | | | | > | | | |
| 8 | Basic skills tests | | > | | > | | | | | | |
| | Other achievement tests | | | | > | | | | | | |
| 9 | Basic skills tests | | > | | > | | > | | | | |
| | Other achievement tests | | | | > | | > | | | | |
| | Aptitude | | | | | | >> | | | | |
| 10 | Basic skills tests | | > | | > | | > | | | | |
| | Other achievement tests | | | | > | | > | | | | |
| 11 | Basic or life skills tests | | | | | | | | > | | |
| | College entrance tests | | | | | | | | | > | |

TABLE 1 (continued)

| Grade / Testing Areas | Purposes | | | | | | | |
|---|---|---|---|---|---|---|---|---|
| | Instructional Management Decisions | | | Entry-Exit Decisions | | Programmatic Decisions | | |
| | Diagnosis | Placement | Guidance | Selection | Certification | Survey Assessment | Formative Evaluation | Summative Evaluation |
| **12** | | | | | | | | |
| College entrance tests | | | | | ✓ | | | |
| Basic or life skills tests | | | | ✓ | | | | |
| Basic skills tests [a] | ✓ | ✓ | | | | | | |
| Basic skills tests [b] | ✓ | ✓ | | | | | ✓ | ✓ |
| Physical abilities tests [b] | ✓ | ✓ | ✓ | | | | | |
| Aptitude tests | ✓ | ✓ | ✓ | | | | | |

NOTE: Whether the basic skills tests are norm-referenced or objective-referenced, tests vary greatly from district to district. Presently norm-referenced tests are most frequently used, but objective-referenced tests are gaining popularity. Hours of testing are likely to range from 2 to 6 each year.

[a] Compensatory Education. The testing shown here most likely occurs each year the student is in the program. This testing is in addition to that shown for students in the regular program, resulting in 2 to 3 times as much testing as the regular students.

[b] Special Education. The testing shown usually occurs when a student is being evaluated to determine his/her need for placement in a special education program. It could occur at any grade level.

two, from first grade through early high school, they take basic skills tests. Results are used for placement in particular educational programs; accountability reporting to the public, school boards, and/or legislators; evaluation of regular school programs; and reporting to students and parents regarding students' progress on particular skills and/or their relative standing to classmates or national norm groups.

A student generally experiences one or two group-administered aptitude tests between grades three and ten. These test results become the basis for selection of gifted and talented students or students in need of special remedial education. In some cases, the results are used to predict achievement test results.

At some point in the middle elementary grades, subject areas other than the basic skills, such as reference skills, science, or social studies, are frequently added to achievement test content. In high school, until recently, basic skills testing had been continually decreasing. With the minimum competency movement, however, renewed emphasis has been placed on basic skills tests, as well as life skills testing. The number of times (or grade levels) students are given the opportunity to pass a minimum competency test varies from school to school. The typical student takes the test once early in high school and passes. Lower performing students may have to take the test repeatedly before passing. In some instances, students are given the opportunity to take competency tests before entering high school.

In their junior and senior years of high school, college bound students take one or more college entrance examinations.

The lower part of Table 1 identifies the additional testing experienced by students referred for or placed into compensatory and special education programs. These students experience two or three times more testing than students in the regular program. The additional testing usually occurs (1) during the initial stages of determining whether a student should be placed in those programs and (2) for program evaluation purposes.

## Departures from the Typical Pattern

Not every district follows the pattern just presented. Variations in the pattern tend to be related to district size and the relative technical expertise of the test coordinator or director. Also, in any setting the degree to which testing specialists help shape the testing program or simply implement plans dictated by key administrators influences the pattern.

School districts may be categorized as small, medium, or large—rural, suburban, or urban. The expertise of the test director is typically low in the small rural schools and high in suburban and large urban districts.

Occasionally well-developed and integrated testing programs are found in small schools, but they seem to be the exception rather than the rule. Small rural schools, especially, tend to have less sophisticated testing programs. In these cases, principals or superintendents are often responsible for testing; they frequently have numerous other duties, and may lack measurement knowledge or experience. As a result, the testing program evolves in response to tradition, the requirements of special programs, and the influence of test salespeople.

The most effective testing programs tend to be in medium-sized school districts. These districts are small enough to permit good communications among test users, yet large enough to afford a knowledgeable, experienced test coordinator—a person with sufficient influence to coordinate and make better use of testing. Medium-sized districts also seem to provide the most congenial atmosphere for local test development. As curricula come to be organized around attainment of specific skills, locally developed, objective-referenced tests become increasingly attractive. Finally, medium-sized districts often have sufficient expertise and human resources to be innovative in their testing programs.

The larger urban districts face a special challenge in the coordination of the many testing purposes inherent in an extremely complex system. Testing programs in these districts range from highly organized and sophisticated testing patterns to those evidencing minimal coordination. The problems of communication between all the various consumers of testing are staggering. The authority that can be exercised by a single test coordinator depends on special kinds of rapport that are especially difficult to establish in larger settings.

## CONCLUSIONS

An overall impression has been drawn of the amount and kinds of testing experienced by students throughout elementary and secondary school. The picture is based on longtime experience in testing administration and an informal questionnaire-survey in fourteen states of the northwest region. In describing a typical testing pattern, the focus was on norm-referenced, and objective-referenced achievement tests and aptitude tests. Other testing, such as teacher-made tests or interest and aptitude measures, was not addressed in detail.

These three major types of tests were discussed in terms of their functions for instructional management, entry-exit decisions, and programmatic decisions, in the light of the many influences on testing, such as federal, state, and local regulations, key administrators, teachers, parents, and the general public. The testing pattern that emerged is depicted in Table 1. It shows that the average student experiences 2 to 6 hours of testing each year throughout elementary and secondary school, but that students in compensatory or special education programs may experience two to three times as much.

Clearly, there is evidence that testing can make a positive contribution to the educational process, when carefully and knowledgeably used. Nevertheless, student aptitude and achievement testing is now in a state of great flux, battered and pushed by many countervailing forces. Public demands for accountability, for the use of unbiased and nondiscriminatory tests, personnel evaluation, demands for greater integration of testing and instruction, advances in technical methodologies for test development, and aggressive test publishing have produced a disquieting controversy and confusion, which must be addressed.

Unless more attention is given to how to better integrate testing with instruction and how to evaluate special programs using tests that also serve instructional needs, testing is likely to continue to proliferate in an increasingly dysfunctional fashion. Research is needed to document the pattern of increased testing, with particular emphasis on the reasons for the increase and the extent to which the results can be effectively used. Research is also needed to identify the conditions—within a system, within a school—which promote good integration of testing, instruction, and program planning. In this connection, changes are needed in the training of teachers and administrators in test use and interpretation of results. At the policy level, funders of special programs and others who make decisions to require further student testing must carefully evaluate the consequences of such decisions—what their mandates mean at the building level in the light of valid educational goals. Is additional testing the best method to accomplish their intended purpose? For example, information about program management or curriculum materials for a special program may be more useful than more student scores. Specifically, this might require a thorough study of testing for statewide assessment.

The need for research efforts along these lines is clearly indicated even by the informal impressions of this report on typical testing patterns in today's elementary and secondary schools. Testing patterns may yet be developed that will allow testing to contribute to education as fully as its advocates promise it can.

## REFERENCES

Brzezinski, E. J., and Womer, F. B. (1978) Testing in Michigan: A Twenty Year Perspective. Paper presented at the National Council of Measurement in Education Annual Conference, Toronto.

Connelly, M., and Casserly, M. (1979) *Minimum Competency Testing in the Great City Schools*. Washington, D.C.: The Council of Great City Schools.

Goslin, D. A. (1967) *Teachers and Testing*. New York: Russell Sage Foundation.

Hiscox, M. D., and Brzezinski, E. J. (1980) A Guide to Item Banking in Education. Paper presented at the 10th Annual Conference in Large-Scale Assessment, Boulder, Colorado.

Houts, P. L. (1975) Standardized testing in America, II. *The National Elementary Principal* 54(6):2-3.

Nafziger, D. H. (1979) Testing in the 1980's: The Impact of Evaluation on Measurement Procedures. Paper presented at the National Council of Measurement in Education Annual Conference, San Francisco.

Pipho, C. (1978) Minimum competency testing in 1978: a look at state standards. *Phi Delta Kappan* 59:585-588.

## APPENDIX
## EXAMPLES OF SCHOOL TESTING PATTERNS

The following testing profiles are based on the actual reports of elementary, junior high and senior high schools throughout the northwest. Let's begin by examining the schools within one district: Elementary Schools A and B, Junior High C, and Senior High D. Readers are asked to keep in mind that the survey information provided here focuses essentially on ability and achievement tests and subtests—not on teacher-made or curriculum-embedded tests. Respondents answered eleven general questions regarding the achievement and ability tests given in their schools, then a series of questions on testing within remedial education programs or classes, testing for special education, and other measures. Here then are the results, beginning with Elementary School A.

---

*The Format*

Respondents' answers to the survey questions are reported under three headings; Achievement/Ability Testing, Testing within Remedial Education Programs/Classes, and Testing for Special Education. The primary focus of this survey was on Achievement/Ability Testing; these results are shown in chart form for each school and broken down test by test. Other responses are provided in brief narrative form.

---

*Test Use Today in Elementary and Secondary Schools* 255

1. Elementary School A
   Grades 1-6
   Approx. School Enrollment: 322
   Approx. District Enrollment: 20,500

**Testing Within Remedial Education Programs/Classes**

| | |
|---|---|
| 1. Diagnostic tests used once a child is placed in remedial program | At least two different tests are used |
| 2. Who administers tests | Learning disability teacher |
| 3. Time per month spent in testing | 1 hour |
| 4. Frequency of testing | Once a week |
| 5. Percent of students in remedial classes | Less than 10 percent |
| 6. Who selects tests | Learning disability teacher |
| 7. Who sees/uses results | Learning disability teacher/ classroom teacher |
| 8. Are all tests commercially published? If no, identify such tests and their source. | No. Some tests are written by district teachers. |

**Testing for Special Education**

| | |
|---|---|
| 1. Tests administered to determine if special education needed | Learning disability |
| 2. Basis for child referral for testing | Teacher referral, learning disability teacher referral, parent referral |
| 3. Testing time | 1-1½ hours |
| 4. Percent of students tested | 5 percent |

Elementary School A—Achievement/Ability Testing

| | SRA Achievement Level B | SRA Achievement Level C, D | SRA Achievement Level E | Managing Reading by Objectives (MRBO) Managing Arithmetic by Objectives (MABO) | SRA Educational Ability Series, Levels C, D, E |
|---|---|---|---|---|---|
| 1. Test name | | | | | |
| 2. Grade | 1 | C-2<br>D-3 | 4, 5, 6 | 1-6 | C-3<br>D-4<br>E-5, 6 |
| 3. Time required | 3 hours | C—2.5 hours<br>D—2.75 hours | 4 and 6—2.5 hours<br>5—5.5 hours | | 5 hours |
| 4. When administered | Winter | Winter | Winter | Throughout the year at teacher's discretion | Winter |
| 5. Students tested | All students at grade level | All students at grade level | All students at grade level | All students at grade level | All students at grade level |
| 6. Use of results at school level | Report to parents and school board; select students for learning disabilities, talented and gifted; decide on curriculum changes. Diagnose strengths and weaknesses. | | | Report to parents, select students, decide on curriculum changes, diagnose strengths and weaknesses | Select students for talented and gifted |

| | | | | | |
|---|---|---|---|---|---|
| 7. Use of results at district level | Report to parents, public, school board; decide on curriculum changes | | | | Report to school board |
| 8. Who sees results | Teachers, parents, school and district administrators, school board | | | Teachers, students, parents, school and district administrators | Teachers, school and district administrators |
| 9. Test construction | National publisher | National publisher | National publisher | District personnel | National publisher |
| 10. Testing initiator | District personnel, school principal | District personnel, school principal | District personnel, school principal | District personnel, teacher | District personnel |
| 11. Test selector | District personnel | District personnel | District personnel | District personnel and project director | District personnel |

## Test Use Today in Elementary and Secondary Schools

2. Elementary School B
   Learning Disabilities 1-6
   Approx. School Enrollment: 500
   Approx. District Enrollment: 20,500

**Testing Within Remedial Education Programs/Classes**

| | |
|---|---|
| 1. Diagnostic tests used once a child is placed in remedial program | For learning disabilities testing, ten different tests are used |
| 2. Who administers tests | The learning disabilities teacher or aide |
| 3. Time per month spent in testing | 40 minutes |
| 4. Frequency of testing | Two times a year, plus ongoing evaluation |
| 5. Percent of students in remedial classes | 6-8 percent |
| 6. Who selects tests | Learning disabilities teacher, speech clinician |
| 7. Who sees/uses results | Learning disabilities teacher, speech clinician, parents, teachers, principal |
| 8. Are all tests commercially published? If no, identify such tests and their source. | No. Managing reading by objectives. Managing math by objectives. |

**Testing for Special Education**

| | |
|---|---|
| 1. Tests administered to determine if special education needed | More than ten different tests |
| 2. Basis for child referral for testing | Teacher referral, parent referral, learning disabilities referral from gross screening scores |
| 3. Testing time | 2.5 hours |
| 4. Percent of students tested | 8-10 percent |

Elementary School B—Achievement/Ability Testing

| | SRA Achievement Test and Educational Ability Series | Managing Reading by Objectives (MRBO) | Managing Arithmetic by Objectives (MABO) | Keymath | Peabody Individual Aptitude Test (PIAT) |
|---|---|---|---|---|---|
| 1. Test name | | | | | |
| 2. Grade | 1-6 | 1-6 | 1-6 | 1-6 | 1-6 |
| 3. Time required | Varies—30 minutes for 6th grade placement | Varies | 80 minutes | 40 minutes | |
| 4. When administered | Fall or Winter | Continuously September through May | Continuously September through May | At placement time with new students | As needed throughout the year |
| 5. Students tested | All students at the grade level | All students at the grade level | All students at the grade level | New students | Gifted or talented, new students, those referred by teacher as having reading difficulty |
| 6. Use of results at school level | Report to parents, public and school board; select students; decide on curriculum changes | Report to parents and public; decide curriculum changes; diagnose students' strengths and weaknesses | Report to parents and the public; diagnose students' strengths and weaknesses | Diagnose students' strengths and weaknesses | Diagnose students' strengths and weaknesses; place students |

| | | | | | |
|---|---|---|---|---|---|
| 7. Use of results at district level | Report to parents, public and school board; select students | Report to parents and public; decide curriculum changes; diagnose students' strengths and weaknesses | Report to parents and the public; diagnose students' strengths and weaknesses | Diagnose students' strengths and weaknesses | Diagnose students' strengths and weaknesses |
| 8. Who sees results | Teachers, parents, public, school and district administrators | Teachers, students, parents, school and district administrators | Teachers, students, parents, school and district administrators | Teachers, students, parents, school administrators | Teachers, students, parents, school administrators |
| 9. Test construction | National publisher | District personnel | District personnel | National publisher | National publisher |
| 10. Testing initiator | District personnel | District personnel | District personnel | School principal and learning disabilities teacher | District personnel, school principal and learning disabilities teacher |
| 11. Test selector | District personnel and school principal | District personnel and school principal | District personnel and school principal | District personnel | School principal and learning disabilities teacher |

# Test Use Today in Elementary and Secondary Schools

3. Junior High School C
   Grades 7, 8, 9
   Approx. School Enrollment: 910
   Approx. District Enrollment: 20,500

## Testing Within Remedial Education Programs/Classes

| | |
|---|---|
| 1. Diagnostic tests used once a child is palced in remedial program | Several different tests are used |
| 2. Who administers tests | Resource Center staff, developmental reading teacher |
| 3. Time per month spent in testing | 2-4 periods (46 minutes) |
| 4. Frequency of testing | 2-4 week interval |
| 5. Percent of students in remedial classes | 10-12 percent |
| 6. Who selects tests | Resource Center teacher, developmental reading teacher |
| 7. Who sees/uses results | Resource Center teacher, developmental reading teacher |
| 8. Are all tests commercially published? If no, identify such tests and their source. | No. The tests come from many printed sources, including extant tests, research and professional material. |

## Testing for Special Education

| | |
|---|---|
| 1. Tests administered to determine if special education needed | A number of tests are used within the building. If the student is referred out of the building, the district level special ed. department determines what tests are given. |
| 2. Basis for child referral for testing | Teacher, counselor, parent, administrator, special ed. person in building or at district level |
| 3. Testing time | 3 hours testing plus more time in observation and interviews |
| 4. Percent of students tested | 4-8 percent |

Junior High School C—Achievement/Ability Testing

| | SRA Educational Ability Series | SRA Achievement Series | Differential Aptitude Test (DAT) | Managing Reading by Objectives (MRBO) |
|---|---|---|---|---|
| 1. Test name | | | | |
| 2. Grade | 7, 8, 9 | 7, 8, 9 | 9 | 7 |
| 3. Time required | 40 minutes | Approx. 5.5 hours | 6.5 hours | 10-15 minutes |
| 4. When administered | Fall and spring | Spring | Fall and winter | Twice monthly |
| 5. Students tested | All new students | All students at the grade level | Students enrolled in career classes | All students at the grade level |
| 6. Use of results at school level | Selecting students for talented and gifted (TAG) program | Reporting to parents, deciding curriculum changes, diagnosing students' strengths and weaknesses | Reporting to parents, diagnosing students' strengths and weaknesses | Diagnosing students' strengths and weaknesses |

| | | | | |
|---|---|---|---|---|
| 7. Use of results at district level | Selecting students for talented and gifted (TAG) | Reporting to parents, public and school board; deciding on curriculum changes; diagnosing students' strengths and weaknesses | None | Diagnosing students' strengths and weaknesses |
| 8. Who sees results | Talented and gifted (TAG) teacher, counselor | Teachers, students, parents, school and district administrators, school board | Teachers, students, parents, school administrators | Teachers, students, school and district administrators, counselors |
| 9. Test construction | National publisher | National publisher | National publisher | District personnel |
| 10. Test initiator | District personnel | District personnel | Guidance counselor | School principal and teacher jointly |
| 11. Test selector | District personnel | District personnel | Guidance counselor | Teacher |

# Test Use Today in Elementary and Secondary Schools

4. High School D
   Grades 10, 11, 12
   Approx. School Enrollment: 1,800
   Approx. District Enrollment: 20,500

---

**Testing Within Remedial Education Programs/Classes**

1. Diagnostic tests used once a child is placed in remedial program — More than eight different tests are used; the testing varies by subject.

2. Who administers tests — Teacher

3. Time per month spent in testing — 2-4 hours—varying

4. Frequency of testing — Twice/week—every three weeks

5. Percent of students in remedial classes — Perhaps 8 percent

6. Who selects tests — Varies—combinations of teacher, department chairman, administrator

7. Who sees/uses results — Same as #6, plus parents and student

8. Are all tests commercially published? If no, identify such tests and their source. — No. A combination of commercial and teacher-made tests is used.

**Testing for Special Education**

1. Tests administered to determine if special education needed — Most classes are multilevel. Two tests per class per month would be a very *rough* average. Classes vary greatly in testing practices, but most test every one to three weeks.

2. Basis for child referral for testing — Teacher, counselor, parent, student referrals

3. Testing time — Average 2 hours

4. Percent of students tested — 8-10 percent

## High School D—Achievement/Ability Testing

| | | |
|---|---|---|
| 1. Test name | Preliminary Scholastic Aptitude Test (PSAT) National Merit Scholarship Qualifying Test (NMSQT) | APP Exams |
| 2. Grade | 11 | Most twelfth graders Some eleventh graders |
| 3. Time required | 3 hours | 3 hours |
| 4. When administered | Fall—one date only | Spring—third week in May |
| 5. Students tested | Those who wish to | Gifted or talented, plus anyone who wants to take the exams |
| 6. Use of results at school level | Report to parents, select students for NMS, SAT practice | Report to parents and the public; provide information for school records |
| 7. Use of results at district level | None | None |
| 8. Who sees results | Teachers, students, parents, school administrators and NMSC | Teachers, students, parents, school administrators and college personnel |
| 9. Test construction | National publisher | National publisher |
| 10. Test initiator | Service offered by CEEB | Service offered by CEEB |
| 11. Test selector | CEEB | CEEB |

## Test Use Today in Elementary and Secondary Schools 269

Schools A, B, C, and D illustrate the range and extent of testing that can—and do—occur within a single district. But of course, testing patterns vary from school to school. The following illustrations, also abstracted from the survey, show some of the different forms these patterns may take.

5.  
Elementary School E  
Grades K-4  
Approx. School Enrollment: 600  
Approx. District Enrollment: 1,700

*And*

Middle School E  
Grades 5, 6  
Approx. School Enrollment: 350  
Approx. District Enrollment: 1,700

**Testing Within Remedial Education Programs/Classes**

1. Diagnostic tests used once a child is placed in remedial program — At least three tests are used

2. Who administers tests — Reading specialist

3. Time per month spent in testing — One-half hour

4. Frequency of testing — Quarterly, semesterly, skill mastery

5. Percent of students in remedial classes — 0.5 percent

6. Who selects tests — Reading specialist

7. Who sees/uses results — Reading specialists, classroom teacher, parent

8. Are all tests commercially published? If no, identify such tests and their source. — Yes

**Testing for Special Education**

1. Tests administered to determine if special education needed — At least six different tests are used

2. Basis for child referral for testing — Teacher referral, parent referral

3. Testing time — The basic education and placement battery generally takes about two hours. If more testing is needed, the time may run as long as 5 hours or more.

4. Percent of students tested — 10 percent

## Elementary School E—Achievement/Ability Testing

| | | | |
|---|---|---|---|
| 1. Test | Iowa Test of Basic Skills | Cognitive Abilities Test | Iowa Test of Basic Skills (Middle School) |
| 2. Grade | 2, 3, 4 | 2, 4 | 5 |
| 3. Time required | 6 hours | 1.75 hours | 6 hours |
| 4. When administered | Fall | Fall | Fall |
| 5. Students tested | All students at the grade level | All students at the grade level | All students at the grade level |
| 6. Use of results at school level | Report to parents, public and school board, select students, decide on curriculum changes | Report to school board, select students | Report to parents, public and school board, select students, decide on curriculum changes |
| 7. Use of results at district level | Report to public and school board, select students | Report to the school board, select students | Report to public and school board |
| 8. Who sees results | Teachers, students, parents, public, school and district administrators, school board | Teachers, school administrators, school board | Teachers, students, parents, public, school and district administrators, school board |
| 9. Test construction | National publisher | National publisher | National publisher |
| 10. Test initiator | District personnel | District personnel | District personnel |
| 11. Test selector | District personnel | District personnel | District personnel |

6. Elementary School F
   Grades K-6
   Approx. School Enrollment: 280
   Approx. District Enrollment: 80,000

**Testing Within Remedial Education Programs/Classes**

| | | |
|---|---|---|
| 1. | Diagnostic tests used once a child is placed in remedial program | At least three tests are used in addition to teacher observation |
| 2. | Who administers tests | Title I teacher |
| 3. | Time per month spent in testing | Varies |
| 4. | Frequency of testing | Several times a month |
| 5. | Percent of students in remedial | 25 percent |
| 6. | Who selects tests | Title I director |
| 7. | Who sees/uses results | Title I teachers, classroom teacher, administrator, specialists |
| 8. | Are all tests commercially published? If no, identify such tests and their source. | No. Some are teacher-made. |

**Testing for Special Education**

| | | |
|---|---|---|
| 1. | Tests administered to determine if special education needed | At least seven tests are used |
| 2. | Basis for child referral for testing | Teacher referral, parent referral, outside agency |
| 3. | Testing time | 4-6 hours |
| 4. | Percent of students tested | 7 percent |

Elementary School F—Achievement/Ability Testing

| 1. Test | BOEIIM | California Test of Basic Skills (CTBS) | Writing Sample | Criterion Science | Criterion Math |
|---|---|---|---|---|---|
| 2. Grade | K | 3, 4, 6 | 3-5 | 6 | 6 |
| 3. Time required | 20 minutes | 50-124 minutes | 50 minutes | | |
| 4. When administered | 3 to 5 times a year | Fall | Winter | Winter | Winter |
| 5. Students tested | All students at the grade level | All students at the grade level | All students at the grade level | All students at the grade level | All students at the grade level |
| 6. Use of results at school level | Diagnosis of students' strengths and weaknesses | Diagnosis | Diagnosis | Diagnosis | Diagnosis |

|  | Report to the public | Report to the public | Report to the public | Report to the public | Report to the public | Report to the public |
| --- | --- | --- | --- | --- | --- | --- |
| 7. Use of results at district level | | | | | | |
| 8. Who sees results | Teachers | School administrators | School administrators | School administrators | School administrators | School administrators |
| 9. Test construction | National publisher | National publisher | District personnel | District personnel | District personnel | District personnel |
| 10. Testing initiator | District personnel | District personnel | District personnel | District personnel | District personnel | District personnel |
| 11. Test selector | District personnel | District personnel | District personnel | District personnel | District personnel | District personnel |

7. Junior High G
   Grades 7, 8, 9
   Approx. School Enrollment: 700
   Approx. District Enrollment: 11,000

**Testing Within Remedial Education Programs/Classes**

| | | |
|---|---|---|
| 1. | Diagnostic tests used once a child is placed in remedial program | Two tests are used |
| 2. | Who administers tests | Remedial teacher, counselors, psychologist |
| 3. | Time per month spent in testing | In most cases, none; children are not tested frequently |
| 4. | Frequency of testing | Twice a year |
| 5. | Percent of students in remedial classes | 4 percent |
| 6. | Who selects tests | No response |
| 7. | Who sees/uses results | Psychologist, remedial teachers, parents, counselors, classroom teachers |
| 8. | Are all tests commercially published? If no, identify such tests and their source. | No response |

**Testing for Special Education**

| | | |
|---|---|---|
| 1. | Tests administered to determine if special education needed | Approximately 14 tests are used |
| 2. | Basis for child referral for testing | Teacher observation, failure notices. To qualify for special education in our program a child must be three grade levels below average |
| 3. | Testing time | 2 hours |
| 4. | Percent of students tested | 5.6 percent |

## Test Use Today in Elementary and Secondary Schools

### Junior High G—Achievement/Ability Testing

| | | |
|---|---|---|
| 1. Test | Cognitive Abilities Test (C.A.T.) | Iowa Test of Basic Skills (ITBS) |
| 2. Grade | 7 (8 and 9 makeups) | 8 |
| 3. Time required | 4 hours | 7-8 hours |
| 4. When administered | Fall | Fall |
| 5. Students tested | All students at the grade level | All students at the grade level |
| 6. Use of results at school level | Report to parents, select students, diagnose strengths and weaknesses | Report to parents, select students, diagnose strengths and weaknesses |
| 7. Use of results at district level | Report to school board, decide on curriculum changes | Report to school board, decide on curriculum changes |
| 8. Who sees results | Teachers, students, parents, school administrators | Teachers, students, parents, school administrators |
| 9. Test construction | National publisher | National publisher |
| 10. Testing initiator | District personnel | District personnel |
| 11. Test selector | District personnel | District personnel |

8. High School H
   Grades 10, 11, 12
   Approx. School Enrollment: 1,485
   Approx. District Enrollment: 13,000

**Testing Within Remedial Education Programs/Classes**

1. Diagnostic tests used once a child is placed in remedial program — There are no Title I programs at this school. Three diagnostic tests are used for the reading program.

2. Who administers tests — Teachers, psychologists, occupational therapists, speech pathologists, or other specialists

3. Time per month spent in testing — As required

4. Frequency of testing — Before placement; then during classes, at end of units; post testing

5. Percent of students in remedial classes — No response

6. Who selects tests — Teachers, psychologists, or other specialists

7. Who sees/uses results — Teachers, parents, students, or specialists

8. Are all tests commercially published? If no, identify such tests and their source. — This depends on program

**Testing for Special Education**

1. Tests administered to determine if special education needed — Approximately twelve different tests are given, based on a student's individual needs

2. Basis for child referral for testing — Teacher referral, past performance present functioning in classes. Student referrals and parent referrals are also accepted.

3. Testing time — 1-2 hours initially, then more if placement is made

4. Percent of students tested — 1-1.5 percent

High School H—Achievement/Ability Testing

| 1. Test | American College Test | College Boards, SAT, ACH | Preliminary Scholastic Aptitude Test | SRA Achievement Series |
|---|---|---|---|---|
| 2. Grade | 11 and 12 | 11 and 12 | 11 | 10-12 |
| 3. Time required | 3.5 hours | SAT—3.5 hours ACH—1 hour per test | 145 minutes | 5.5 hours |
| 4. When administered | 3-5 times a year | 3-5 times a year | Fall | Fall |
| 5. Students tested | Student elects to take test | Student elects to take test | 11th graders elect to take test | Random sampling |
| 6. Use of results at school level | Report to parents | Report to parents | Report to parents | Diagnose strengths and weaknesses |
| 7. Use of results at district level | Decide on curriculum changes | Decide on curriculum changes | Decide on curriculum changes | Diagnose students' strengths and weaknesses |
| 8. Who sees results | Students, parents, public and school administrators | Students, parents, public and school administrators | Students, parents, public and school administrators | School and district administrators |
| 9. Test construction | National publisher | National publisher | National publisher | National publisher |
| 10. Testing initiator | Colleges | Colleges | Colleges | District personnel |
| 11. Test selector | Colleges | Colleges | Colleges | District personnel |

*Test Use Today in Elementary and Secondary Schools* 279

9. High School I
   Grades 9-12
   Approx. School Enrollment: 1,500
   Approx. District Enrollment: 60,000

**Testing Within Remedial Education Programs/Classes**

| | |
|---|---|
| 1. Diagnostic tests used once a child is placed in remedial program | One test is used |
| 2. Who administers tests | Teacher |
| 3. Time per month spent in testing | 1.5 hours |
| 4. Frequency of testing | Twice monthly |
| 5. Percent of students in remedial classes | 40 percent |
| 6. Who selects tests | Math Department head |
| 7. Who sees/uses results | Teachers |
| 8. Are all tests commercially published? If no, identify such tests and their source. | No. San Francisco Math Inventory Test developed by San Francisco Math Department heads and teachers. |

**Testing for Special Education**

| | |
|---|---|
| 1. Tests administered to determine if special education needed | Varies, depending on need and parent approval |
| 2. Basis for child referral for testing | Teacher and parent request |
| 3. Testing time | 2 hours |
| 4. Percent of students tested | 20 percent |

High School I—Achievement/Ability Testing

| 1. Test | Statewide assessment | CTBS | High school proficiency | Math inventory |
| --- | --- | --- | --- | --- |
| 2. Grade | 12 | 9-12 | 9-12 | 9 |
| 3. Time required | Half hour | 4 hours | 3 hours | 1 hour |
| 4. When administered | Fall | Fall and winter | Winter | Fall |
| 5. Students tested | All students at the grade level | All students at each grade level | All ninth graders; students at other grade levels below certain percentile on previous test | Only those below a certain percentile on a previous test |
| 6. Use of results at school level | Statewide assessment | Evaluation of Title I programs | Report to parents, public, school board; diagnose strengths and weaknesses; decide on curriculum; certify students | Select students; diagnose students' strengths and weaknesses |

| | Statewide assessment | Report to public and school board; evaluate special programs | Report to parents, public, school board; diagnose strengths and weaknesses; decide on curriculum; certify students | None |
|---|---|---|---|---|
| 7. Use of results at district level | | | | |
| 8. Who sees results | The public | Teachers, parents, the public, school administrators | Teachers, parents, public, students, school and district administrators, school board | Teachers and students |
| 9. Test construction | State | National publisher | District personnel | District personnel |
| 10. Testing initiator | State agency | State agency and district personnel | State agency | School principal and teacher |
| 11. Test selector | State agency | District personnel | District personnel | School principal and project director |

*Test Use Today in Elementary and Secondary Schools* 283

10. High School J
    Grades 10, 11, 12
    Approx. School Enrollment: 1,729
    Approx. District Enrollment: 76,000

**Testing Within Remedial Education Programs/Classes**

| | | |
|---|---|---|
| 1. | Diagnostic tests used once a child is placed in remedial program | At least four different tests are used |
| 2. | Who administers tests | Perceptual communication teachers |
| 3. | Time per month spent in testing | Depends on students |
| 4. | Frequency of testing | Depends on students |
| 5. | Percent of students in remedial classes | 1.9 percent approx. |
| 6. | Who selects tests | Reading specialists and other special educators |
| 7. | Who sees/uses results | Teachers |
| 8. | Are all tests commercially published? If no, identify such tests and their source. | No. Math and English developed by school personnel. |

**Testing for Special Education**

| | | |
|---|---|---|
| 1. | Tests administered to determine if special education needed | Specialists—psychologists, speech therapists and others—choose appropriate tests. At least four different tests are used. |
| 2. | Basis for child referral for testing | School difficulties—academic or otherwise—which have not responded to classroom intervention. Sometimes parent or self referral. |
| 3. | Testing time | 1 to 10 hours. (Estimated cost child: $500 for evaluation and placement.) |
| 4. | Percent of students tested | Some only have partial evaluations, but approximately 1+ percent are given such testing. |

High School J—Achievement/Ability Testing

| 1. Test | Test of Everyday Math | CTBS T/4 | Adult Performance Level (APL) | Writing Sample | AAHPER Physical Education Tests | Vocabulary | CTBS S/4 |
|---|---|---|---|---|---|---|---|
| 2. Grade | 10 | 10 | 12 | 11 | PE classes | 11 | New to school dist. |
| 3. Time required | Untimed | 49 minutes | Untimed (estimate 55 minutes) | 40 minutes | | Untimed (estimate 30 minutes) | 46 minutes |
| 4. When administered | Fall | Fall | Winter | Winter | End of semester and year | Fall | At time of enrollment |
| 5. Students tested | Entry level math | All students at grade level | All students at grade level | All students at grade level | All P.E. students | Optional: school choice | All new students |
| 6. Use of results at school level | Report to parents, public and school board; evaluate special programs; diagnose students' strengths and weaknesses | Report to parents and school board; select students; decide on curriculum changes; diagnose students' strengths and weaknesses | Report to school board; decide on curriculum changes; diagnose students' strengths and weaknesses | Diagnose students' strengths and weaknesses | Report to parents, public and school board; diagnose students' strengths and weaknesses | Diagnose students' strengths and weaknesses | Diagnose students' strengths and weaknesses; provide basis for class placement |

| | | | | | | | |
|---|---|---|---|---|---|---|---|
| 7. Use of results at district level | Report to parents, public and school board; decide on curriculum changes; evaluate special programs | Report to public and school board | Report to parents and public; decide on curriculum changes; evaluate special programs; certify students | Evaluate special programs; diagnose students' strengths and weaknesses | Report to school board; diagnose students' strengths and weaknesses | Decide on curriculum changes; evaluate special programs; diagnose students' strengths and weaknesses | NA |
| 8. Who sees results | Teachers, students, school and district administrators, school board | Teachers, students, parents, school and district administrators, school board | Teachers, students, parents, district administrators, school board | Teachers and students | Teachers, students, parents, school administrators, school board | Teachers | Teachers, students, and counselors |
| 9. Test construction | District personnel | District personnel | National publisher | District personnel | National publisher | District personnel | National publisher |
| 10. Testing initiator | District personnel | District personnel | District personnel | District personnel | District personnel | Teacher | Guidance counselor |

RODNEY SKAGER
# On the Use and Importance of Tests of Ability in Admission to Postsecondary Education

**INTRODUCTION**

The role of testing for postsecondary admissions is a significant educational issue at the beginning of the 1980s. The previous decade witnessed a diminution of confidence in the academic grade point average (GPA), the other quantitative predictor of future academic performance. Generally lower standards in the grading process in both secondary schools and postsecondary institutions have been well documented. But while grades have inflated, test scores have retained the same meaning. If predicted academic performance continues to be the primary admissions criterion for most selective institutions, then the movement against testing on the one hand and traditional institutional values on the other are on a collision course.

That vocal and potentially influential groups in the United States distrust or even openly oppose the use of tests of ability in postsecondary admissions is hardly news. Rightly or wrongly, tests themselves, rather than the way in which they are used, are viewed by many as the primary obstacle to the achievement of representative distributions of different ethnic or other groups throughout higher and professional education.

In the light of such extensive criticism, certain questions arise. How significant is performance on tests of ability for applicants to 4-year undergraduate institutions, graduate schools, and professional schools of business, law, and medicine? Is the assumption valid that tests are a heavily weighted factor in the admissions process, or is the picture mixed,

# Tests of Ability in Admission to Postsecondary Education

with test performance more important in certain situations and for certain categories of applicants? It will be the objective of this report to answer these questions, insofar as currently available information permits.

Tests used in postsecondary admissions measure what Anastasi (1980) has referred to as "developed abilities"—cognitive performance reflecting systematic learning, whether directly from schooling or indirectly through interaction with the environment. The concept of developed abilities covers a fairly broad spectrum of test content ranging from generalized verbal skills measured by reading comprehension through tests that are closely tied to particular subjects such as physics or mathematics.

## ANALYZING TEST USE IN SIX MAJOR ADMISSIONS TESTING PROGRAMS

At present, the six major postsecondary admissions testing programs in the United States include: at the undergraduate level the Scholastic Aptitude Test (SAT) and the American College Testing Program (ACT); for general graduate education and many professional schools the Graduate Record Examination (GRE); the Graduate Management Admission Test (GMAT) in schools of business and management; the Law School Admission Test (LSAT); and the Medical College Admission Test (MCAT). All of these tests are administered nationwide. Policy relating to their content and use is under the authority of national organizations, usually comprised of member institutions who contract or have similar arrangements with technical organizations for services such as test development, score reporting, and, in some cases, research.

There is no single, across-the-board answer to the question of how much weight a given test carries in admissions. However, inferences can be made from data about specific aspects of test use, such as the number of institutions requiring a test, the usual selection ratio in such institutions, the kind of admissions model typically used, as well as current research on test use. This report is organized around four questions that are posed for each of the six testing programs:

1) How many examinees took the test last year, and what trends in volume are apparent in comparison with the recent past and immediate future?

2) What proportion of the institutions in a given category require that test scores be submitted with the application? Are there subcategories of institutions that require test scores more frequently than other institutions?

3) What, if any, is the typical admissions model used by institutions

requiring the test, and how do test scores fit into that model in relation to other types of information?

4) What does research tell us about the importance of test scores compared to other types of information and in relation to the applicant's chances of being admitted to an institution of choice?

More information is available for some testing programs than for others, and the answers, which will be generalized for each program, will vary accordingly.[1] Exceptions to common practice do exist, of course. They are surprisingly rare and will be mentioned only briefly.

## Undergraduate Admissions

The SAT and ACT account for virtually all admissions testing at the undergraduate level. The SAT is of course the progenitor of all other national admissions tests. It yields two broad-gauge scores, Verbal (V) and Mathematical (M), in addition to the more recently developed Written Test of Standard English. SAT-V combines performance on vocabulary, verbal reasoning, verbal relationships, and reading comprehension. The SAT-M score is more closely related to school content in arithmetic, algebra, and geometry and requires competency in computation, application of principles, and original problem solving. The ACT assesses competencies in the four subject fields of English, mathematics, social studies, and natural sciences. It is designed to provide work samples of content-related activities that are likely to be useful in college work. For example, the English test measures the use and understanding of principles of correct and effective writing.

While the ACT subtests are intended to be tied more closely to academic curricula than are the SAT tests, especially the SAT Verbal, both ACT and SAT provide stable measures that change relatively little between the junior and senior years of high school. In the general population, scores on the two tests are highly correlated, with the sum of the ACT English, natural sciences, and social studies subtests correlating .82 with SAT Verbal in a recent national sample of about 15,000 applicants who

---

[1] Most of the information presented in this report was obtained or identified through the generous assistance of individuals at the American College Testing Program, the College Board, the American Association of Medical Colleges, and the Educational Testing Service, as well as from colleagues in university administration and higher education research. A number of important observations and conclusions in this paper reflect the experience and judgment of these individuals rather than the findings of quantitative research. Opinions by experts will be identified as such.

had taken both tests.[2] In other words, applicants score about as well on one test as on the other.

## Volume of Test Use

Just under 2.5 million examinees took these tests at least once during 1978-1979 (1,519,345 for the SAT and 940,397 for the ACT). This number includes many who took both tests.

Approximately 4.86 million SAT score reports were sent to colleges. This means that, in order to receive at least one offer of admission, many SAT examinees apply to three or more institutions. The picture is likely to be similar for ACT examinees. This is surprising in view of the fact that a large majority of undergraduate applicants are offered admission to the institutions to which they apply. It seems that applicants may overestimate the difficulty of being admitted to their first-choice institution. Both ACT and SAT programs allow students to send score reports to three institutions as part of the registration fee. How much this practice encourages multiple applications is not known.

## Extent to Which Tests are Required

Summary data provided by the American College Testing Program reveal that either the SAT or the ACT test is required by approximately nine out of ten 4-year undergraduate institutions. These data are listed in Table 1, broken down by the highest degree offered at the institution, e.g., bachelor's, master's, or doctoral.

While patterns of test use vary between the three types of institutions, there is a remarkable degree of consistency. Either the ACT or SAT is required at 89.5 percent of the bachelor's degree only institutions, while 91 percent of the master's and Ph.D. granting institutions require one or the other test. Given the common pattern of applying to more than one institution, it can be concluded that virtually all applicants to 4-year undergraduate institutions take either ACT or SAT or both.

## Typical Admissions Model

Few national studies have been conducted of undergraduate admissions procedures. The diversity, especially in size, of the approximately 1,700

---

[2] Personal communication from the Higher Education Research Institute, Inc., October 1979.

TABLE 1  Undergraduate Admissions Testing Requirements for Bachelor's Only, Master's, and Ph.D. Level U.S. Colleges and Universities

| Test(s) Required | Bachelor's Only f | % | Master's f | % | Ph.D. f | % | Total f | % |
|---|---|---|---|---|---|---|---|---|
| ACT | 98 | (13) | 57 | (10) | 34 | (12) | 189 | (11.9) |
| SAT | 35 | ( 5) | 67 | (12) | 43 | (15) | 145 | ( 9.1) |
| ACT (SAT)[a] | 133 | (17) | 65 | (12) | 37 | (13) | 235 | (14.8) |
| SAT (ACT)[b] | 91 | (12) | 69 | (13) | 40 | (14) | 200 | (12.6) |
| ACT = SAT[c] | 326 | (43) | 240 | (44) | 109 | (38) | 675 | (42.4) |
| Other test | 33 | ( 4) | 16 | ( 3) | 14 | ( 5) | 63 | ( 4.0) |
| None | 42 | ( 5.5) | 28 | ( 5) | 6 | ( 2) | 76 | ( 4.8) |
| Unknown | 5 | ( 1) | 3 | ( 1) | 6 | ( 2) | 14 | ( 0.9) |

[a]ACT (SAT) indicates ACT preferred, SAT accepted.
[b]SAT (ACT) indicates SAT preferred, ACT accepted.
[c]ACT = SAT indicates either test accepted with no preference.

undergraduate colleges and universities in the United States might lead to the expectation that there are a variety of admissions models in operation, but this may not be the case. Although administrative procedures vary widely, observers associated with testing programs describe a single, dominant model for the majority of undergraduate institutions, whether small or large.

Most undergraduate colleges and universities use some variation of a three-category model in which applicants are initially classified into (a) presumptive-admit, (b) hold, and (c) presumptive-deny status. Presumptive-admit applicants have strong academic credentials. These individuals are denied admission only if further scrutiny of the record turns up some sort of negative information. Hold applicants are academically less outstanding but may, on further examination, be found to have special qualifications. The latter would include all other indicators of achievement, including academic and nonacademic accomplishments as revealed by letters of recommendation, special awards, and the like. Finally, applications in the presumptive-deny category would be screened for "special admissions" applicants. The latter might be disadvantaged students, students who are handicapped, children of alumni, or athletes.

Final decision criteria differ substantially among the three categories. The picture that emerges, albeit impressionistic, reveals substantial flexibility in the dominant admissions model. This is important, since the nature of the model relates directly to the openness of the system.

Two aspects of the context of the admissions process would seem to justify the wide use of the three-category model. First, there is considerable pressure to meet affirmative action guidelines, especially for institutions heavily dependent on federal grants and contracts. The "special admissions" label is undoubtedly an offspring of affirmative action, even though special consideration of varying degrees has long been given to applicants supported by influential people, children of prominent alumni, athletes, and others. It is generally agreed that special admissions procedures exist in one form or another in virtually all large public institutions, and probably in most other types of institutions as well. It is not unusual for a standard admissions policy to be described in application materials as if there were only one admissions policy. For example, the 1979-1980 published admissions criteria for the University of California require the attainment of progressively higher scores on the SAT to the extent to which the applicant falls below a 3.3 grade point average (GPA). But the university also allocates small percentages of slots at the freshman and upper division level to special admissions applicants, who are admitted on the basis of criteria not mentioned in the admissions materials.

The second aspect justifying the three-category model, especially in the case of presumptive-deny applicants, is the fact that most institutions must dip rather deeply into their pools of applicants in order to ultimately enroll a full entering class. This presumes a real need on the part of most institutions to look at almost all members of the applicant pool.

In spite of this general picture, there are probably instances in which arbitrary cut-off scores on tests and grades are routinely applied without further examination of the applicant's record. There are also a relatively small number of institutions, chiefly private and of high prestige, where the number of applicants is large in spite of the institution's reputation for selectivity. In these institutions the presumptive-deny category or its equivalent might be very large with a concomitantly low probability of gaining admission.

## Admissions Research

The importance of test scores in undergraduate admissions can be investigated by considering several questions, most of which are discussed in a current national study. The full report of that study, sponsored jointly by the College Board and the American Association of Collegiate Registrars and Admissions Officers (AACRAO), is currently in preparation.[3]

---

[3] I am most grateful to the College Board for making these and other data available in advance of publication of the survey. This preliminary report was authored by W. D. Van Dusen, J. E. Nelson, E. C. Jacobson, and S. H. Ivens.

The study began when questionnaires were sent to all the nearly 1,700 public and private 4-year institutions listed in the *U.S. Education Directory*. After various types of follow-up, replies were received from 333 or 63.1 percent of the public 4-year institutions and 648 or 56.8 percent of the private institutions. Any biases characterizing the group of responding institutions would be difficult to determine precisely, because individual institutions were not identified in constructing the data base. However, College Board research staff were willing to speculate that the sample was biased in the favor of board member institutions (not all of whom require the SAT, by the way) and more selective institutions. (This was confirmed in data showing that nearly 100 percent of the respondents required test scores as compared to 90 percent nationally.) Their speculation was borne out as well because so many items dealt with issues pertaining to selectivity, and certain "open-door" institutions reported to the board that the questionnaire was not relevant to their situation. These factors tend to give greater weight to those institutions in which test scores are relatively important. In view of the purpose of the present report, however, such a bias is in an acceptable direction.

(1) *Has the widely recognized inflation of grades at the secondary level significantly reduced the validity of the high school record as a predictor of later academic performance?* If grades are less valid than formerly, then greater reliance may be placed on test scores as the only alternative objective indicator of academic potential. A report by Ford and Campos (1977) covering the 10-year period from 1964 to 1974 shows that, in one hundred and one 4-year institutions participating in the Admissions Testing Program's Validity Study Service, the median correlation between high school record and freshman GPA slumped somewhat from about .55 or .56 for the first 2 years of the period (accounting for 31 percent of the variance in freshman grades) to an apparently stabilized .50 (25 percent of the variance) in the last 2 years of the period. At the same time, validity coefficients for SAT Verbal and Mathematics rose slightly to about .40 (16 percent of the variance) and .38 (14 percent of the variance), respectively. Although summary data were not available on median regression weights for high school record vs. test scores, the general impression at the College Board is that, while weighting for GPA has declined slightly and weighting for test scores has shown a parallel increase, grades are still weighted significantly more heavily in prediction equations calculated for the typical undergraduate college or university. It would seem that, even if grade inflation has caused some institutions to depend more on test scores, the overall effect is likely to be slight.

(2) *What proportion of applicants are denied admission by 4-year in-*

## Tests of Ability in Admission to Postsecondary Education 293

*stitutions?* Objective indicators such as grades and test scores are likely to assume greater importance to the extent that applicant pools exceed the number of available places in entering classes. Most colleges and universities, however, admit substantial proportions of their applicants. Staff at the College Board report that the median proportion of applicants accepted by public 4-year institutions runs at about 80 percent. The figure is above 70 percent for private 4-year institutions (College Entrance Examination Board 1979). For the College Board/AACRAO respondents the median was slightly over 80 percent for both types of institutions. Unpublished data at the College Board for a group of 255 public institutions (likely to be more selective than the average) showed that only 28 (or 11 percent) accepted less than 50 percent of their applicants. In contrast, 60 (23.5 percent) accepted 91 percent or more; 62 (or 24 percent) accepted 81 to 90 percent; 65 (or 25 percent) accepted 71 to 80 percent of the applicants.

While the overall picture is one of surprising accessibility, it is changed somewhat by applicant self-selection. For example, one distinguished private institution accepts 80 percent of its applicants because mainly academically outstanding students choose to apply.

(3) *How frequently are minimum scores used by institutions and how high are those scores?* In the College Board/AACRAO study, participating institutions were asked if there were minimum high school GPAs or minimum SAT or ACT scores beyond which "an applicant is generally not considered for admission?" Approximately 38 percent of public and 42 percent of private 4-year institutions replied in the affirmative for the SAT, with the corresponding figures for the ACT at 29 percent and 36 percent, respectively. However, the mean cut-off scores used by these institutions were surprisingly low. In the case of the SAT-total, the average was 740 for public and 754 for private 4-year institutions (out of a possible score of 1600). For ACT composites, the averages were also low, 16.2 for public and 16.4 for private (out of a possible 36). In all cases, the so-called cut-off scores averaged well below national averages for undergraduate admissions test takers as a whole.

In contrast, it was found that minimum GPAs equal to or less than "C" were used more frequently as cut-off points, especially by private 4-year institutions (58 percent) and to a lesser extent by public institutions (43 percent).

(4) *How commonly are test scores used in making admissions decisions and how much weight do they carry?* The College Board/AACRAO data reveal that for 64 percent of public and 78 percent of private institutions, test scores are "routinely considered in reaching an overall judgment regarding admissibility for practically all freshmen." Another 20

percent of public and 9 percent of private "check only when other application credentials fall below some specified level." It is likely that the latter institutions use test scores mainly when applicants' grades are low. Finally, only 12 percent of public and 7 percent of private institutions indicated that tests were required but "seldom play any role in the admissions decision."

Test scores are clearly second in importance to high school grades in both public and private institutions. Only 3.6 percent of the public and 1 percent of the private institutions ranked scores as the single most important factor, while about 60 percent of public institutions and 50 percent of private describe test scores as a "very important factor." This is undoubtedly the picture that has existed for many years, and other information in the College Board/AACRAO study reveals that little or no change is anticipated in the weight given to tests during the next decade.

(5) *What types of information other than tests and grades are considered?* To the extent that other types of information are considered in the admissions process, tests and grades lose some of their potential importance. The College Board/AACRAO study found that other credentials commonly required for some or all applicants included personal interviews in a surprising number of institutions (42 percent for public and 54 percent for private) and letters of recommendation (33 percent for public and 82 percent for private).

When asked whether subjective judgments of personal qualities were considered, presumably as derived from the above types of information, most institutions, especially private institutions, answered in the affirmative. For example, evidence of motivation or initiative was of interest to 59 percent of the public and 91 percent of the private institutions. Citizenship and moral character were considered by 38 percent of public and 83 percent of private institutions. Evidence of special skills and abilities was also seen as important by 57 percent and 80 percent of the public and private institutions, respectively. In fact, all of the other subjective factors, including work experience, community or church involvement, and leadership capabilities were taken into consideration by more than half of the private institutions and substantial proportions of the public institutions. How much weight these factors carry is unknown, but their consideration is clearly compatible with the use of the three-category admissions model as described earlier, as well as with the relatively high selection ratio at most institutions, and the relatively low average cut-off scores on tests and grades reported by institutions using this particular administrative device.

In general, undergraduate admissions policies seem to reflect consid-

## Tests of Ability in Admission to Postsecondary Education

erable flexibility in their use of test scores relative to other forms of application credentials. Nationally, most applicants are admitted to the college or university of their choice. Rigid cut-off points, for either test scores or high school grades, are surprisingly low, if used, and indeed are used by very few institutions. A handful of the most prestigious institutions continue to turn away significant numbers of qualified applicants. The College Board/AACRAO study turned up no evidence, however, that test scores per se were the dominant factor in this process in any substantial number of institutions.

## Graduate Admissions: The Graduate Record Examination

The Graduate Record Examination (GRE) is published by the Educational Testing Service (ETS) under the sponsorship of the Graduate Record Examinations Board. The Aptitude Test, the subject of this section, is most widely used, although most applicants take one or more of the twenty advanced subject matter tests also published by ETS. The Aptitude Test is composed of three subtests: verbal, quantitative, and analytical reasoning. The verbal subtest is similar to the SAT Verbal, but requires a higher level of performance, and contains items measuring vocabulary, verbal relationships, and reading comprehension. The quantitative subtest assesses basic mathematical skills in arithmetic, algebra, and geometry as well as problem solving and data interpretation skills (charts, graphs, etc.). The analytical reasoning test measures thinking skills including relationships, inferences, and analysis of evidence; scores are being reported, but because it is still new, interpretation is still being investigated.

### Volume of Test Use

Approximately 279,700 examinees took the GRE in 1978-1979, down from 285,800 the previous year. Wild (1979) informs us that only about 222,000, or 78 percent, of the test takers in 1977-1978 were potential applicants to graduate school, so the total GRE volume figure, in terms of applications, should probably be revised downward by approximately 20 percent. There has been a downward trend since the peak year of 1973-1974, and the projected drop for 1979-1980 is between two and three thousand examinees. Since graduate faculties are not likely to contract significantly in response to short-term fluctuations in the number of applicants, the prospect is for somewhat diminished selectivity in order to fill places in some graduate school departments.

*Extent of Test Use*

In most graduate schools, decision-making authority for admissions rests with individual departments or schools or even specific programs. For this reason, it is extremely difficult to discover the actual proportion of graduate applicants who are required to take the GRE. A large graduate institution might easily comprise thirty different schools and departments, each with its own set of requirements for admission.

While approximately 700 institutions offer graduate degree programs, a relatively small subset of those institutions confers most of the degrees, especially at the doctoral level. The Council of Graduate Schools (CGS), with 360 member institutions, awards well over 95 percent of the doctorates and 85 percent of the master's degrees, according to GRE program staff. The Association of Graduate Schools (AGS), joint founder with the CGS of the GRE Board and responsible for the appointment of one-quarter of its members, is a much smaller organization of only forty-eight U.S. member institutions. However, AGS membership includes most of the largest and most prestigious graduate schools, both public and private. GRE program staff report that about two-thirds of the annual GRE score reports are sent to this small group of mainly large institutions.

In this report focusing on the relative importance of tests in postgraduate admissions, the AGS institutions are obviously of particular interest. A publication of the GRE Board (1979), intended for prospective graduate applicants or their advisors, lists pertinent data about 695 U.S. graduate schools, among them the AGS institutions (GRE Board 1979). Listings are made by program (e.g., general education, special education, elementary education, etc.) rather than department or school and include an indication of whether the GRE is required for all, some, or no applicants, as well as whether the GRE Advanced Test or some other test is also required. Since this information comprises four volumes of material, one commonly offered program area each from the liberal arts, life sciences, natural sciences, and professional curricula was selected in an effort to create a representative general picture. Accordingly, humanities, biology, chemistry, and general education were singled out, and Table 2 shows the number of AGS institutions at which the GRE was required for all or some candidates within each of these programs.

The GRE is required or recommended by a significant majority of the AGS institutions in connection with biology, chemistry, and humanities programs, but by just over 50 percent in education. However, an additional third of the AGS schools or colleges of education require that at least some applicants submit GRE scores. There are no institutions not

TABLE 2  Association of Graduate Schools, 1979-1981 GRE Requirements for Four Selected Fields

| Field of Study | Required or Recommended for All | | Required for Some | | Not Required | | Number of AGS Institutions with Program |
|---|---|---|---|---|---|---|---|
| | f | % | f | % | f | % | |
| Biology | 36 | (86) | 6 | (14) | — | — | 42 |
| Chemistry | 35 | (74) | 4 | (8.5) | 7 | (15) | 47 |
| General education[a] | 18 | (51) | 11 | (31) | 6 | (17) | 35 |
| Humanities | 39 | (91) | — | — | 4 | (9) | 43 |

[a] Refers to general study of the field of education.

requiring the GRE for any candidates in biology and relatively few in the other three programs surveyed.

While the GRE is the largest testing program, the Miller Analogies Test (MAT), published by the Psychological Corporation, is also used on a national scale. In addition, some programs require the GRE advanced test in the proposed field of study rather than the aptitude test. For example, of the six general education programs not requiring the GRE for any applicants, one required the advanced test, three required some other test (probably the MAT), and only two required no test at all.

It seems reasonable to conclude that virtually all applicants to the forty-eight AGS institutions take some form of admissions test, especially if they apply to more than one institution. While forty-eight is a small proportion of the 695 graduate institutions, among them are the largest and most eminent private institutions, including the two most respected technological institutions, as well as a substantial majority of the largest public institutions.

## Typical Admissions Model

Given the vast number and diversity of graduate institutions and programs, generalizations about how admissions decisions are made are far more difficult to formulate than in the case of business, law, or medical schools. Still, it can reasonably be assumed that the diffusion of authority in admissions, especially likely in large and highly prestigious institutions, probably gives graduate faculty control over admissions standards as well as the decision process itself. The typical decision-making body in graduate admissions is a faculty committee supported by administrative staff.

GRE program personnel believe that the three-category model described for undergraduate admissions is also dominant in graduate admissions, although administrative procedures may be considerably less formalized. If this is the case, admissions committees are likely to devote most of their time to deciding whether to admit the middle "hold" group of candidates, whose academic history and potential does not place them in the presumptive-admit category. This group plus special admissions candidates are likely to be examined in the light of prior experience, recommendations, or autobiographical statements. Such a process tends to generate flexibility in the use of information.

The GRE program does not provide statistically derived prediction indices based on prior grades and test scores. GRE staff report that standard, numerically weighted formulas are rarely used in graduate admissions. However, they do suspect occasional arbitrary (nonvalidated) use of cutoff scores on the GRE, especially where there is outside pressure to admit large numbers of applicants in certain categories.[4] This practice is contrary to the stated policies of the GRE Board.

*Admissions Research*

The only national study of the use of the GRE in graduate admissions was reported by Burns (1970). It was based on an 85 percent response to questionnaires sent to the 287 institutions then belonging to the Council of Graduate Schools. This group included almost all of the Ph.D.-granting institutions in the country and a somewhat smaller proportion of the master's only institutions.

Although the Burns study is unfortunately 10 years old, there is no apparent reason to believe that admissions practices have changed during the last decade. A perhaps more significant qualification regarding the data stems from the fact that the data source was reports from graduate school administrators, rather than directly from schools and departments, and was therefore somewhat removed from actual admissions process but perhaps not so far as to produce misleading conclusions.

Burns divided the responding institutions into (a) master's only, (b) low Ph.D., i.e., doctorate-granting institutions awarding less than the average number of doctorates per year, and (c) high Ph.D. The latter group included almost all of the large public and private universities.

---

[4] Schools of education, for example, may sometimes be pressured to admit certified personnel from local school districts who must secure advanced degrees in order to obtain salary increases. Minimum standards based on test scores may in such instances be used as a convenient administrative device for resisting outside pressure.

What do Burns's data tell us about the extent to which the GRE was required 10 years ago? First, 52 percent of the high Ph.D. institutions reported that at least some departments required the GRE and another 20 percent used it if scores were available, although across-the-board requirements were reported by only 31 percent of these institutions. Low Ph.D. (47 percent) and masters only (55 percent) institutions required the GRE for all departments more frequently.

For those high Ph.D. institutions where the GRE was used at least to some extent (70 percent of the respondents), ratings of its importance averaged 4.0, or of above average importance, on a five-point scale, and only slightly lower for masters only and low Ph.D. institutions. Table 3 reproduces from Burns the percentages of the total group of institutions giving the most common responses to a question about use of the GRE Verbal Test, broken down for humanities, social science, and science departments. Two other uses reported by more than 10 percent of the institutions were as a cut-off score, and for "positive decisions" rather than for denial. For all three modes of test use, science departments put more weight on the GRE Verbal than did humanities departments. Finally, slightly under 20 percent of the institutions reported that the GRE was not used at all in admissions.

Burns's data do not permit adding percentages for the three modes of test use in Table 3, since within any institution all three modes could have been used by different departments. Yet, when the figures were broken down by numbers of departments, they were found (Burns's data not shown here) to parallel fairly closely the percentages for institutions, suggesting that many of the respondents may have been answering "mod-

TABLE 3   Most Frequent Institutional Responses to Questions on Use of the GRE Verbal Ability Score[a]

| Use of GRE Results When Available or Required | Humanities (%) | Social Science (%) | Science (%) |
|---|---|---|---|
| Not at all in admissions decisions | 17 | 16 | 18 |
| For all candidates with other data | 50 | 52 | 57 |
| Primarily to make positive decisions, not for denial | 13 | 16 | 17 |
| To provide a minimum standard | 15 | 17 | 17 |

[a]From Burns (1970: Table 24).

ally" for humanities, social science, and science departments. Taken together, these responses to the test use question suggest that a substantial proportion of the departments in the majority of institutions surveyed used the GRE in some way in making admissions decisions. This extrapolation from Burns's summary data is consistent with the relatively high ratings given to the importance of GRE scores by the GRE manual. It should be kept clearly in mind, however, that GRE scores are almost never used in the absence of other credentials and have hardly ever been rated as the most important factor in admissions decisions.

*Inferences*

In sum, the GRE appears to be widely, though not universally, used in graduate admissions. At the largest and most prestigious of the public and private institutions, the GRE or some other test is likely to be required or recommended by most academic programs. At most institutions conferring more than the average number of Ph.D. degrees, the GRE is generally taken seriously as an indicator of academic potential. There are apparently some instances in which GRE scores are used as cut-offs, but this does not appear to be the norm. The admissions process typically is relatively informal, is administered by faculty, and allows for considerable flexibility in the way in which test scores and other information are weighted in reaching decisions. However, since mainly faculty seem to be involved in graduate admissions, the real importance of test scores at the graduate level would be best researched by a study of graduate faculty admissions committees and their views on the validity of the GRE aptitude test as a predictor of postbaccalaureate performance and career potential.

**Medical Admissions: The Medical College Admission Test**

The MCAT now in use has recently replaced an earlier test administered since 1962. The new test has moved away from the general ability test used previously to an instrument designed to assess the specific knowledge and skills judged to be important for successful performance in medical school and in the later practice of medicine. The test was developed by the American Institutes for Research under the sponsorship of the Association of American Medical Colleges (AAMC) and assesses (a) science knowledge in biology, chemistry, and physics, (b) the ability to solve problems in the three science fields, (c) reading skills including comprehension, evaluation, and the ability to use information presented in narrative form, and (d) quantitative skills of comprehending, evalu-

## Tests of Ability in Admission to Postsecondary Education

ating, and applying information presented numerically or graphically. Six scores are reported: biology, chemistry, physics, science problems, reading, and quantitative.

### Volume of Test Use

Current annual MCAT test volume is approximately 48,000, excluding roughly 6,000 repeat testings. The competition is for about 15,000 places. During the next three years the number of test takers is expected to drop by at least 3,000 and possibly as much as 5,000, but it is unlikely that this decline will make it easier to be admitted to the most prestigious schools. Those who decide not to apply to such schools may do so because they judge their own chances of admission to be relatively poor, a conclusion supported by Gordon's (1979) report on the 1977-1978 applicant pool.

### Extent of Test Use

Applicants to all but two of the 126 U.S. medical schools are required to take the MCAT. Gordon reports that, in 1977-1978, 83 percent of the applicants applied to two or more schools. In fact, significant numbers applied to as many as twenty or more institutions (with the individual winner in this particular category of endeavor applying to an even 100).

### Typical Admissions Model

AAMC research staff report that about 95 percent of U.S. medical schools interview prospective applicants. This standard use of the interview, unique among postsecondary institutions, results in a two-stage admissions process. The first is an initial screening to determine who will be interviewed, with the result that most medical schools typically interview about two and one-half times the number of applicants who will eventually receive offers of admission. The administrative device at the first stage is usually an admissions committee, sometimes including students, which considers prior grades, test scores, the quality of the applicant's undergraduate institution, letters of recommendation, and, in the case of many public institutions, whether or not the applicant is a resident of the state. The interview during the second stage is usually structured around a more detailed examination of the same material.

There are few exceptions to this almost universal admissions model that is so different from the three-category model used in undergraduate admissions, and less systematically, in graduate admissions as well. The standard use of interviews makes the initial screening process critical for those applicants not advanced to stage two. It is conceivable that, for institutions with many applicants for the number of positions available, objective factors, such as test scores and prior grades, could be quite significant at the initial stage. There has been no research on this hypothesis, however.[5]

## Admissions Research

Applicants to medical schools are undoubtedly more highly self-selected than any other postsecondary applicant group. Data on the 1978-1979 applicant pool show that 57 percent had undergraduate GPAs of 3.3 or better (AAMC 1979). Moreover, a surprisingly high 45 percent of the total pool received at least one offer of admission. Where there is such high self-selection, an overall selection ratio is a misleading indicator of how difficult it is to gain admission to many schools. Gordon (1979), for example, reports that forty-three of the forty-eight private medical schools admitted less than 10 percent of their applicants in 1977-1978.

The chances of receiving at least one offer of admission are shown in Table 4 for various intervals of prior GPA and in Table 5 for test scores, along with the number of applicants in each interval. It is immediately apparent from Table 4 that, while high grades do not insure admission, the probabilities go up dramatically for applicants with GPAs above 3.3 (B+). Applicants in the 3.3 to 3.99 range have slightly over a 60 percent chance of being admitted, while even for the relatively small group of applicants with 4.0 GPA the chances, at slightly over 80 percent, are still not perfect. However, the probability of being offered admission drops precipitously when GPA is below 3.3, with applicants in the 3.0 to 3.29 range having only a 28 percent chance. About 79 percent of the 14,471 applicants offered admission to medical schools for the 1978-1979 entering class had GPAs of 3.3 or above. Yet, in the same year, over 7,000 applicants in the same GPA range were turned down. Other selection factors must have been operating when there was such a surplus of apparently academically qualified applicants.

MCAT scale scores are reported on a range of 1 to 15, with the score of 8 containing the median. Table 5 shows the probabilities of receiving at least one offer of admission for applicants reporting scores in the lowest (1-4), middle (8), and highest (12-15) scale score ranges on each of the six MCAT tests. (Percentile values for the scale scores differ slightly be-

---

[5] AAMC researchers are conducting a study of admissions practice in U.S. medical schools, but their conclusions were not available for the preparation of this paper.

TABLE 4  Probability of Receiving at Least One Offer of Admission to a Medical College by Level of Undergraduate GPA (1978-1979 Entering Class)[a]

| Undergraduate GPA | Total Applicants (N = 31,812)[b] | Proportion of Total | Probability of Offer (N = 14,471) |
|---|---|---|---|
| 4.0 | 363 | .01 | .81 |
| 3.30-3.99 | 18,064 | .57 | .61 |
| 3.00-3.29 | 6,857 | .22 | .28 |
| 2.30-2.99 | 5,843 | .18 | .19 |
| 2.00-2.99 | 557 | .02 | .08 |
| 1.99 | 128 | .01 | .03 |

[a]Calculated from frequency distributions provided by Association of American Medical Colleges (1979, Table 3-A).
[b]Total N in this table is lower than total test volume because the 13 percent of applicants with unreported test scores have been excluded.

tween tests, and approximate percentile ranges are indicated in the second column of the table.) Table 5 shows that, for any one of the six tests, (a) individuals who score around the 10th percentile had only about a 10 percent chance of being admitted, (b) individuals who scored around the middle of the range (45th to 55th percentile) had about a 40 percent chance of receiving an offer, and (c) those who scored at the top of the range (or above the 90th percentile) on any test had a little under a 75 percent chance of an offer.

The findings reported in Tables 4 and 5 do not differ in any substantial way from those reported by Gordon (1979) for the last year in which the old MCAT test was used. In the case of both grades and test scores,

TABLE 5  Probability of Receiving at Least One Offer of Admission to a Medical College for Applicants with Low, Middle, and High Scale Scores on the Six MCAT Tests (1978-1979 Entering Class)[a]

| Score Range | Approximate Percentile Rank | MCAT Test | | | | | |
|---|---|---|---|---|---|---|---|
| | | Biol. | Chem. | Phys. | Sci. Probs. | Read. | Quant. |
| 1-4 | 9th-10th | .09 | .10 | .11 | .09 | .12 | .13 |
| 8 | 45th-55th | .39 | .41 | .42 | .39 | .43 | .41 |
| 12-15 | 92nd-95th | .74 | .75 | .73 | .75 | .68 | .69 |

[a]Calculated from frequency distributions provided by Association of American Medical Colleges (1979: Table 3-A).

increments of performance significantly increase the chance of being admitted. However, the relationship is not as strong for any single test as it is for grades, nor is there a dramatic increase, as in the case of GPA, in the probability of being admitted once a particular scale score is obtained on the MCAT. This is not surprising. While there is only one overall GPA, there are six MCAT scores.

Frequency distributions for the 1978-1979 entering class show quite clearly that, for any given test score, there is a sharp drop in the proportion of applicants admitted (as well as the number who apply) below the critical GPA of 3.3. For example, at the top range of the biology test (scale score 12 to 15) 1,403 out of 1,691 (or 82 percent) of the applicants with GPA of 3.33 to 3.99 were admitted. Dropping down only one interval on GPA to 3.00 to 3.29, but retaining the same test score, only 168 out of 340 applicants (or 49 percent) were admitted. The decrease is dramatic, not only in the number of applicants in the category, but also in the chance of being admitted for those who do apply. While test scores are clearly considered in medical school admissions, it seems that being at or above the critical barrier of an average grade of B+ is the single most important factor, because of self-selection by applicants as well as selection by the medical schools. It also appears to be possible, in comparing current data with that reported by Gordon (1979) for the last administration of the old test, that the shift to six reported scores without any combined index reduces the likelihood that cut-off test scores might be used. The distribution of the 1977-1978 science subtest (old MCAT) showed a quite marked drop-off in percentage admitted below the top score level. This phenomenon is not apparent for the new test.

It could be argued that admissions decisions could be made entirely on grades, and it would still appear that test scores were a selection factor, since those admitted would tend to have high test scores. Correlations between MCAT test and GPA provided by AAMC research staff are in the .30 to .40 range for the applicant pool. However, this notion seems unlikely, certainly for the most prestigious of the medical schools. At these institutions self-selection is likely to produce an applicant pool with very high grades and test scores, and with concomitant low correlations between tests and grades. Tests in this situation would contribute information that is independent of GPA. (See Dawes 1979 and Goldberg 1977 for discussions of the effects of self-selection and the optimum weighting of predictors.)

*Inferences*

The MCAT is taken by practically all applicants to medical school. Over the nation as a whole this pool of applicants is characterized by a significant degree of self-selection, especially on prior academic performance. The two-stage admissions model that appears to be used at most medical schools incorporates an initial screening process from which a subset of the applicants is advanced to a second stage for interviewing. The initial screening process is generally based on objective information (GPA and test scores) as well as qualitative information.

It is certainly possible that at some institutions cut-offs on tests or grades might be applied in the first stage, since a relatively large second-stage pool is generally identified. If this practice is used, GPA is probably the critical indicator. Among individuals extended at least one offer of admission, there is a very sharp drop-off below the B+ average, both in the number who apply and in the proportion offered admission. There is no similar drop-off for any single MCAT score, and no composite score is reported.

## Admission to Law School: The Law School Admission Test

The LSAT is developed, administered, and scored by the Educational Testing Service under contract to the Law School Admission Council. It yields a single score reflecting the ability to understand and draw inferences from reading and to reason logically both verbally and quantitatively. While there is a separate writing ability section, this report will deal with the general aptitude score, which is by far the most widely used in admissions decisions.

### Volume of Test Use

The number of LSAT candidates tested has dropped from a high of about 133,000 in 1974-1975 to 115,284 for the 1978-1979 year, competing for about 43,000 places. While there has been a parallel drop in the number of candidates ultimately completing their applications to one or more ABA-approved law schools, it is unlikely that the high prestige schools, including many large public schools, will become noticeably less selective as a result. Their applicant pools, like those of comparable medical schools, contain far more qualified candidates than can be admitted.

### Extent of Test Use

All of the 168 law schools approved by the ABA require the LSAT for all applicants. According to the 1979 *Pre-Law Handbook* (Association of American Law Schools 1979), 160 of the schools also require that applications be submitted through the Law School Data Assembly Service

(LSDAS). Currently, LSDAS provides 150 schools with their own admissions index predicting first year law grades for each applicant. The index is derived from undergraduate GPA and LSAT scores. In contrast to medical schools, the overwhelming majority of law schools thus have at their disposal a quantitative index derived from objective data. Such an index readily lends itself to use as an initial screening device for schools where applicant pools are very large compared to the number of places available. It is important to determine, insofar as possible, how this index is used and how much weight tests carry as compared to undergraduate GPA.

*Typical Admissions Model*

The great surge in applications to law schools in the 1960s, plus the fact that very few law schools regularly interview applicants, apparently directed admissions practice toward the three-category or presumptive-admit/ hold/presumptive-deny model. In an in-depth study of admissions at five major law schools selected for variance in such important dimensions as large vs. small, public vs. private, and student body mainly resident vs. substantial nonresident, Turnbull et al. (1972:322) concluded that

Application volume, readily available admissions indices from LSDAS, and severe understaffing of law school admissions offices have created pressure toward a highly mechanical, computerized admission procedure.

All five schools used some form of the three-category admission model, with the decision on classification of applicants into the top or bottom categories (except for the small school in the study) made by administrative personnel using the admissions index derived from GPA and LSAT scores. Qualitative indices were also used, but mainly for the hold group, which in all cases was examined by an admissions committee composed mainly of academic personnel. While the Turnbull et al. study was conducted at the beginning of the decade, current experience of LSAT program staff confirms that the three-category model is still typical.

How the LSDAS index can be used to implement the three-category model is illustrated in the following example. A hypothetical law school in a large state university receives about 5,000 applications for the 300 seats in the next entering class. Applicants are first ordered from highest to lowest on predicted GPA as provided by the LSDAS index. The presumptive-admit group is then identified by selecting the top 270 applicants on the index, since prior experience has shown that about 200 acceptances will be generated by that number of offers. Next, the middle group is identified, and by noninclusion, the presumptive-deny group. The admissions office does this by going down another 800 applicants on the index of predicted GPA. This large group is then reviewed by the admissions committee, which offers admission to enough individuals to assure an additional 100 acceptances. At this point qualitative information is likely to enter significantly into the decisions. It may also have been used to some extent to reverse the initial decision on a few individuals in the presumptive-admit or presumptive-deny groups.

The cost of this review process is significant in terms of time and effort expended, especially by faculty. It is likely that (a) there will be relatively small differences between the predicted performances of individuals at the top and bottom of the hold category and that (b) many of the almost 3,500 individuals in the presumptive-deny category will differ only slightly in predicted performance from those in the hold category.

This situation is probably not uncommon in law school admissions. The large numbers of applicants for a limited number of seats mean that some kind of initial selection has to be made and, consequently, that not all applications will receive the same amount of attention. The similarity among most applicants on objective measures means that many will be turned away whose academic potential on such measures is only slightly lower than at least some individuals who are accepted. There is no doubt that objective indices, such as tests and GPA, could assume considerable importance in this context.

*Admissions Research*

Is the LSAT likely to be more important than GPA in law school admissions? One of the conclusions reached by Turnbull et al. (1972) was that GPAs from different institutions often should be adjusted if comparisons between their respective graduates are to be fair. Two of the schools in their study did this by adjusting each applicant's undergraduate GPA according to the mean LSAT score for applicants from his or her college or university. This underscores the fact that, for many law schools, the LSAT may represent a more stable measure of potential than do grades. Although there was no evidence in the schools studied that the LSAT was weighted more heavily than GPA, the analyses of each school's admissions data showed that the index based on the two variables was easily the most powerful selection measure, especially for very high or very low applicants.

Evans (1977) provides frequency distributions from which can be calculated the probability that individuals at different score ranges of the LSAT will receive at least one offer of admission. Table 6 provides these

TABLE 6 Proportion of Examinees Receiving at Least One Offer of Admission from an ABA-Approved Law School by LSAT Score Interval (1975-1976 Applicants)

| LSAT Scores | Total Number of Applicants | Probability of Offer of Admission |
|---|---|---|
| 750+ | 762 | .93 |
| 700-749 | 3,494 | .90 |
| 650-699 | 8,095 | .88 |
| 600-649 | 13,215 | .81 |
| 550-599 | 15,156 | .69 |
| 500-549 | 13,908 | .49 |
| 450-499 | 9,474 | .31 |
| 400-499 | 5,960 | .20 |
| 350-399 | 3,224 | .13 |
| 300-349 | 1,775 | .06 |
| 300 or less | 998 | .02 |

SOURCE: Evans (1977:Table 6).

probabilities plus the number applying to one or more LSDAS-participating law schools for each 50-point interval on the LSAT score range. Clearly, applicants with high test scores had a very good chance of receiving at least one offer. Applicants in the 700-749 LSAT score range had a 90 percent chance of receiving an offer, and the chances were only slightly lower for the 650-699 group. There is also a regular progression in the probability of receiving an offer of admission at progressively higher score intervals (when plotted the $p$ values form a flat S curve) that does not reveal any score level where a cut-off might be commonly applied. There is some evidence of self-selection on the LSAT, however, since there is a sharp jump in the number of applicants beyond the 500 level. There is also strong evidence in Evans's data of an even greater degree of self-selection on GPA, although it is not quite as marked as was the case for medical school applicants.

Finally, LSAT program staff familiar with the LSDAS index over recent years report that LSAT scores are being weighted more heavily in comparison to GPA. This trend is confirmed in a report by Schrader (1977), who showed that for most schools the LSAT was by the early 1970s already a more useful predictor than GPA.

If that is true, then the grade inflation that began in the 1960s is bound to be a major contributing factor. It is widely believed that grades in social sciences and liberal arts have been inflated more severely than grades in the sciences, which would affect meaning of the undergraduate

GPA more seriously for applicants to law school than for applicants to medical school. Added to this is the effect of self-selection in restricting the range of GPA among applicants and thus lowering its reliability, although this phenomenon would admittedly operate even more forcefully for medical applicants. Lastly, there is the problem of comparability among GPAs earned at different undergraduate institutions, perhaps greater for social sciences than for natural or physical sciences, although no direct evidence for this speculation was uncovered.

*Inferences*

Although typical practice does not appear to be inflexible with respect to use of admissions data, a number of pressures acting on law school admissions probably have led in the last decade to increased reliance on LSAT scores and concomitant decrease in reliance on GPA. These are: (a) the large numbers of applicants for relatively few places at most ABA-credited schools, which have led to the common use of an admissions model that places most applicants in presumptive-admit or presumptive-deny status early in the review process, (b) the availability of an objective predictive admissions index for all institutions in the LSDAS service, (c) an inflation in undergraduate grades that has resulted in the LSAT becoming a more accurate predictor than undergraduate GPA for many law schools, (d) the longstanding problem of poor comparability of GPAs from different undergraduate institutions, and (e) self-selection among applicants that is apparently more marked on GPA than on the LSAT.

## Admission to Graduate Management Programs: The Graduate Management Admission Test

The GMAT is a rapidly growing postsecondary testing program. Although the program was established in the early 1950s, its volume has soared in recent years because of the heightened interest in graduate training programs in management and public policy fields. It was developed and is administered and scored by the Educational Testing Service under contract to the Graduate Management Council, an organization composed of 57 graduate schools of management. All of the latter, chiefly large and highly regarded institutions, require the GMAT. But, beyond that, something over 600 schools or departments require the GMAT. About 150 of these are accredited by the American Assembly of Collegiate Schools of Business. Other users are schools of public health, public administration, or accounting.

Little is known about admissions practices of user institutions, but the

GMAT program is currently conducting a study that should answer the sort of questions addressed in this report. One factor that may differentiate some schools of business and management from other types of professional schools is their recognition of, and preference for, some work experience prior to admission. In general, students do not move directly from undergraduate programs into schools of management. In some instances, recent undergraduates with excellent academic credentials may be given deferred admission status and advised to gain such work experience.

Test volume of the GMAT (including repeat takers) was approximately 190,000 for 1978-1979, significantly above the figures for 5 years earlier. This rapid growth is consistent with shifts to business and management fields by applicants who formerly might have selected law school or some other type of graduate training.

## Alternatives in Admissions

Although there is little question about the widespread use of tests in postsecondary admissions, there is at the same time considerable interest in alternative qualitative indicators and models of the admissions process. The investigation on which this report was based found that a few institutions have developed radically different approaches in response to criticisms of testing and traditional selective admissions practices. Though rare, the alternatives may well presage practices that will be widely used in the future.

The Carnegie Council on Policy Studies in Higher Education (Willingham et al. 1977) provides a comprehensive list of qualitative indicators, some of which have been used since selective admissions began. Most institutions in each of the six categories just surveyed consider qualitative information for at least some of their applicants, although usually in combination with test scores. Special allowances for "disadvantagement," based on parent's income or educational level, are currently of particular interest because they provide an indirect alternative to admissions indices based directly on race or ethnicity. Astin (1978) has explored various systematic ways of using disadvantagement measures along with test scores and grades.

A variety of alternative admission models are described in Fuller et al. (1978). Manning (1977) proposes a two-stage admissibility model, which involves an initial determination of whether or not each applicant is likely to succeed in the institution. Those who pass the first cut, primarily because of adequate performance on quantitative indices, are further examined with the object of achieving cultural, geographic, and other types of diversity in the entering student body. This approach is of course most pertinent for selective institutions with large numbers of applicants for the spaces available.

A number of alternative admissions models described in Fuller et al. (1978) use arbitrarily weighted quantitative formulas, which combine indices based on tests and grades with various qualitative indices. The standard use of admissions indices thus weighted could protect institutions from charges that admissions criteria are applied unevenly for different groups of applicants. With increased public scrutiny over postsecondary admissions, the future may bring the use of formula admissions procedures by more institutions as they seek to avoid potential challenges in the courts.

## CONCLUSIONS

Recent moderate declines in the volume of most testing programs in higher education reflect smaller applicant pools overall and, possibly, a shift in student interest to management and business fields at the postgraduate level. There is no evidence of a trend away from the use of tests in any of the programs. Instead, it appears that test scores are almost universally required in undergraduate, graduate, and professional school admissions, especially by institutions that have a surplus of qualified applicants and even by those that use admissions procedures that are radically different from the norm.

The fact that tests are required for almost all applicants at all levels, in itself, tells relatively little about their significance in gaining admission to higher education. The critical factor is clearly how test scores are used in making admissions decisions, in relation to the type of admissions model, the use of cutoffs, prior academic records, and the universal phenomenon of self-selection on the part of applicants.

There was ample evidence in the data from more than one program that applicants engage in a significant degree of self-selection, presumably based on their beliefs about the weight attached to test scores or GPA by a given institution. The public image of the selectivity of an institution, whether accurate or not, is a potent factor in determing the nature of the applicant pool. In some cases this phenomenon may significantly restrict the number of applicants. High selection ratios may thus be a misleading indicator of selectivity for leading undergraduate colleges, as well as for law, medical, and business schools.

The evidence reviewed in this report further suggests that, except for law schools, more weight is given to prior academic records than to test scores, in both self-selection by individual applicants and criteria used by the institutions. For example, where minimum cutoffs on quantitative measures are used, the GPA is likely to be more heavily weighted than test scores for both undergraduate and postgraduate programs. Even prospective law students appear to weigh grades more heavily in self-selection, although for this particular program grade inflation has brought about a situation in which the test is considered more predictive of first year grades than is prior academic record.

Particular instances in which applicants may have been accepted or rejected primarily because of test scores doubtless occur, but these do not emerge out of the general picture. Test scores are likely to be more important in decisions about individual applicants to the extent that the scores are either very high or very low. Unless standard, numerical formulas are used, extremeness tends to increase the weight given to performance on tests. This is also true for the GPA.

While specific administrative procedures may vary, almost all undergraduate, graduate, and professional institutions use a procedure in which applicants are initially classified into "presumptive-admit," "hold," and "presumptive-deny" categories. Prior academic records and test scores are most important in this initial classification, with qualitative indices playing a larger role in the final scrutiny of all three categories. This common model can be quite flexible depending on how large the hold category is relative to the number of spaces available and the extent to which the other two categories are scrutinized and reversals made in the light of subjective measures.

The only other commonly used model appears to be a two-stage model used by colleges of medicine with their very large applicant pools and some highly selective undergraduate colleges. Here an initial determination of admissibility is followed by a stage of closer scrutiny in which qualitative indices (including interviews in the case of medicine) become more important. This model also is flexible enough to be able to address affirmative action goals effectively, again depending on how it is applied.

In general, most selective institutions, especially large public institutions, are likely to have more than one policy of admissions.

In those few institutions where alternative admissions models are used, it appears that greater emphasis is placed on such qualitative indices as nonacademic achievements, diversity, and disadvantagement. This occurs to the extent that (a) diverse members of the academic community are involved, especially students, (b) the indices themselves are used openly and systematically, e.g., when quantified and assigned numerical weights, and (c) the underlying model of the admissions process assures that all types of information are considered equally for all applicants.

With or without tests, selective admissions policies are likely to endure

## Tests of Ability in Admission to Postsecondary Education

in universities and professional schools. The chaos that developed in Italian higher education recently as a result of a national open admissions policy is a sobering example, if one is needed, of why selective admissions will not be abandoned in this country. Our system will also continue to give prospective students the freedom to choose the institutions to which they apply. The prestigious institutions, whose degrees and credentials have the most value in the meritocracy, will, as a result, continue to be selective in times of declining national enrollments. In this context, quantitative indices will remain useful.

## REFERENCES

Anastasi, A. (1980) The place of abilities in the conception and measurement of achievement. In *Proceedings of the 1979 Invitational Conference on Testing Problems*. Princeton, N.J.: Educational Testing Service.

Association of American Law Schools and Law School Admissions Council, Inc. (1979) *79-80 Pre-Law Handbook*. Washington, D.C.: Association of American Law Schools.

Association of American Medical Colleges (1979) *Medical School Admissions Requirements, 1980-81, United States and Canada*, 30th ed. Washington, D.C.: Association of American Medical Colleges.

Astin, A. W. (1978) Quantifying "disadvantagement." In A. W. Astin, B. Fuller, and K. C. Green, eds., *Admitting and Assisting Students After Bakke*. San Francisco: Jossey-Bass.

Burns, R. L. (1970) *Graduate Admissions and Fellowship Selection Policies and Procedures*, Vols. 1 and 2. Princeton, N.J.: Educational Testing Service.

College Entrance Examination Board (1979) *College Guide to the ATP Summary Reports*. Pamphlet distributed by the Admissions Testing Program of the College Board.

Dawes, R. M. (1979) The robust beauty of improper linear models in decision-making. *American Psychologist* 34(7):571-582.

Evans, F. R. (1977) *Applications and Admissions to ABA Accredited Law Schools: An Analysis of National Data for the Class Entering in the Fall of 1976*. Princeton, N.J.: Law School Admission Council.

Ford, S. F., and Campos, S. (1977) *Summary of Validity Data from the Admissions Testing Program Validity Study Service*. New York: College Entrance Examination Board.

Fuller, B., McNamara, P. P., and Green, K. C. (1978) Alternative admissions procedures. In A. W. Astin, B. Fuller, and K. C. Green, eds., *Admitting and Assisting Students After Bakke*. San Francisco: Jossey-Bass.

Goldberg, L. R. (1977) Admission to the Ph.D. program in the department of psychology at the University of Oregon. *American Psychologist* 32(8):663-668.

Gordon, T. L. (1979) Study of U.S. medical school applicants, 1977-78. *Journal of Medical Education* 54:677-702.

Graduate Record Examination Board, Council of Graduate Schools in the United States (1979) *Graduate Programs and Admissions Manual, 1979-81*. Four manuals of profiles on graduate programs (copyright by Educational Testing Service 1972, 1979). Princeton, N.J.: Educational Testing Service.

Manning, W. H. (1977) The pursuit of fairness in admissions. In Carnegie Council on Policy Studies in Higher Education, *Selective Admissions in Higher Education*. San Francisco: Jossey-Bass.

Schrader, W. B. (1977) Summary of law school validity studies, 1948-1975. *Reports of*

*LSAC Sponsored Research*, Vol. III. Princeton, N.J.: Law School Admission Council, 519-549. (Microfiche/LSAC-78-8).

Turnbull, A. R., McKee, W. S., and Galloway, L. T. (1972) Law school admissions: A descriptive study. *Reports of LSAC sponsored research*, Vol. II. Princeton, N.J.: Law School Admission Council, 265-332. (Microfiche/ LSAC-72-7).

Wild, C. L. (1979) *A Summary of Data Collected from Graduate Record Examinations Test-takers During 1977-78* (No. 3). Princeton, N.J.: Educational Testing Service.

Willingham, W. M., Breland, H. M., and Associates (1977) The status of selective admissions. In Carnegie Council on Policy Studies in Higher Education, *Selective Admissions in Higher Education*. San Francisco: Jossey-Bass.

Eric Gardner
# Some Aspects of the Use and Misuse of Standardized Aptitude and Achievement Tests

## INTRODUCTION

Much criticism of tests and testing is related more to the effect of the use of tests on personal, social, and political issues than to their educational relevance. In fact, one of the points most often stressed at a recent Phi Delta Kappa Symposium (Merwin, in press) on "Measurement in Education for the 1980s" was that the problems facing measurement today and throughout this decade are primarily political rather than technical in nature. Within such a context there is a tendency to single out one variable (often test scores) from the schooling context as the prime agent of educational practice or the major cause for unacceptable personal or educational outcomes.

In order to make sense of the claims and counterclaims about aptitude and achievement tests, it seems desirable to step back from the quantities of emotional and value-laden material that have been written about their use and misuse and to consider the debate on more general grounds. In so doing, it is essential to keep in mind the definition of a test and the implications of that definition for the frequently voiced concerns about standardized tests, and the less frequently expressed but equally real

---

Due to my other commitments and short notice, this paper does not represent a position paper on the use and misuse of standardized tests. It is, rather, an attempt to present background material that would be useful in considering the use and misuse of tests in any particular area.

concerns about alternative information-gathering procedures. A test is essentially a measure of a sample of behavior obtained under specified conditions that is used to make inferences about what the performance would be within a larger domain of behavior. This definition and its implications are central in considering the appropriate use of tests and test data and have served as basic guidelines for the present paper. Although this discussion deals only with testing in the educational setting, much of the criticism, as well as the aspects of use and misuse, could be applied to employment testing as well.

## ASPECTS OF THE USE OF APTITUDE AND ACHIEVEMENT TESTS

The use and misuse of aptitude and achievement tests cannot be considered independently of each other. A commentary on misuse of a certain test often suggests an appropriate change in its use. Since testing provides some of the most reliable, useful, and efficiently obtained information available in making evaluations for many different purposes and there is at present no adequate substitute, improved understanding of test misuse requires information on some claimed uses.

The similarities and differences between aptitude and achievement tests are important for our purposes here. Some of the criticism and misuse arise from a misunderstanding of what these tests actually measure, especially what the relationship is between aptitude and achievement tests and, to a lesser degree, between different types of achievement tests (survey, so-called norm-referenced, criterion-referenced, and diagnostic).

The term "intelligence test" became so closely identified with the commonly held concept of innate intelligence that its use is no longer politically and socially viable. Hence, what have been called intelligence tests are now generally referred to (and actually more appropriately so) as aptitude tests. There is no test (nor is there likely to be one) that measures innate intelligence. Neither the original authors of the Stanford-Binet nor any of their successors made such claims. Their purpose was to provide tests that would help predict success in the mental processes required in school settings. The Scholastic Aptitude Test (SAT) was the most appropriately named initially and rests its case on its effectiveness in concert with other important variables, such as previous achievement and motivation, in predicting success in academic subjects, principally during the college freshman year. It is possible, however, to design tests based on particular behaviors that will permit inferences about various aspects of intelligence. The technical manual of the Otis-Lennon Mental Ability Test (Otis and Lennon 1969), a widely used single score "intelligence" or aptitude test, gives a good presentation of the test rationale

## Use and Misuse of Standardized Aptitude and Achievement Tests

and a description of the aspects of cognitive ability it does and doesn't attempt to measure.

The line of demarcation between aptitude and achievement tests is not as clear-cut as popularly believed. Each presents stimuli that require responses from the subject, and both types call for responses based on previous background and experience. The major difference has been well stated by Anne Anastasi (1976:17): "Today the difference between these two types of tests is chiefly one of degree of specificity of content and extent to which the test presupposes a designated course of instruction."

Although there is a tendency for professionals in the measurement field to assume that the similarity between aptitude and achievement tests is a recent discovery, Truman L. Kelley (1927:27), made a number of comments that are worthy of note:

When allowance for chance errors is made, the correlation between a good battery achievement test [the total score] and an intelligence test is found to be very high. . . . The writer finds not so much occasion to criticize the practical conclusions of those who consider that intelligence tests in the main measure innate differences as he does the conclusions of those who consider achievement tests to measure in the main acquired differences.

To reiterate, aptitude tests cannot be designed that are completely independent of past learning and experience (achievement), and achievement tests cannot be constructed that are completely independent of aptitude. Performance on an aptitude test gives a score that only permits inference about aptitude. It does not measure aptitude directly.

Aptitude tests, such as the SAT, are used to predict future performance in schooling. There is considerable empirical evidence as to the extent of their success. As indicated earlier, they represent a valuable, but not the most important, component in such prediction. They are not always (and should not be) used as the sole basis for selection or admission but rather in conjunction with other evidence, such as academic record and personal recommendations.

Aptitude tests are also used in conjunction with achievement tests in analyzing and interpreting the performance of pupils. Although there is a high degree of relationship between aptitude and achievement test scores, there are numerous situations in which there is substantial discrepancy for particular pupils. In these situations, pupil problems are identified and remedial procedures attempted. For example, a high aptitude score and poor performance in the classroom often indicate lack of motivation or the need for special attention on the part of counselors or teachers.

Achievement tests, especially those most recently produced, vary from one to another in both form and purpose. The claimed uses for standardized achievement tests may be placed in three general categories: l) those used for the classroom purposes, 2) those used for supervisory and administrative purposes within school systems, and 3) those related to administrative or legislative uses outside the individual school systems.

In the first category are such claimed uses as:

1. To assess the learning achieved by pupils and classes.
2. To provide diagnostic information about learning problems of pupils and classes.
3. To assist teachers in selecting the most effective instructional approach.
4. To provide data for parents and pupils in educational and career choices.
5. To aid in decisions involving grouping for instructional purposes.
6. To aid in decisions identifying pupils with special needs.

These and similar claimed uses relate primarily to decisions made by teachers in the classroom. In discussing the validity of these claims, it is necessary to take into account the different types of standardized achievement tests and the recent changes and trends in testing. Standardized survey achievement tests (early standardized achievement tests were all of this type) sample general constructs with relatively few items. Hence, they are not particularly useful in providing precise diagnostic information about learning problems within academic subjects. They should not be the sole basis for grouping pupils or determining the instructional program a pupil should follow. They do provide limited evidence about relative performance in the different school subjects. Test results are not always accurate in their assessment of pupils, but neither are teachers. In most cases, teacher judgments and test results will agree, but in cases where they do not, the teacher is alerted to a possible problem needing attention. Since each represents fallible and imperfect estimates of pupil characteristics, using both should benefit both the teacher and the pupil.

More specific in content are so-called criterion and norm-referenced tests. The recent turn to more use of criterion-referenced tests has caused a number of changes in achievement testing. Two important contributions made by the criterion test movement were a greater emphasis on specified instructional objectives and the use of a different frame of reference for interpretation. Two entirely different frames of reference for test interpretation have been proposed, used, and discussed by professionals in the measurement field since the beginning of the achievement testing movement in the early 1900s. One is referred to frequently as a relative or normative frame of reference and the other as an absolute or content frame of reference. Criterion-referenced tests offer the content frame of reference for interpretation of test scores, while norm-referenced tests are used to offer the performance of a normative population sample for interpretation. As is obvious, the dichotomy based on the type of frame of reference is not a realistic one, since recently many criterion-referenced tests have been normed and the most recently published, so-called norm-referenced tests have blueprints giving specific instructional objectives and have methods of interpretation based on the content. However, the controversy during the last fifteen years about the relative merits of criterion-referenced vs. norm-referenced tests has caused considerable confusion among test users and has resulted in specific misuses both in terms of test selection and interpretation. For example, tests have been selected merely because they had the label "criterion-referenced test," whether or not they were the most suitable test for a particular purpose. To infer what information can be obtained from a current achievement test merely from the labels norm-referenced or criterion-referenced is a major misuse in itself. Mehrens and Ebel (1979) have discussed this issue in detail in a recent publication written for the practitioner.

Criterion-referenced tests designed to measure the elements in a specific school curriculum will usually contain more items focusing on the specific objectives of that curriculum than will the so-called norm-referenced test. Hence, they will give more information with greater depth for that particular system. They will be of greater use for decisions relating to grouping and changes in instruction. The most recent standardized norm-referenced achievement tests are designed to meet instructional objectives, as are criterion-referenced tests, but focus on content that is common to the curricula of the various states and cities. Hence, they should be supplemented, especially in localities where the curriculum and the objectives are unique.

The third kind of achievement test, of which there are very few, is a diagnostic test. These tests, which are essentially restricted to reading and mathematics, are designed to probe deeper with more items into categories included in other achievement tests and into more detailed subcategories where problems and errors are defined more specifically. The final, and most important, level of diagnosis is provided by the teacher buttressed with as much information as can be obtained in a one-to-one relationship with the pupil.

In general, all types of achievement tests have their own role and, if properly used, provide needed information for the decisions a teacher must make. Their most important contribution is to provide an additional source of evidence about pupils to corroborate the teacher's judgment, to suggest unnoticed problems, and to provide, as do diagnostic tests, suggestions for more one-to-one, in-depth diagnosis. Diagnosis usually takes place in a sequential order with tests providing information in the initial stages and the teacher-pupil interaction in the final and most crucial stage. It is important to note that in some circumstances it may be a misuse not to rely on tests or some other independent assessment to confirm teacher judgments.

The uses of achievement tests outside the classroom for administrative purposes within the school system and for administrative and legislative purposes outside the system are quite similar. For principals and superintendents, tests can be a means of identifying classrooms and programs where additional resources are needed (Rudman 1977). For state legislatures and boards of education, test scores are used for various types of accountability decisions, the basis for staff reduction, merit raises, allocation of funds, assessment of school effectiveness, awarding high school diplomas, and evaluations in connection with federal programs. In such extremely complex areas, test usage varies widely from district to district as local administrators try to cope with burgeoning public demands and still fulfill the unique needs of their own schools.

This brief description of test use today provides the context for current criticism of testing and the background for real or alleged misuse of tests. It has included ideas and concepts endorsed by most of the commentators on educational testing and supported in the empirical literature. However, in focusing specifically on test misuse, the presentation cannot avoid becoming more subject to the biases of the presenter. Use, according to one person, could become misuse in the eyes of another.

## CRITICISM OF STANDARDIZED TESTS

That criticism of standardized tests is extensive and far-reaching is obvious. The reasons are less so. In many instances, especially with regard to political issues, tests provide a handy target on which to focus criticism. They are external; they are commercial; they are standardized; they are largely norm-referenced (many criterion-referenced tests have norms); and they are summative in nature. These descriptors, completely independent of test use, conjure up all kinds of condemnatory images of inhumanness, corporate state, assembly line, coerciveness, competition, big business, loss of individuality, standardized educational requirements, and many others. In addition, tests are used for a variety of purposes, sometimes correctly and sometimes incorrectly, that have different effects on different publics. Finally, standardized tests do have limitations and are subject to misuse. The misuse has been compounded by the decrease in training in the technical aspects of testing (construction and use) and measurement concepts and skills offered by teacher training institutions as well as by the public's lack of real knowledge about what tests can or cannot be expected to accomplish. These are some of the major reasons for the extensive criticism of tests, which must be taken into account in assessing use and misuse.

A graduate student at Boston College, who has undertaken an exhaustive literature review of testing criticism to determine the number and type, has identified over sixty specific criticisms and is still adding to his list. More useful for our purposes here, however, is the following statement taken from a recent publication (1979:3) of the National Education Association (the American Federation of Teachers has a different policy with regard to test use; this group would stress some of the same issues but would propose remediation for the situation rather than elimination of tests):

The Association opposes the use of standardized tests, and continues to seek to eliminate their use, because they:
- are often biased against those who are economically disadvantaged or who are culturally and linguistically different;
- are often used for tracking;
- are often invalid, unreliable, and restricted to the measurement of cognitive skills;
- are often used as a basis for the allocation of federal, state, or local funds;
- are often used by book publishers and testing companies to promote their financial interests rather than to improve measurement and instruction;
- are used by the media as a basis for invidious public comparisons of students and schools;
- are often used to standardize educational expectations arbitrarily; and
- are often used in a way which diminishes performance motivations.

Another approach consists of a few selected issues that classify criticisms: l) on the basis of what the tests measure or what they don't measure, and 2) on the basis of their effects on pupils, teachers, and the educational process.

## Category 1

1. Standardized tests measure the ability to function in a competitive situation.
2. Standardized achievement tests assume that everyone agrees that the most important skills are included.
3. Standardized tests measure only unimportant characteristics.

4. Standardized aptitude tests assume all pupils have the same background.
5. Standardized tests mean that half the pupils are failures.
6. Standardized aptitude and achievement tests are undemocratic.
7. Standardized achievement tests measure only a small portion of the school's objectives.
8. Standardized tests really measure cultural background.
9. Standardized aptitude tests are useful in predicting success in college.
10. Standardized aptitude tests are really intelligence tests.
11. Standardized achievement tests are not diagnostic.
12. Standardized aptitude tests do not measure innate intelligence.
13. Standardized aptitude tests are harmful when used to predict success in college.
14. Standardized tests do not measure creativity.
15. Standardized tests do not take personality into account.

## Category 2

16. Standardized tests "label" pupils.
17. Standardized tests "mislabel" pupils.
18. Standardized achievement tests determine the curriculum.
19. Standardized achievement tests involve teaching for the tests.
20. Standardized achievement tests foster competition.
21. Standardized tests reduce pupils' self-concepts.
22. Standardized tests arouse fear and satisfy greed.

It is obvious that there are a number of inconsistencies among the items. One public will criticize a standard test because it measures a trivial, relatively unimportant dimension of the entire pupil. The same test will be criticized by others because the score reflects too many pupil characteristics, such as social class, vocabulary, ability to work and think quickly, emotional and social security, etc. Secondly, it seems that some of the criticisms are justified, at least in some circumstances, and that some criticism could be overcome by the appropriate selection of tests and the supplementation of test results with other kinds of data. It seems equally obvious that no test, as a sample of behavior, can measure all the characteristics of a human being.

The main point is that, although related, criticism of tests is not identical to test misuse. There are a number of criticisms of tests that are not only unrelated to test use but are so general that the criticisms cannot be examined for their appropriateness. Other criticisms are generalizations

## Use and Misuse of Standardized Aptitude and Achievement Tests

based on an observation of only one test or one item. Criticisms such as "Standardized achievement tests are not diagnostic" or "Standardized tests do not measure creativity" are not meaningful unless the purpose for which the test is to be used is stated explicitly. If, in the first instance, a short standardized survey test in reading comprehension is used to determine the reading level of third graders in a particular school system, the criticism that it is not diagnostic produces a non sequitur since diagnosis is not intended. However, if the test were used with the intention of obtaining detailed diagnostic information about reading difficulties, it would be a misuse of the survey test.

### PRINCIPAL MISUSES OF STANDARDIZED TESTS

1. Improper or inappropriate reporting of test results to the public through the press and other media.
2. Failure to report to parents in a meaningful fashion.
3. Using test scores to rank schools or to identify "good" or "poor" school systems.
4. Coaching or teaching for the test.
5. Using test scores in isolation for decision making (use of grade equivalents for grade promotions, and entry and exit from high school), investing tests with a precision beyond what they may possess.
6. Using test results to identify "good" and "poor" teachers. Using tests as threats to teachers and pupils. Using test scores to label pupils.
7. Misinterpreting measure of change over a period of time by comparison of results from tests dissimilar in content or norming procedures.
8. Use of grade equivalents (and vertical scale scores) for profiling across tests in a battery.
9. Misuse of tests in out-of-level situations—inappropriateness of content, normative misinterpretations.
10. Misuse of item and objective cluster information, lack of reliability.
11. Sloppy and inappropriate test administration practices—ignoring the limits; giving clues; setting the stage, "This test won't count in your course grades."
12. Misuse of test results by "poorly prepared" teachers and guidance counselors. Misunderstanding of the purposes of interest measures, e.g. "Interest measures are tests that tell you what you are good at."
13. Misunderstanding the purposes and limitations of screening de-

vices, such as McCarthy Screening Test, leading to misuse of gross indicators for in-depth diagnosis.
14. Proliferation of testing at state, district, and local levels, especially for pupils in titled programs.
15. Administering achievement tests, reporting back results in the form of numbers, but not involving the pupils in the interpretation of their performance. Failure to make available to students and/or parents scored tests, booklets, and answer sheets.

The above list of test misuses was compiled from suggestions of concerns about testing made by the professional staff of the Psychological Corporation, and it demonstrates amply the overwhelming multiplicity of claimed misuses of tests and the impossibility of cataloguing them all, let alone considering each one separately.

In addition, not all claimed misuses are in fact real misuses. For example, a popularly claimed misuse is, "the influence of test results in labeling children." Airasian, in a recent address, pointed out that labeling, based on any type of information, is not intrinsically bad, incorrect, or harmful. Ebel (1976) and Lennon (1978), in recent articles addressed to the educational practitioner, have included discussions of the same issue. However, the word "labeling" has taken on a derogatory meaning for many educators and, thus, has a highly emotional connotation. Critics of testing almost always cast labeling in a negative, detrimental light, while the proponents of testing focus on its positive, enhancing qualities. The empirical evidence about the influence of test information in labeling pupils, however, is equivocal at best. Furthermore, teachers label pupils either with or without test information and either explicitly or implicitly. Some kinds of labels are needed for classroom operations.

The bulk of the research on the influence of test information on teachers' perceptions is concerned with raised expectation and subsequent performance, while much of the present debate focuses on lowered expectations and performance. Madaus and Airasian are currently doing extensive research in this area. They have been especially interested in the pygmalion effect (Rosenthal and Jacobson 1968) and in following up on the refutation of Rosenthal and Jacobson's findings (Madaus 1979) by Snow (1969) and Thorndike (1968). There is substantial evidence of a high degree of agreement between pupil test performance and teacher rating and also some evidence that, when discrepancies occur between test information and teacher perceptions, teachers tend to give credence to the piece of information most favorable to the pupil (Airasian et al. 1977). When considering the influence of standardized tests on the labels pupils receive, it might be argued that for some pupils, namely those judged more favorably after testing, it is a misuse not to test. Test scores are related to the labels attached to some pupils, but the proportion of pupils involved, whether or not the labels are beneficial or injurious, and the complex interaction between test results and teacher judgments need further study before it is possible to know whether standardized tests are important elements in the labels attached to pupils.

When separated from such general misunderstanding, most testing misuse would seem to fall into one of the following six general areas.

## 1. Acceptance of a Test Title for What the Test Measures

There is a tendency for unsophisticated test users to accept the name assigned to a test as an accurate and complete description of the variable being measured. Since titles must be brief, they cannot convey all that the user needs to know about the kind of behavior to be measured. All tests are open to this kind of uncritical abuse. Since there are so many facets of cognitive ability, it is obvious that no test can be an adequate measure of them all. Only full knowledge of the items can reveal what is being measured. Furthermore, the testing situation may completely change the expected behavior. If a non-English speaking or blind pupil is given an "aptitude" test in printed English, it obviously doesn't measure *any* aspect of "aptitude" or "intelligence" except lack of knowledge of English or lack of vision. In a less obvious area, a test labeled "Science Achievement" may be an acceptable test to sample the science curriculum for students in a particular fifth grade science course but fail to function as a science test at all for most pupils if the reading difficulty is at the high school level. A test producer's claims for an achievement test or an aptitude test do not mean that it will function as such in all circumstances with all pupils. Failure to examine the manual and the items carefully in order to know the specific aspects of cognitive ability to be tested (memory, vocabulary, type of reasoning, etc.) can result in misuse by virtue of selecting an inappropriate test for a particular purpose or situation.

## 2. Ignoring the Error of Measurement in Test Scores

Every test score contains an error of measurement. It is a misuse of any test score or any observation to accept it as a fixed, unchanging index containing no error. It is impossible to say with certainty that an individual's observed score gives his "true" performance on the general domain about which inferences are to be made. The best that can be done is to estimate experimentally the standard error of measurement and then use that value to set up a band within which a probability can be stated about the "true" score's being within that band. That 1) we cannot accept an SAT score of 550 as a precise measure, 2) we must accept a range of scores, and 3) we must then expect to be wrong a certain proportion of the times does not mean that the SAT does not furnish useful data. It does mean that the test score is being misused if knowledge of the size of the errors of measurement is not used in interpreting the score. In the case of most standardized test scores, the magnitude of the errors is made explicit, not hidden or unknown. In fact, the errors in essay grading or any other type of evaluative data have far larger but usually unknown errors of measurement.

Some people reject the notion of basing decisions on probabilistic data. However, probability estimates are involved in almost all decisions. For example, the decision to cross a busy street at a particular instant is not made with a probability of 1.0 of doing so safely.

### 3. Use of a Single Test Score for Decision Making

Misuse of tests occurs when scores are not considered and interpreted in the full context of the various elements that characterize pupils, teachers, and the general educational environment involved. For a test score represents only a sample from a limited domain and does not include the variety of factors that might influence that score. For example, in decisions determining admission to college, SAT scores should not be used in isolation and are in fact usually considered along with the pupil's high school record and other relevant data, such as teacher's or supervisor's recommendations concerning motivation, leadership ability, creativity, involvement in extracurricular activities, etc. All of these can then be evaluated against the student's socioeconomic background, along with consideration of any social obstacles or unusual physical demands required of the student to reach his current educational level (Fruen 1978).

### 4. Lack of Understanding of Test Score Reporting

There is substantial misunderstanding, not just among laymen, but also among many educators, of the meaning of test scores. Most people believe that they understand the meaning of a raw score or of that particular raw score converted to a percent of items answered correctly, as in the case of many criterion-referenced tests. However, even in this most elementary illustration, more is involved than a single number indicates. Forty-five items answered correctly out of fifty easy items has a substantially different meaning than forty-five items answered correctly out of a sample of fifty very difficult items from the same domain.

The interpretation of a raw score converted to a percentile score causes even more problems. The statement that "In a norm-referenced test half the pupils must fail" is a good illustration. A percentile score of 20, by itself, represents neither a good nor a poor performance. It merely indicates that among the group used as a frame of reference this score was higher than that reached by 20 percent of its members. If the group were of high ability or had unusual skills, a percentile rank of 20 might indicate an excellent or even remarkable performance.

The misinterpretation of grade equivalents is even more common. A grade equivalent is the score that was exceeded by 50 percent of the normative group and not attained by the other 50 percent of the group at the specific time when the test was given. It does not represent a standard to be attained. It does not represent the grade in which the pupil should be placed.

To compensate for the decreasing emphasis on test construction and test interpretation in teacher training institutions, there have been efforts by the National Council on Measurement in Education[1] and other organizations to provide workshops and reading material on measurement issues. Both parents and professional educators stand to benefit, since both are involved in the misuse of testing based on misinterpretation of scores.

## 5. Attributing Cause of Behavior Measured to Test

It is common, especially for critics of testing, to confuse the information provided by a test score with interpretations of what caused the behavior described by the score. A test score is a numerical description of a sample of performance at a given point in time. A test score gives no information as to why the individual performed as reported. Claiming that it does, whether intended as a positive attribute or a criticism, is tantamount to test misuse. Furthermore, no statistical manipulation of test data, even though combined with the best additional data, will permit more than probabilistic inferences about causation or future performance. The current reports (Beaton et al. 1977; College Entrance Examination Board 1977) on the decline of SAT scores is an excellent example of the difficulty

---

[1] The National Council on Measurement in Education (NCME) is a national organization of professionals concerned with testing and measurement issues. It publishes *The Journal of Educational Measurement* and *Measurement in Education*.

in ascribing causation to known performance. The charge given the researchers by the investigating panel was to explain the causes of the drop in SAT scores. They were able to describe the drop and offer changes in test populations as a plausible partial explanation for the initial drop but could only speculate on the effect of other variables and the reasons for the continued drop.

## 6. Bias

There is an enormous literature on bias associated with tests, which bears chiefly on two aspects of test use or misuse: bias in a selection process using test scores; and test bias or the bias ascribed to a particular test or test item (Gardner 1978). The first situation is one in which the test is used to predict a criterion. A test is biased for members of a subgroup of the population if, in the prediction for which the test was designed, the predicted score is consistently too high or too low for members of that subgroup. The second involves bias in the test itself, in the sense that the score does not represent a measure of the "true" ability being tested.

The problem of bias in selection, whether for admission to educational institutions or for employment, has been, and still is, troublesome for a society in which equality of opportunity has been a major accepted philosophy. A number of approaches have been proposed as solutions to this problem, ranging from a least squares regression method to various types of procedures based on specific ratios and probabilities. In a recent volume of the *Journal of Educational Measurement* devoted entirely to bias in selection, Peterson and Novick (1976) analyzed and evaluated the most widely used models and then proposed a threshold utility model, which selects those applicants with highest expected utility. The utilities differ for the various subpopulations, and the prediction equations may also differ from subpopulation to subpopulation. They were especially concerned that some of the models, which seemed to produce desirable results, might be doing so for the wrong reasons and under other circumstances would produce undesirable results that could be used to justify discrimination against some minority groups.

Their model has the virtue of forcing a definition of bias or lack of bias in terms of utility for some social need. However, it does not eliminate the bias issue. It merely separates the political and social issues from the statistical. To quote Cronbach, "If discussion within the psychometric community helps the philosophers and lawyers to put more substantial arguments behind competing rules for attaining equity, we will have done our part" (1976:41).

Part of the difficulty with statistical selection models such as the Constant Ratio or Conditional Probability Model (or, for that matter, the Regression of Equal Risk Models) is that they attempt to provide a purely technical resolution to an issue that involves value judgments. Values are implicit in many models, but they need to be dealt with explicitly. Decision theory provides a framework for doing this, and that is the approach advocated by Peterson and Novick. Note that it provides a framework for making a decision, but it doesn't automatically provide the decision or answer. The answer involves a value judgment, which implies bias by somebody against A and for B or vice versa.

The literature on test bias or set- and culture-free tests is far more voluminous than that on bias in selection. The use of the word bias in this context has even more connotations than it does when associated with selection, as the possibility of bias is present in all tests. In some instances bias does exist; it may fail to be claimed, or it may be claimed for the wrong reasons. But more often when it doesn't exist at all, it may be claimed for irrelevant reasons. For example, as Ebel has pointed out (1976), some standardized educational achievement tests have been attacked for their alleged bias against cultural minorities and pupils of low socioeconomic status because such pupils tend to score lower.

Lower scores alone do not signify bias in an achievement test. If they did, then every spelling test would be biased against poor spellers, every vocabulary test against persons who had poor vocabularies, and every shorthand test against persons who had never learned shorthand. The fact that a group of pupils who do poorly on a particular language test might do better if the test were in a Chicano dialect does not mean that the original test is biased against them. It means that they have poor English language skills, a situation that needs remediation. Because a pupil does poorly on a reading comprehension test, but well on a comparable listening comprehension test, does not mean the reading comprehension test is biased. The two contrasting scores give important information about him for instructional purposes. An achievement test is designed to measure the competence of pupils in specifically defined areas under conditions described in the manual. The score of each pupil indicates how adequately the questions defining the domain tested were answered. For a test to have satisfactory content validity, it is important that aspects of the variable the test was designed to measure not be deleted in the name of bias.

In contrast, a test designed to measure achievement in elementary science, in which the items are presented in language and syntax far above the level of the pupils tested, is biased, especially against the poor readers. A distinction must be made here between that aspect of reading difficulty based on science vocabulary that was part of the curriculum and other vocabulary that was not. The score on the test should measure knowledge of science, including appropriate scientific vocabulary, but not general reading ability. This is a case of bias introduced by complex reading material, which can be recognized and corrected.

Recently, the lowest age grade level of a diagnostic reading test was rejected by a state committee because of sex bias. The primary criticism was that the items portrayed males and females in mostly traditional roles. The criticism was not made of the higher level tests. Here is an illustration where trade-offs are necessary. If the objective of the test was to promote the concept of sexual equality and to teach that sex is irrelevant to a person's roles in life, then it is clear that the test was not designed for that purpose. If the purpose was to present stimuli familiar to very young children just beginning to learn to read, then females in the roles of mother and teacher and males as father, mail carrier, and fire fighter are reasonable, as the aim should be to avoid distraction from the reading task.

Most very young children have not been exposed to many males or females in atypical roles, e.g., male first grade teachers are not common. Their experiences have been limited to what takes place at home or in school, and for the most part these are female dominated. This situation may change in time, but has not to date. It seems that efforts to promote a broader acceptance of sex role changes can better be achieved in other parts of the curriculum than by introducing this issue in a situation that is bound to make the reading task more difficult. Here is a value judgment. The decision could be made either way, but should be done explicitly, not because the label "sex bias" has been attached to a good diagnostic reading test.

## CONCLUSIONS

Concern about the misuse of tests is justified. The heat of the controversy testifies to the interest of the public in one of this country's most widely used educational tools. A missing element, however, in almost all the debates on the use and misuse of tests is a reasonable degree of humility. Such statements as "I don't know," or "We need to find out about that" are rare. Without some recognition of the fallibility of humans and human minds—profitable, meaningful, and intelligent dialogue is impossible.

The recent proliferation of testing for accountability, program evaluation, and minimum competency has opened new areas to controversy, for tests used for these purposes relate to decisions that have the potential for affecting adversely the life changes of pupils, teachers, and administrators and thereby fostering a wide variety of responses from teaching geared to the tests to demands for their abolition.

This creates a strong temptation to withdraw from this unpleasant situation by suggesting that standardized achievement tests not be used in making accountability decisions about teachers, pupils, administrators, or schools. Such a recommendation is not politically feasible or desirable. The public wants and has a right to seek information about the adequacy and effectiveness of its institutions, including schools. The world in which we live is a competitive world in which comparisons among individuals and institutions are demanded by most elements of society: taxpayers, parents, administrators, and legislators alike. In general, they are unwilling to accept testimonials about the goodness of education from teachers and administrators whom they view as having a vested interest. They desire some external, objective data, which at this point is most readily available through standardized testing. Further support for this rationale stems from one of the unique characteristics of American education, namely the principle of local control. There are no national syllabi (although data have been obtained that show much greater uniformity among elementary curricula, probably due to common textbooks, than one would expect) nor common tests with which to make desired comparisons. Good standardized tests provide a common frame of reference. It is important to keep in mind, however, that standardized tests can provide only a portion of the information needed to evaluate a curriculum, program, teaching method, or educational staff.

There is reason for concern about the misuse of standardized achievement tests as the sole criterion for making decisions involving accountability, graduation, and promotion. Yet at present they are the most publicly acceptable, politically viable, and probably most technically appropriate instruments we have. Improved instruments are needed for this purpose, but change for change's sake is not the answer. Change should be considered as a vector where concern is focused not only on the magnitude of the change but especially on whether the change is in the right direction and is capable of producing a better result.

There are many well-constructed tests that provide highly reliable and valid information for certain specific purposes. For a number of these tests, revisions or modifications would at best result in minimum improvement, and the substitution of other types of data-gathering devices for the same purpose would definitely produce less reliable and valid information. Society would benefit most from better instruction in the proper use and interpretation of tests and from the development of ways of obtaining information (tests and other devices) about important variables for which there are currently no measures.

# REFERENCES

Airasian, P. W., Madaus, G. F., Kellaghan, T., and Pedulla, J. J. (1977) Proportion and direction of teacher rating changes of pupils' progress attributable to standardized test information. *Journal of Educational Psychology* 69(6):702-709.

Anastasi, A. (1976) *Psychological Testing*, 4th ed. New York: Macmillan Co., Inc.

Beaton, A. E., Hilton, T. L., and Schrader, W. B. (1977) *Changes in the Verbal Abilities of High School Seniors, College Entrants, and SAT Candidates between 1960 and 1972.* Princeton, N.J.: Educational Testing Service.

College Entrance Examination Board (1977) *On Further Examination.* A Report of the Advisory Panel on the Scholastic Aptitude Test Score Decline. New York: College Entrance Examination Board.

Cronbach, L. J. (1976) Equity in selection—where psychometrics and political philosophy meet. *Journal of Educational Measurement* 13:1.

Ebel, R. L. (1976) A paradox of educational testing. *Measurement in Education* 7:4.

Fruen, M. (1978) The use of tests in admissions to higher education. *Measurement in Education* 9(Fall):4.

Gardner, E. F. (1978) Bias. *Measurement in Education* 9 (Summer):3.

Kelley, T. L. (1927) *Interpretation of Educational Measurements.* Yonkers-on-Hudson, N.Y.: World Book Co.

Lennon, R. T. (1978) Perspective on intelligence testing. *Measurement in Education* 9(Spring):2.

Madaus, G. F. (1979) The Effects of Standardized Tests on Pupils: The Expectancy Phenomenon. A report presented at the annual meeting of the American Educational Research Association, San Francisco.

Mehrens, W. A. and Ebel, R. L. (1979) Some comments on criterion-referenced and norm-referenced achievement tests. *Measurement in Education* 10(Winter):1.

Merwin, J. C., ed. (in press) *Phi Delta Kappa Research Symposium on Measurement in Education for the 1980's.* Bloomington, Ind.: Phi Beta Kappa, Inc.

Otis, A. S., and Lennon, R. T. (1969) *Technical Handbook of the Otis-Lennon Mental Ability Test.* New York: Harcourt, Brace and World, Inc.

National Education Association (1979) *Parents and Testing.* Washington, D.C.: National Education Association.

Peterson, N. S., and Novick, M. R. (1976) An evaluation of some models for culture fair selection. *Journal of Educational Measurement* 13:3-29.

Rosenthal, R., and Jacobson, L. (1968) *Pygmalion in the Classroom: Teacher Expectations and Pupils' Intellectual Development.* New York: Holt, Rinehart and Winston.

Rudman, H. C. (1977) The superintendent and testing: Implications for curriculum. *Measurement in Education* 8:4.

Snow, R. E. (1969) Unfinished Pygmalion. *Contemporary Psychology* 14:197-199.

Thorndike, R. L. (1968) A review of *Pygmalion in the Classroom. American Educational Research Journal* 5:708-711.

# Psychometric Issues

ROBERT LINN
# Ability Testing: Individual Differences, Prediction, and Differential Prediction

## INTRODUCTION

Individual differences in abilities are apparent to the most casual observer. Whether the task is running a hundred-yard dash, playing the piano, solving mathematical problems, or preparing a legal brief, the differences in individual performance are substantial. The origins, malleability, and implications of individual differences are longstanding topics of intense debate, but their existence is not.

Systematic efforts at measuring individual differences have a lengthy history, which can be traced back more than 4,000 years (DuBois 1970). The development and rapid growth of group-administered ability tests with procedures similar to many of those that are currently used, however, started with the Army Alpha test in World War I. Today testing in the United States is a widespread activity that often looms importantly in a variety of educational decisions. Test results play a role in the admission of students to colleges, graduate and professional schools; they are used in selection and placement of employees in business and industry; and they are heavily used by the military and other governmental agencies in making personnel decisions.

Although commonplace, the use of ability tests in selection and placement decisions is also quite controversial. The validity of ability tests, especially for members of minority groups and for groups of lower socioeconomic status, has been frequently and forcefully challenged. The controversies over testing are neither created by, nor will they be resolved by, the results of investigations of test validity (Cronbach 1975). Empirical investigations can determine how well an ability test predicts grades in college or supervisor ratings on the job and whether it is a better predictor for whites than for blacks, or for women than for men. But the study findings will not determine whether or how an ability test should be used to make selection or placement decisions.

Justification of test use obviously depends upon much more than the predictive validity of a test. Potential benefits and losses for the individual, the institution, and the society at large need to be considered, and the relative importance of the benefits and losses can be expected to vary greatly in the eyes of these various interests. Nonetheless, information about the degree of relationship of test scores to particular criterion measures and about the degree to which the observed relationship is generalizable across situations and from one population to another is an important component in the evaluation of the use of tests for selection and placement and, as such, is the subject of this paper.

## CRITERION-RELATED VALIDITY

Validity is not a property of a test that is independent of the uses that are made of it. It is an interpretation of test results for a given population that is validated, rather than the test in isolation. Thus, a single test may have many validities associated with the many interpretations made of its results. Evidence of the validity of a particular interpretation of a single test for a given population may be irrelevant for other interpretations of that test, for the interpretation of other tests, or for the interpretation of that test for other populations. There are so many types of tests, of criterion measures to be predicted, of settings in which the predictions take place, and of groups of persons tested that no single statement regarding criterion-related validity could be expected to hold true across all combinations of these factors.

The potential dependence of validity on the particular ability test, on the criterion measure, on the situation, and on the population makes summarization difficult. There are, however, a number of common features that are shared by many of the most widely used ability tests and, as will be seen, there is more consistency in the results across situations and populations than might be expected. Thus, some useful generalizations are possible.

Because correlation coefficients play a prominent role in the summarization of criterion-related validity study results, a few brief comments about these coefficients are in order. Correlation coefficients are subject

## Prediction and Differential Prediction

to a variety of interpretations. For the purposes of this paper, however, the primary consideration is what a correlation coefficient of a given magnitude implies about the predictive value of a test. One way of making this link is through the study of expectancy tables associated with correlations of various magnitudes. An expectancy table summarizes the distribution of scores on a criterion variable for persons with a particular score or range of scores on the test.

Expectancy tables may be constructed directly from the observed distribution of pairs of test and criterion scores. Alternatively they may be constructed from summary statistics using assumptions about the form of the distribution. The latter approach will not correspond precisely to any observed sample results. It is useful, however, for gaining an understanding of the predictive meaning of correlation coefficients.

Under idealized circumstances (in particular, assuming that the test and criterion have a bivariate normal distribution), 44 percent of the people who are in the top fifth of the distribution of test scores would be expected to also be in the top fifth of the distribution of criterion scores when the correlation is .50. For correlations of .10, .20, .30, and .40, the corresponding percentages are 24, 28, 33, and 38, respectively (Schrader 1965). The chances of predicting correctly that someone standing in the top fifth on the test will also be in the top fifth on the criterion measure improve steadily as the correlation increases. There obviously is still a large margin of error in the prediction for a correlation of .50, however.

The expected chances of being in the top fifth, the top half, and the top four-fifths on the criterion are summarized in Table 1 for several points in the test score distribution and several values of the correlation between the test and the criterion. Once again these values are based on an assumption that the distribution of the test and criterion has an idealized form.

From an inspection of Table 1 it can be seen that, even with a correlation as high as .60, some persons with quite low test scores can be expected to rank among the top fifth on the criterion. Conversely, the expectation is that a few people with very high test scores will not rank among even the top 80 percent on the criterion. Nevertheless, prediction based on the test is clearly better than could be accomplished without prior information, even when the correlation is as low as .20. For example, prediction that persons who stand at the 90th percentile on the test will be among the top fifth on the criterion would be expected to be right 28 percent of the time for a correlation of .20, compared to an expectation of only 20 percent of the time for the same prediction for persons selected at random.

TABLE 1  Expectancy Table for Selected Percentile Ranks on a Test and Selected Values of the Correlation Between Test and Criterion

| Correlation Coefficient | Percentile Rank on Test | Expected Probability of Standing in Each Range on the Criterion | | |
|---|---|---|---|---|
| | | Top Four-fifths | Top Half | Top Fifth |
| .2 | 90 | .87 | .60 | .28 |
|    | 50 | .80 | .50 | .20 |
|    | 10 | .72 | .40 | .13 |
| .3 | 90 | .90 | .66 | .32 |
|    | 50 | .81 | .50 | .19 |
|    | 10 | .68 | .34 | .10 |
| .4 | 90 | .93 | .71 | .36 |
|    | 50 | .82 | .50 | .18 |
|    | 10 | .64 | .29 | .07 |
| .5 | 90 | .96 | .77 | .41 |
|    | 50 | .83 | .50 | .17 |
|    | 10 | .59 | .23 | .04 |
| .6 | 90 | .98 | .83 | .46 |
|    | 50 | .85 | .50 | .15 |
|    | 10 | .54 | .17 | .02 |

## Prediction of School Achievement

Teacher marks provide one, perhaps the most, commonly used criterion measure for evaluating the predictive validity of ability tests. Teachers clearly are in a good position to make judgments about the achievement of their students. They generally have access to a considerable amount of information about student performance. There are, nonetheless, a number of limitations on teacher marks that should be recognized. Teachers' standards vary, with some being much more generous with high marks than others. Teachers also use different ways to assign marks. Some attempt to assign them solely on the basis of performance, while others attempt to take effort into account. Finally, despite their best efforts, teachers may be influenced in marking by prejudices, expectations based on early impressions, or personal preferences. Since the need for standardized tests rises at least in part from the limitations of teacher marks, it may seem somewhat ironic that teacher marks serve as the primary criterion measure for evaluating the predictive validity of tests.

The relationship between ability tests and teacher marks for school children has been investigated in innumerable studies, which have revealed substantial variability in the size of the observed correlations. Much of the variability is associated with the type of test, the subject matter for which the marks are obtained, the grade level, and the group studied. A large amount of the variability is due also to simple sampling error. Despite this variability, some clear patterns emerge.

The Differential Aptitude Tests (DAT) (The Psychological Corporation 1972) provide an illustration of a widely used and much studied battery of tests. The DAT was originally published in 1947, with revisions in 1962 and 1972. The DAT is a battery of eight tests, including:

| | |
|---|---|
| Verbal Reasoning (VR), | Space Relations (SR), |
| Numerical Ability (NA), | Spelling (SP), |
| Abstract Reasoning (AR), | Language Usage (LU), and |
| Mechanical Reasoning (MR), | Clerical Speed and Accuracy (CSA). |

Correlations with teacher marks are reported in the technical manual (Bennett et al. 1974) separately for boys and girls and by subject matter areas. Within each subject matter area, correlations are reported for groups of students from various schools in grades eight through eleven. For example, correlations with marks in English/literature are reported for sixty-nine groups of boys with the number of boys within a group ranging from twenty-seven to 298. The median correlation between VR and marks in English/literature for the sixty-nine groups of boys is .46. The comparable figure for girls is .52.

Large variability in median correlations might be expected as a function of the subject matter in which the marks are obtained and the particular one of the eight tests that is used. This expectation is only partially realized, however. For the academic subjects (English/literature, mathematics, science, and social studies/history), the pattern of correlations for the several tests shows a good deal of similarity. This is illustrated in Figure 1 for two of the subjects, English/literature and mathematics. The median correlations of these subjects with grades are plotted separately for boys and girls across the eight subtests.

Grades in English/literature are predicted about equally well by VR, NA, and LU for both boys and girls. Mathematics grades are predicted best by NA. The VR, AR, and LU subtests are all about equally good at predicting grades in mathematics, albeit not so good as NA. CSA is a poor predictor of grades in both English/literature and mathematics. The remaining tests have correlations in between the ones mentioned above in both subjects.

The finding that verbal and numerical tests correlate with grades at about the level indicated in Figure 1 is representative of what has been

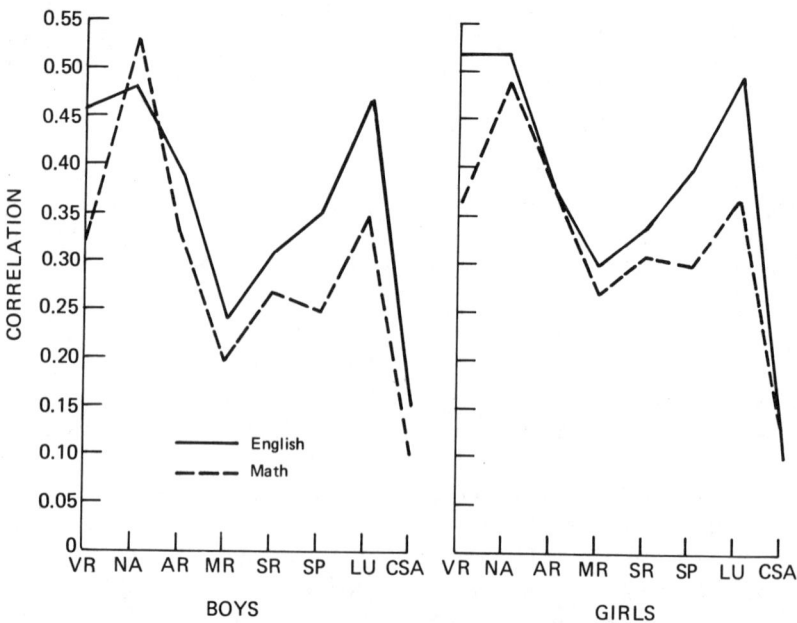

**FIGURE 1** Median correlations of DAT with grades in English and literature and for grades in mathematics.

found in other academic subjects and for other tests. For boys a composite of VR + NA has median correlations of .51, .48, .54 and .56 in English/literature, mathematics, science, and social studies/history, respectively. The corresponding values for girls are .56, .51, .53, and .58. These values are fairly typical of those reported over the years for a number of high-quality tests of general ability.

There is, of course, variability in the correlations from group to group. For example, correlations of VR + NA with grades in English/literature range from .00 to .73 for the sixty-nine groups of boys for which results are reported. However, only five of the sixty-nine correlations are less than .30, and only six of them are above .65. Much of the variability in the correlations can be attributed to simple sampling error. In the above example the median number of boys per group was 99. If sixty-nine samples of 99 persons each were drawn from a single population with a correlation of .51, one would expect that by chance five of the samples would have correlations larger than .61 and another five samples would have correlations smaller than .39.

The distinction between aptitude and achievement tests is not sharp, but when a distinction is made, it refers to the functions of the tests. Achievement tests are more often interpreted as samples, while aptitude

## Prediction and Differential Prediction

tests are interpreted as signs. Despite their similarities, standardized achievement tests are often used as criterion measures to investigate the validity of aptitude tests. Correlations of aptitude tests are typically much higher with standardized achievement tests than with teacher marks. For example, the correlations of VR with reading achievement scores on several tests are typically in the .60s and .70s. Correlations of NA with arithmetic and mathematics achievement test scores are generally in the .70s or low .80s.

The high relationship between scores on aptitude tests and those on achievement tests may be illustrated by results reported for another well-known ability test. Three types of reasoning tasks that yield moderately distinct results are verbal, numerical or quantitative, and spatial or figural. Various mixtures of these tasks are found in most tests of general ability, as exemplified by the Cognitive Abilities Test (CAT) (Houghton-Mifflin 1974). This test is a revision and expansion of the Lorge-Thorndike intelligence tests. Correlations of the CAT with scores on the Iowa Tests of Basic Skills (ITBS) and the Tests of Academic Progress (TAP) are reported in the CAT manual. The ITBS and TAP are achievement test batteries that were normed on the same sample as the CAT. Verbal, quantitative, and nonverbal (consisting of figural tasks) scores on the CAT were correlated with the composite scores on the ITBS and TAP within grade level. The verbal score typically correlated .80 to .85 with the achievement test composite. The correlations of the other two ability scores with the achievement composite scores were lower than those found for the verbal scores, but still quite substantial. Typical values were between .70 and .80 for quantitative and between .65 and .70 for nonverbal.

In summary, a large body of results has demonstrated that ability test scores, especially tests of verbal reasoning and numerical or quantitative ability, are related to school achievement as measured by teacher marks or standardized achievement tests.

### College Admissions

*Correlations Between Tests and College Grades*

Most students who plan to attend college must take the College Board's Scholastic Aptitude Test (SAT) and/or the tests of the American College Testing Program (ACT). Although described in somewhat different terms and consisting of different numbers of tests, the SAT and ACT are both measures of developed ability, and they are both used primarily for predicting performance in college. Two scores are reported for the SAT: a verbal score and a mathematics score. The ACT reports scores for tests of English Usage, Mathematics Usage, Natural Sciences Reading, and Social Studies Reading, as well as a composite score.

Although the SAT and ACT have been correlated with a variety of other measures in studies conducted over the years, the dominant criterion measure has always been grades in college, in particular the grade point average (GPA) for the freshman year or the first semester or quarter. Literally hundreds of validity studies are conducted routinely each year through the Validity Study Service run by Educational Testing Service (ETS) for the SAT, the Research Services Program provided by ACT, and by many individual colleges.

Distributions of correlations of SAT-V (verbal) and SAT-M (mathematical) with first term or first year GPAs for students in liberal arts or general programs are summarized in Figure 2. The distributions of correlations depicted in Figure 2 are based upon 310 groups of students. The median (i.e., the 50th percentile) of the 310 correlations for each test is indicated by the horizontal lines. The range of correlations between the 25th and 75th percentiles is depicted by a wide vertical bar, while a narrow vertical bar shows the range of correlations between the 10th and 90th percen-

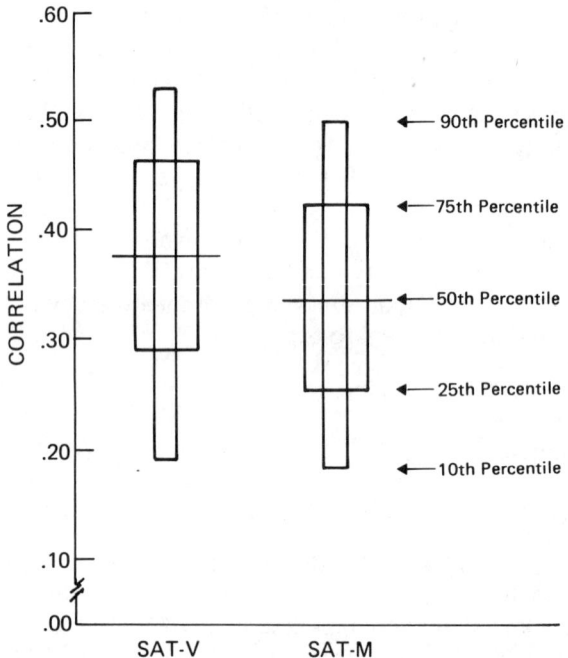

**FIGURE 2** Distributions of correlations of SAT-V and SAT-M with freshman GPA for 310 groups (based on Schrader 1971).

tiles. That is, 10 percent of the 310 correlations are smaller than the lower end of a narrow vertical bar and 10 percent are larger than the upper end of that bar. The median correlation of SAT-V with freshman GPA is .38, and for 80 percent of the 310 groups of students the correlation falls between .19 and .53. The median for SAT-M is .34, and 80 percent of the correlations fall between .18 and .50. As was true of the variability of the DAT correlations discussed above, a sizeable fraction of the variability in the correlations shown in Figure 2 may be attributed to simple sampling error.

Based on what was indicated earlier about the relationship between the size of a correlation coefficient and the accuracy of prediction, it is clear that people with the same SAT scores will have wide variability in their GPAs. There are many factors that influence the size of these correlations, however. The criterion is far from perfect. Unreliability of grades tends to deflate the validities. Another important consideration is that the results are based on selected samples of students. College students are more able than the general population, and student ability level varies greatly from college to college. Both these factors lead to greater homogeneity of ability of students within a college than is found for the general population. The homogeneity tends to reduce the correlation between the test scores and GPA.

The effect of variability on the magnitude of correlation coefficients is well known. If selection leads to a reduction in the spread of test scores, then a reduction in the correlation with the criterion variable is to be anticipated. This effect is clearly illustrated in Figure 3 where the distributions of correlations of SAT-V with freshman GPA are shown for groups of students that are categorized by the amount of variability in the SAT-V scores.

The results in Figure 3 are based on the same 310 groups used in Figure 2. For Figure 3, however, the groups are divided into categories of small, medium, and large variability on the SAT-V. Small variability is defined as a SAT-V standard deviation of 74 or less (SD $\leq$ 74). There are 105 groups with SD $\leq$ 74, and the median correlation for these groups is .31. The median correlation for the 92 groups with medium variability (75 $\leq$ SD $\leq$ 84) is .37, and that for 113 groups with large variability (SD $\leq$ 85), however, is .44. From an inspection of Figure 3, it is clear that correlations based on groups of homogeneous ability do not provide an adequate indication of the correlations typically found for more heterogeneous groups.

Correlations of the best combination of four ACT test scores (i.e., the multiple correlations) with grades in college are summarized each year in the Research Summary Tables prepared by ACT. Multiple correlations

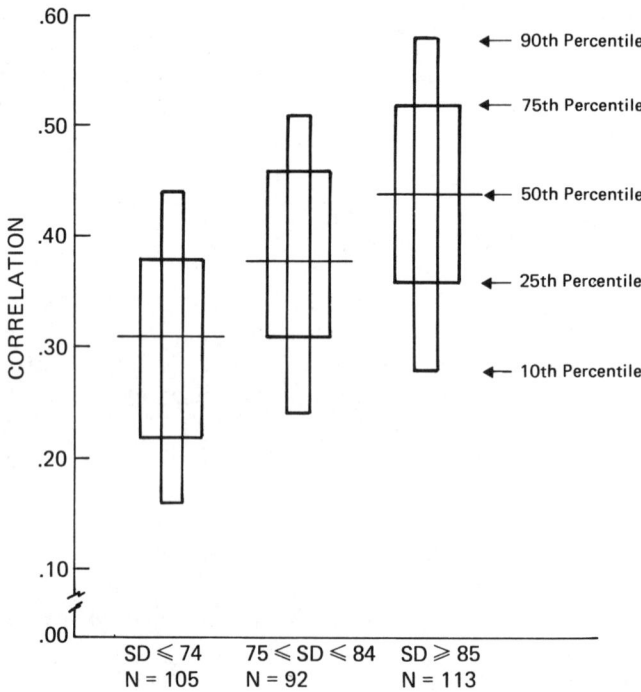

**FIGURE 3** Distributions of correlations of SAT-V with freshman GPA for 310 groups categorized by the size of the standard deviation of the SAT-V scores (based on Schrader 1971).

are reported separately for grades in English, mathematics, social studies, natural sciences, and overall. The median multiple correlations with overall GPA and number of colleges on which the medians are based are listed for several 3-year periods in Table 2. The median values in Table 2 each summarize multiple correlations from over 300 participating colleges reporting results for over 200,000 students. Thus, they are highly stable results, which reflect a great degree of summarization.

As is shown in Table 2, the median correlation of the combination of four ACT scores with freshman GPA has been close to .50 in every 3-year period. There is, of course, considerable variability in the multiple correlations from college to college. For example, for the most recent 3-year period for which data were available, the median multiple correlation was .51, but 10 percent of the 312 colleges had multiple correlations of .35 or less, and another 10 percent had multiple correlations of .61 or greater. Again, variation spread in the magnitude of the correlations is to be expected as the result of sampling error.

## Prediction and Differential Prediction

TABLE 2   Median Multiple Correlations of ACT Scores with College GPA for Colleges Participating in ACT Standard Research Service

| Years | Number of Colleges | Median Multiple Correlation |
|---|---|---|
| 1965-1967[a] | 437 | .479 |
| 1968-1970[a] | 419 | .465 |
| 1972-1974[b] | 389 | .489 |
| 1973-1975[b] | 349 | .500 |
| 1974-1976[b] | 328 | .509 |
| 1975-1977[b] | 317 | .513 |
| 1976-1978[b] | 312 | .512 |

[a]Based on Technical Report (American College Testing Program 1973).
[b]Based on Research Services Summary Reports.

### Correlations of High School Grades with College Grades

The results summarized in Figures 1 and 2 and in Table 2 document the consistent positive correlation between the SAT or ACT and freshman GPA. Typically, neither of these tests has been found to be a better, or even as good, predictor of freshman GPA, however, as high school grades or high school rank in class (Schrader 1971, American College Testing Program 1973). The most recent results from the ACT Research Service show that the distribution of correlations of high school grades with freshman GPA is very nearly the same as the distribution of multiple correlations of ACT scores with freshman GPA.

In Figure 4, the distributions of correlations of the combination of ACT scores with GPA and of the correlations between high school grades and overall GPA are summarized for the 312 colleges that provided the results between 1976 and 1978. Comparison of the percentiles for these two sets of correlations indicates that the distributions of the correlations are very similar.

Since high school records can predict college GPA at least as well as, if not better than, the SAT or ACT, it might well be asked what is gained by the use of the tests. How much higher is the multiple correlation with college GPA for the combination of high school grades and test scores than the simple correlation between high school grades and college GPA? It should be recognized of course that there may be arguments other than increments in validity that favor the addition of tests. For example, grades at one high school may not mean the same thing as grades at another, whereas test scores are comparable regardless of the high school that the

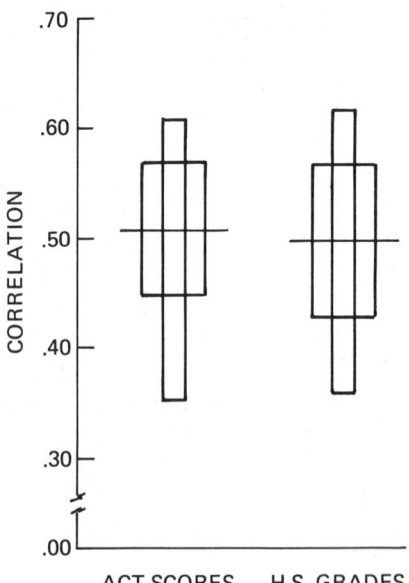

**FIGURE 4** Distributions of multiple correlations of ACT scores with freshman GPA and correlations of high school grades with freshman grades for 312 colleges included in ACT Research Services Summary Tables for 1976-1978.

student attended. When test scores are used in combination with high school grades to predict college performance, the test scores, in effect, adjust for differences in high school grading standards (Linn 1966). Of chief interest here, however, is their contribution to validity.

*Increase in Validity Due to the Addition of Test Scores*

The multiple correlation of high school grades and SAT or ACT scores with freshman grades is necessarily at least as high as, or higher than, the simple correlation of high school grades and college GPA. The increment need not be large, however.

For the 310 groups included in Schrader's (1971) summary of predictive validities involving the SAT, the addition of SAT scores to high school grades typically increased the correlation by about .05 to .10. The distributions of correlations for high school grades alone and for the combination of high school grades plus SAT scores are summarized in Figure 5. These results are for the same 310 groups of students that were included in the SAT results shown in Figures 2 and 3. The median correlation for high school grades alone is .51, while the median multiple correlation for high school grades plus SAT scores is .59.

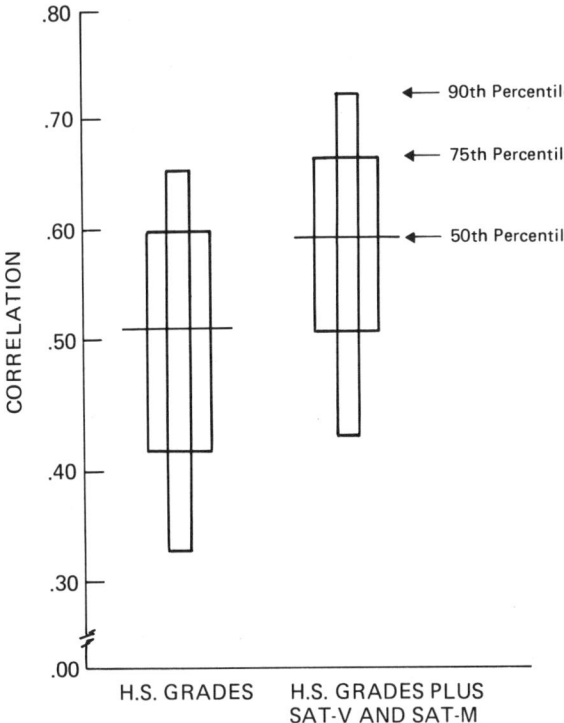

**FIGURE 5** Distributions of correlations of high school grades with freshman GPA and of multiple correlations of high school grades and SAT scores with freshman GPA for 310 groups (based on Schrader 1971).

The results for the 312 colleges that participated in the ACT Standard Research Service between 1975-1976 and 1977-1978 show that combining ACT scores with high school grades yields increments in validity over high school grades alone similar to those found for SAT. The distribution of correlations of high school grades with college grades and the distribution of multiple correlations of high school grades and ACT scores are depicted in Figure 6. There is less variability in the correlations for the ACT data set than there is in the SAT data set (Figure 5). The median correlations are very similar, however. For high school grades alone the median correlation in the ACT data set is .50. The median multiple correlation for high school grades and ACT combined is .59.

The increments in validity due to the combination of SAT or ACT scores

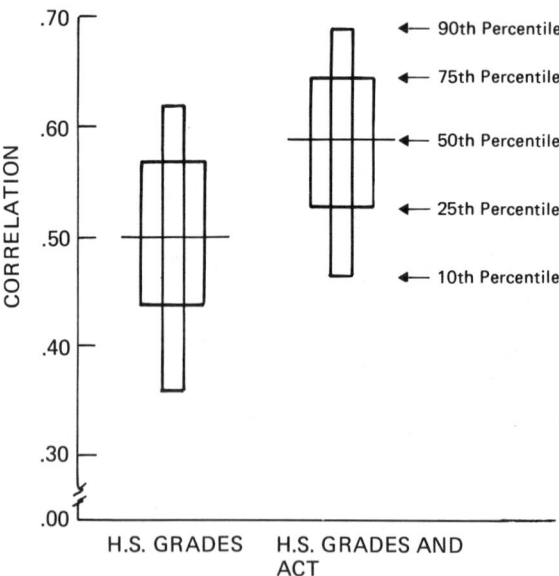

**FIGURE 6** Distributions of correlations of high school grades with freshman GPA and of multiple correlations of high school grades and ACT scores with freshman GPA for 312 colleges participating in the ACT Standard Research Service in 1975-1976, 1976-1977, and 1977-1978.

and high school grades shown in Figures 5 and 6 are typical of results that have been obtained in recent years. The consistency of these results over time is indicated by the median correlations listed in Table 3 for seven sets of results from the ACT Standard Research Service, each of which involves an accumulation over a 3-year interval. Even discounting the stabilizing effect caused by overlapping data sets, there is obviously a high degree of consistency of results with the possible exception of the 1965-1967 time period, when the median correlation for high school grades alone was somewhat higher than during other time periods. For every time interval, however, the addition of ACT scores yields an improvement in the prediction of grades in college over what can be accomplished with high school grades alone.

A rough indication of the typical gain in predictive power through the use of the ACT or SAT in combination with high school grades is provided by comparing the expectancy tables for correlations of .5 and .6 that are provided in Table 1. The Table 1 results are, of course, an idealization based on a theoretical distribution. Also the difference of .5 to .6 is somewhat on the generous side. Nonetheless, this comparison may pro-

TABLE 3  Median Correlation of High School Grades with College GPA and Median Multiple Correlations of High School Grades and ACT Scores with College GPA for Colleges Participating in ACT Standard Research Service

| Years | Number of Colleges | H.S. Grades Alone | H.S. Grades and ACT |
|---|---|---|---|
| 1965-1967[a] | 437 | .541 | .603 |
| 1968-1970[a] | 419 | .512 | .576 |
| 1972-1974[b] | 389 | .514 | .584 |
| 1973-1975[b] | 349 | .506 | .585 |
| 1974-1976[b] | 328 | .506 | .586 |
| 1975-1977[b] | 317 | .509 | .588 |
| 1976-1978[b] | 312 | .502 | .587 |

[a]Based on Technical Report (American College Testing Program 1973).
[b]Based on Research Service Summary Tables.

vide some intuition about the improvement in predictive power when these well-known college admissions tests are included in the prediction equation.

In contrast to the abundance of investigative studies of the validity of high school grades and college admissions test scores for predicting freshman GPA, relatively few have examined the prediction of grades after the freshman year. The available results, however, lead to the conclusion that high school grades and college admissions test scores are better predictors of freshman GPA than they are of GPA in subsequent years. For a large sample of University of Illinois students, Humphreys (1968) found that the predictive validities of both types of predictors declined fairly steadily from one semester to the next. For example, the correlation of the ACT Composite scores with eighth semester GPA was only .17, compared to .38 with first semester GPA and .30 with second semester GPA. The best single predictor of GPA for any single semester was consistently GPA in the immediately preceding semester. Adjacent semester GPAs were found to correlate between .49 and .56. Even the relationship between grades in college declines over time, however. Thus, the correlation between first semester GPA and eighth semester GPA was only .34.

The relatively low intercorrelations between semester grades observed by Humphreys is partially due to the selected nature of the sample of students who continued through all eight semesters. For example, for the sample with complete data for the eight semesters, the correlation betweeen first and second semester GPA was .56, whereas the correlation for the sample with grades in at least the first two semesters was .66. The latter figure is also apt to be reduced somewhat by the selective nature of college dropouts between the first and second semesters. (Almost 1,100 of the original 8,336 students with first semester grades did not have second semester grades.) Even allowing for the effects of selection, however, it is clear that academic performance in college, as measured by semester GPAs, is not highly stable.

Grades in college have generally been found to have little or no relationship to measures of nonacademic performance during college (Holland and Richards 1965). As discussed in greater detail below, college grades are useful in predicting subsequent performance (once again as measured by grades) in graduate and professional schools. Prediction of success outside of school is more problematic. Hoyt (1965, 1966) reviewed a variety of studies relating college grades to various measures of success as an adult, such as earnings and supervisor ratings in such occupations as teaching, medical practice, and engineering. Hoyt acknowledged that there were many limitations in his studies, but stated nonetheless that "despite the limitations of these studies, we can safely conclude from them that college grades have no more than a very modest correlation with adult success, no matter how defined" (1966:72). A similar conclusion was reached more recently by Munday and Davis (1974). Great weight continues to be given, however, to college GPA, especially first term or first year GPA, in college admissions research. The most ample justification for this practice rests in the value attributed to academic performance in its own right rather than its relationship to later-life accomplishments.

### Graduate and Professional Schools

Test results are required for admission to most graduate and professional schools. The graduate school admissions process is often highly decentralized, and the use that is made of test scores varies greatly, not only from school to school, but from department to department within the same university or even from one specialization to another within a single department. There are several factors that limit the value of criterion-related validity studies in graduate school. Graduate school grading systems often provide little discrimination. The high degree of specialization makes comparisons across specialties problematic, and the number of students within a specialization is frequently too small to yield reliable results. In addition, the admitted students are highly selected, and as was illustrated in Figure 3, less variability in scores results in lowered correlations. Thus, it is not surprising that the compilation of evidence of

## Prediction and Differential Prediction

predictive validity is less straightforward for graduate and professional schools than for tests used in undergraduate college admissions.

*Law Schools*

Validation in law schools stands out as a notable exception to the more usual situation in other graduate and professional schools. Certainly, results for law schools are strongly affected by the homogeneity in the measured ability of their students. Many law schools receive several times more applications than they can accept. Selection from a pool of applicants that is already highly self-selected and relatively homogeneous in ability results in restricted variability in ability as measured by test scores and undergraduate records. However, law school grading systems do not yield the uniformity of grades often observed in graduate schools, first year classes are of adequate size to conduct validity studies, and there is sufficient commonality in the first year curriculums to make comparisons reasonable. Consequently, the empirical evidence that test scores and undergraduate grades predict grades in law school is stronger than it is for most graduate school specializations.

Schrader (1976) summarized the results of several hundred validity studies conducted for law schools between 1948 and 1975. The criterion used in these studies was first year grade average in law school (FYGA). The predictors used in these studies were the Law School Admissions Test (LSAT) and undergraduate grade point average (UGPA). Seventy-nine law schools participated in validity studies at least once between 1971 and 1974. The 25th, 50th, and 75th percentiles of the distributions of correlations of UGPA, LSAT, and the multiple correlations of UGPA and LSAT combined with FYGA are shown for these seventy-nine schools in Figure 7.

Several generalizations can be made from the results summarized in Figure 7. Both LSAT and UGPA are positively related to FYGA. The combination of LSAT and UGPA in a multiple correlation provides a better prediction of FYGA than either UGPA or LSAT alone. There was an erosion in the predictive power of UGPA between the 1963-1970 period and the 1971-1974 period, possibly due to so-called grade inflation. During the same time periods, the predictive power of LSAT remained fairly stable or possibly even increased. A consequence of the combination of the last two results is that the increment in validity due to the combination of LSAT and UGPA over UGPA alone was larger in the 1971-1974 interval (increase in median correlation from .25 to .45) than it was in 1963-1970 (increase in median correlation from .33 to .48).

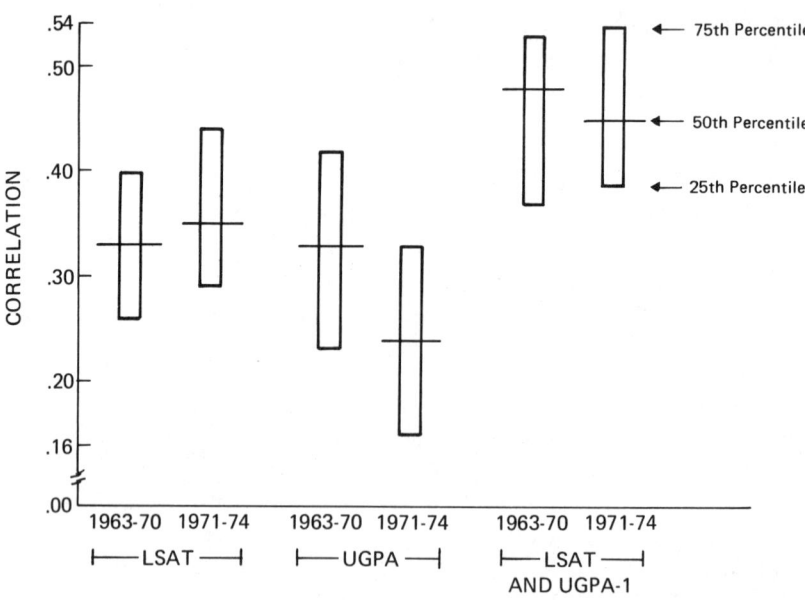

**FIGURE 7** Distributions of correlations of LSAT, UGPA, and multiple correlations of UGPA and LSAT with first-year average grade in law school (based on Schrader 1979).

*Medical Schools*

Medical school admissions are also extremely competitive. The competition starts as far back as the choice of undergraduate school and undergraduate curriculum and continues with intense pressure to earn high pre-med grades and to score well on the Medical College Admissions Test (MCAT).

The MCAT recently underwent a major revision. Since the new MCAT was first administered only in the Spring of 1977, little has accumulated in the way of predictive validity studies. The new MCAT represents a fairly major departure from the old MCAT, which was a general ability test. The new test, however, places more emphasis on the assessment of science knowledge and includes separate scores for biology, chemistry, and physics. Scores are also reported for skills analysis in reading, quantitative skills analysis, and science problems. The new interpretive manual discourages the use of a single composite score (Association of American Medical Colleges 1977).

The Interpretive Manual reports the results of concurrent validity studies that were conducted in four medical schools by administering the new MCAT to students who were already enrolled. Although these results are not a substitute for the predictive validity studies that are currently being

## Prediction and Differential Prediction

analyzed, they do provide preliminary evidence that the new MCAT scores have a substantial positive relationship with grades in specific courses in medical school. Correlations in the .30s, .40s, and .50s were common between the six specific test scores and grades in individual courses. A more complete analysis of the criterion-related validity of the new MCAT must await the accumulation of the results of additional validity studies.

### Graduate Schools

Despite their limitations, grades still constitute the most commonly used criterion measure for the validation of tests used in graduate school admissions. Ratings of dissertation quality, comprehensive examinations, and degree attainment have also been used as criteria, but all of them have weaknesses. (See Hartnett and Willingham 1978 for a detailed discussion of the "criterion problem" in graduate education.)

Validity studies using the Graduate Record Examinations (GRE) as predictors have been summarized by Willingham (1974) and more recently by Wilson (1979). Seven major fields from six or more departments were included in the GRE board's cooperative validity studies between 1974 and 1976. The median correlations of the verbal and quantitative tests of the GRE with graduate school GPA for these seven fields are summarized in Figure 8. The number of studies on which the median correlations in each field are based is shown in parentheses above the major field designation.

The median validities displayed in Figure 8 are somewhat lower than the median validities that were reported above for SAT-V and SAT-M with undergraduate GPA as the criterion. The relative predictive power of the quantitative test in comparison to the verbal test, however, is better for sciences and engineering at the graduate level than at the undergraduate level. As has been noted previously, the magnitude of a correlation coefficient is affected by the size of the variability of the scores being correlated. Differences in the degree of homogeneity of test scores from field to field may explain at least some of the differences in predictability from one field to another. Differences in homogeneity also affect the relative magnitude of the correlations for the two types of tests. Thus, for example, the fact that the verbal test predicts graduate school GPA as well as, or slightly better than, the quantitative test for math majors may be because math majors are more homogeneous on the quantitative test than on the verbal test.

Wilson clustered major fields into two general categories labeled "verbal" fields and "quantitative" fields. The median correlations with graduate GPA for the seventy studies in verbal fields were .31 for GRE-verbal

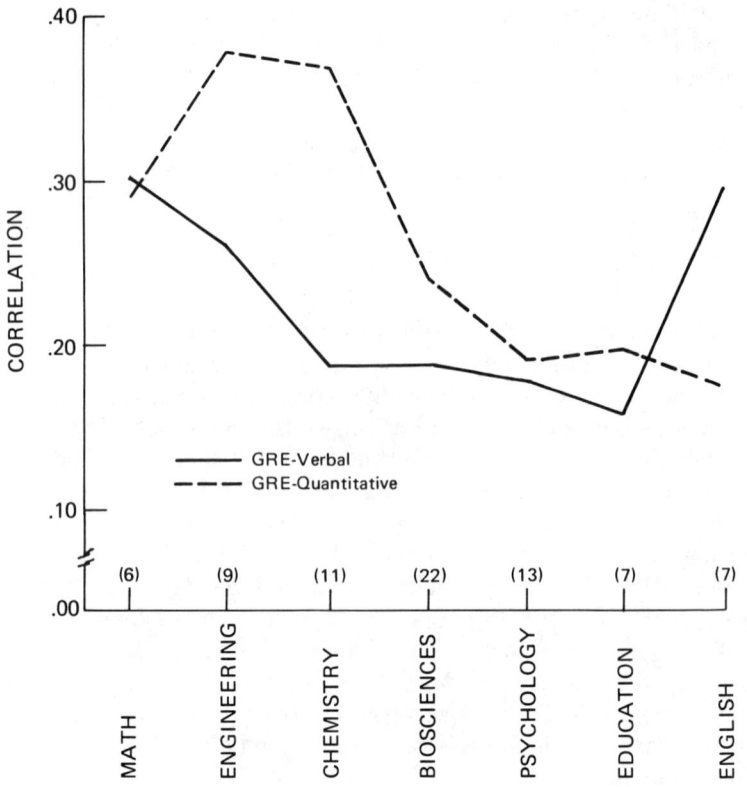

**FIGURE 8** Median correlations of GRE-verbal and GRE-quantitative with graduate school GPA (based on Wilson 1979).

and .25 for GRE-quantitative. The corresponding figures for the sixty-three studies in fields classified as quantitative were respectively .20 and .31 for GRE-verbal and GRE-quantitative. The median correlations between undergraduate GPA and graduate GPA were .30 for 46 verbal fields and .29 for 38 quantitative fields. Not all studies included in the GRE results also had results for undergraduate grades.

Another test that is commonly used in graduate school admissions is the Miller Analogies Test (The Psychological Corporation 1970). The predictive validity of the MAT for grades in graduate school is generally similar in magnitude to those of the GRE-verbal test. For one sample of 436 science students in a nationwide fellowship project, the correlation between the MAT and GRE-verbal was .83. Thus, similarity in the correlations of these two tests with other variables is to be expected.

## Prediction and Differential Prediction

The results of prediction of graduate grades from ability test scores fall into a familiar pattern. There are consistent positive correlations of a magnitude that is of some utility in prediction. The predictions are subject to large errors, however. Prediction based on previous academic performance, i.e., undergraduate GPA, is generally about as good as the prediction based on tests alone. The combination of the two is better than either one alone (Willingham 1974).

The GRE-advanced tests have generally been found to have a somewhat higher correlation with graduate school GPA than either the GRE aptitude or undergraduate grades. The GRE-advanced tests are achievement tests in the subject matter corresponding to major fields of study such as chemistry or mathematics. In four major fields, for which at least five studies with correlations between the GRE-advanced test for that field and graduate GPA were summarized by Wilson (1979), the median correlations were as follows: chemistry, .45; bioscience, .37; psychology, .32; and English, .40. These results, generally favoring the advanced test over the aptitude tests of the GRE, are consistent with results reported previously by Willingham (1974).

## Prediction of Occupational Performance

Since the introduction of the Army Alpha test, innumerable studies have investigated the relationships between performance on various ability tests and occupational level and performance within an occupation. Stewart (1947) reported results showing between-occupation differences in median scores on the Army General Classification Test for over 80,000 enlisted men during World War II. These often-cited results show a hierarchy of occupations in terms of median ability scores, with professions such as accountants and lawyers at the high end, followed by white-collar jobs such as bookkeepers and cashiers. Groups with the lowest median scores were farm workers and lumberjacks.

Although the difference in median scores for occupations at the high end of the distribution and those at the low end is quite large, there is also considerable spread within occupations. The overlap in scores for individuals in different occupations is substantial. For example, policemen as a group had a median score only slightly above the general average. An individual policeman who scored at the 75th percentile of the distribution of policemen, however, would have a score higher than 25 percent of the lawyers, which is an occupation with one of the highest medians.

Thorndike and Hagen (1959) also found substantial differences in the average abilities of members of various occupations. Their results are based on a 1955 follow-up study of approximately 10,000 men who were tested in 1943 when they volunteered for pilot, navigator, and bombardier training programs. The Thorndike and Hagen sample was more educated (all were high school graduates) and more able than a general cross section of their age cohorts. Even for this more homogeneous group, however, there were large differences in mean test scores between some occupational groups. On a general intellectual ability measure, for example, the highest scoring group (chemical engineers) had a mean almost two standard deviations above that of the lowest scoring group (production assemblers).

The profiles of mean performance across different occupations revealed patterns that were generally consistent with expectations. For example, architects had scores that were above the mean of the entire sample on almost all of the tests in the battery, but were especially high in visual perception. College professors were well above the mean on general intellectual ability, but below the mean on mechanical ability. Miners, on the other hand, were well above the combined groups mean on mechanical and psychomotor ability, but below the mean on general intellectual ability.

The between-occupational differences in ability test scores are consistent with common stereotypes, but they do not imply any necessary connection between test score and occupational performance. Test scores are correlated with the amount of formal education persons have obtained, as well as with other measures of educational performance such as grades. Thus, the between-occupational differences in average test performance may reflect, at least in part, differences in the educational requirements of various occupations. Sewell and Hauser (1976) have estimated that about 80 percent of the apparent effect of ability on occupational attainment is mediated through the effects of ability on grades in school, amount of education, perceived expectations of significant others, and aspirations. The remaining 20 percent is attributed to the direct effect of ability on occupational status.

Scores on tests of general ability have also been found to be positively correlated with earnings. Taubman and Wales (1974) reported a 17 percent differential in the 1955 earnings of the top and bottom fifths in ability for the Thorndike and Hagen sample. The comparable figure for their own 1969 follow-up of that sample was 25 percent. Jencks et al. (1972) estimated the correlation between the Armed Forces Qualification Test and income to be .33. Much of the relationship between ability test scores and earnings reported by these and other authors, however, may be attributed to other factors and/or be mediated through the effects of ability on years of education and occupation. Sewell and Hauser (1975) estimated that about half the effect of ability on earnings is mediated through education (40 percent) and occupational status (11 percent). Griliches (1976) attributed even less of the relationship between measured ability and earnings to the direct effect of ability. But the Griliches sample was quite young and the effect of ability on earnings has been found to be larger 12 to 14 years after high school graduation than at younger ages (Hauser and Daymont 1977). In any event, it is clear that the modest overall correlation between scores on ability tests and later earnings becomes considerably smaller when occupation and educational level are held constant.

Evidence of the validity of ability tests for performance within an occupation comes from the host of criterion-related validity studies that have been conducted in private industry, the military, and governmental agencies. Earnings provide only one of the many criterion measures that have been used in these studies. Ghiselli (1966) systematically summarized the results of virtually all criterion-related validity studies in occupational settings that appeared in the literature between 1919 and 1964. Jobs were classified for purposes of the summary according to the *Dictionary of Occupational Titles* and the General Occupational Classification System. The latter system employs broader categories and consequently yields summary results that are somewhat more comprehensible.

Ghiselli used two broad categories of criterion measures: training criteria, such as grades in occupational training courses and ratings by instructors; and job performance criteria including supervisor ratings, measures of productivity, and accident rates. Tests were classified broadly as measures of intellectual abilities, spatial and mechanical reasoning, perceptual accuracy, motor abilities, and personality traits. Within each of these general categories of tests, results were also reported for subcategories, such as immediate memory and arithmetic under the category of intellectual abilities.

Ghiselli computed the average correlation between tests classified as measures of intellectual abilities with training criteria and performance criteria by applying Fisher's Z transformation and computing the mean Z, which was then transformed to the average correlation. These average correlations are listed in Table 4 for the eight major occupational categories of the General Occupational Classification System and are positive with each type of criterion measure in every instance. It is clear, however, that the correlations are generally a good deal higher for training criteria (often .40 or higher) than they are with proficiency criteria (typically closer to .20).

Tests of intellectual ability had higher average correlations with the

TABLE 4  Average Validity Coefficients for Intellectual Abilities Tests for Major Categories of Jobs Classified According to the General Occupational System (Based on Ghiselli 1966)

| Occupational Category | Training Criteria | Performance Criteria |
|---|---|---|
| Managers | NA | .25 |
| Clerks | .47 | .27 |
| Sales | NA | .18 |
| Protective service | .35 | .23 |
| Personal service | .54 | .03 |
| Vehicle operators | .15 | .14 |
| Trades and crafts | .41 | .19 |
| Industrial workers | .40 | .16 |

criterion measures than any other of Ghiselli's categories of tests for many of the occupations. For some occupations, however, one of the other categories of tests proved to be a better predictor. The test with the highest correlation with either the training or performance criterion for a particular type of occupation was used to define what Ghiselli called "maximal validity" coefficients. The average over occupations of these maximal validities was .47 for training criteria and .33 for proficiency criteria.

The average correlations in Table 4 or the average maximal validity do not reveal the variability in validity coefficients that has been found from study to study within a given occupational category. Such variability in validities has generally been viewed as quite large and has been used to support the dictum that the validity of a test should be investigated in each feasible setting. Feasibility has been interpreted by some to mean that a sample of thirty or more can be obtained for a validity study. Since correlations based on samples as small as thirty are quite unreliable, the validities are commonly viewed as highly situation specific. Otherwise, more reliance would be placed on generalizations from situation to situation for a particular job-test combination and less reliance on empirical studies in situations with small samples.

Ghiselli (1966) examined the variability in validity coefficients for a given job from one organization to another and for the same organization from one time to another. He reported the distributions of validity coefficients for four jobs. Each distribution consisted of between 72 and 191 coefficients. The range of coefficients in each case was large indeed. Both positive and negative coefficients were included in each distribution. In each distribution one or more coefficients fell outside the extremes of $-.25$ and $+.75$. Such large fluctuations in validities led Ghiselli and

## Prediction and Differential Prediction

others to conclude that generalizations regarding validities, even for a single occupation and a given test, are unwarranted.

The conclusion that validity for a single job-test combination lacks generalizability has recently been challenged by Schmidt and Hunter (1977, 1978). These authors enumerate seven factors that contribute to the variability in observed coefficients (1978:219). Three of the factors are: 1) differences in the reliability of the criterion measure from one study to another, 2) differences in range restriction, i.e., degree of homogeneity in ability of the group, from one study to another, and 3) sampling variability.

Schmidt and Hunter (1977) used the above three factors to model the distribution of validity coefficients that would be obtained assuming that the true population validity was constant across studies for a given job-test combination. That is, they generated a hypothetical distribution of reliabilities of criterion measures and a hypothetical distribution of the amount of range restriction for a set of studies. They used these two hypothetical distributions, along with information about sample size, to compute a distribution of correlations that would be expected to be observed over a set of studies in which the true population validity had a single value. When Schmidt and Hunter modeled Ghiselli's distributions of validity coefficients for four jobs, they found that a large percentage of the observed variability could be simulated by the three factors included in their model. They argued that much of the remaining variability could be explained in terms of the other factors not included in their model.

By showing that considerable variability in validity coefficients is to be expected simply because of artifacts such as range restriction and sampling error, Schmidt and Hunter have made a strong case for validity generalization within a specific job and test combination. The utility of summary results, such as those provided by Ghiselli, is enhanced to the extent that validity is generalizable across situations and populations. The Hunter and Schmidt results obviously depend upon the starting assumptions about distributions of criterion reliability and range restriction. Thus, they cannot be considered clear proof of validity generalization. They do show, however, that considerable variability in validities from study to study is to be expected, even where validity generalization is appropriate.

The final example of this section suggests that, at least in the case of training criteria, a measure of general ability has reasonably good validity over a wide range of occupational specialties. Valentine (1977) summarized the results of validity studies in forty-three occupational specialties in the Air Force. Included among the specialties were such diverse jobs as metal working, computer systems, and personnel. The criterion variable for each job was the final grade in the specialty training school. The sample consisted of "all air force non-prior service enlisted accessions in September 1973 through October 1975." The number of personnel per job averaged 1,023 and ranged from 103 to 4,736. The median correlation between the Armed Forces Qualification Test (AFQT) and final school grade was .34 for all forty-three jobs. The range of correlations was .10 to .50. However, all but three of the correlations were between .24 and .43. Thus, the correlations between tests of intellectual abilities and training criteria for these Air Force jobs are generally similar in magnitude to those reported in other settings.

**Summary: Criterion-Related Validity**

Tests of verbal and quantitative ability have consistently been found to be moderately good predictors of academic achievement as measured by grades in school, in college, and in graduate and professional schools. The power of ability tests to predict academic performance is matched, if not exceeded, by the predictive power of previous academic performance. The combination of the two provides more accurate prediction of subsequent performance than either alone.

Performance on general ability tests is positively related to occupational status and to earnings. Ability test scores are also related to the amount of formal education. After reviewing a variety of sources, Jencks et al. (1972), for example, estimated the correlation between intelligence test scores at age 11 and eventual years of schooling to be .55. Much, but not all, of the association between scores on ability tests and occupational status may be explained by the links between ability and education, on the one hand, and education and occupational level, on the other (Sewell and Hauser 1976). Similarly, much of the correlation between measured ability and earnings can be attributed to the mediating effects of education and occupational status.

Within an occupation, the prediction of performance from scores on ability tests is much better for training criteria than for measures of performance on the job. Training criteria are often quite similar to the main criteria used in educational settings. Hence, it is not particularly surprising that tests of intellectual ability are often found to have correlations with occupational training criteria that are similar in magnitude to those with grades in educational institutions.

Correlations between scores on ability tests and occupational performance criterion measures are quite modest, commonly in the .20s. In the

## Prediction and Differential Prediction    361

case of correlations as low as .2 or .3, it is reasonable to ask whether tests have enough predictive power to be of any practical utility. From an inspection of Table 1, it is clear that the chance of correctly predicting whether or not a person will rank in the top half on the criterion measures is only slightly improved over a coin flip by knowledge of test scores, when the correlation is as low as .20. The potential value of using a test for purposes of selection, however, depends on other factors than the size of the relationship with a criterion. For example, the value depends on the selection ratio, that is, on the proportion of applicants who are selected. If the selection ratio is very small, say .05 or .10, the average performance of selected persons on the criterion measure can be markedly improved by using a test, even one that has a small correlation with the criterion. On the other hand, a much higher correlation would be required to realize a comparable gain in average performance on the criterion when the selection ratio is large.

Another factor that influences the value of using a test for selection is the level of criterion performance necessary for someone to be considered successful. (The proportion of all applicants who would be considered successful is called the base rate.) A stringent requirement for classification as a success results in a low base rate, while a lenient requirement yields a high base rate. Whatever the requirement, the base rate provides an indication of the proportion of people who would be successful if applicants were selected at random. The potential value of using a test can be gauged by a comparison of the expected success rate (i.e., the proportion of selected people who are successful) with the base rate.

Taylor and Russell (1939) reported extensive tables showing the expected success rate for various combinations of base rate, selection ratio, and correlation between predictor and criterion. Their results demonstrate that a correlation of even .2 or .3 can be quite useful for certain combinations of base rate and selection ratio. Conversely, a test that correlates considerably higher with a criterion would have little value for some other combinations. For example, in a situation where half the applicants would be considered successes if given an opportunity, i.e., the base rate is .50, a test with a correlation of only .25 with the criterion would be expected to result in a success rate of .70, an improvement of .20 over the base rate, when only the top 5 percent of the applicants were accepted.

A few additional examples based on the Taylor and Russell tables may help clarify the interplay between the base rate, the selection rate, and the size of the correlation in determining the usefulness of a test for purposes of selection. With a base rate of .5, a success rate of .7 could be achieved with any of the following pairs of conditions:

| Selection Ratio | Correlation |
|---|---|
| .05 | .25 |
| .20 | .35 |
| .40 | .50 |
| .50 | .60 |
| .60 | .70 |
| .70 | .90 |

Note that if 70 percent of the applicants are accepted (selection ratio = .70), an extraordinarily high correlation (.90) would be required to achieve a success rate of .70. A correlation of .90 is obviously much higher than any that have been encountered in the results summarized above.

From a study of various combinations of base rate, selection ratio, and correlation, some general principles may be readily discerned. With a small base rate and small selection ratio, substantial gains in the success rate can be achieved by the use of a test with a modest correlation with the criterion. For example, a test with a correlation of .3 would yield a success rate of .41 when the base rate is .2 and the selection ratio is .05. That is, the success rate is over twice as good when the test is used for selection than it would be without it. When the base rate and selection ratio are high, however, even a test with a high correlation with the criterion will yield gains in the success rate that are too small to justify using the test for purposes of selection. For example, a test with a correlation of .60 with the criterion would yield an increase in the success rate of only .04 when the base rate is .8 and the selection rate is .9.

Because the Taylor and Russell tables describe artificial situations, they should be used "to afford a perspective, primarily, rather than supply precise values" (Lord and Novick 1968:276). The tables are of greatest use in demonstrating the importance of other factors than the strength of association between a test and a criterion in determining the potential value of a selection test. It is clear that in situations where only the rare applicant can succeed and where there is an abundance of applicants a test with even a modest correlation can be quite useful in improving the success rate. On the other hand, when most applicants are accepted and most of those accepted are later considered successful, there is little to be gained by using even a highly valid test to make selections.

## GROUP DIFFERENCES IN ABILITY TEST RESULTS

When identifiable subgroups of the population such as men, women, children with parents from different clusters of occupations, or members of different racial or ethnic groups are compared, differences in average

## Prediction and Differential Prediction

performance on ability tests are usually found. Although the variability between subgroups may be relatively small in comparison to the variability among individuals within a single subgroup, these differences in average performance can have potentially important implications for test use. In particular, if group differences on a test used for selection do not reflect differences that are observed in performance in college or on the job, then the use of the test for selection may unfairly exclude a disproportionately large number of members of the group with the lower average test score.

The purpose of this section is to provide an indication of the magnitude of some group differences in average scores on ability tests that may be of use as background in understanding the potential adverse impact that use of a selection test might be anticipated to have. Group differences in test scores are *not* evidence of innate differences. They may, however, reflect differences in probabilities of success in school or on the job, which must be recognized in order to develop sound educational and social policy.

### Socioeconomic Differences

The fact that children of the rich tend to score higher than children of the poor on tests of general ability has been known almost from the time Binet introduced his first test. Since the early work showing mean differences on the Binet (e.g., Stern 1914) for lower- and upper-class children, differences favoring the higher status group have been found repeatedly on a wide variety of aptitude and achievement tests, whether groups are defined in terms of parental occupational status, education, or income.

Correlations between indices of parental socioeconomic status and children's scores on general ability tests are typically about .30 (Spaeth 1976). Translated into mean differences, this correlation implies that children from families whose socioeconomic status is in the top 20 percent have an average test score at roughly the 65th percentile of the general population, whereas children from the bottom 20 percent of the socioeconomic distribution average at about the 35th percentile.

The strength of the relationship between socioeconomic status and test scores varies somewhat as a function of the type of ability. The relationship tends to be somewhat higher with verbal ability than with quantitative or spatial ability. The direction of the difference in group means is the same, however, for a wide variety of general ability and educational achievement tests.

## Sex Differences

Mean differences on ability tests for males and females are generally smaller than those between groups of high and low socioeconomic status. Also, the direction of the differences is not constant across different types of intellectual ability tests. Sex differences in verbal, quantitative, and spatial abilities have been reported in various studies. Males have generally been found to score higher on quantitative and spatial ability tests, while females score higher on tests of verbal ability (Maccoby and Jacklin 1974).

The size of sex differences changes as a function of age. Studies have generally found few or no sex differences in quantitative abilities for young children. Differences in quantitative scores begin to appear in adolescence and to increase during the high school years. Sex differences in spatial abilities begin to appear at about ages 6 to 8 and to increase with age through high school. Female superiority in verbal ability has been observed for very young children. The difference appears to diminish for a time and then increase again after about age 11.

Norms are presented separately for boys and girls on a number of standardized ability tests. The separate norms on the Differential Aptitude Tests (Bennett et al. 1974) provide some indication of the size and direction of differences that are obtained for tests of various aptitudes. An individual with a score at the 50th percentile on every test using the fall grade 12 norms for boys would have scores equal to the following percentiles when compared with the fall grade 12 norms for girls:

| | |
|---|---|
| Verbal reasoning | — 50th percentile, |
| Numerical ability | — 55th percentile, |
| Abstract reasoning | — 55th percentile, |
| Clerical speed and accuracy | — 30th percentile, |
| Mechanical reasoning | — 85th percentile, |
| Space relations | — 60th percentile, |
| Spelling | — 30th percentile, |
| Language usage | — 35th percentile. |

As can be seen, the larger group differences occur on the more specialized aptitudes such as mechanical reasoning, clerical speed and accuracy, and spelling.

Sex differences on ability tests are often attributed to differences in interests and experiences, which perhaps are based on differential expectations. While these suggested explanations seem plausible, the etiol-

## Prediction and Differential Prediction

ogy of the observed sex differences is not an issue for the purposes of this paper. Neither are the other differences described in this section. Rather the issues here involve the question of adverse impact when a test is used for selection and whether the tests have the same predictive meaning for members of different groups.

From the above results, it is clear that, if people were selected from the DAT norm groups on the basis of high scores on the mechanical reasoning test, fewer girls than boys would be selected. That is, the mechanical reasoning test would be expected to have an adverse impact on girls. Adverse impact requires that the evidence of test validity be given close scrutiny, which might involve investigations of differential validity and prediction. The latter issues will be addressed below following a brief summary of racial and ethnic group differences in average scores on ability tests.

### Racial and Ethnic Differences

It was noted above that it has been repeatedly documented that children from families of lower socioeconomic status tend to score lower on standardized ability and achievement tests than do children from families of higher socioeconomic status. Similar and not unrelated are the many studies that have shown that members of certain racial/ethnic groups tend to score lower on standardized ability and achievement tests than do members of the white majority.

The Coleman report (Coleman et al. 1966) provided detailed comparisons of several racial and ethnic groups. A large national sample of children was tested in grades 1, 3, 6, 9, and 12. Schools enrolling large numbers of minority children were intentionally overrepresented in the sample to provide stable estimates of performance for blacks, Oriental-Americans, Indian-Americans, Mexican-Americans, and Puerto Ricans, as well as for whites.

Notable differences between the groups were found on both the verbal and nonverbal ability tests at every grade level. With some exceptions, the ordering of the groups and magnitude of the group differences were similar on the reading, mathematics, and general information achievement tests. At grade 12, the rank ordering of the groups in terms of median scores on the verbal ability test was whites, Oriental-Americans, Mexican-Americans, Indian-Americans, Puerto Ricans, and blacks. On a scale with a mean of 50 and a standard deviation of 10, the median 12th grade verbal ability scores for these six groups were 52.1, 49.6, 43.8, 43.7, 43.1, and 40.9, respectively. Although there is a great deal of overlap in the distribution of scores for all groups, the above differences in medians are large indeed.

The difference in medians for blacks and whites of roughly one standard deviation typifies the results of a number of comparative studies of these two groups. Contrary to a common belief, this difference is not noticeably larger on the verbal ability test than on tests in several other areas. The 12th grade difference in median scores was at least 10 points on the nonverbal ability test, the mathematics achievement test, and the general information test; and the difference was almost as large (9.7 points) on the reading achievement test. Assuming that the score distributions are approximately normally distributed, the roughly one standard deviation difference between the groups indicates that only about 16 percent of the blacks would score above the mean for whites.

The potential adverse impact implications of group differences as large as those between whites and blacks should be apparent. A cutoff score on an ability test that would select half the whites from the general population would select only about 16 percent of the blacks. One that would select 20 percent of the whites would select only about 3 or 4 percent of the blacks. The potential adverse impact for other minorities (with the exception of Oriental-Americans, who score higher than whites on tests of nonverbal ability and mathematics) is also substantial.

The suggested reasons for the differences in group means that have been observed are highly controversial. Many people have placed part or all of the blame for the differences on the tests. It is argued that the tests are a reflection of the white middle-class culture and are inappropriate for members of other groups. In short, the tests are said to be biased.

Tests are indeed culture dependent. This culture dependence clearly makes some inferences inappropriate. For example, a mean difference between groups on a test provides no basis for inferring that one group is inherently inferior to the other. The results merely describe a current state of affairs and may be useful in drawing certain inferences regarding likely behaviors in other situations. Such inferences must, of course, be justified. Providing the evidence to support inferences made from test scores is what the process of test validation is all about.

The claim that people who have low scores on a test are apt to perform poorly on a job must be supported by evidence. It does not logically follow that, because such a claim can be supported for one group, it can also be supported for another. Indeed, it has frequently been claimed that commonly used tests are not valid for members of certain demographic groups: that members of those groups would perform better on the job or in the educational institutions than is predicted on the basis

## Prediction and Differential Prediction

of tests. The possibility that tests may be differentially valid for members of different groups and that they may have different predictive meanings is central to the discussion of fair test use.

### DIFFERENTIAL VALIDITY

Criterion-related validities for separate demographic groups have been compared in a considerable number of studies in the past dozen years. These studies, which have been conducted in both academic and employment settings, have most often compared the validities for blacks and whites or for men and women. A few studies have included comparisons involving groups that have been labeled as Spanish-surnamed, Mexican-Americans, or Chicanos. Still fewer studies have included other racial or ethnic minorities.

Two general types of studies have typically been made to compare the criterion-related validity for different groups. One type involves comparisons of the correlations between the test(s) and the criterion measure(s) and is commonly referred to as in investigation of differential validity. The second type of comparison is addressed more specifically to the question of whether test scores have the same predictive meaning for members of different groups. This question is generally approached by comparing within-group regression equations and determining whether the equation for the majority group or the combined group tends to predict criterion performance that is higher (overprediction) or lower (underprediction) than that which is actually achieved. This second type of comparison is referred to as an investigation of differential prediction.

Differential validity and differential prediction are related but not identical issues. A test could have the same correlation with a criterion measure for two subgroups, yet the prediction equation based on one group could greatly over- or underpredict the criterion performance of the other. Differential prediction is clearly the more crucial of the two issues, because differences in the predictive meaning of a test score have more direct bearing on considerations of fairness in selection than do differences in correlations (Bartlett et al. 1978, Linn 1978). Indeed, a strong case can be made that, if the prediction systems are the same for two groups, differences in correlations for the two groups are of little consequence. Conversely, if the prediction equations differ, little or no solace can be provided by the observation that the correlations are equal.

Despite the more limited value of comparing correlation coefficients rather than regression equations and standard errors of estimate, the topic of differential validity has received considerable attention in the literature, especially in the literature dealing with employee selection. Partially for this reason, and partially because some studies have provided information on differential validity but only incomplete information about differential prediction, the results of differential validity studies will be reviewed here. The results are of some interest because of the relationship between differential validity and differential prediction. It should also be noted that some researchers consider differential validity an important issue in its own right (e.g., Hunter et al. 1979).

## Differential Validity: Correlations with College GPA

### Sex Differences

Correlations of SAT and ACT scores with freshman GPA are typically somewhat higher for women than for men. Schrader (1971) reported distributions of correlations of SAT scores with freshman GPA and multiple correlations of SAT scores and high school records for 116 groups of men and 143 groups of women. The values of these coefficients clearly tend to run higher for women than for men, whether the predictor is SAT-Verbal alone, SAT-Mathematical alone, or the combination of the two test scores with high school record. Median correlations were as follows: SAT-V, .33 for men and .41 for women; SAT-M, .30 for men and .36 for women; SAT and UGPA multiples, .55 for men and .62 for women. Comparisons of other percentile points reveal similar differences, and consistent results have been reported more recently by Ford and Campos (1977). Results for the ACT also show a consistent tendency for freshman GPA to be slightly more predictable for women than for men (American College Testing Program 1973).

### Differences for Minority and Majority Group Students

Results of studies comparing the predictive validities of ACT and SAT for minority and majority group students were summarized by the American College Testing Program (1973) and more recently by Breland (1978). Since the bulk of the studies in which validities for blacks and whites were compared was conducted prior to 1973, there is a great overlap in the two summaries. There is somewhat less overlap in the summaries of comparisons involving Chicano and Anglo samples.

The two summaries together provide a total of thirty-four pairs of multiple correlations of either SAT or ACT scores with freshman or first semester GPA for blacks and whites. Of the thirty-four comparisons, the multiple correlation for whites was larger than the one for blacks twenty-five times, smaller eight times, and equal to two decimal places the remaining time. The median multiple correlation for blacks was .302, and the median multiple correlation for whites was .385.

The frequency of occurrence of higher multiple correlations for whites than for blacks is statistically significant.[1] ACT and SAT scores are related to freshman GPA for both whites and blacks, but the relationship tends to be somewhat higher for whites than for blacks. The observed difference in predictability cannot be explained by differences in homogeneity of the two groups on the test scores. The standard deviations of the test scores are larger for blacks than for whites in slightly over half of the colleges where this information was reported. For the difference in predictability to be potentially attributable to differences in variability, the standard deviations would have to be consistently smaller for blacks than for whites.

When high school grades are combined with test scores, the tendency for grades to be predicted somewhat better for whites than for blacks is still observed. Comparisons of twenty-eight pairs of multiple correlations of high school grades and either SAT or ACT scores with freshman GPA for blacks and whites can be made from the results summarized in the ACT technical manual (American College Testing Program 1973) and by Breland (1978). In these twenty-eight comparisons, the multiple correlation is higher for whites twenty times, higher for blacks seven times, and equal to two decimal places once. The median multiple correlation is .430 for blacks and .548 for whites.

The ACT and Breland summaries together include eighteen pairs of multiple correlations of high school grades and either SAT or ACT scores with freshman GPA for samples of Anglos and Chicanos within the same colleges. As with the above comparisons for pairs of white and black samples, the multiple correlations tend to be somewhat higher for the majority group than for the minority group. The median multiple correlation is .440 for the eighteen Anglo samples and .388 for the eighteen Chicano samples. Of the eighteen comparisons, the multiple correlation was larger for Anglos in thirteen cases and larger for Chicanos in five cases.

As will be seen below, the finding that freshman GPA is somewhat less predictable for minority than majority students does not generalize to law school or employment settings. The difference for freshman grades in college suggests, however, that nonsystematic errors in prediction tend

---

[1] In this paper, a result will be referred to as statistically significant when there is less than one chance in twenty of obtaining a sample difference as large as that observed when there is no difference for the population values.

to be larger for minority students than for majority students. The question of whether the use of a single prediction equation for all applicants to a college results in systematic errors for minority students will be addressed below in the section on differential prediction.

**Differential Validity: Graduate and Professional Schools**

With the exception of law schools, there is a paucity of evidence regarding the questions of differential validity or differential prediction in graduate and professional schools. One of the problems in conducting studies at this level, that of small sample size, is, of course, compounded at the graduate and professional levels when samples are subdivided. This applies particularly to minority groups, not only because they represent a small fraction of the general population, but because they are underrepresented in graduate and professional schools. Because of the very limited nature of the evidence in other areas, the remainder of this section will be devoted to results obtained for law schools. The extent to which the findings in law schools may be generalizable to other professional or graduate schools is problematic.

*Sex Differences*

The comparison of the criterion-related validities of traditional predictors of first year grades in law school for men and women yields results that are similar to those found for predicting freshman grades in college. That is, whether the LSAT is considered as the sole predictor or in combination with UGPA, there is a tendency for first year grades in law school to be predicted somewhat better for women than for men. Pitcher (1974) summarized the results for twenty-one law schools participating in the law school validity study service in 1974-1975 that had fifty or more women students. For these twenty-one law schools, the median correlation between the LSAT and was .45 for women and .35 for men. The median multiple correlation of LSAT and undergraduate GPA with first year grades in law school was .53 for women and .47 for men.

*Differences Between Minority and Majority Group Students*

Comparisons of correlations of LSAT and multiple correlations of LSAT and undergraduate GPA with first year grades in law school for whites and blacks are available for a total of forty-two law schools in three studies (Schrader and Pitcher 1973, 1974, Powers 1977). The results for

## Prediction and Differential Prediction

these forty-two law schools contrast greatly with those obtained at the undergraduate levels for they indicate that the predictive power of the LSAT is at least as good, if not better, for blacks than for whites. The median correlation between the LSAT and FYGA was .27 for the forty-two samples of black students and .21 for the forty-two samples of white students.

Although the difference in the median correlations for blacks and whites is statistically significant, it is probably attributable to differences in the restriction of range of test scores for the two groups. The LSAT standard deviation was larger for blacks than for whites in thirty-five of the forty-two law schools. Using standard procedures to estimate what the correlations would have been for the black sample at each school, if the standard deviation of the LSAT for blacks had been equal to the standard deviation for whites, results in a median adjusted correlation of .22 for blacks. This adjusted median is very close to the median correlation actually observed for whites (.21).

When LSAT and undergraduate grades are combined, the observed multiple correlations with FYGA are quite similar. The median multiple correlation is .34 for blacks and .32 for whites. The multiple is higher for blacks in twenty-eight law schools and higher for whites in fourteen law schools. Even this small apparent difference is probably caused by differences in homogeneity of the two groups. Thus, it is concluded that law school grades for blacks and whites are about equally predictable from LSAT scores and undergraduate GPA. This conclusion must be qualified, however, because the sample of schools with large enough numbers of black students to enable comparisons is not representative of the population of law schools. One indication of this lack of representativeness is the fact that the correlations for both whites and blacks tend to be a good deal lower than is typical (see Figure 7) of all law schools participating in the validity study service.

The evidence regarding possible differences in predictive validity for Chicano law students in comparison to Anglos is less extensive than the above results for blacks. The results that are available, however, suggest that the LSAT alone or the LSAT in combination with undergraduate GPA predict grades in law school as well for Chicano students as they do for their Anglo classmates. The median correlation of the LSAT with first year grades in thirteen law schools studied by Schrader and Pitcher (1974) or Powers (1977) was .29 for Chicanos and .25 for Anglos. The multiple correlations of LSAT and undergraduate GPA with first year grades in law school had median values of .40 and .30 for Chicanos and Anglos respectively.

## Differential Validity: Employment Settings

Numerous reviews of investigations of differential validity for minority and majority group employees have been published (Boehm 1972, Hunter and Schmidt 1978, Katzell and Dyer 1977, Schmidt et al. 1973). With the exception of Katzell and Dyer, there is widespread agreement in the reviews and elsewhere that differential validity is not a commonplace phenomenon. The most comprehensive analysis of differential validity study results for blacks and whites examined 866 pairs of correlations between employment tests and criterion measures from thirty-nine studies (Hunter et al. 1979). They reported analyses that indicate that the incidence of differential validity in the 866 pairs could be attributed to chance plus a few statistical artifacts. Based on this analysis, Hunter et al. concluded that, for black and white job applicant populations, differential validity "probably is nonexistent."

If taken literally, Hunter et al.'s conclusion is probably too strong. The evidence is nonetheless clear that whatever differences do exist are of small magnitude. Furthermore, the differences are not consistently in one direction. Even the one review that reached a contrary conclusion (Katzell and Dyer 1977) found that the direction of the differences was inconsistent.

In their recent analysis of 866 pairs of test-criterion correlations for blacks and whites, Hunter et al. (1979) classified criterion measures into objective criteria (e.g., job sample measures, errors, quality, and quantity of output) and subjective criteria (e.g., supervisor ratings). The mean difference between validity observed for blacks and that for whites for the 334 test-criterion pairs involving objective criteria was .01, with blacks having the higher mean correlation. The corresponding mean difference for the 532 test criterion pairs involving subjective criteria was .04, with blacks again having the higher mean. It is evident that the common expectation that tests are better predictors for whites than for blacks does not hold up in employment testing situations.

## Differential Validity: Air Force Training Criteria

The results of the validation of the Armed Services Vocational Aptitude Battery against final school grade (FSG) in air force technical training were reported separately for subgroups defined by race (Valentine 1977). Validities were reported separately for whites and blacks in thirty-nine job areas and are quite discrepant with the results just reviewed for studies in employment settings. On the other hand, they are consistent with the results reviewed above for predicting freshman GPA in college, in that

## Prediction and Differential Prediction

there is a consistent tendency for FSG to be predicted better for whites than for blacks.

The correlation between the Armed Forces Qualification Test (AFQT) and FSG was higher for whites than for blacks in thirty-seven of the thirty-nine job areas where comparative results were available. The median correlation for whites was .33, compared to a median correlation of .18 for blacks. A part of the difference in the correlations may be attributed to differences in homogeneity of the test scores for the two groups. In all but five of the job areas, the AFQT standard deviation was larger for whites than for blacks. And the differences remained, even after adjusting the correlations by estimating what they would have been in each job area if the standard deviation for the black sample equaled that of the white sample. The median adjusted correlation for blacks is .20, and the observed correlations for whites are larger than the adjusted correlation for blacks in thirty-four of the thirty-nine job areas. The number of blacks was large enough in most job areas to yield reliable results. The average number of blacks per job area was 270, which is considerably larger than most differential validity studies. Thus, the finding of differential validity for grades in the air force technical schools is well established.

### Summary of Differential Validity Results

The results of studies of differential validity for minority group members (in most studies black) and majority group members are not consistent from one setting to another. Freshman grades in college are typically predicted somewhat better for whites than for blacks or Chicanos. Final grades in Air Force technical training schools for enlisted personnel are also predicted somewhat better for whites than for blacks. On the other hand, the prediction of first year grades in law school is typically as good, if not better, for blacks and Chicanos as it is for whites, and there is little evidence of differences in validity coefficients for whites and blacks in civilian employment settings.

Differences in correlation coefficients suggest that the groups differ in the magnitude of nonsystematic errors of prediction that are typically made. They say nothing about possible systematic errors of prediction for members of an identifiable subgroup when a single equation is used to make predictions for everyone. Comparisons of regression equations are needed to investigate the possibility of systematic errors of prediction. Not only can the issue of possible systematic errors be addressed by comparing regression systems for different groups, but the issue of differences in the size of nonsystematic errors for members of various groups can be addressed more directly than by the use of correlation coefficients. The latter may be accomplished by comparing the size of the variability of scores actually obtained on a criterion measure for fixed predicted values.

## DIFFERENTIAL PREDICTION

Prediction of performance on the job or grades in college from scores on tests or other predictors is usually accomplished by means of a linear regression equation. The regression equation provides an estimate of the average score on the criterion measure for people with any particular score on the test or other predictor. This estimated average score on the criterion for people with a given score on the test is used as the predicted criterion score. It is, of course, possible that a prediction system developed for one group of people will be inappropriate for another group.

If a linear regression model and a single predictor were assumed for each group, the prediction systems for two groups could still differ in three important ways: (1) the variability of criterion scores for fixed predicted scores could be unequal, that is, the standard error of estimate might differ from one group to the other; (2) the regression lines could differ in slope; (3) the regression lines could have different intercepts.

Differences in standard errors of estimate imply that the magnitude of the nonsystematic errors of prediction tends to be larger for members of one group than for members of another. The standard errors of estimate provide a more direct index of differences in predictability between two groups than is provided by correlation coefficients. Differences in slope imply that the predicted criterion scores changed more with changes in the test score for the group with the steeper slope than they did for the group with the flatter slope. With equal slopes, a difference in intercepts implies that the predicted criterion score associated with any particular test score is higher for one group than the other. In other words, use of an equation based on one group would tend to systematically over- or underpredict the criterion performance for members of the other group.

When equations for two groups have substantially different slopes and/or different intercepts, the implication follows that use of a single equation for all persons regardless of group membership will result in some systematic errors of prediction, although near compensation on average might occur. Thus, when differences in slopes and/or intercepts are found, it is important to determine the direction and magnitude of the systematic errors.

## Differential Prediction of College GPA

*Sex Differences*

The standard error of estimate is generally smaller for women than for men, when traditional predictors are used to predict freshman GPA (American College Testing Program 1973). This result is consistent with what would be expected in light of the previously discussed finding that correlations between traditional predictors and freshman GPA are usually higher for women than for men.

Unfortunately, available studies of sex differences in the prediction of grades in college have often not reported results of statistical tests of the equality of standard errors of estimate, slopes, and intercepts. Systematic errors of prediction due to the use of a single equation for men and women were found consistently, however, in results summarized by Linn (1973) and by the American College Testing Program (1973).

The use of the regression equation for men with SAT scores as predictors to predict GPA for women underpredicted the actual GPA of women in all ten colleges for which results were reviewed by Linn. For women with average SAT scores, the predicted GPA based on the equation for men was between a quarter (.24) and a full (.98) standard deviation below the actual mean GPA for women. In terms of a 4-point grade scale, the equation for men typically underpredicted the women's GPA by .36.

Results reported by the American College Testing Program (1973) are consistent with the above. Use of a combined equation for men and women was found to underpredict the actual GPA in all nineteen colleges included in the analysis, when ACT scores were used to make the predictions. Underprediction averaged .27 over the nineteen colleges for women with ACT scores equal to the mean. When predictions were based on high school grades and ACT scores combined, the tendency for women to perform better than predicted on the basis of a common equation was reduced somewhat, but remained the consistent outcome with an average underprediction of .20.

The amount of systematic error that is introduced by the use of a single equation for men and women is large, relative to the size of predicted differences in GPA for people with different predictor scores. For example, the difference between the predictions based on the equation for men and those based on the equation for women is typically about as large as the difference in predicted GPA for women with average SAT scores and women with SAT scores a full standard deviation below the mean (approximately the 16th percentile) in the ten colleges included in Linn's (1973) review.

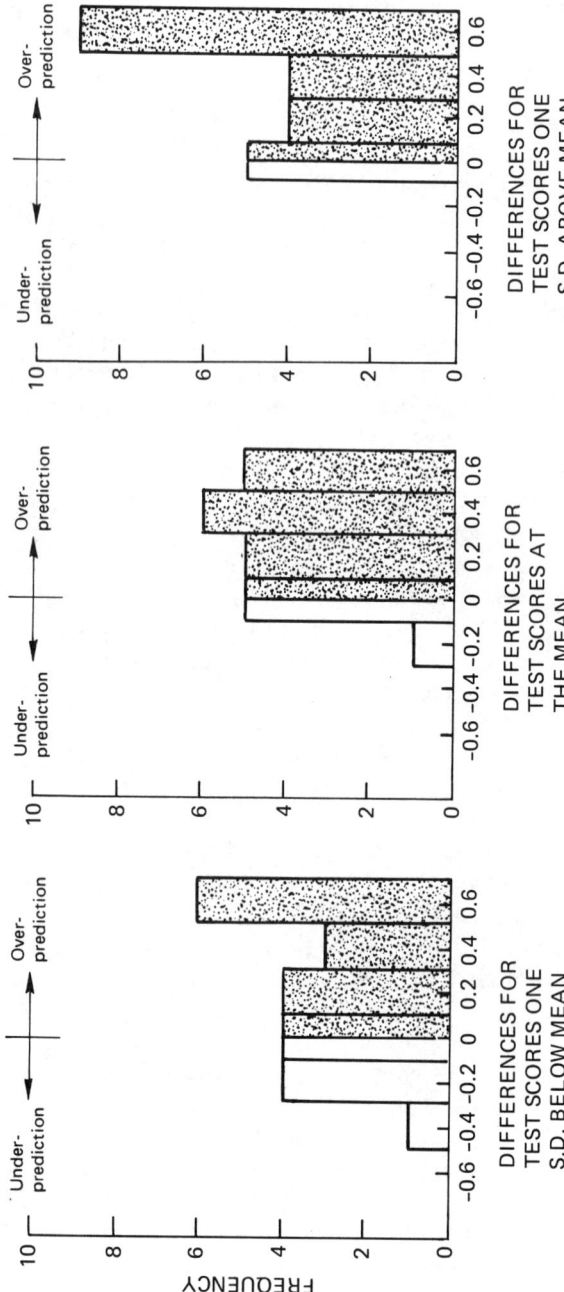

**FIGURE 9** Distributions of differences between predicted GPA's based on equation for white students and equation for black students divided by the GPA standard deviation of black students (based on a secondary analysis reported by Linn 1973).

## Prediction and Differential Prediction

### Minority and Majority Group Differences

Statistical comparisons of prediction systems for minority and majority group college students more often than not lead to the conclusion that the systems have significantly different standard errors of estimate, slopes, or intercepts. In a recent review, Breland (1978) found that the regression systems differed significantly on at least one of these three factors in nineteen of twenty-five comparisons involving samples of blacks and whites and in ten of twenty-four comparisons involving samples of Chicanos and Anglos. The sample size was relatively small in some of the comparisons, which makes it unlikely to find significant differences in the regression systems for the two groups even if they, in fact, differ. This limited power to detect differences, coupled with the frequency of significant outcomes, supports the inference that regression systems for majority and minority group students are not the same.

Given that the regression systems are not identical, the key issues are the direction and magnitude of the differences. In most cases, the equation for whites or a combined equation for whites and blacks yield predicted GPAs somewhat higher than would be obtained from the equation for black students. For black students with SAT scores at the mean for their group, the equation for whites overpredicted actual GPA in eighteen of the twenty-two colleges studied by Cleary (1968), Davis and Kerner-Hoeg (1971), and Temp (1971). The distribution of differences between predicted GPA based on the equation for whites and the predicted GPA based on the equation for blacks divided by the GPA standard deviation for black students is shown in Figure 9 for SAT scores one standard deviation below the mean of black students, and SAT scores one standard deviation above the mean for black students. A positive difference (cross-hatched area of Figure 9) indicates that the equation for whites overpredicts the actual GPA of blacks.

As can be seen in Figure 9, the equation based on white students tends to overpredict the GPA of black students, whether their test scores were above, below, or at the mean. The amount of overprediction is generally smaller for low than for high test scores. This reflects the tendency for the slope to be somewhat less for blacks than whites. At many of the colleges it would require an increase of about 50 points on both the SAT-Verbal and SAT-Mathematical to yield an increase in predicted GPA of about a quarter of a standard deviation. Thus, the amount of overprediction is often relatively large in comparison to the difference in predicted GPAs associated with sizeable changes in test scores. Whether the differences are large enough to be of practical importance is a matter of some debate, but it is clear that systematic errors resulting from the use of a single equation for blacks and whites will generally favor black students.

The results shown in Figure 9 using SAT scores are consistent with those that have been reported using ACT scores (American College Testing Program 1973). When high school grades are combined with either SAT or ACT scores, the tendency for a single equation to overpredict GPAs of black students is still observed. A combined equation for blacks and whites with high school grades and test scores as predictors was found to overpredict the GPAs of black students with predictor scores at the mean by an average of .15 on a 4-point scale in twenty-four comparisons summarized by Breland (1978). The combined equation underpredicted the mean GPA of blacks in only two of the twenty-four comparisons.

The tendency to overpredict for black students apparently does not generalize to other minorities. At least for Chicano students, a combined equation is at least as likely to underpredict as overpredict the actual mean GPA, when predictions are based on a combination of high school grades and test scores. In the ten comparisons summarized by Breland that involved "Spanish-surnamed" or "Chicano" students, the combined groups equation for high school grades and test scores underpredicted the mean performance of Chicano students in six cases with differences between predicted and actual mean GPA averaging −.02 on a 4-point scale.

*Socioeconomic Status*

Differences in plans to attend, actual attendance, and graduation from college have been found among various socioeconomic levels, even after adjusting for measured differences in ability (Sewell and Shah 1967). These results, combined with the well-known finding that people from lower socioeconomic backgrounds tend to score lower on ability tests than those from higher socioeconomic backgrounds, raise the question of whether test scores have the same predictive meaning regardless of socioeconomic level. The best set of results for answering this question for the prediction of freshman GPA is provided in the ACT technical manual (American College Testing Program 1973).

In comparisons of both high and low income men and high and low income women at nineteen colleges, a combined equation did not consistently over- or underpredict the mean GPA of either income group. Furthermore, the over- or underpredictions for high or low income groups within a single college were never large. Hence, it was concluded that separate equations are not needed for applicants from families with different incomes.

## Age Differences

The evidence regarding differential prediction for subgroups defined by age is quite limited. The main source is again the ACT technical manual, which includes age comparisons in which adults were defined as anyone 21 years or older and youths as anyone under 21. Although limited to comparisons in only five colleges, the prediction systems for youths and adults were consistently different. Whether based on ACT scores alone, high school grades alone, or a combination of the two, use of a combined group equation underpredicted the mean GPA of adults in all five colleges. The amount of underprediction was quite consistent from college to college, ranging from a low of .26 to a high of .36, when predictions were based on grades and test scores combined. Such differences represent approximately one-third of the GPA standard deviation in each college. In selective admissions, a difference of this magnitude would have a large effect on the probability of older students' being accepted.

## Differential Prediction of First Year Grade Average in Law School

### Sex Differences

Pitcher (1974, 1975) has reported a total of twenty-nine comparisons of regression equations for men and women, based on results from twenty-three law schools, six of which provided data for two different years. When FYGA were regressed on LSAT scores and undergraduate GPA, significant differences in standard errors of estimate, slope, and/or intercepts were obtained in six of the twenty-nine comparisons. (This offers essentially no evidence of true differences, since 4.4 significant differences would be expected by pure chance.)

Over the twenty-nine data sets there was a slight, but nonsignificant, tendency for a single equation based on the combined group of men and women to predict a FYGA that was lower than the actual mean for women with average scores on the predictors. The common equation underpredicted the grades of women in twenty of the twenty-nine cases. The differences between predicted and actual average grades for women based on the combined groups regression equation ranged from $-2$ to $+2$ with a median of $-.4$. The grade averages in each law school were scaled to have a standard deviation of 10. Thus, a difference of $-2$ implies that the actual average grades of women were .2 standard deviations better than predicted from the common equation. Positive values imply that predictions are higher than actual performance.

## Minority and Majority Group Differences

The comparisons of regression equations for minority students (either blacks or Chicanos) with those for majority students indicate that the equations are not the same. Thirty-eight of forty-two comparisons of regression systems for blacks and whites differed significantly when LSAT and UGPA were used together as predictors of FYGA in law school. With LSAT used alone as the predictor, forty-one of the comparisons had significant differences in standard errors of estimate, slopes, and/or intercepts. The most common difference was in intercepts (Linn 1975, Schrader and Pitcher 1973, 1974, Powers 1977). Results for comparisons involving Chicano and majority law students also consistently revealed significant differences in regression systems, especially in intercepts, in each of the thirteen law schools observed (Schrader and Pitcher 1974, Powers 1977).

Differences between the regression equations for minority and majority group law students are consistently in one direction. Use of the majority group equation or a single equation based on the combined groups tends to overpredict the actual FYGA of minority group law students. The amount of overprediction is greater with LSAT used as the only predictor than with LSAT and UGPA used together. In either case, however, the tendency to overpredict is clear, and the amount of overprediction is substantial in some law schools.

The distributions of these differences are shown in Table 5. The combined groups equation typically overpredicts the average FYGA by slightly more than a quarter of a standard deviation and occasionally by as much as a half a standard deviation when the equation is based on LSAT and UGPA together. The advantage in predicted FYGA afforded by using a combined equation rather than a separate equation based on minority students is roughly equivalent to the addition of 50 points to the LSAT score of minority students at the typical school. In other words, if 50 points (an amount that corresponds to the difference between a score at about the 30th percentile and one at the 50th percentile) were arbitrarily added to the LSAT scores obtained for minority students and the original equation for that group were used to make predictions, the amount of overprediction would be approximately a quarter of a standard deviation at the typical school.

Evans (1977) used the Law School Data Assembly Service files to estimate the proportion of candidates taking the LSAT between September 1975 and August 1976 who were admitted to at least one law school. The estimated proportions for the 4,299 black candidates and for the 66,994 white or unidentified candidates are plotted in Figure 10 for various score intervals on the LSAT. As would be expected, the proportion of candidates, both black and white, offered admission to at least one

TABLE 5  Distributions of Difference Between Predicted and Actual Average Grade (Amount of Overprediction) for Minority Group Law Students Based on the Combined Groups Regression Equation in Each School[a]

|  | Frequencies for Black Students | | Frequencies for Chicano Students | |
|---|---|---|---|---|
| Difference | LSAT Alone | LSAT and UPGA | LSAT Alone | LSAT and UPGA |
| 8 or more | 2 | 0 | 2 | 0 |
| 7 | 5 | 0 | 1 | 0 |
| 6 | 13 | 2 | 4 | 1 |
| 5 | 9 | 1 | 0 | 1 |
| 4 | 9 | 7 | 4 | 3 |
| 3 | 3 | 11 | 0 | 3 |
| 2 | 0 | 17 | 2 | 3 |
| 1 | 1 | 3 | 0 | 1 |
| 0 | 0 | 1 | 0 | 1 |
| MEAN | 5.2 | 2.7 | 6.0 | 3.0 |

[a]Results are based on Schrader and Pitcher (1973, 1974) and Powers (1977). First year grade average is scaled to have a standard deviation of 10 for the combined group at each law school.

law school increases as the LSAT scores increase. The proportion is higher for blacks than for whites in every score interval except the next to highest, where the black proportion was based on only six candidates. Over all score intervals, a total of 1,697 of the 4,299 black candidates were estimated to have been offered admission to at least one law school. If the proportion for black candidates had been equal to that for whites, however, only 824 black candidates would have been offered admission to at least one law school.

Obviously, minority students on the average are not penalized by the use of a single prediction equation for all students rather than separate equations for minority and majority groups. If anything, a single, combined equation is an advantage for minority students. Even so, strict reliance on the traditional predictors to select law students, without regard to minority group status, would result in the exclusion of many minority students who even now attend law schools and meet their requirements.

## Differential Prediction: Employment Settings

Results from studies in business and industrial settings, where regression systems for minority group employees have been compared to those for majority group employees, have generally been similar to results in ac-

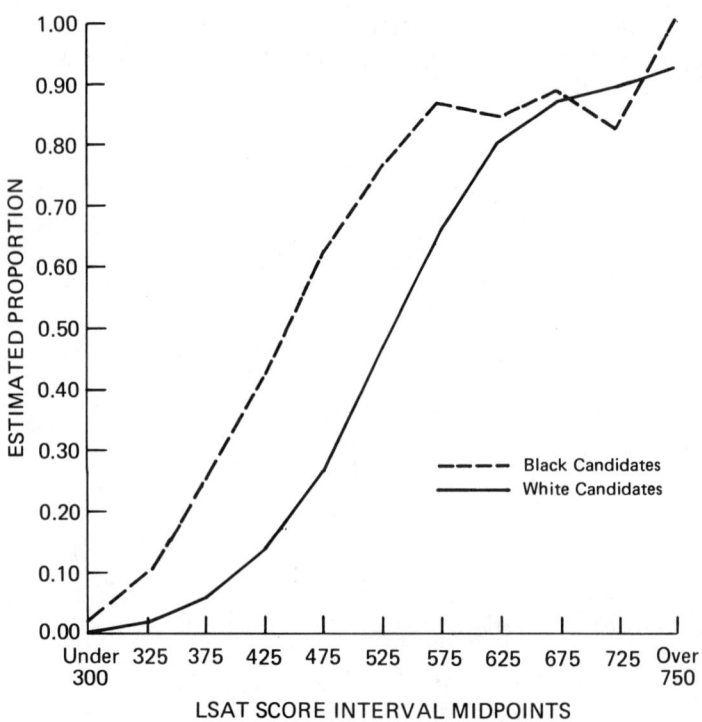

**FIGURE 10** Estimated proportion of black and white LSAT candidates who are offered admission to at least one law school (based on Evans 1977).

ademic settings. The frequency of significant differences in employment settings is somewhat less, but where differences are found, a single equation based on the majority group or the combined minority and majority groups usually tends to overpredict the actual criterion performance of minority group employees (Bartlett et al. 1978). In the bulk of the studies, the minority group has been composed of blacks, although samples of Chicano employees have been included in a few.

Twenty studies that provided sufficient information to compare standard errors of estimate, slopes, and intercepts for minority and majority group employees were reviewed by Ruch (1972), who compared 618 pairs of regressions of individual criterion measures on individual tests. Significant differences were found in standard errors of estimate, slopes, or intercepts in 223 of the comparisons. Where significant differences were found, the standard error of estimate was usually larger for whites than blacks (92 percent of the significant differences). Slopes were generally steeper for whites than for blacks (91 percent of the significant

## Prediction and Differential Prediction

differences), and intercepts were higher for whites than blacks (95 percent of the significant differences). The generally higher intercepts for whites imply that a single regression equation would tend to overpredict the actual criterion scores of black employees.

Major studies of four job categories that have been completed since Ruch's review (cartographic technicians, inventory management specialists, telephone operators, and clerical jobs) lend further support to the general conclusion that prediction systems for minority and majority group employees are often different. Where differences occur, the equation for the majority or combined groups generally overpredicts the criterion scores of the minority employees. (See Campbell et al. 1973, Gael et al. 1975a, 1975b).

As noted by Mollenkopf (1975), the studies of these four jobs were exemplary in several respects. The studies of cartographic technicians and inventory management specialists (Campbell et al. 1973) included sizeable samples of whites, blacks, and Mexican Americans. The studies of telephone operators and clerical jobs included sizeable samples of white, black, and Spanish-surnamed employees. Studies of all four jobs were most notable, however, for the effort that went into the development of high-quality criterion measures and the choice of tests.

## Differential Prediction: Air Force

The general findings of studies in employment settings are strongly reinforced, at least for training criteria, by the recent results for Air Force technical training reported by Valentine (1977). To evaluate the effect of using the equation based on white Air Force personnel to make predictions for blacks, Valentine focused on twenty-four job areas that included at least 100 black and 100 white trainees. The regression systems for blacks and for whites were found to be significantly different in twenty of these twenty-four job areas. With samples as large as those in Valentine's analyses (an average of 406 black and 1,153 white trainees per job area), even fairly small differences in the regression equations can be detected. Thus, it is more useful to look at the direction and magnitude of the differences in prediction.

For a person with average scores on the predictors, which included the AFQT, the Armed Services Vocational Aptitude Battery, and an index of educational background, the predicted final grade in the technical training school was found to be higher in all twenty-four job areas using the equation for whites than it would be using the one for blacks. The distribution of differences in predicted grades resulting in use of the equation for whites and that for blacks is shown in Figure 11. The predictions

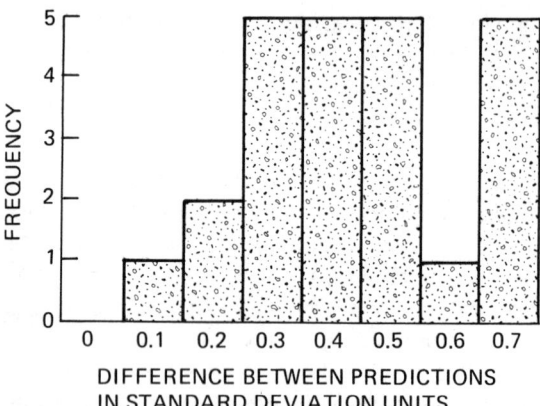

**FIGURE 11** Distribution of differences between predicted final school grade using the equation for white trainees and the predicted value using the equation for black trainees (based on Valentine 1977). Differences are expressed in standard deviation units using the observed standard deviation of final school grades for black trainees in each job area. Predictions were made based on predictor scores equal to the combined group's mean.

were made for predictor scores equal to the combined group mean, and differences are expressed in terms of standard deviation units. A positive difference indicates that the equation for whites tends to overpredict the grades of black trainees, who had predictor scores near the mean of all trainees. As noted by Valentine, the use of separate regression equations for blacks and whites would result in reduced rates of qualification of black air force enlisted personnel for the technical training courses in all twenty-four job areas.

## Summary of Differential Prediction Results

Whether the criterion to be predicted is freshman GPA in college, first year grades in law school, outcomes of job training, or job performance measures, carefully chosen ability tests have *not* been found to underpredict the actual performance of minority group persons. Contrary to what is often presupposed, the bulk of the evidence shows either that there are essentially no differences in predictions based on minority or majority group data, or that the predictions based on majority group data give some advantage to minority group members. In most instances, the use of separate equations for purposes of selection would reduce, rather than increase, the number of minority group members selected. On the other hand, differences between groups in distributions of test scores are such that, despite the tendency to overpredict actual performance, strict reliance on ability test scores to select applicants for jobs or further education would likely reduce the number of selected minority group members in comparison to current practice.

Results of differential prediction studies may dispel some common myths about ability tests and, in so doing, provide some necessary background for policy decisions regarding test use. They obviously do not provide a sufficiently complete basis for such judgments, however. What relevance the results have for policy depends largely on the value that is attached to the criterion measure. How important is it, for example, to select students who will receive high grades? The question of the value of grades and their relationship to other valued outcomes has been given relatively little consideration here.

Interpretation of differential prediction results should be tempered by a recognition of the limited predictive power of ability tests for any of the criteria involved in the studies. It should be recalled that a correlation of about .4 is commonplace in predicting academic grades or job training criteria. Correlations with job performance criteria are usually much smaller. Because of the relatively large differences between groups, tests with such modest correlations with criterion measures might still lead to the exclusion of the preponderance of minority group applicants who, in fact, could perform quite satisfactorily if given the opportunity, an outcome forcefully indicated by Thorndike (1971). Thus, it is essential that the use of tests be evaluated not only in terms of predictive value, but also in terms of possible social consequences.

## REFERENCES

American College Testing Program (1973) *Assessing Students on the Way to College: Technical Report for the ACT Assessment Program*, Vol. 1. Iowa City, Iowa: American College Testing Program.

Association of American Medical Colleges (1977) *New Medical College Admission Test: Interpretative Manual.* Washington, D.C.: Association of American Medical Colleges.

Bartlett, C. J., Bobko, P., Mosier, S. B., and Hannon, R. (1978) Testing for fairness with a moderated multiple regression strategy: An alternative to differential analysis. *Personnel Psychology* 31:233-241.

Bennett, G. K., Seashore, H. G., and Wesman, A. G. (1974) *Fifth Edition Manual for the Differential Aptitude Tests.* New York: The Psychological Corporation.

Boehm, V. R. (1972) Negro-white differences in validity of employment and training selection procedures. Summary of the research evidence. *Journal of Applied Psychology* 56:33-39.

Breland, H. M. (1978) Population Validity and College Entrance Measures. College Board Research and Development Report (RDR 78-79, No. 2); also Research Bulletin RB78-19. Princeton, N.J.: Educational Testing Service.

Campbell, J. T., Crooks, L. A., Mahoney, M. H., and Rock, D. A. (1973) *An Investigation of Sources of Bias in the Prediction of Job Performance: A Six-Year Study.* PR-73-37. Princeton, N.J.: Educational Testing Service.

Cleary, T. A. (1968) Test bias: Prediction of grades of Negro and white students in integrated colleges. *Journal of Educational Measurement* 5:115-124.

Coleman, J. S., Campbell, E. Q., Hobson, C. J., McPartland, J., Mood, A. M., Weinfeld, F. D., and York, R. L. (1966) *Equality of Educational Opportunity.* Washington, D.C.: U.S. Department of Health, Education, and Welfare.

Cronbach, L. J. (1975) Five decades of public controversy over mental testing. *American Psychologist* 30:1-14.

Davis, J. A. and Kerner-Hoeg, S. (1971) Validity of Pre-Admission Indices for Blacks and Whites in Sex Traditionally White Public Universities in North Carolina, ETS Project Report PR-71-15. Princeton, N.J.: Educational Testing Service.

DuBois, P. H. (1970) *A History of Psychological Testing.* Boston: Allyn and Bacon, Inc.

Evans, F. R. (1977) Applications and admissions to ABA accredited law schools: An analysis of national data for the class entering in the fall of 1976. In *Law School Admission Council Annual Council Report.* Washington, D.C.: Law School Admission Council.

Ford, S. F., and Campos, S. (1977) *Summary of Validity Data for the Admissions Testing Program Validity Study Service.* New York: College Entrance Examination Board.

Gael, S., Grant, D. L., and Ritchie, R. J. (1975a) Employment test validation for minority and nonminority telephone operators. *Journal of Applied Psychology* 60:411-419.

Gael, S., Grant, D. L., and Ritchie, R. J. (1975b) Employment test validation for minority and nonminority clerks with work sample criteria. *Journal of Applied Psychology* 60:420-426.

Ghiselli, E. E. (1966) *The Validity of Occupational Aptitude Tests.* New York: Wiley.

Griliches, Z. (1976) Wages of very young men. *Journal of Political Economy*, S69-S85.

Hartnett, R. T., and Willingham, W. W. (1978) The criterion problem: What measure of success in graduate education. GRE Research Report No. 7704. Princeton, N.J.: Educational Testing Service.

Hauser, R. M., and Daymont, T. N. (1977) Schooling, ability, and earnings: Cross-sectional findings 8 to 14 years after high school graduation. *Sociology of Education* 50:182-206.

Holland, J. L., and Richards, J. M., Jr. (1965) *Academic and Nonacademic Accomplishment: Correlated or Uncorrelated?* ACT Research Report No. 2. Iowa City, Iowa: American College Testing Program.

Houghton-Mifflin (1974) *Cognitive Abilities Test.* Boston: Houghton-Mifflin Company.

Hoyt, D. P. (1965) *The Relationship Between College Grades and Adult Achievement: A Review of the Literature.* ACT Research Report, No. 7. Iowa City, Iowa: American College Testing Program.

Hoyt, D. P. (1966) College grades and adult accomplishment. *Educational Record* 47:70-75.

Humphreys, L. G. (1968) The fleeting nature of the prediction of college academic success. *Journal of Educational Psychology* 59:375-380.

Hunter, J. F., and Schmidt, F. L. (1978) Differential and single group validity of employment tests by race: A critical analysis of three recent studies. *Journal of Applied Psychology* 63:1-11.

Hunter, J. E., Schmidt, F. L., and Hunter, R. (1979) Differential validity of employment tests by race: A comprehensive review and analysis. *Psychological Bulletin* 86:721-735.

Jencks, C., Smith, M., Acland, H., Bane, M. J., Cohen, D., Gintis, H., Heyns, B., and Michelson, S. (1972) *Inequality: A Reassessment of the Effect of Family and Schooling in America*. New York: Basic Books, Inc.

Katzell, R. A., and Dyer, F. J. (1977) Differential validity revived. *Journal of Applied Psychology* 62:137-145.

Linn, R. L. (1966) Grade Adjustments for prediction of academic performance: A review. *Journal of Educational Measurement* 3:313-329.

Linn, R. L. (1973) Fair test use in selection. *Review of Educational Research* 43:139-161.

Linn, R. L. (1975) Test bias and the prediction of grades in law school. *Journal of Legal Education* 27:293-323.

Linn, R. L. (1978) Single group validity, differential validity and differential prediction. *Journal of Applied Psychology* 63:507-512.

Lord, F. M., and Novick, M. R. (1968) *Statistical Theories of Mental Test Scores*. Reading, Mass.: Addison-Wesley.

Maccoby, F. E., and Jacklin, C. N. (1974) *The Psychology of Sex Differences*. Stanford, Calif.: Stanford University Press.

Mollenkopf, W. G. (1975) Some Observations on Validity and Validation. Presidential address to the Division of Evaluation and Measurement of the American Psychological Association Annual Meeting, Chicago.

Munday, L. A., and Davis, J. C. (1974) *Varieties of Accomplishment After College: Perspectives on the Meaning of Academic Talent*. ACT Research Report No. 62. Iowa City, Iowa: American College Testing Program.

Pitcher, B. (1974) Predicting law school grades for female law students. In Law School Admission Council *Annual Council Report*. Washington, D.C.: Law School Admission Council.

Pitcher, B. (1975) A further study of predicting law school grades for female law students. In Law School Admission Council *Annual Council Report*. Washington, D.C.: Law School Admission Council.

Powers, D. E. (1977) Comparing predictions of law school performance for black, Chicano, and white law students. In Law School Admission Council *Annual Council Report*. Washington, D.C.: Law School Admission Council.

The Psychological Corporation (1970) *Miller Analogies Test*. New York: The Psychological Corporation.

The Psychological Corporation (1972) *The Differential Aptitude Tests*. New York: The Psychological Corporation.

Ruch, W. W. (1972) A Re-analysis of Published Differential Validity Studies. Paper presented at the symposium on Differential Validation Under EEOC and OFCC Testing and Selection Regulations. American Psychological Association, Honolulu, Hawaii.

Schmidt, F. L., Berner, J. G., and Hunter, J. E. (1973) Racial differences in validity of employment tests: Reality or illusion? *Journal of Applied Psychology* 53:5-9.

Schmidt, F. L., and Hunter, J. E. (1977) Development of a general solution to the problem of validity generalization. *Journal of Applied Psychology* 62:529-540.

Schmidt, F. L., and Hunter, J. E. (1978) Moderator research and the law of small numbers. *Personnel Psychology* 31:215-232.

Schrader, W. B. (1965) A taxonomy of expectancy tables. *Journal of Educational Measurement* 2:29-35.

Schrader, W. B. (1971) The predictive validity of College Board admission tests. In W. H. Angoff, ed., *The College Board Admissions Testing Program: A Technical Report on Research and Development Activities Relating to the Scholastic Aptitude Test and Achievement Tests*. New York: College Entrance Examination Board.

Schrader, W. B. (1976) Summary of law school validity studies, 1948-1975. In Law School Admission Council *Annual Council Report.* Washington, D.C.: Law School Admission Council.

Schrader, W. B., and Pitcher, B. (1973) Predicting law school grades for black American law students. In Law School Admission Council *Annual Council Report.* Washington, D.C.: Law School Admission Council.

Schrader, W. B., and Pitcher, B. (1974) Prediction of law school grades for Mexican American and black American students. In Law School Admission Council *Annual Council Report.* Washington, D.C.: Law School Admission Council.

Sewell, W. H., and Hauser, R. M. (1975) *Education, Occupation and Earnings: Achievement in the Early Years.* New York: Academic Press.

Sewell, W. H., and Hauser, R. M. (1976) Causes and consequences of higher education: Models of the status attainment process. In W. H. Sewell, R. M. Hauser, and D. L. Featherman, eds., *Schooling and Achievement in American Society.* New York: Academic Press.

Sewell, W. H., and Shah, V. P. (1967) Socioeconomic status, intelligence, and the attainment of higher education. *Sociology of Education* 40:1-23.

Spaeth, J. L. (1976) Characteristics of the work setting and the job as determinants of income. In W. H. Sewell, R. M. Hauser, and D. L. Featherman, eds., *Schooling and Achievement in American Society.* New York: Academic Press.

Stern, W. (1914) Children of different social strata. In *The Psychological Methods of Testing Intelligence.* Translated by G. M. Whipple. Baltimore: Warwick and York, Inc.

Stewart, N. (1947) AGCT scores of army personnel grouped by occupation. *Occupations* 26:5-41.

Taubman, P., and Wales, T. (1974) *Higher Education and Earnings: College as an Investment and a Screening Device.* New York: McGraw-Hill.

Taylor, H. C., and Russell, J. T. (1939) The relationship of validity coefficients to the practical effectiveness of tests in selection: Discussion and tables. *Journal of Applied Psychology* 23:565-578.

Temp, G. (1971) Test bias: Validity of the SAT for blacks and whites in thirteen integrated institutions. *Journal of Educational Measurement* 8:245-251.

Thorndike, R. L. (1971) Concepts of culture fairness. *Journal of Educational Measurement* 8:63-70.

Thorndike, R. L., and Hagen, E. (1959) *Ten Thousand Careers.* New York: John Wiley & Sons.

Valentine, L. D. (1977) *Prediction of Air Force Technical Training Success from ASVAB and Educational Background.* AFHRL-TR-77-18. Lackland AFB, Tex.: Personnel Research Division, Air Force Human Relations Laboratory.

Willingham, W. W. (1974) Predicting success in graduate education. *Science* 183:273-278.

Wilson, K. (1979) *The GRE Cooperative Validity Studies: 1976-78.* GRE Research Report No. 75-8R. Princeton, N.J.: Educational Testing Service.

Nancy Cole
# The Implications of Coaching for Ability Testing

## INTRODUCTION

The term "coaching" is used to refer to a wide variety of test preparation activities undertaken by individuals in an attempt to improve test scores. The term sometimes has negative connotations, in that coaching is perceived as a vaguely inappropriate or illicit activity. At the same time, many high schools provide test preparation activities for their students prior to administering college admissions tests; commercial test preparation courses for college, graduate school, or professional examinations are available in all major cities; numerous "How to Take the _____ Test" books can be purchased in bookstores everywhere; and most teachers prepare their students in a variety of ways for standardized school achievement tests, sometimes with materials supplied by the test publisher. Given its wide use, in spite of its sometimes suspect image, coaching has become an important component of the present controversy about ability testing.

The concern with coaching is not new. In 1959 the trustees of the College Entrance Examinations Board "issued a detailed statement asserting that the general finding of the coaching studies was that increases

---

The author wishes to acknowledge the invaluable assistance of Pamela Ross and Fred McHale in locating sources, suggesting conceptual issues, and reacting to earlier drafts of this paper.

in SAT scores resulting from coaching are negligible" (Fremer and Chandler 1971:147). The statement concluded with two concerns: (1) that students who cannot afford coaching will purchase it with little gain or feel they are at a disadvantage in not doing so, and (2) that coaching is a corruption of the educational process "to gain ends which we believe to be not only unworthy, but ironically, unattainable" (College Entrance Examination Board 1959:3).

## Social Implications

At present, the concern with coaching is rooted in the social implications voiced so long ago by the College Board and in the validity implications for the tests themselves. If students who can afford expensive coaching schools gain an advantage on admissions or professional certification tests, testing could contribute to an exacerbation of economic stratification in the society—a result completely counter to testing's traditional goal of offering opportunity to the most capable regardless of economic background.

These potential social implications have received wider attentions in the last two decades in view of their relationship to the civil rights movement of the 1960s and, more recently, to the entrance of consumer groups into the testing controversy. Thus, the possibility of direct advantage to some students in admissions and certification tests because of their being able to afford expensive coaching has become a serious threat to such testing. The crucial questions raised by this social concern are the extent to which expensive, commercial coaching is an advantage over other types of very inexpensive, or even free, test preparation and the effect of coaching's differential availability, even in the latter case.

## Validity Implications

In addition to its social implications, coaching raises issues concerning the validity of the tests for their intended use. Each individual enters the testing situation with his own assortment of skills, knowledge, and characteristics. The testing situation is intended to produce a sample of that individual's performance in order to infer something more general about him or her, for example, that he or she knows a certain amount about high school algebra, has a certain level of scholastic ability, is ready to perform at a certain level in college, or knows enough about law to be admitted to the bar. To the extent that such samples of performance (test scores) can be correctly generalized to the desired interpretation, the test is considered valid for that interpretation.

## The Implications of Coaching for Ability Testing

Coaching can affect test validity in three respects. First, if coaching were to raise an individual's score above the level of his ability, his score could not be interpreted as a valid measure of his ability. Second, even if coaching were only to enable a person to achieve his maximal level of performance, but were differentially available, the differences in the extent to which near maximal performance was achieved would be accentuated and would affect the validity of interpretation of the scores. The third case pertains only to tests purporting to measure relatively stable characteristics. If coaching were to produce a gain in score, that score surely could not be considered a valid measure of a fixed or stable characteristic.

That some studies have shown gains in test scores after coaching has been considered evidence against the validity of tests as measures of stable characteristics and is a matter of particular concern to the College Board, which states in its Technical Manual (see Fremer and Chandler 1971:147):

In the case of the SAT, coaching efforts typically attempt to improve test scores within a time period that is too short for there to be any reasonable expectation of improvement in the underlying ability that the test was designed to measure. . . . The average student who might consider such coaching has spent 15 to 17 years, including 10 or more school years, developing the skills and abilities measured by the SAT. A coaching course of a few weeks is not likely to have much effect on his ability level at this point in time. One of the principal aims in constructing the SAT is to make it resistant to attempts to increase scores by means of short-term cram courses. Indeed, the usefulness of the SAT as an indicator of a student's potential for college work depends in large measure on the fact that the SAT measures general ability as it has developed over the full range of experiences in a person's life.

Even so, the validity implications of coaching remain: Is it necessary for the admissions purpose to assume that tests are measuring fixed characteristics? How much change with instruction and learning does the aptitude construct allow? And is the amount of change produced by coaching sufficient to negate this stable trait interpretation?

### WHAT IS COACHING?

In general, coaching can be considered instructions given in preparation for taking a test that are designed to elicit maximum performance on the part of the individual coached. In fact, it takes so many forms that it can probably be best defined by specifying its various components. Pike (1978) approached such a specification by defining potential components of test score variance and analyzing them as true score or error components. Table 1 employs several of Pike's suggestions adapted to a definition in terms of the type of skill or information that is the subject of coaching. Included are supplying answers, taking the test for practice, maximizing motivation, optimizing test anxiety, instructing test wiseness, and instructing test content. Together, they provide a framework for an examination of coaching.

**Supplying Correct Answers (Cheating)**

Should coaching include this component, it would appropriately be viewed in a negative light. If individuals were supplied with answers without having to demonstrate the skills being tested, the meaning of the score as a measure of the presumed skill or ability would be invalidated, for it would only measure whether or not answers were available to the individuals. If answers were available to some individuals and not to others, it would, in addition, be obviously unfair and inappropriate. For these reasons, test security is important, especially for admissions and certifying tests, and some test publishers go to considerable lengths to protect test security and detect cheaters. Supplying answers to actual questions to be used on the test, however, is rarely possible as a method of coaching. It is universally viewed as inappropriate as a coaching practice, even if possible, and is presented here only to illustrate one extreme of test preparation that might explain some of the negative connotations of the term coaching. None of the studies of coaching reviewed here even refer to this component.

TABLE 1   Possible Components of Test Preparation

1. Supplying Correct Answers (Cheating)
2. Taking the Test for Practice
3. Maximizing Motivation
4. Optimizing Test Anxiety
5. Instructing Test Wiseness
   a. general test wiseness (being careful, following directions, using good guessing strategies, using time well, etc.)
   b. taking advantage of test construction flaws and cues
   c. using special strategies appropriate to a novel or complex question format
6. Instructing Test Content
   a. instructing in areas related to the interpretation to be made from the scores (the content domain for an achievement measure, the ability being measured, requisite skills or knowledge for eventual success for an admissions or selection measure)
   b. reviewing previous instruction in areas related to the interpretation to be made
   c. instructing test-specific content unrelated to the interpretation to be made

## Taking the Test for Practice

Typically, test takers improve their performance on a second testing, apparently just because of the experience during the first testing with the nature of the test and the testing situation. This component (2 in Table 1) could be considered a subpart of test wiseness, but the two are distinguished here because test-wiseness training often includes directed practice with sample test questions, while practice involves only taking the test under actual test conditions without any special instruction or assistance.

A small but consistent average improvement in scores typically occurs the second time an ability test is given, even without intervention or time for growth and learning. This so-called practice effect could surely be considered a form of coaching. In fact, students involved in highly competitive college admissions, for example, are advised to take the admission test first in the junior year for practice and again in the senior year when the scores are actually used in college applications. At issue in studies of coaching, however, is the question of how much score gain a coaching intervention can produce over and above the practice effect. Thus, in this review the practice effect will be distinguished from other types of coaching, although it is included here for conceptual completeness as a possible component of test preparation or coaching.

## Maximizing Motivation

Some people try harder to do well on tests and care more about testing outcomes. Thus, individual motivation potentially affects test scores directly and can be considered a component in coaching (3 in Table 1). Some people also care more about doing well and try harder in all aspects of the educational or work setting. In this way, motivation affects test scores indirectly as well as through a more general motivation to develop the abilities measured by the test.

### Effects of Need Achievement

One aspect of motivation has been studied for many years under the label "need for achievement" proposed by Murray (1938) and developed by McClelland et al. (1953). It is thought to be an intrinsic motivational force (a learned pattern of responding) eliciting achievement-related behaviors that are fulfilled by successful achievement. As such, it is learned from the expectancies and demands placed on children by their parents and significant others and, consequently, seen to vary within cultural background, race, sex, or socioeconomic status.

Motivation to achieve may be a direct potential extraneous influence on test scores if some test takers, lower in need achievement, achieve less well on a test than they would if better motivated. However, the direct effects of need achievement on test performance are thoroughly confounded with its indirect effects on learning the abilities being tested, as shown by the consistent finding that need achievement is related to academic performance measured by school grades, not tests (Littig and Yeracario 1963, McClelland et al. 1953, Robinson 1964).

Further complications are added by the findings that (a) need achievement differs by socioeconomic status level and ethnic background (Davis and Havighurst 1946, Douvan 1956, Glick 1970, Rosen 1956), and (b) need achievement adds to the prediction of college performance over and above its effect on test scores (Lowell 1952, McClelland et al. 1953). The latter finding suggests that the direct need achievement effects on test performance may be valid in some admissions tests, as presumably are many of the indirect effects of need achievement on learning in other test uses. However, in the case of instructional uses of tests, achievement inferences from test scores, or inferences about ability traits, the direct effects of need achievement on test performance (over and above its indirect effects on prior learning) represent an extraneous (not valid) influence on test scores.

Need achievement is thought to be a stable characteristic developed over a long period of time and therefore not likely to be developed within the short time spans associated with coaching. Need achievement is very likely related, however, to which test takers seek and profit from coaching assistance and which do not. Such self-selection would tend to accentuate differences in test performance due to need achievement.

*Effects of Extrinsic Motivations*

These are the types of extrinsic rewards that promote academic achievement, in general, and test achievement, in particular. Extrinsic rewards have been used to improve student performance in school learning (Benowitz and Busse 1970, Dalton et al. 1973, Rosenbaum and Breiling 1976, Thomson and Galloway 1970) and on tests (Ayllon and Kelly 1972, Elam 1970, Quay 1975, Simons and Bibbs 1974, Tuinman et al. 1972, Ward et al. 1970, Zigler and Butterfield 1968), especially for elementary school-age groups.

Extrinsic motivation has been presumed to be maximal when much is at stake for the individual test taker, as in admissions or selection testing, professional certification testing, and minimum competency testing. The extrinsic rewards are far less direct in standardized achievement testing, testing used for instructional decisions, and ability-trait testing, which involve chiefly teacher and/or parental approval.

Not only does it appear safe to conclude that extrinsic rewards can increase test performance in some students, but it may well be that such rewards have greater effects on students of lower socioeconomic status (SES) and some racial-ethnic backgrounds. This supposition is supported by evidence that: (1) reward characteristics relate to racial-ethnic and SES characteristics (Mischel 1958, Price-Williams and Ramirez 1974, Schultz and Sherman 1976, Walls and Smith 1970), with the typical test situation rewards (time delayed, abstract) less likely to be effective in lower SES and some minority ethnic groups; and (2) intrinsic need achievement is lower in the same students. This raises the possibility that extrinsic rewards might move such students closer to maximal performance.

Coaching might be used to alter the extrinsic reward system—to add different types of rewards that would prove more motivating to some groups than those afforded by the usual test situation. The concern that achievement motives may fail to produce maximal performance seems especially important in achievement testing, using tests for instructional decisions, and measuring ability traits in elementary and secondary schools rather than in admissions and selection tests. When the primary purpose of the testing is external to the student (reporting to parents, judging school quality for administrators and school boards, or evaluating educational programs), these concerns increase.

## Optimizing Test Anxiety

The test anxiety construct (component 4 in Table 1) refers to learned motivational responses to such stressful, evaluative situations as testing. In the seminal work on test anxiety, Mandler and Sarason (1952) theorized that test situations arouse two types of learned patterns of response or drives: (1) task drives that evoke responses leading to task completion (called motives to achieve in this paper), and (2) anxiety drives that elicit both relevant (task-facilitating) and irrelevant (task-interfering) responses.

According to Mandler and Sarason, the irrelevant, task-interfering anxiety components are "manifested as feelings of inadequacy, helplessness, heightened somatic reaction, anticipations of punishment or loss of status and esteem" (Mandler and Sarason 1952:166). These authors assumed that the task-relevant responses are elicited in all persons but are interfered with for some persons by the task-irrelevant responses. This notion produced the expectation of a curvilinear relation between test anxiety and performance (the inverted U hypothesis): to produce maximal performance, a situation must be stressful enough to arouse facilitating anxiety but not so stressful as to arouse debilitating anxiety as well. Alpert and Haber (1960) raised the possibility that the type of stressful, evaluative situations that evoke debilitating anxiety for some people evoke facilitating anxiety for others.

More recently, in a review of test anxiety research, Wine (1971:2) considered its adverse affects in the light of a person's dividing "attention between self-relevant and task-relevant variables"; persons of low debilitating anxiety were found to focus more fully on the task, while those with high debilitating anxiety focused on irrelevancies, primarily on the self.

Though it can be altered, test anxiety is usually considered a habit pattern or trait of an individual, which has been shown to relate consistently to school performance (Gaudry and Fitzgerald 1971, Gaudry and Spielberger 1971, Gjesme 1972, Hill 1971, Simons and Bibbs 1974), classroom and study skills behavior (Allen et al. 1972, Nottleman 1975, Wittmaier 1972), external locus of control (Allen et al. 1974, Bauer 1975, Clark 1971, Prociuk and Breen 1973), self-depreciating behaviors (Sarason and Ganzer 1963, Sarason and Koenig 1965), and, of course, test performance (Allison 1970, Boor 1972, Gaudry and Bradshaw 1970, Newmark et al. 1975, Nighswander and Beggs 1971, Osterhouse 1975). However, consistent results correlating with sex, race, or socioeconomic status have not been found.

Test anxiety therapies designed to change the debilitating test anxiety habit pattern have focused on desensitization techniques and, more recently, on attention to task-relevant variables (Sarason 1972a, 1972b, 1975b) and have frequently produced changes in measured test anxiety. Attention to task-relevant variables would seem rather promising in relation to instruction (or coaching) designed to reduce debilitating test anxiety.

Test anxiety can also be viewed as a product of the external evaluative or testing situation. Evaluative directions have been shown to increase test anxiety and produce poorer test performance in persons of high debilitating anxiety (Bauer 1975, Long and Bessemer 1971, Feehley 1970). However, the use of nonevaluative directions may result in lower scores for those who are not given to test anxiety (Young and Brown 1973).

In general, the voluminous test anxiety literature indicates considerable individual variability in test anxiety and many ways to alter it noticeably. Existing research has not been directed, however, to estimating the amount of change in real testing situations produced by coaching designed to reduce test anxiety. It is thus difficult to gauge the potential magnitude of such coaching. For most test uses, however, test anxiety is clearly an extraneous factor leading to incorrect test score interpretation (lower than maximal performance) for persons of high debilitating anxiety. The possible exception is college or graduate admissions, in which debilitating effects of test anxiety on the admissions test scores may parallel similar debilitating effects in the evaluative situations of college or graduate school performance.

In summary, it should be noted that the issue goes far beyond the ability testing situation—the test anxiety construct could just as appropriately be labeled evaluation anxiety (anxiety aroused by a stressful, evaluative situation), as any evaluative situation could produce the same effects. In fact, at least half the existing studies of test anxiety have used evaluative tasks rather different from the typical ability testing situation (e.g., memory tasks, problem solving, concept formation, perceptual motor tasks, and programmed instruction).

**Instructing Test Wiseness**

In a recent review of test wiseness, Sarnacki (1979) adopted the often quoted definition of Millman et al. (1965:707) that test wiseness is "a subject's capacity to utilize the characteristics and formats of the test and/or test-taking situation to receive a high score." According to the same authors, "Test wiseness is logically independent of the examinee's knowledge of the subject matter for which the items are supposedly measured." Further, Millman et al. (1965:707) outlined the components of test wiseness in two major categories:

1. General test wiseness: elements independent of test constructor or test purposes (time use, following directions, guessing, and answer elimination strategies) and,

2. Test-specific test wiseness: elements dependent upon the test constructor or purpose (constructor intent, flaws and cues).

These two categories correspond to categories 5a and 5b of Table 1. An additional category, 5c, might have been included in the first two but is singled out here because of the special problems raised by unusual and coachable test item formats.

Measures of test wiseness have focused on the use of flaws and cues in tests. With these measures, test-wiseness skills have been shown to increase over the late elementary school grades but not over the high school years, suggesting the effect of experience with tests (Crehan et al. 1974, Slakter et al. 1970a). Test wiseness has been found to correlate positively with verbal achievement (Bajtelsmit 1975b, Diamond and Evans 1972, Rowley 1974) and negatively (Bajtelsmit 1975b) or not at all (Millman 1966) with test anxiety. However, studies of the relationship with intelligence have been mixed, with low relationships found for some aspects of test wiseness (Ardiff 1965, Diamond and Evans 1972, Dunn and Goldstein 1959). It is clear from a variety of studies that test wiseness can be taught, resulting in higher test-wiseness scores (Bajtelsmit 1975a, Gibb 1964, Langer et al. 1973, Moore et al. 1966, Slakter et al. 1970b, Woodley 1973) and higher scores on objective tests (Callenbach 1973, Moore 1971, Oakland 1973, Omvig 1971, Wahlstrom and Boersma 1968). In this light, test wiseness can be considered a component of coaching.

The size of the test-wiseness effect on performance on common standardized tests has been studied very little. From the perspective of test construction flaws, it is clear that the size of the effect of test wiseness depends upon the frequency of flaws and cues in a particular test. Teacher-made tests are more subject to test construction flaws than are well-constructed, professionally developed tests, although flaws and cues have been found in widely used, commercially available tests as well (Metfessel and Sax 1958). Only two studies involving test-wiseness instruction were found to have used common standardized tests and reported the results in a way that gains due to the instruction could be gauged. Callenbach (1973) used the almost 150-item Stanford Reading Test (Primary Level I) and reported a mean difference of 5.5 points between a randomly assigned grade group instructed in test wiseness and one not so instructed. This difference, although .25 standard deviations, represented less than 5 percent of the test items at an age level when maximal effects of instruction could be expected. Omvig (1971) compared performance on the Iowa Tests of Educational Development of a noncounseled group with that of randomly assigned, ninth-grade students, who had received test-wiseness instruction from a guidance counselor. The differences were significant on correctness of expression (1.45 raw score points) and quantitative thinking (1.55), but not significant on seven other subtests or the composite, all of which showed less than one item difference between the two groups.

In general, studies of test wiseness support the meaningfulness of the test-wiseness construct, although it is found to be multidimensional, and the relative importance of its various components is not clear. Measures have focused on test construction flaws and cues (Millman et al. 1965). There are no comparable measures for other aspects of test wiseness, such as being careful, following directions, guessing effectively, using time well, marking answers with care, etc., although typical test-wiseness

# The Implications of Coaching for Ability Testing

instruction includes these areas and has frequently been shown to affect scores on test-wiseness measures, and, less frequently, on some standardized tests. It is not clear, however, which aspects of the instruction are most crucial (the general or test flaw instruction), what size effect can be expected to result, or what types of tests are most subject to it.

Lack of test wiseness in any of its components would presumably be an invalid factor in most test interpretations, with the possible exception of admissions tests, in which test wiseness might also be reflected in future school performance and hence a valid part of the predictor tests. Even if so, however, the influence of test wiseness, though predictively valid, would be misleading since the test names and contents imply the measurement of other predictive abilities than test wiseness.

Given the typical tendency for increase in test-wiseness levels, it appears that many students develop test-wiseness skills on their own through exposure to tests in school, although the variability in test wiseness is certainly not automatically eliminated by such exposure.

Many authors (e.g., Downey 1977, Sarnacki 1979) have therefore suggested instruction in test wiseness for test takers in order to attempt to eliminate or minimize the test-wiseness variable in test score interpretations. Some commercially available tests, such as the Scholastic Aptitude Test (SAT) and American College Test (ACT), provide supplementary materials on several aspects of the general test-wiseness category (time use, guessing, marking). An examination of the use of such information over the last 10 to 20 years by both SAT and ACT administrators shows movement toward more complete and more honest discussion of advantageous test-taking strategies, although strategies for using flaws and cues (category 2 of test wiseness) are not typically covered. For other types of tests, there is a great deal more variation in the instruction in test wiseness given students.

## Instructing Test Content

Instructing test content (component 6 in Table 1) involves at least three distinguishable categories, each with possibly different implications. Instructing in areas related to the interpretation to be made from the scores (6.a in Table 1) is usually associated with instruction, as such, rather than coaching. For example, for professional certification, 6.a would involve instruction in the skills and knowledge involved in practicing that profession; for standardized achievement testing, instruction in the skills and knowledge taught in the classroom; for admissions and selection, instruction in the requisite skills and knowledge required for college, graduate or professional education, or a job. Component 6.a is obviously legitimate instruction, whether or not a part of a coaching enterprise. It has the characteristic of being associated with a relatively long-term instructional effort if the test is measuring abilities that require time to acquire. The exception to this would be the review of previously learned material as described by component 6.b, in which case a short-term review might be expected to increase the level of test performance as well as the factor the test is intended to measure. Because of the time factor, only the review portion (6.b) has typically been considered coaching, although conceptually longer term, in-depth instruction could be as well.

Test-specific instruction (component 6.c) represents instruction in content that is important to know in order to do well on the test, but is not related to the interpretive factor the test is intended to measure. In this sense, 6.c is clearly distinguishable from 6.a and 6.b. For some types of test content, it is difficult to imagine a 6.c component. For example, aside from test-wiseness aspects, it is difficult to imagine instruction in the types of questions that might be included in a standardized achievement test of reading comprehension without also instructing in reading comprehension per se. It is easier, however, to imagine instruction in vocabulary for a verbal analogies test that might or might not improve the verbal skill needed for college work. If such vocabulary instruction affected test performance, but not college readiness, it would be classified under 6.c. If such vocabulary instruction also increased college readiness, it would be classified under 6.a (or 6.b). In one case (6.a or 6.b), the coaching or instruction would produce valid results; in the other case (6.c), the instruction would decrease test validity for the use.

## Summary of Coaching Components

Components 1 (supplying correct answers) and 6.c (test-specific instruction) are coaching activities most clearly related to the negative connotations of the term. They involve instruction that invalidates the meaning of the test score for an individual so coached by resulting in a higher score than the person's capability for the intended factor would warrant. By contrast, components 2, 3, 4, and 5 (practice, maximizing motivation, optimizing test anxiety, and instructing test wiseness) do not produce scores higher than "deserved" but enable some test takers to achieve their maximal performance, while others with nonoptimal levels of these components may not achieve maximal performance. This latter group may score lower than "deserved," in terms of the factor being measured, thereby threatening test validity. Likewise, preparation in components 2, 3, 4, and 5 may be differentially available in that some test takers have

# The Implications of Coaching for Ability Testing

access to test preparation because of economic or social advantages, whereas others do not.

Components 6.a and 6.b (instruction and review in the factor being measured) are valid components, which are desirable and positive. Typically, schools or other learning experiences are relied on to provide this instruction. Inequities occur, however, in school quality or home learning experiences, and there is similarly no assurance that all individuals can benefit equally from such instruction. So, too, if instruction in 6.a and 6.b beyond the usual, generally available channels (e.g., in expensive coaching schools) occurs and is effective, inequities arise because of the differential availability of such instruction, even though test validity is not threatened. These instances of inequity are matters of social concern, but in no sense are they produced by the tests themselves.

## HOW MUCH GAIN DOES COACHING PRODUCE?

This question is quite difficult to answer and, not surprisingly, existing research evidence does not provide many clear answers. The bulk of the research on practice, instruction in test content, motivation, text anxiety, and test wiseness has been directed to showing that the effects occur rather than to estimating the size of the effects, with the possible exception of the research on coaching in college admissions testing. This research has been primarily directed toward coaching for one college admissions examination, the SAT, and in examining this research, we will attempt to estimate, at least for this test, the size of the coaching effect. It is expected that results for the SAT would generalize at least to a number of admissions tests and, to some extent, to most ability tests.

An important condition is whether the researcher decides who is to receive coaching or studies individuals who have decided on their own to be coached. When volunteers are studied and compared to groups not seeking out coaching, any differences may be attributable to differences in the personal characteristics of the groups compared rather than to coaching. These nonexperimental studies not involving random assignment of subjects must then be interpreted carefully in the light of this important design feature.

## Baseline Studies of Practice and Growth

Because much of the concern with the coaching issue has involved the social implications of differential access to commercial coaching, it is important to look first at scoring gains due simply to practice and normal growth without any coaching intervention. Several studies have been directed specifically to estimating practice and growth effects; in addition, in experimental studies of coaching, the control group gains provide estimates of practice and growth. Both types of studies are reported in Table 2. Although there is some variation in results from study to study, there is a clear and consistent average increase in scores without coaching, attributable presumably to practice and normal school achievement. The average over the five studies listed of combined practice and 6-month

TABLE 2  Gains on the SAT Due to Practice and Growth

| Authors | Sample Size | Practice and Growth Gains | | Time Between Testing |
|---|---|---|---|---|
| | | SAT-V | SAT-M | |
| Dyer (1953) | ~200[a] | 50 | 15 | 6 mo |
| Evans and Pike (1973) | 165[b] | — | 18 | several wk |
| Fremer and Chandler (1971) | | | | |
| 1962 | —[c] | 24 | 23 | 7 mo |
| 1963 | —[c] | 16 | 18 | 7 mo |
| 1964 | —[c] | 21 | 27 | 7 mo |
| 1965 | —[c] | 19 | 18 | 7 mo |
| 1966 | —[c] | 13 | 9 | 7 mo |
| Levine and Angoff (1958)[d] | | | | |
| practice | — | 10 | 10 | 0 |
| growth | — | 20 | 10 | 8 mo |
| Pearson (1948)[e] | 7,000 | | | |
| practice | | 20 | — | 0 |
| growth | | 21 | — | 6 mo |
| Average Practice and Growth Over 6 Mo | | 26 | 21 | |
| Roberts and Oppenheim (1966)[f] | | | | |
| six schools | 111 | −8 | — | 6 wk |
| eight schools | 122 | — | −6 | 6 wk |
| four schools | 113 | −1 | 0 | 6 wk |

[a] All senior boys at a private school for boys.
[b] High school junior volunteers from 12 schools randomly assigned to a no-coaching control group.
[c] Average gains from May of the junior year to December of the senior year of volunteer retakers of the SAT in the years given. Number of students ranged from 96,000 in 1962 to 193,000 in 1966.
[d] Based on several groups of students tested at various times between May 1955 and March 1957, as reported by Fremer and Chandler (1971).
[e] Based on students repeating the SAT-V between 1942 and 1945 as reported by Fremer and Chandler (1971).
[f] Volunteers from 18 predominantly black high schools in Tennessee with average SAT scores near 300.

## The Implications of Coaching for Ability Testing

growth effects is estimated to be 26 for SAT-V (Verbal) and 21 for SAT-M (Mathematical) on the 200 to 800 SAT score scale.

One discrepant finding listed in Table 2 showed no gains or negative gains in a group of very low-scoring black Tennessee high school students. It is possible that inadequate motivation or achievement levels too low to profit from practice account for these results. The results are not included in the averages, since all the other studies involved probable college-bound students. However, the study is a useful reminder that the typical practice effect may not apply to all students.

### Coaching Study Results

As noted above, coaching studies can be divided into two groups: (1) those in which students were randomly assigned to coaching or no coaching groups and (2) those in which volunteers for coaching were studied and matched roughly with some other group who were not volunteers for coaching.

#### Experimental Research on Coaching

The experimental studies in the published literature share the following characteristics: (1) a group of students first took the SAT; (2) then the researcher assigned some of the group to some type of coaching; and (3) subsequent to the coaching all were retested. The effect of the coaching is gauged by comparing the pre/post score change in the coached group to the pre/post change in the uncoached group. In these studies, coaching probably did not include all the test preparation components outlined in Table 1. In particular, coaching was relatively short-term (ranging from 2 hours to 30 hours) and consisted of group practice with test items similar to SAT items and other unspecified activities at the discretion of the particular instructor and, occasionally, commercial coaching.

The results from these studies are summarized in Table 3, which indicates that most, but not all, showed gains due to coaching. The average coaching effect was 9 points for SAT-V and 15 points for SAT-M. A major difficulty with summarizing such studies is the possible variable quality of the coaching. Most of the studies left the coaching to schools, and the time devoted to coaching as well as the content varied greatly. Two studies with the most intensive instruction in math (French and Dear 1959, Evans and Pike 1973) showed the greatest gain—26 and 25 points, respectively. In a recent monograph, Messick (1980) focused on the length of time spent in coaching and noted the strong relationship between time spent and gains shown.

TABLE 3  Gains on the SAT in Experimental Comparisons of Coaching-No Coaching Groups

| Authors | Coached Group Size | Coaching Gains | | Time Between Testing | Hours of Coaching |
|---|---|---|---|---|---|
| | | SAT-V | SAT-M | | |
| Alderman and Powers (1979) | | | | | |
| A | 28 | 28 | — | | 5 |
| B | 39 | 8 | — | | 14 |
| C | 22 | −3 | — | | 9 |
| D | 48 | 7 | — | | 8 |
| E | 25 | −1 | — | | 8 |
| F | 37 | 1 | — | | 5 |
| G | 24 | 18 | — | | 14 |
| H | 16 | 12 | — | | 72 |
| Dyer (1953) | 200[a] | 5 | 13 | 6 mo | 10 |
| Evans and Pike (1973) | 337 | — | 25 | several wk | 21 |
| French and Dear (1959) | | | | | |
| private school study | 225 | 5 | 13 | 6 mo | 18 |
| public school study | 161 | 18 | 6 | 6 mo | 18 |
| intensive math study | 71 | — | 26 | 6 mo | 24 |
| Roberts and Oppenheim (1966)[b] | | | | | |
| six schools | 154 | 14 | — | 6 wk | 8 |
| eight schools | 188 | — | 8 | 6 wk | 8 |
| Average Coaching Gains | | 9 | 15 | | |

[a]All senior boys at a private school for boys
[b]Volunteers from 18 predominantly black high schools in Tennessee.

## Studies Not Using Random Assignment

In this group of studies, persons volunteering for coaching in a natural setting were compared with some roughly equivalent but not volunteer groups. These studies are separated from the others because of the very real possibility that volunteer groups differ fundamentally from the control groups in motivation to achieve and aspirations—a possibility that might heighten the effectiveness of coaching.

In Table 4 the average gain attributed to coaching by these studies in which volunteer characteristics are confounded with coaching effects is 17 points on SAT-V and 13 on SAT-M. It should be noted that these figures give disproportionate weight to a 1978 study of the Boston Regional Office of the Federal Trade Commission (FTC). When only the later reanalysis of that data by the Federal Trade Commission (1979) are

TABLE 4  Gains on the SAT in Studies of Volunteer Coaching with Nonvolunteer, Nonrandom Comparison Groups

| Authors | Coached Group Size | Coaching Gains SAT-V | Coaching Gains SAT-M | Time Between Testing | Hours of Coaching |
|---|---|---|---|---|---|
| Boston Regional Office (1978)[a] | | | | | |
| Test taken once (with prior coaching) | | | | | |
| School 001A | 72 | 55 | 40 | Variable | [b] |
| School 022 | 37 | 0 | 25 | Variable | [b] |
| Test taken twice (coached in between) | | | | | |
| School 001A | 155 | 40 | 25 | Variable | [b] |
| School 022 | 75 | 15 | 0 | Variable | [b] |
| Federal Trade Commission (1979)[a] | | | | | |
| School 001A[c] | | 30 | 19 | Variable | [b] |
| School 022[c] | | −2 | 5 | Variable | [b] |
| Frankel (1960) | 45 | 8 | 9 | 7 mo | 30[b] |
| Lass (1958)[d] | | 3 | 11 | 12 mo | [e] |
| | | 12 | −1 | 12 mo | [e] |
| Whitla (1962) | 52 | 11 | 0 | 5 mo | [b] |
| Average Coaching Gains (all 10 values) | | 17 | 13 | | |
| Average Coaching Gains (eliminating Boston Regional Office results) | | 10 | 7 | | |

[a]The Boston Regional Office (1978) study and the Federal Trade Commission (1979) study are different analyses of the same data. The results reported here are for major subsamples highlighted by each report and do not represent identical groups.
[b]Regular coaching in a commercial coaching school.
[c]Figures reported are those for subsample five, which apparently involved 417 students in both schools combined and were representative of other subsamples analyzed.
[d]As reported by Pike (1978); sample size is not given.
[e]Commercial coaching but of short duration.

used, the average coaching effect is 10 points on SAT-V and 7 on SAT-M.

The widely discussed reports of the Boston Regional Office of the Federal Trade Commission (1978) and the Federal Trade Commission (1979) reanalysis of the Boston Regional Office data deserve special mention. In the original study, some of the largest coaching gains in the literature were reported for one New York City coaching school. However, the coached groups differed in several systematic ways from the uncoached group. Using regression procedures to control for such differences as initial test scores, high school record, and some demographic characteristics, the second study reported greatly reduced coaching effects. In one school, the gains decreased to 30 points on SAT-V and 19 points on SAT-M, and in the other, to almost none. See Messick (1980) for a detailed examination of these analyses.

Several possible differences between the coaching volunteers and nonvolunteers in the two FTC studies have been raised. First, the original report emphasized the fact that the comparison group of nonvolunteers may have actually received some coaching in unidentified coaching schools (a potentially very small effect) or in their regular schooling (a potentially much larger effect). Such a possibility would serve to reduce the coaching effect estimated by the study as an overall effect of coaching but would not reduce it as an estimate of the effect of commercial coaching schools over and above typically existing free coaching.

Second, the hypothesis has frequently been advanced that students who score lower than expected on a first test (negative errors of measurement) may be overrepresented among those seeking coaching. If so, part of a supposed coaching effect would be a result of regression to the mean, not coaching. The second FTC report considered this possibility and found that the students being coached at the effective coaching school had, in fact, scored lower on their first SAT (raising the regression possibility), but also on their previous preliminary SAT. This latter result identified the group not as negative measurement errors but as individuals who consistently scored lower on tests than would be expected from their other performance records, which refuted the regression hypothesis. The report goes on to suggest that such consistently poor test performers may be especially coachable (the second school studied, for which no effects were found, had not coached this type of student).

Third, it has been hypothesized that highly motivated students, aspiring to prestigious colleges, whose families support such motivations and aspirations, can profit most from coaching. The background characteristics of the coached group in the FTC study were consistent with this hypothesis. Further support is found in the relatively small gains in the Roberts and Oppenheim (1966) study of low-achieving students.

## Summary of Coaching Gains

The bulk of the evidence from a variety of studies is that coaching can often produce detectable differences in students' scores, especially if the

## The Implications of Coaching for Ability Testing

students wish to improve and the instruction is good. At issue then is whether commercial coaching is an advantage over free, generally available forms, what type of students profit from coaching, and what types of coaching are most effective.

### Implications of the Size of Coaching Gains

The position of the College Board has been that the typical 10-point SAT gain shown in experimental coaching studies is not an important gain. In light of the SAT score scale (200 to 800), the error of measurement on that scale (approximately 30 to 35 points) and the typical gain due to practice and growth without coaching (20 points), this position is not unreasonable. If the 10 SAT points were translated further to the number of items answered correctly, it would probably represent a difference of less than one test question due to coaching in some parts of the 200 to 800 scale. In terms of the technical integrity of the SAT as a relatively stable measure of scholastic ability, a gain in the range of 10 to 20 points (1 to 3 test items) does not seem a serious threat to the construct.

The studies showing larger gains may have reflected special characteristics of the test takers, which made them more subject to higher gains to reach their proper maximal performance. In the first case, the gains may have been largely due to coaching a group who had never achieved as well on tests as they had in other academic situations, and as such, would be appropriate and desirable in terms of the ability construct. In the second case, mathematics instruction and review may be especially important for students who have not had math courses recently (Pike 1978). Again, such review would enable students to show maximal performance appropriately.

Any reasonable scholastic ability construct allows for some flexibility stemming from schooling, special instruction, and maturity, even if viewed as relatively stable. It is this author's conclusion that the level of gain that typically results from coaching is not a serious threat to the ability construct interpretation or to the admissions use.

Although these gains (typically averaging close to 10 points and only rarely averaging as high as 25 points) are relatively small technically, they have rather different implications for the issue of whether or not students should be advised to seek some form of test preparation or coaching. Those students, most strongly seeking admissions in a highly competitive situation, would probably choose to make the effort to add 10 to 25 points to their scores. Such differences in score might even look important to some colleges, primarily because the 200 to 800 scale is so inflated. The same differences on a less inflated scale (1.0 or 2.5 points on a 20 to 80 scale) would seem less important to both students and admissions officers.

Regardless of whether or not commercial coaching is required, it is this author's opinion that students seeking their maximal possible score should be advised to take the test for practice and to seek coaching if gains of 10, 20, or 30 points are potentially important to them.

*Commercial Versus Free Coaching*

Informal evidence suggests that most schools with a large college-bound student population provide some form of free coaching for college admissions tests by regular teachers. Several of the coaching studies reported here used school coaching systems already in place; others provided coaching materials to be implemented by teachers. An important social issue is the extent to which school-based coaching is as effective as commercial coaching.

First, it must be noted that neither free, school-based coaching nor commercial coaching is a single phenomenon. With each type, coaching varies in many ways, such as length of time or quality of instruction. As in studies of any instructional program, the results show that some produce greater gains than others. At the same time, there seems to be no consistent evidence that commercial coaching is superior. The evidence is limited, but even the Federal Trade Commission (1979) study found gains in only one of two commercial coaching schools studied.

Differential availability remains an issue, however, if not all schools provide admissions test coaching. For example, schools with small numbers of college-bound students may not offer any school-based coaching. Test publishers have responded to this inequity by providing more test preparation material directly to the students who register to take a test. Such material provides much the same type of information as coaching sessions, although probably less of it and with less emphasis on special test-taking strategies. It seems likely that a highly motivated student could profit from self-instruction with such materials, but there have been no studies comparing such individual efforts to more structured coaching.

*Who Can Be Coached?*

There is little direct evidence on this issue, but the indirect evidence suggests that not all students can be expected to gain equally from coaching. Those who consistently do poorly on tests in comparison to other performance measures and those highly motivated to achieve may improve most. Those for whom the test is very difficult may lack the necessary basic knowledge on which to base improvement. Those taking regular school instruction which reviews basic skills (such as mathematics) may profit less from a review through a coaching school than those not taking the regular high school mathematics course (Pike 1978).

## SUMMARY

Coaching has been a volatile issue because of its social implications of differential availability and validity implications for the predicton of future performance and for a relatively stable ability construct. The most disappointing aspect of the coaching literature is that the components of coaching have been so poorly identified. We cannot determine which of the test preparation components described in Table 1 have been included in a particular coaching study. We would like to be able to distinguish test-wiseness coaching from instruction of the types in components 6.a and 6.b. We are left to guess from indirect evidence that some types of test questions on the SAT are more subject to test-wiseness and test-specific instruction than others, but beyond the area of analogy items we know little about which ones. It is clear that only two components, supplying correct answers (component 1) and providing test-specific instruction unrelated to the test score interpretation (component 6.c), are fundamentally inappropriate, but available evidence does not allow the determination of how much effect, if any, these components have on coaching gains. Although they may decrease the validity of scores if differentially available to students, all other components can be viewed as desirable for all test takers as an aid in obtaining their deserved maximal performance. The ideal situation would allow all test takers to take any ability test after practice with the test, with maximal motivation, with optimal levels of test anxiety, with maximal test wiseness, and after review of relevant, previously learned material or new substantive learning.

A review of the research indicates that coaching often produces detectable results, although they are small in relation to total individual variation on the measures and therefore not a serious threat to the interpretation of the scores as a predictor of future academic success or as a relatively stable ability construct. At the same time, the size of the coaching effects (usually around 10 to 25 points on the inflated 200 to 800 SAT scale) appears significant enough to some students and some colleges to make it worthwhile for students in highly competitive admissions situations to seek coaching, and they should not be discouraged.

The potential disadvantage to students unable to afford commercial coaching has been a major concern. Studies reviewed, however, show little reason to prefer commercial coaching to free, school-based coaching, although quality in both types varies considerably. Of even more social concern than the commercial versus school-based coaching issue is the likelihood that school-based coaching is more generally available in schools with many college-bound students than it is in those with fewer such students. Other social issues are less closely related to coaching. The need to achieve, the motivational effect of external rewards, and test anxiety are all felt to have at least an indirect effect on coaching results. The extent of such effects, however, and how much they in turn are related to individual differences in experience, SES, and ethnic background have been shown to vary widely and have not thus far been thoroughly examined.

Finally, it is important to remember that all the components of coaching have counterparts in any method (test or nontest) of evaluating individuals' abilities. Motivation to achieve in both its intrinsic and extrinsic components and its social implications is fundamental to schooling and its many evaluative techniques. Test anxiety is really evaluation anxiety and would remain as a direct problem in any nontest form of evaluation. Test wiseness would undoubtedly have a counterpart in preparation for any nontest evaluative procedure. If the evaluation of individuals continues to be viewed as socially constructive, then, whether tests or other methods are used, these various components must be considered and differences in them minimized to improve the validity of such evaluations. Whether an evaluation method other than tests could reduce such differences more effectively would have to be examined for each evaluation method proposed. Objective test scores at least give a way to discover and explore the fact that such components exist. In the case of less formal evaluative procedures, the problems would be potentially the same, but more difficult to isolate and study.

## REFERENCES

Alderman, D. L., and Powers, D. E. (1979) The effects of special preparation on SAT-Verbal scores. *College Board Research Report RR-79-1*. Princeton, N.J.: Educational Testing Service.

Allen, G. J., Lerner, W. M., and Hinrichsen, J. J. (1972) Study behaviors and their relationship to test anxiety and academic performance. *Psychological Reports* 30(2):407-410.

Allen, G. J., Giat, L., and Chuerney, R. J. (1974) Locus of control, test anxiety, and student performance in a personalized instruction course. *Journal of Educational Psychology* 66(6):968-973.

Allison, D. E. (1970) Test anxiety, stress, and intelligence-test performance. *Canadian Journal of Behavioral Science* 2(1):26-37.

Alpert, R., and Haber, R. N. (1960) Anxiety in academic achievement situations. *Journal of Abnormal and Social Psychology* 61:207-215.

Ardiff, M. B. (1965) The Relationship of Three Aspects of Test-Wiseness to Intelligence and Reading Ability in Grades Three and Six. Unpublished Master's Thesis, Cornell University.
Ayllon, T., and Kelly, K. (1972) Effects of reinforcement on standardized test performance. *Journal of Applied Behavior Analysis* 5:477-484.
Bajtelsmit, J. W. (1975a) The Efficacy of Test-Wiseness and Systematic Desensitization Programs for Increasing Test-Taking Skills. Paper presented at the annual meeting of the National Council on Measurement in Education, Washington, D. C.
Bajtelsmit, J. W. (1975b) Development and Validation of an Adult Measure of Secondary Cue-Using Strategies on Objective Examinations: The Test of Obscure Knowledge (TOOK). Paper presented at the annual meeting of the Northeastern Educational Research Association, Ellenville, N. Y.
Bauer, D. H. (1975) The effect of instructions, anxiety, and locus of control on intelligence test scores. *Measurement and Evaluation in Guidance* 8(1):12-19.
Benowitz, M. L., and Busse, T. V. (1970) Material incentives and the learning of spelling words in a typical school situation. *Journal of Educational Psychology* 61:24-26.
Boor, M. (1972) Relationship of test anxiety and academic performance when controlled for intelligence. *Journal of Clinical Psychology* 28(2):171-172.
Boston Regional Office of the Federal Trade Commission (1978) *The Effect of Coaching on Standardized Admission Examinations.* Boston: Federal Trade Commission.
Callenbach, C. (1973) The effects of instruction and practice in content-independent test-taking techniques upon the standardized reading scores of selected second grade students. *Journal of Educational Measurement* 10:25-30.
Clark, N. C. (1971) Test Anxiety, Locus of Control, and Feedback in Self-Instruction. Ph.D. dissertation, George Peabody College for Teachers.
College Entrance Examination Board (1959) A statement by the College Board of Trustees on test "coaching." *College Board Review* 38:3.
Crehan, K. D., Koehler, R. A., and Slakter, M. J. (1974) Longitudinal studies of test-wiseness. *Journal of Educational Measurement* 11:209-212.
Dalton, A. J., Rubino, C. A., and Hislop, M. W. (1973) Some effects of token rewards on school achievement of children with Down's syndrome. *Journal of Applied Behavior Analysis* 6:251-259.
Davis, A., and Havighurst, R. J. (1946) Social class and color differences in child rearing. *American Sociological Review* 11:698-710.
Diamond, J. J. and Evans, W. J. (1972) An investigation of the cognitive correlates of test-wiseness. *Journal of Educational Measurement* 9:145-150.
Douvan, E. (1956) Social status and success strivings. *Journal of Abnormal and Social Psychology* 52:219-221.
Downey, G. W. (1977) Is it time we started teaching children how to take tests? *The American School Board Journal* (January):26-31.
Dunn, T. F., and Goldstein, L. G. (1959) Test difficulty, validity, and reliability as functions of selected multiple-choice item construction principles. *Educational and Psychological Measurement* 19:171-179.
Dyer, H. S. (1953) Does coaching help? *College Board Review* 19:331-335.
Evans, F. R. and Pike, L. W. (1973) The effects of instruction for three mathematics item formats. *Journal of Educational Measurement* 10:257-271.
Elam, S. (1970) The age of accountability down in Texarkana. *Phi Delta Kappan* 51:509-514.
Federal Trade Commission (1979) *Effects of Coaching on Standardized Admission Examinations: Revised Statistical Analysis of Data Gathered by the Boston Regional Office of the Federal Trade Commission.* Washington, D.C.: Federal Trade Commission.

Feehley, C. J. (1970) Test Anxiety, Task Complexity, Cue Position and Evaluative Instructions As They Affect Performance on a Learning Task. Ph.D. dissertation, Catholic University of America.

Frankel, E. (1960) Effects of growth, practice, and coaching on SAT scores. *Personnel and Guidance Journal* 38:713-719.

Fremer, J., and Chandler, M. O. (1971) Special studies. Chapter VI in W. H. Angoff, ed., *The College Board Admissions Testing Program: A Technical Report on Research and Development Activities Relating to the Scholastic Aptitude Test and Achievement Tests*. New York: College Entrance Examination Board.

French, J. W., and Dear, R. E. (1959) Effect of coaching on an aptitude test. *Educational and Psychological Measurement* 19:319-330.

Gaudry, E., and Bradshaw, G. D. (1970) The differential effect of anxiety on performance in progressive and terminal school examinations. *Australian Journal of Psychology* 22:1-4.

Gaudry, E., and Fitzgerald, D. (1971) Test anxiety, intelligence and academic achievement. In E. Gaudry, and C. D. Spielberger, eds., *Anxiety and Educational Achievement*. New York: Wiley.

Gaudry, E., and Spielberger, C. D. (1971) *Anxiety and Educational Achievement*. New York: Wiley.

Gibb, B. G. (1964) Test-Wiseness as a Secondary Due Response. Ph.D. dissertation, Stanford University. Ann Arbor, Mich.: University Microfilms, No. 64-7643.

Gjesme, T. (1972) Sex differences in the relationship between test anxiety and school performance. *Psychological Reports* 30:907-914.

Glick, O. (1970) Sixth graders' attitudes toward school and interpersonal conditions in the classroom. *Journal of Experimental Education* 38:17-22.

Hill, K. T. (1971) Anxiety in the evaluative context. *Young Children* 27:97-116.

Langer, G., Wark, D., and Johnson, S. (1973) Test-wiseness in objective tests. In P. O. Nacke, ed., *Diversity in Mature Reading: Theory and Research. Vol. I, 22nd Yearbook of the National Reading Conference*. Milwaukee, Wis.: National Reading Conference.

Lass, A. H. (1958) Unpublished report. Abraham Lincoln High School, Brooklyn.

Levine, R. S., and Angoff, W. H. (1958) The effects of practice and growth on scores on the Scholastic Aptitude Test. *ETS Research Bulletin*. Princeton, N.J.: Educational Testing Service.

Littig, L. W., and Yeracario, C. A. (1963) Academic achievement of achievement and affiliation motivations. *Journal of Psychology* 55:115-119.

Long, K. K., and Bessemer, D. W. (1971) An analytical investigation of instructions designed to elicit test anxiety. *Psychological Reports* 29:283-294.

Lowell, E. L. (1952) The effect of need for achievement on learning and speed of performance. *Journal of Psychology* 33:31-40.

Mandler, G., and Sarason, S. B. (1952) A study of anxiety and learning. *Journal of Abnormal and Social Psychology* 47:166-173.

McClelland, D. C., Atkinson, J. W., Clark, R. A., and Lowell, E. L. (1953) *The Achievement Motive*. New York: Appleton-Century-Crofts, Inc.

Messick, S. (1980) *The Effectiveness of Coaching for the SAT: Review and Reanalysis of Research from the Fifties to the FTC*. Princeton, N.J.: Educational Testing Service.

Metfessel, N. S., and Sax, G. (1958) Systematic biases in the keying of correct responses on certain standardized tests. *Educational and Psychological Measurement* 18:787-790.

Millman, J. (1966) *Test-Wiseness in Taking Objective Achievement and Aptitude Examinations*. Final Report. New York: College Entrance Examination Board.

Millman, J., Bishop, C. H., and Ebel, R. L. (1965) Analysis of test-wiseness. *Educational and Psychological Measurement* 25:707-726.

Mischel, W. (1958) Preference for delayed reinforcement: An experimental study of a cultural observation. *Journal of Abnormal and Social Psychology* 56:57-61.

Moore, J. C. (1971) Test-wiseness and analogy test performance. *Measurement and Evaluation in Guidance* 3:198-202.

Moore, J. C., Schutz, R. E., and Baker, R. L. (1966) The application of a self-instructional technique to develop a test-taking strategy. *American Educational Research Journal* 3:13-17.

Murray, H. A. (1938) *Explorations in Personality*. New York: Oxford University Press.

Newmark, C. S., Wheeler, D., Newmark, L., and Stabler, B. (1975) Test-induced anxiety with children. *Journal of Personality Assessment* 39:409-413.

Nighswander, J. K., and Beggs, D. L. (February 1971) *A Study of the Relationships between Test Order, Physiological Arousal, and Intelligence and Achievement Test Performance*. Unpublished manuscript. ERIC No. ED 046 983.

Nottlemann, E. B. (1975) *Test Anxiety and Off-Task Behavior in Evaluation Situation*. Unpublished manuscript. ERIC No. ED 113022.

Oakland, T. (1973) The effects of test-wiseness materials on standardized test performance of preschool disadvantaged children. *Journal of School Psychology* 10:355-360.

Omvig, C. P. (1971) Effects of guidance on the test results of standardized achievement testing. *Measurement and Evaluation in Guidance* 4:47-52.

Osterhouse, R. A. (1975) Classroom anxiety and the examination performance of test-anxious students. *Journal of Educational Research* 68:247-249.

Pike, L. W. (1978) *Short-term Instruction, Test-wiseness, and the Scholastic Aptitude Test: A Literature Review with Research Recommendations*. Research Bulletin RB-78-2. Princeton, N.J.: Educational Testing Service.

Price-Williams, D. R., and Ramirez, M. (1974) Ethnic differences in delay of gratification. *Journal of Social Psychology* 93:23-30.

Prociuk, T. J., and Breen, L. J. (1973) Internal-external control, test anxiety and academic achievement: Additional data. *Psychological Reports* 33:563-566.

Quay, L. C. (1975) Reinforcement and Binet performance in disadvantaged children. *Journal of Educational Psychology* 67:132-135.

Roberts, S. O., and Oppenheim, D. B. (1966) *The Effects of Special Instruction upon Test Performance of High School Students in Tennessee*. Research Bulletin 66-36. Princeton, N.J.: Educational Testing Service.

Robinson, W. P. (1964) The achievement motive, academic success, and intelligence test scores. *British Journal of Social and Clinical Psychology* 4:98-103.

Rosen, B. C. (1956) The achievement syndrome: A psychocultural dimension of social stratification. *American Sociological Review* 21:203-211.

Rosenbaum, M., and Breiling, J. (1976) The development and functional control of reading-comprehension behavior. *Journal of Applied Behavioral Analysis* 9:323-333.

Rowley, G. L. (1974) Which examinees are favored by the use of multiple choice tests? *Journal of Educational Measurement* 11:15-23.

Sarason, I. G. (1972a) Experimental approaches to test anxiety: Attention and the uses of information. In C. D. Spielberger, ed., *Anxiety: Current Trends in Theory and Research*, Vol. 11. New York: Academic Press.

Sarason, I. G. (1972b) Test anxiety and the model who fails. *Journal of Personality and Social Psychology* 22:410-413.

Sarason, I. G. (1975a) Test anxiety and the self-disclosing coping model. *Journal of Consulting and Clinical Psychology* 43:148-153.

Sarason, I. G. (1975b) Test anxiety, attention, and the general problem of anxiety. In C. D. Spielberger, and I. G. Sarason, eds., *Stress and Anxiety*, Vol. 1. Washington, D.C.: Hemisphere.

Sarason, I. G., and Ganzer, V. J. (1963) Effects of test anxiety and reinforcement history on verbal behavior. *Journal of Abnormal and Social Psychology* 67:513-519.

Sarason, I. G., and Koenig, K. P. (1965) The relationship of test anxiety and hostility to description of self and parents. *Journal of Personality and Social Psychology* 2:617-621.

Sarnacki, R. E. (1979) An examination of test-wiseness in the cognitive domain. *Review of Educational Research* 49:252-279.

Schultz, C. B., and Sherman, R. H. (1976) Social class, development, and differences in reinforcer effectiveness. *Review of Educational Research* 46:25-59.

Simons, R. H., and Bibbs, J. J. (1974) Achievement motivation, test anxiety, and underachievement in the elementary school. *Journal of Educational Research* 67:366-369.

Slakter, M. J., Koehler, R. A., and Hampton, S. H. (1970a) Grade, level, sex, and selected aspects of test-wiseness. *Journal of Educational Measurement* 7:119-122.

Slakter, M. J., Koehler, R. A., and Hampton, S. H. (1970b) Learning test-wiseness by programmed texts. *Journal of Educational Measurement* 7:247-254.

Thomson, E. W., and Galloway, C. G. (1970) Material reinforcement and success in spelling. *Elementary School Learning* 70:395-398.

Tuinman, J. J., Farr, R., and Blanton, R. E. (1972) Increases in test scores as a function of material reward. *Journal of Educational Measurement* 9:215-223.

Wahlstrom, M., and Boersma, F. J. (1968) The influence of test-wiseness upon achievement. *Educational and Psychological Measurement* 28:413-420.

Walls, R. T., and Smith, T. S. (1970) Development of preference for delayed reinforcement in disadvantaged children. *Journal of Educational Psychology* 61:118-123.

Ward, W. C., Kogan, N., and Pankove, E. (1970) *Motivation and Capacity in Children's Creativity*. ETS Research Bulletin. Princeton, N.J.: Educational Testing Service.

Whitla, D. K. (1962) Effect of tutoring on Scholastic Aptitude Test scores. *Personnel and Guidance Journal* 41:32-37.

Wine, J. (1971) Test anxiety and direction of attention. *Psychological Bulletin* 76:92-104.

Wittmaier, B. C. (1972) Test anxiety and study habits. *Journal of Educational Research* 65:357-364.

Woodley, K. K. (1973) Test-Wiseness Program Development and Evaluation. Paper presented at the annual meeting of the American Educational Research Association, New Orleans, Louisiana.

Young, F. A., and Brown, M. (1973) Effects of test anxiety and testing conditions on intelligence scores of elementary school boys and girls. *Psychological Reports* 32:643-649.

Zigler, E., and Butterfield, E. C. (1968) Motivational aspects of changes in I.Q. test performance of culturally deprived nursery school children. *Child Development* 39:1-14.